Cultural Memory

in

the

Present

Mieke Bal and Hent de Vries, Editors

ALL THE DIFFERENCE IN THE WORLD

POSTCOLONIALITY
AND THE ENDS
OF COMPARISON

Natalie Melas

STANFORD UNIVERSITY PRESS

STANFORD, CALIFORNIA

2007

Stanford University Press
Stanford, California

Publication of this book has been supported by the Hull Memorial
Publication Fund of Cornell University.

Printed in the United States of America on acid-free, archival-quality paper

Library of Congress Cataloging-in-Publication Data

Melas, Natalie.
All the difference in the world : postcoloniality and the ends of comparison / Natalie Melas.
    p.cm. — (Cultural memory in the present)
    Includes bibliographical references and index.
    ISBN-13: 978-0-8047-3197-3 (cloth : alk. paper)
    ISBN-13: 978-0-8047-3198-0 (pbk. : alk. paper)
    1. Caribbean literature—20th century—History and criticism.   I. Title.
PN849.C3M45 2006
860.9'9729—dc22
                                                                    2006017972

Typeset by Newgen in 11/13.5 Garamond

For my father,
C. Michael Melas

and my mother,
Herta Dammer Melas
in memoriam
(1927–1993)

Contents

Preface

A doorbell rings and a woman opens the door to find two distinguished professors of comparative literature at Harvard, Harry Levin and Renato Poggioli, in blue workmen's coveralls. She calls to her husband, a graduate student of theirs, and says, "Honey! The men are here to compare the literature." This, by Harry Levin's own account in *Grounds for Comparison*, was what the graduate student's wife dreamed one night. The anecdote puts us in mind of a time when comparative literature, like all the humanities, was the exclusive preserve of a white male elite and part of its effect derives from the improbable transformation of these two eminent professors into manual laborers. What is most apposite for my purposes, however, is the vigorous, transitive use of the verb "compare" in the wife's announcement that "the men are here to compare the literature." Unmistakably an instance of wish-fulfillment, the wife's dream world presents the act of comparison with all the referential certainty and confidence it lacks in the disciplinary practice of comparative literature in the waking world. Like others associated with the discipline to this day, she no doubt was unable to answer satisfactorily persistent questions about her husband's studies, such as "so, what exactly does he compare?"

The idea of comparison, as name, method, and practice, is the starting point for this study. In the first chapter I undertake a historical analysis of comparison in disciplinary formations of knowledge. The qualifier "comparative" has its origin in what was considered one of the great innovations of scholarship in the nineteenth century, the comparative method. Applied across disciplines, it provided a comprehensive and systematic approach to the totality of objects in a given field and replaced the directionlessness of a merely taxonomic comparison with a positivist evolutionary teleology. When comparative literature abandoned the objective of studying all the literature in the world, its adjectival appendage gradually fell into amnesia.

The matter of scope has now, however, reasserted itself and with it the adjective "comparative," partly in response to the concerted critique of Eurocentrism over the last twenty years, and partly in response to the exigencies of the rapid pace of globalization in contemporary life. Whereas a temporal scheme of evolution unified the comprehensive field of an earlier positivist comparatism, a spatial scheme of sheer extensiveness undergirds this new attention to comparative scope. The question then shifts from "what do you compare?" to "on what grounds do you compare?" The general argument I develop in this book is that comparison, under these conditions, involves a very particular form of incommensurability: space offers a ground of comparison, but no given basis of equivalence.

My objective is neither to compare one literature or culture to another nor to propose a new model for comparative analysis, but rather to examine various instances of postcolonial comparison by analyzing figures of incommensurability in a set of literary and theoretical texts. The approach developed in this book is premised on a particular view of postcoloniality as a condition linked to the cultural logic subtending the history of European conquests begun five hundred years ago, conquests that brought, for the first time, the world as an empirical totality into human apprehension. This history, whose extraordinary violence and almost unmitigated exploitation persist in various forms to this day, nonetheless also initiated an unprecedented dynamic of cultural ruptures and cultural contacts. For a long time the conquering powers asserted their cultures as a unified and universal expression for the whole of the world, but the increasing presence of other views and other voices, most especially in the extraordinary proliferation of literature (as well as music and art) from formerly colonized regions in the post-WWII period, fundamentally challenges that unicity. The voices I have in mind and that I address in the book are not the voices of pure difference. These writers are in constant dialogue with European literary forms and with colonial discourses, but they put these to the purpose of articulating particular positions in the world that are not assimilable to a single picture of the world. The totality of the world that conquest first revealed is, in this restricted and cultural sense, not systematizable. We exist, we think, we write in the presence of all the cultures in the world, without possessing them in a single concept or idea. Glissant writes that in this condition, the "multiple poetics of the world" present themselves as "equivalences that do not unify." In this spirit, I attempt to bring the various texts addressed in this study into relation over a ground of comparison that is in common but not unified.

Each chapter develops a literary-theoretical figure for that incommensurability in which there is ground for comparison but no basis for equivalence: "the foil," "dissimilation," "*com-paraison*," "Relation," "ruined metaphor," and "catastrophic miniaturization". The foil designates a mode of comparison in Joseph Conrad's work in which the moment of recognition in narrative closure is interrupted by a slight slippage between foreground and background with the result that, rather than assimilating their hearers, the stories dissimilate them. Chapter 3 develops dissimilation in reference to the postcolonial reception of Conrad's work. The aim here is to explore the ramifications of a mode of postimperial reading that takes place in the absence of unified or consensual cultural recognition. I link dissimilation to Jean-Luc Nancy's concept of *com-paraison* (co-appearance) to theorize how dissimilation might be understood not only as alienation but also as a mode of relation that does not depend on the recognition of sameness. This finds further development in Édouard Glissant's notion of "Relation," which expresses at one and the same time the realization of a comparative and relational cultural logic of decolonization and also the depropriating and fitfully postnational world of late capitalism. Chapter 4 extends the analysis of this co-incidence in a reading of Derek Walcott's *Omeros*, which, I argue, develops a narrative of postcolonial cultural politics and historical injury within a framework that explicitly addresses the neocolonial/global circumstance of tourism. Walcott's particular ruination of the Homeric metaphor marshals the opacity of a flaunted incommensurability against the platitude of commodified space. Chapter 5 articulates a spatial figure of incommensurability, catastrophic miniaturization, in Aimé Césaire's *Notebook of a Return to the Native Land* and two novels of Simone Schwarz-Bart. This figure, I argue, elaborates on the comparison of colonial inferiorization through the trope of scale. In Schwarz-Bart's novels scale also carries a particular gendered connotation and gives a reflection on gender as an incommensurable fissure in the postcolonial allegorization of an Antillean collectivity.

In a movement that mirrors the argument around comparative method in the first chapter, the subsequent chapters develop a meditation on the postcolonial ramifications of a shift from time to space as an organizing category of experience and a basis for cultural comparison, here mediated through literary form. The imperial traveler, like the imperial anthropologist, translates the geography of empire into the evolutionary scale of civilization and, moving through space, imagines himself visiting the former ages of mankind. Conrad's imperial narrator, however, must strain to keep his narrative from succumbing to the unthinkable comparisons his dislocation invites. The co-presence of inassimilable figures in colonial space ultimately foils Marlow's narrative authority. Walcott elaborates a polemically anti-historical postcolonial aesthetic only to confront the transformation of St. Lucia from backwater of colonial history to a tourist Mecca. In *Omeros* he elaborates an extraordinary edifice of partial similitudes, which function, I argue, like ruins in a landscape as an appropriation of space. Aimé Césaire and Simone Schwarz-Bart, within the strictures of the different colonial and postcolonial cultural problematics they each confront, develop a complex response to what I call the "catastrophic miniaturization" in which colonial inferiority is conflated geographically with insular space. Emplacement, that minimal requirement for the development of an embodied perspective, becomes the object of literary figuration and for Schwarz-Bart it crucially involves a comparative disposition of gender differentiation that operates in a complex dialogue across her two Antillean novels, *Pluie et vent sur Télumée Miracle* and *Ti Jean L'horizon*.

The sequence of these chapters describes a postcolonial itinerary that proceeds from the breakdown of imperial comparison in the colonial narratives of Joseph Conrad to the moment of postcolonial response, or "writing back," and from there to adumbrations of the possibility of intercultural community beyond domination. This arc of what one might call a postcolonial comparatist's desire for an emancipated comparatism is qualified and undercut by a focus on the incursion of contrary and incommensurable forces upon it. These include the effects on culture, particularly literature, of global capitalism, as well as the difficulty for influential Caribbean ideologies of cultural difference to make place for the intercommunal difference of gender. Inevitably this postcolonial itinerary, and comparison itself, is also a meditation on community and collectivity as literature represents its aspirations, its fissures, and its reflection in the process of reading.

Acknowledgements

A stationary stone gathers more moss than it can see its way through and must despair of naming all those who nudged, coaxed, and inspired it. I would like to thank my colleagues Anne Adams, Calum Carmichael, Debra Castillo, Walter Cohen, Jonathan Culler, Brett de Bary, Peter Hohendahl, William Kennedy, Barry Maxwell, Jonathan Monroe, Timothy Murray, Naoki Sakai, and, above all, Neil Saccamano for their patience, encouragement, advice, and the example of their work. Thanks to Sue Besemer for cheering from the sidelines. Leslie Adelson, David Lloyd, and Anne Anlin Cheng offered rigorous readings in the earlier stages. A whole set of anonymous readers provided encouragement and helpful commentary, but Mieke Bal amazed me by grasping my intent better than I could. I am grateful to Helen Tartar, erstwhile editor *extraordinaire*, for the care and commitment with which she shepherded this project as far as she could. I extend my gratitude in admiration to Maryse Condé for her inspiration, support, and help with references. Paz Nachon and Katherine Jentleson provided expert research assistance. Bill and Gail Shaw, and especially the cabin that Jack Shaw built, provided a perfect refuge for the first writing.

Akin Adesokan, David Agruss, Sze Wei Ang, Tarek El-Arris, Ian Bogost, Zahid Chaudhary, Ainsworth Clarke, Jolisa Gracewood, Sondra Hausner, Nina Hien, Tsitsi Jaji, Junyoung Kim, Sheetal Majithia, Gabrielle McIntyre, Yoshi Mihara, Larraine Patterson, Shital Pravinchandra, Stanka Radovic, Leah Rosenberg, Estelle Tarica, Jamie Trnka, Meg Wesling, Jennifer Wilks, and Chi-ming Yang are only a few of the indispensable interlocutors I was privileged to discuss this material with in and out of various seminars. Their work has been a constant stimulus and inspiration to me. As this project took shape, a year at Cornell's Society for the Humanities afforded me the intellectual stimulation and companionship of Ernst van Alphen, Emily Apter, Mieke Bal, Timothy Brennan, Susan Buck-Morss,

Cesare Casarino, Dominick LaCapra, Steven Rubenstein, John Tagg, Karenedis Barzman, Cathy Vasseleu, and Shelley Wong. Ranjana Khanna and Srinivas Aravamudan passed through a few years later and brought their fellowship, encouragement, and the invaluable inspiration of their work. Michael, Emily, Sophia, and Eva followed this labor lovingly from afar, since the days, now long past, when Sophia awed me with her ability to write a book in ten minutes. On another continent, Maria, Christina, and Theodora Chorafas kept me good company to the end, at which time sister Theoktisti also made her surprise appearance.

This writing was a solitary endeavor until it was almost finished when it couldn't have gone on without the sustenance, emotional and alimentary, of my friends Viranjini Munasinghe and Shelley Wong and their families or the ease, labor, and tender constancy of Ramez Elias, who put up with all this in the midst of greater woes.

Portions of chapters 2 and 4 have appeared previously in *Qui Parle* and *Callaloo*, respectively.

ALL THE DIFFERENCE IN THE WORLD

Grounds for Comparison

> But no sooner have they been adumbrated than all these groupings
> dissolve again, for the field of identity that sustains them, however
> limited it may be, is still too wide not to be unstable; and so the sick
> mind continues to infinity, creating groups then dispersing them
> again, heaping up diverse similarities, destroying those that seem
> clearest, splitting up things that are identical, superimposing differ-
> ent criteria, frenziedly beginning all over again, becoming more and
> more disturbed, and teetering finally on the brink of anxiety.
> —Michel Foucault, *The Order of Things*

Those affiliated with comparative literature are probably familiar
with an encounter like this. At a cocktail party, a reception, or a family
dinner, someone leans over and asks what you study. "Comparative literature," you answer, to which the interlocutor responds, "Oh, and what
exactly do you compare?" Besides the usual discomforts of having to explain academic work, there is always a particular shock of nonrecognition
associated with the sudden spotlight on the word "compare." One might
answer the question simply enough by replying, "literatures" or "cultures,"
but one hesitates at the verb: in what sense does the act of comparing describe what one does in this discipline? The adjectival appendage has been
a source of some consternation over the last eighty years or so. Lane Cooper, who balked at using the name for the program he headed at Cornell in
the 1920s, took "comparative" strictly as an attribute of the object "literature" and found it a "bogus term" that no more "sense [or] syntax than say
'comparative potatoes,' or 'comparative husks.'"[1] A few decades later, René
Wellek, taking "comparative" as a characterization of the act of a practitioner, or a "method of comparison," remarked that scholars of literature
do many things besides compare ("reproduce, analyze, interpret, evoke,

evaluate, generalize, etc."), and advocated changing the discipline's name to "general literature" or just "literature."[2] But despite its insufficiencies, or out of sheer institutional inertia, the "comparative" sticks throughout the years of the discipline's postwar consolidation. It is notable therefore that it should make such a stunning comeback in the 1993 Bernheimer report, where it supplants the term "literature" as the focal point for a discipline equal to the challenges of "the age of multiculturalism," in the words of the title of the volume under which the report and a collection of responses to it was published. "Comparison" occurs in various guises thirteen times in this brief report. But while sheer repetition would seem to make of it the discipline's new "standard," its meaning is far from clear, for comparison is no longer a misplaced adjective or a method of analysis but a space:

The space of comparison today involves comparisons between artistic productions usually studied by different disciplines; between various cultural constructions of those disciplines; between Western cultural traditions, both high and popular, and those of non-Western cultures, between the pre- and postcontact cultural productions of colonized peoples; between gender constructions defined as feminine and those defined as masculine, or between sexual orientations defined as straight and those defined as gay; between racial and ethnic modes of signifying; between hermeneutic articulations of meaning and materialist analyses of production and circulation and much more.[3]

The "space of comparison" seems to be a synonym or a kind of toponym for this long paratactic sentence's last words "and much more," in the sense that comparison here above all connotes inclusiveness in the form of a potentially limitless serial extension. But if the association of the noun comparison with an inclusive space comes out clearly, the meaning of the verb "to compare" as a practice or an act is obscure. In some of the examples listed, the comparative dimension or approach seems constitutive to the point of redundancy: it is hard to imagine a study of gay sexual orientation without some comparative reference to heterosexuality, or of the construction of femininity without comparative reference to masculinity, though the precise nature of the comparison is complicated by the very particular and vexed nature of the comparability in question (masculinity and femininity are intrinsically comparative just as they are precisely not equivalent). In other examples, the elements under comparison seem at least initially to be incomparable or at least incommensurable. Is not the very point, in the practice of cultural studies for instance, of studying "low" or popular culture *not* to compare it with "high" culture, but rather to refuse binary relation high/low and define the parameters of popular culture's own positivity? A similar incommensurability obtains, as an initial standpoint with respect to the binary Western/non-Western, where, in addition, the very determination of equivalent categories to bring into comparison is highly problematic. If comparison as a space or an ethos of inclusiveness suggests itself to the discipline of comparative literature as a corrective, if not a kind of panacea, to the discipline's exclusionary and elitist Eurocentric institutional past, comparison as a method or a practice presents itself as a perplexing problem.

Indeed comparison comes through most clearly as an attribute—not a practice—of a person, the "comparatist," where it indexes the productive anxiety of "unhomeliness" or dislocation. As Charles Bernheimer puts it in his introduction (itself entitled "The Anxieties of Comparison"), "multicultural comparatism begins at home with a comparison of oneself to oneself," in other words, with "the hybrid constitution of the comparatist subject" (Bernheimer, 11). Indeed most of those essays that embrace the multiculturalist turn (as opposed to those that lament the perceived dethroning of literature), stress the positionality of the practitioner of comparative literature.[4] As a method, comparison for Bernheimer is defined, or undefined, as an ellipsis, the typographical equivalent for perplexity itself: "Comparison is indeed the . . . what is it?—activity, function, practice? all of these?—that assures that our field will always be unstable, shifting, insecure, and self-critical" (Bernheimer, 2). This un-definition of comparison as a kind of conduit for uncertainty and instability contrasts sharply with the supreme positivity of the comparative method that defined comparative literature at its very institutional beginnings in the United States. Compare Charles Chauncey Shackford in the first known lecture on comparative literature delivered in the United States at Cornell University in 1871:

And the method in which this study can be best pursued is that which is pursued in anatomy, in language, in mythology, and recently applied by Mr. Freeman to politics, namely the comparative. The literary productions of all ages and peoples can be classed, can be brought into comparison and contrast, can be taken out of their isolation as belonging to one nation, or one separate era, and be brought under divisions as the embodiment of the same aesthetic principles, the universal laws of mental, social and moral development: the same in India and in England; in Hellas, with its laughing sea, and Germany with its sombre forests.[5]

The intellectually estranging effect of this juxtaposition is all the more powerful when one considers that it is precisely something like Shackford's comparative method, a practice of comparison that classifies, differentiates and assimilates, and finally evaluates its objects in a universal field, that haunts the activity of comparison as it is described in the passage of the Bernheimer report. In giving central place to "comparison," the late twentieth-century self-definition of comparative literature unknowingly returns to its institutional origins in the comparative method, which subsist as a kind of ruin buried just below the surface of the text. The 1993 report returns to the earlier comprehensive scope of comparison, except that to Shackford's 1871 "literary productions of all ages and peoples," it would add non-literary productions (and much more), but, and this stands out in starkest relief, without his basic unifying concept, namely the "universal laws of development." Where comparison was once indissociably temporal—a matter of development through time—it now seems firmly if indistinctly associated with space. In the broadest sense, the conditions for and the ramifications of the shift of the scope of comparison from time to space will be the central concern of this chapter.

Institutional memory of early champions of the comparative method at the moment of the discipline's initial institutionalization during the last quarter of the nineteenth century seems to have faded from its dominant self-perception. With a single cursory exception, none of the contributors to *Comparative Literature in the Age of Multiculturalism* or its recent successor, *Comparative Literature in an Age of Globalization* (2006), make mention of pre-WWII origins of the discipline. In the tacitly accepted version of the story of origins, the discipline begins with the arrival on American shores of the great émigré Romance philologists fleeing fascism and persecution (Leo Spitzer, Renato Poggioli, René Wellek, et al., and of course most prominently, Erich Auerbach) in the 1930s and 1940s. The model of comparative literature they fostered generally held sway until the advent of deconstruction and the discipline's identification with literary theory. Deconstruction, in turn, is followed by the prominence of a panoply of approaches, many of them originating in other disciplines, all of them advocating various kinds of historicism or contextualization and often articulating minoritarian or oppositional positions (Marxism, postcolonialism, feminism, new historicism, etc.), more or less accommodated under the broad rubric of multiculturalism. It is not surprising that comparatists' sense of the discipline's trajectory should extend little beyond the time of their own institutional formations, as comparative literature seems to exceed the requisite amnesia for institutional reproduction. More than other disciplines it has been almost constitutively formed around displacement.[6] One need only consider, for instance, that (arguably) the most influential successors to Auerbach in terms of their formative impact on the discipline, Paul de Man and Edward Said, are themselves both émigrés, and that the decisive changes they brought to the discipline result, to a large extent, from their lives and educations elsewhere (for De Man the intellectual culture of Europe in the 1930s and 1940s, for Said the colonial world and in particular the fate of Palestine in the 1940s and 1950s) and are thus ultimately discontinuous with the disciplinary practice already established in U.S. universities.[7] Nor is this particular amnesia regarding the positivist comparative method limited to this generation. In an essay from 1956, René Wellek already notes a distinct forgetfulness: "fifty and sixty years ago the concept of evolution dominated literary history; today, at least in the West, it seems to have disappeared almost completely. Histories of literature and of literary genres are being written without any allusion to the problem and apparently with no awareness of it."[8] While he cannot in the compass of this short essay account for this fact, he speculates that it may in part have to do with the success of positivism's critics in the early decades of the twentieth century, such as Henri Bergson and Benedetto Croce, to which might add the rise of "vitalism" or "*Lebensphilosophie*" around figures such as Wilhelm Dilthey and Georg Simmel. My own interest will not be so much to explore the causes of this amnesia as to speculate on the disciplinary narrative of comparison it makes possible, particularly at the moment of the disciplines' consolidation in the postwar years. I should make clear also that the disciplinary self-definition I address here is one that has been dominant but by no means exclusive. It is overwhelmingly associated with what one might call the East Coast establishment (the authors of the four successive reports on standards for the American Comparative Literature Association (ACLA) hail from Harvard, Yale, and Penn, and were all, in addition, educated at Harvard and Yale). What I am calling amnesia is neither complete nor entirely involuntary, but rather a matter of selective omission and disregard. The growth of the discipline in the 1960s occasioned a spate of introductory handbooks, many of which included the writings of positivist precursors. These precursors were, thus, not so much strictly unknown as without echo.[9] This has in part obviously to do with a turn at the time from historicism to formalism, but, as I will argue further on, I do not think this can by itself account for the amnesia. Furthermore, the institutional context I address is, like that of my sources, almost exclusively

American. The discipline of comparative literature has a history outside the United States, in Europe, of course, but also outside Europe, particularly in Asia and the Middle East, which most commentators on the discipline pass over in silence.[10]

The existence of the positivist precursors and the comprehensive comparative scope they envisioned unsettles the one "truth" about the discipline that seems universally shared amongst contemporary practitioners: that comparative literature has until now encompassed mainly European literatures. In his witty contribution to the Bernheimer volume, "*Geist* Stories," Anthony Appiah rightly points out that the discipline would be more accurately named "comparative European literatures" and suggests that it content itself with this historically and regionally coherent scope and leave comparably transnational assemblages to other disciplinary formations.[11] The name "comparative European literatures" certainly characterizes the practice of most U.S. departments, which, with few exceptions, until recently rarely offered the option of studying literatures in any language besides French, German, and English, but it does not represent the historical scope of comparison in the discipline. To assume that it does has one important consequence—namely, that calls for an inclusive multicultural scope of comparison are understood as recent innovations that develop from critiques of Eurocentrism. Such a claim is no doubt accurate in its broadest terms, since the directions for the discipline advocated in the Bernheimer report are unimaginable without the pressures of an "age of multiculturalism," if only because of the unprecedented movement and migration of peoples characteristic of the postcolonial or global moment. But while the nature of this multiculturalism and the conditions of its possibility are novel, its scope is not. By attending closely to the structures of comparison that mediated a previous era's comprehensive scope, I hope to arrive at a more precise analysis of the problem of comparison today.

Comparative Reaches Unimagined

> The world was never better worth preparing for.
> The panorama unrolled before the mind was
> never more gorgeous: a new renaissance reveal-
> ing reaches unimagined; prophesying splendor
> unimagined; unveiling mysteries of time and
> space and natural law and human potency.
> —Charles Mills Gayley, *Idols of Education* (1910)

If we do not take comparative literature's exclusively European scope for granted, then the relative absence of non-Western literatures and languages in the discipline's formation after WWII becomes a real question. The discipline's growth during the 1960s coincides with the final phase of a period of decolonization that by itself would suggest an extension of comparative literature's cosmopolitan scope. Indeed already in 1952, no less a figure than Erich Auerbach himself writes (however ambivalently) of the need to extend the notion of *Weltliteratur* beyond Europe's immediate vicinity.[12] Wellek too echoes such a view in passing, while emphasizing the substantial practical obstacles to it.[13] And yet no one elaborates upon this possibility, but for the exception that proves the rule, René Etiemble, whose polemical writings advocating, in the words of one of his titles, "un comparatisme planétaire" [a planetary comparatism], seem to extract little more than faint ridicule from his American counterparts.[14] Auerbach and Wellek are to a significant extent driven toward what we would call a multicultural direction as a logical extension of the historicist philology that grounds their scholarship, a historicism with roots in universal history. One might well argue that the a- or counter-historicism shared by such dominant movements as new criticism, structuralism, and deconstruction largely overwhelmed the historicist impulses that might have broadened the discipline's scope. One the other hand, nothing intrinsically prevents formalist criticism from approaching non-Western works. Institutional factors, particularly those related to cold war politics, extrinsic to the immediate intellectual history of the discipline go at least part of the way toward accounting for the discipline's exclusively European scope in its most recent incarnation.

The postwar period saw a tremendous expansion of higher education in the United States together with an increased bureaucratization of the humanities, particularly in those fields, like comparative literature, language departments, and area studies, that benefited so handsomely from the National Defense Education Act (1958), a law explicitly designed to help meet the U.S. government's expansive cold war national "security" requirements. Such exigencies also fueled the growth of area studies and perhaps, institutionally at least, account for their strict separation from a transnational discipline in the humanities like comparative literature. In addition, and perhaps most importantly, the propaganda requirements of the cold war spurred renewed interest in the Western tradition for general education. As Gerald Graff points out, the common values such an education was to inculcate in citizens were articulated quite overtly as "expression[s] of cold war anti-Communism."[15] Though the purpose of general education is perhaps definable as a national one, that is to say, as the formation of patriotic and anti-Communist national subjects, the *content* that such influential figures as Harvard's James Bryant Conant proposed for them was by no means limited to American works, but rather drew on the whole Western tradition. There is a sense in which, as John Guillory elegantly argues, this tradition is always called upon, particularly in public debate, to support a national agenda, which its champions accomplish by, in John Guillory's words, "representing the ideational content of the great works as an expression of the same ideas which are realized in the current social order, with its current distribution of cultural goods."[16] In the 1950s and 1960s, thus, as the United States is consolidating its role as "leader of the free world," and waging the cold war in part over emergent decolonizing nations, a great tradition that is specifically limited to the West is far more apposite for the purpose of justifying such key terms as "democracy" and "freedom" in the new imperial context than one that would include comparably "great" non-Western civilizations. I do not mean to claim a simple causal relationship between the United States' strategic uses for particular configurations of internationalism during the cold war and comparative literature's exclusively European scope. Indeed, I think that the discipline's close association with expatriate Europeans and the practice of scholarship they brought with them, both in fact and in spirit, distanced it from the overt expressions of Americanism in other parts of the university, even as, on the whole, the major figures in the discipline tend to be markedly hostile to communism and vice versa.[17] What I want to mark is a conjuncture between the exclusively European scholarly scope of the expatriate philologists that is crucial to the formation of comparative literature as we have inherited it and the particular cold war context in which the discipline flourished.

If nothing else, this scenario urges caution toward any uncomplicated opposition between cosmopolitanism and parochialism or transnationalism and nationalism in the constitution of the discipline, an opposition that is so crucial to comparative literature's self-perception. There is no question that its prominent practitioners have articulated powerful critiques of parochial and reductive approaches to their subject or that they have elaborated comparative works that remain exemplary in their scope and sympathy. Nonetheless, the narrow parochialism that is the field's great other seems to correspond to little in the postwar geopolitical field, which was dominated not by nationalist contests, but by the delicate maneuvering of diplomats in a war that figured the world into two huge "blocs" and whose atomic weapons aimed west to east and east to west threatened total annihilation for everyone and everything equally, without regard to national identity. This is not to understate the strength of national identification, but simply to point out that of all the periods the discipline of comparative literature passed through in the United States from 1871 to the present, the postwar period seems to be the one during which the discipline's "oppositional" cosmopolitan self-identification corresponded least directly to external political conditions. What I want to propose here, in a schematic and speculative mode, is that the cold war created a kind of deferral or a screen between the status of national languages and cosmopolitanism in the university's bureaucratic arrangements and the force of those categories in the geopolitical world and so contributed to diverting the discipline from what might have been a broader comparative scope. The end of the cold war has brought a very sudden change in this ghostly survival of autonomous national units (departments) that now in many cases face dissolution or consolidation into composite disciplinary assemblages, just as it has lifted the curtain to spotlight a globalization, which, in its economic and to an extent political form, had been developing apace all along.[18] From a post–cold war perspective, the nationalist parochialism comparative literature defined itself against seems to finds its most direct reference in internal bureaucratic arrangements (turf battles with national literature departments and interdisciplinary programs over courses, students, funds, intellectual prominence, status). My point here is that, particularly in view of the growth of the university's bureaucracy, internal institutional factors must seriously be taken into account in any attempt to historicize the cultural content of a discipline.

For those of us weaned on the anti-parochial view of comparative literature, it can come as something of a surprise that the discipline did not make its first appearance in the U.S. university after or in reaction to modern national literature departments, but in concert with them. Before addressing larger epistemic questions, I want to take a short detour through the institutional history of comparative literature in the United States in order to ground this reflection on comparison in the very institutional framework from which it most directly issues. This is important not only because the discipline is mediated in its relation to society and to the world by its place in an institution, but also because certain factors that barely emerge in a conceptual account loom larger and more clearly in an institutional account, most particularly in this case, gender. The decisive event for modern literatures and indeed for the very notion of disciplines governed by distinct methodologies and divided into departments was the introduction of the German model of the research university in the 1870s (Graff, 55–64). Prior to this professionalization of scholarship with its rigorous scientific practice and training, the Greek and Latin classics dominated classroom teaching while modern literatures were pursued and discussed outside the university's curriculum in literary societies and debating clubs. While the primary function of the old college had been the socialization of the elite, the primary function of the modern university was the training and certification of specialists. For Graff, the establishment of the modern or research university initiates a contest between specialists and "generalists" or scholars and humanists; that is, between a scientific or empirical approach to literature associated with philology and a generalist or interpretive approach, a split that, according to him, structures literary culture in the academy until the time of his own writing in the late 1980s. While useful as a general distinction, this polarization is often complicated and this is particularly the case with the field of comparative literature insofar as, on the one hand, the comparative method that Charles Chauncey Shackford champions in his lectures (and one must surmise as he elaborated it in his course, the first of its kind—as far as is known—in the United States) aligns with the new emphasis on rigorous method while, on the other hand, the breadth of comparative literature's scope clearly contests the *narrow* specialization associated with philology. To the distinction between generalist humanism and specialized scholarship, one must add the distinction between narrow specialization and broad systematization, both of which will lay competing claims to the mantle of scientificity. For Charles Mills Gayley, a crucial figure in the institutionalization of comparative literature at the turn of the century, the practice of comparative literature was quite explicitly a means toward wresting philology away from myopic pedantry.[19] In Gayley's work, a systematic approach to literary study goes hand in hand with a general appreciation of literature, as important for maintaining the socializing function of the old college as it was for educating the general public. I focus on Gayley here because he was perhaps the most vigorous and influential proponent of a comprehensive and positivist comparatism at the moment of comparative literature's institutional consolidation as a discipline. In current discussions of the discipline that reach beyond the postwar period, Gayley is most often forgotten or erased in favor of his high humanist East Coast counterpart, George Woodberry at Columbia.

In the period between 1880–1915, the height of Gayley's activity, the U.S. university experienced substantial growth in enrollment spurred by the entrance of a broader spectrum of the middle class lured by the promise of careers in business (Graff, 105). The humanists, then as now, bemoan the new philistine students "impervious to humanistic education," in Graff's words (Graff, 106–107). Gayley sounds precisely such themes in his writings, but in his pedagogical practice he finds in comparative literature a solution both to the loss of the old college's elite socialization as well as to the problem of educating a utilitarian-minded professional managerial class. When Gayley is brought to the University of California at Berkeley in 1889 to chair the English department and reform its curriculum, he inherits a hodgepodge of course offerings including some of the old college's instruction in rhetoric, some philologically inflected courses centered on language, and others specialized in various authors and periods. Gayley's main action is to expand and systematize these offerings so that the department would offer, in his words, "a synoptical view of English literature as the outcome of, and the index to, English thought in the course of its development."[20] This meant not only the addition of courses in periods and genres, but more importantly in "Aesthetics of Literature, Principles of Criticism, and Comparative Literature," all of which extended the primary materials far beyond the literature of England.[21] The national literature, in other words, was to be studied in a comparative context. I have found no record of Gayley attempting to establish a separate department of comparative literature, and it may well be that in the institutional conception of the time such strict correspondence between discipline and department was less secure than it has, until recently, been for us. Nor were scholars as intimately identified with departments during this formative period (Gayley himself graduated from the department of literature and science at the University of Michigan, where he concentrated on Greek and Latin and later underwent the requisite training in philological methods during a year's study in Germany). Comparative literature in its scientific dimension provided a model of specialized study, and in its generalist dimension a model both for a livelier version of the old college's course in rhetoric and for the courses in general education designed for the university's new middle-class entrants. Gayley offered a course on "Oral Debates upon Literary Topics" for students in the English department and his popular course on "Great Books" (which, initiated in 1901, was one of the first of its kind in the nation), for the larger college population.

It is not the conflict between the middle class and the elite in the humanities that looms largest as a problem for Gayley in his institutionalization of comparative literature, but rather the contaminating presence of women and more generally of the feminine gendering of modern literature itself. In a short pamphlet, Gayley notes that "the disrepute into which the humanities have fallen" follows from what he calls "the feminization of education" (owing to low salaries for secondary school teachers). "For entrusted to women," he continues, "the languages, literature, and history have come to be regarded as feminine and ineffectual studies," partly to blame for the "undisciplined character of the rising generation of men."[22] The question of women in higher education is a broad one and has been treated or analyzed in depth elsewhere.[23] General institutional histories, however, tend not to treat the question separately. Though Graff comments briefly throughout his analysis on the femininity attributed to modern literature, pointing out, for instance, that part of the attraction of philology was that it endowed the study of modern languages and literatures with "manliness" necessary to make it a respectable subject, he never treats the question in depth. Judging by the references to this subject by Gayley's biographer, his student and collaborator Benjamin P. Kurtz, one could well conclude, reading against the grain, that Gayley's greatest accomplishment with the institution of comparative literature was the defeminization of modern literature. Kurtz reports, for instance, that for "Oral Debates upon Literary Topics," Gayley had recourse to the stratagem of "setting up certain prerequisites to which he adhered with the women but he neglected for the men."[24] For those "fortunate" and "privileged" enough to participate, it was, Kurtz avers, an unforgettable course: "From its vivid discipline they gained a lifelong masculine interest in great literature" (Kurtz, 110). If Gayley felt it to be expedient to keep women away from "great literature" in the effete confines of the English curriculum in order to conserve a corner for the masculine interests so vital to the elite socialization of the old college, he also invited them to leave the site where great literature was made available to the unclean philistine masses, his lecture course on "Great Books." I quote Kurtz at some length:

To stimulate such reading, to rescue reading from subservience to the professional technique of a narrow scholarship, and especially to develop such reading among students in the colleges of applied sciences, he instituted a one-hour course in Great Books. . . . And there was a story of some venturesome engineers who discarded jumpers and overalls, washed the laboratory grime from their hands, and sallied forth to a literary lecture room, *only to find it so crowded with girls, women, coeds, pelicans, old maids, and females of every other sort and description, that they fled back to their hill fastness.* As a matter of fact, to keep the new course for the students in the applied sciences and in commerce, it became necessary to limit the attendance of women. This limitation aroused such a storm of protest, in which the lecturer was repeatedly accused of being a woman-hater, that the course was given one term for the men of the University and the alternate term for all and sundry. Until this device was invented, there was trouble enough. (Kurtz, 151–152; emphasis added)

It is worth considering John Guillory's point that what is transmitted in the university is not so much a particular content, but the culture of the school itself and access to the production and distribution of "cultural capital." The social relations the university contains and reproduces must be considered alongside how it defines and organizes objects of knowledge. I have encountered no discussion, whether biographical or analytical, of women's experience in the rise of the discipline of comparative literature or in its institutional life.[25] The literary theory that dominated comparative literature during the 1980s has often been criticized from an institutional point of view for the full technocratization of literary studies it produced—highly specialized jargon, the successful marketing of expertise for its own stake, the star system, etc. Yet it must also be observed that, to my knowledge anyway, during its founding moment it welcomed and promoted women and a certain strain of feminism in comparative literature on an unparalleled scale, thus perhaps finally breaching the subtle and implicit cordon between the feminine (intrinsically parochial) social graces of modern national literatures and the virility of cosmopolitanism.[26]

In Gayley's important programmatic essay "What is Comparative Literature?" (1903),[27] the adjective "comparative" indicates first a scientific approach that is at once systematic and historical, and second a global scope for the study of literature, a scope so all-encompassing that it depends upon broad-based collaborative work. Gayley calls for the formation of a "Society of Comparative Literature," in which he imagines each member pursuing the study of a "given type, species, movement, or theme" and collectively piecing together a "comparative investigation into the nature of literature, part by part" (Gayley, 85), in time resulting in the discovery of the "common qualities of literature, scientifically determined" (Gayley, 86), a true and universal canon of criticism. He optimistically felt that "this dream is now in a fair way to be realized" (how quaint this seems retrospectively

from this most uncollaborative of disciplines). This notion of the collaborative nature of the comparative enterprise is important in part because
by aligning the academic practice of comparative literature with that of
experimental science, it replaces single all-knowing humanist able to syn-
thesize his learning through a kind of historical intuition with the limited
and specialized investigator.[28] It is easy to caricature Gayley's propositions,
but they are in fact quite nuanced. For Gayley, the comparative method has
a fundamental and dynamic historical or temporal component. It is this
stress on development, or (the term Gayley prefers) "permutation," that
most distinguishes his scientific version of comparative literature from the
high humanism of early comparatists more readily remembered today, such
as George Woodberry, who held the first chair in comparative literature
established in the United States, at Columbia. Gayley quotes from Woodberry's editorial comments on the purpose of the discipline of comparative
literature in the inaugural issue of the *Journal of Comparative Literature*
(1903): "To disclose the necessary forms, the vital moods of the beautiful
soul, is the far goal of our effort, to help in this, in the bringing of those
spiritual unities in which human destiny is accomplished."[29] Gayley comments, "with this the genuine student of literary science must agree," even
as he delicately faults Woodberry for entirely ignoring the possibility of
"growth" (Gayley, 101). The very discrepancy in tone and diction between
the seeker after the "beautiful soul" and the student of "literary science" goes
a long way toward showing the gulf that divided the humanist comparatists
from the scientific practitioners. The question of "growth," a unifying and
roughly evolutionary temporality, is decisive for it will underwrite Gayley's
insistence on the inclusion of all literary expression "wherever found" as
the proper subject matter for the discipline, a stand that will earn him the
acerbic criticism of East Coast philologists and humanists alike. Indeed he
defines the task of this society as "the comparative investigation of literary
growths," and hesitates between "Society of Comparative Literature" and
"Society of Literary Evolution" for its name. Throughout the essay Gayley
stresses the comprehensive scope of comparison and its dependence upon
a notion of "growth":

To repeat, the comparison is not alone between diverse national literatures, but
between any elements involved in the history of literature, or any stages in the
history of any element. There have been, within my own knowledge, those who
would confine the word literature to the written productions of civilized peoples
and consequently would exclude from consideration aboriginal attempts at verbal

art. But students nowadays increasingly recognize that the cradle of literary science is anthropology. The comparative method therefore sets civilized literatures side by side with the popular, traces folklore to folklore, and these so far as possible to the matrix in the undifferentiated art of human expression. (Gayley, 92)

For Gayley the comparative method is not limited to various inter-actions of European national literatures because it applies across time. A progressive or teleological temporality allows for the commensuration of a comprehensive array of verbal artifacts, the "aboriginal" and "civilized," the written and oral verbal arts. Gayley's insistence that "the cradle of liter-ary science is anthropology" is key here. Besides giving us a glimpse into the range of interdisciplinarity possible at the moment of disciplinarity's institutionalization, this assertion reinforces the intrinsically temporal na-ture of the comparative method. The comparative method that dominated late-nineteenth-century anthropology applied across a single civilizational scale where all the world's cultures had their place in an evolutionary hier-archy progressing from the simple or "savage" to the complex and highly differentiated societies of "civilization." In what Johannes Fabian has cri-tiqued as a "spatialization of time," savages were, culturally speaking, the "ancestors" of civilized man, a view that made possible the recovery of the past in the present.[30] Despite hesitation in some quarters about impos-ing upon what is visibly only a coexistence of phenomena in geographical space with the assumption of a consecutive sequence in time,[31] comparison along the civilizational scale allowed all differences in *kind* to be measur-able as differences of *degree* in development or growth.[32] It is this tempo-ralized comparison that underwrites the ubiquity of non-Western subject matter in Gayley's work on aesthetics and comparative literature. To give just two examples, when Gayley delivers a series of lectures on aesthetics at the University of California in 1890–1891, the first half are devoted to learned definitions and disquisitions in the philosophy of aesthetics, with prominent attention to Aristotle, G. W. F. Hegel, Arthur Schopenhauer, and Hutcheson Macaulay Posnett, while the second half introduces an ap-plication or an example of the development of the form of the lyric in the context of environmental factors over three progressive stages: (1) naïve, (2) reflective, and (3) spiritual, with examples from folk songs of South-ern India and lyric from China and Japan, respectively, to illustrate each stage.[33] But this is just a sampling of Gayley's comprehensive scope. The second volume of his *An Introduction to the Methods and Materials of Liter-ary Criticism*, subtitled "Lyric, Epic and Allied Forms of Poetry" (the first volume is devoted to "Aesthetics and Poetics") gives the full panoply. The chapter on "Historical Development" of the lyric is divided into two main sections; the first lays out areas of analysis (e.g., "Beginnings of the Lyric," "Principles of Growth"), while the second is subheaded: "Historical Study by Nationality: Special References," and comprises thirty-three different "nationalities." I reproduce the list in full:

The Greek Lyric

The Roman Lyric

The Byzantine Lyric

Christian Greek and Latin Hymns of the Dark and Middle Ages

Other Latin Christian Lyric Poetry from the 2d to the 14th Century

Latin Poetry of the 15th and 16th Centuries

The French (including Provencal) Lyric

The Italian Lyric

The Spanish Lyric

The Portuguese Lyric

The English Lyric

The Celtic Lyric (Irish, Scottish, Welsh, etc)

The German Lyric

The Dutch Lyric

The Scandinavian Lyric in General

The Icelandic Lyric

The Swedish Lyric

The Danish-Norwegian Lyric

Lyric Poetry of the Lapps and Finns

The Russian Lyric

Serbian Cheskian, Magyar, and Polish Lyrics

The Turkish Lyric

The Afghan Lyric

The Syriac and Armenian Lyric

The Lyric of Arabia

The Persian Lyric

The Indian Lyric

The Sumerian and Babylonian Lyric

The Egyptian Lyric
The Ancient Hebrew Lyric
The Chinese Lyric
The Japanese Lyric
Lower Races
Special Forms[34]

Such a list appears comprehensive: it provides panoramic perspective on all the lyric in the world. Each "nation" is certainly not treated in equal depth (English lyric at 41 pages leads the pack, whereas the Afghan, Syriac, and Armenian lyric, at a single page amongst them, bring up the rear) and the sequence of sections follows roughly three ordering principles: linguistic, racio-geographic, and evolutionary and these are discrepant, as even a cursory look at this list shows. The main tradition of the Western European lyric is presented more or less chronologically and grouped by language families (e.g., Greek, Latin, Romance, Anglo-Saxon, Germanic, etc.) followed by the margins of Caucasian Europe (Scandinavia, Russia, Eastern Europe), then, starting with Turkish lyric, come the darker races of the East, listed at first geographically, then starting with the Summerian and Babylonian lyric, grouped by antiquity. This is followed by the Far East, which remains consistent with linguistic and geographical unities but falls off the temporal scale. The list ends with the "lower races," which include such diverse peoples as Andamanese, Veddas, Australians, Malays, Africans, Esquimaux, and North and South American Indians (Gayley and Kurtz, 369). Race, as it appears here, exists outside the boundaries implicit in all the previous rubrics, outside of unities of language, nationality, geography, and temporal progression. It stands by itself as the bare signifier for that which fails to correspond to any of the other criteria apparent in the inventory, a "none of the above," eluding even the overarching idea of "growth" itself. This inconsistency is irksome enough to warrant Gayley and Kurtz's only explicit comment on their sequence. Noting that the lyric of "the lower or so-called 'primitive' races" ought to come first since it belongs at the origin of the art, they aver without further explanation that an outline according to "nationalities" is more "perspicuous" than one ordered strictly according to "the order of development" (Gayley and Kurtz, 369). The term "nationalities" seems to refer loosely to linguistic unities rather than politico-geographic ones, since, for instance, the list includes Irish, Scottish, Welsh, etc, under the single rubric of "Celtic Lyric," but even this basic index of consistency is foiled by developmentalism's implicit racial distinction. For what else could distinguish "Lapps and Finns," for instance, from "Lower Races"? The inventory's departure from the principle of growth so crucial to Gayley and Kurtz's conception of comparison reveals the limit of their particular positivist humanism, and that limit is the replacement of the Greek with the African at the head of any list.[35] In this comparative scheme, the lower races must remain fundamentally *undifferentiated*. A civilizational progress underlies the list, but it must be read backward (or from the bottom up) from the "lower races" to the modern European languages.

If a fundamental principle of temporal and (if one may say so) Euro-directional development legitimates comparison's comprehensive scope, a supreme confidence in the cumulative and progressive nature of positivist knowledge underlies the scientific comparatists' sense of the discipline's purpose. Throughout the handbook the authors offer directives for future research, in full confidence that once enough literary data has been collected, the proper categories or types will be defined and, submitted to comparison, will at last positively manifest general laws of literature. These grand plans were to be very short-lived. WWI dashed the unquestioned cosmopolitan unity of the European nations so vital to comparative literature's project both in its humanist and its scientific guises, and broke the hold of German philology on the U.S. academy. The anti-positivism of post-WWI intellectual currents, furthermore, turned humanist scholarship away from the systematic and comprehensive approach it had shared with the emergent social sciences. The discipline of comparative literature generally waned during the interwar period.[36]

Compared to post-WWII handbooks of comparative literature, the range and diversity of nations gathered together under the rubric of a genre or, as Gayley would say, a "type" is quite remarkable. René Wellek and Austin Warren's *Theory of Literature*, a very influential handbook continuously in print since it was first published in 1942, is entirely organized around concepts and methods, with no separate heading whatsoever relating to national or cultural scope. The literature of Europe is to such an extent given as the unified field of comparative literature that it neither requires argumentation nor prompts even the shadow of a question. Gayley and Kurtz's *An Introduction to the Methods and Materials of Literary Criticism* and Wellek and Warren's *Theory of Literature* thus mark a clear shift from a geographically comprehensive or global Euro-centered comparatism to a uniquely European comparatism. Besides expanding the perspective of the discipline's institutional history, attention to positivist comparatism has important consequences for contemporary practice. One concerns post-colonial critique. Aimed at the idealist, high humanist stance of the early comparatists, this critique indicts them for what one might call a geographical elision; that is, for excluding the better part of the globe in their comparative, general articulation of human creative endeavor. Edward Said in *Culture and Imperialism* faults George Woodberry, for instance, for waxing eloquent on the unity of mankind without any reference whatsoever to the high imperialism of his time and points to the exclusive focus on the European historical unity of "Romania" as the limited geographical grounding of the work of Erich Auerbach.[37] What is left out, Said shows, is precisely the contemporary imperial relations that carve out the globe and make it unavoidably present as a totality. The "comparative literature of imperialism" centered on an innovative "contrapuntal" reading of texts from the imperial metropoles and the former colonies that Said elaborates in this study aims to restore the historical imbrication of imperialism's geographical extent occluded in the restricted scope of a strictly European comparatism (*CI*, 18–19). As we have seen, however, the relation of positivist comparative literature to contemporary political and economic imperial hegemony is direct, no less so than that of its disciplinary "cradle," anthropology. Its methodology, furthermore, draws its authority from a particular reading of imperial history, as we shall explore further. There is, of course, no critique of imperialism in this methodology, and no attention or even mention of relations of domination and coercion. What stands out starkly, however, is that a comprehensive geographical scope is neither novel nor sufficient in and of itself as a response to Eurocentrism. Needless to say, Said's approach offers much more than such an unmediated inclusivity. Nonetheless, attention to the dimension of the comparative project that is not grounded in the representative universalism of high humanism opens a slightly different angle onto the paths a postcolonial comparatism might take, particularly because the idea of comparison as a method features so prominently in the positivist approach.

The Time of Comparison

How much will it still take before the mines of the past have rendered all the treasures they enclose? The work of modern erudition will only be accomplished when all the faces of humanity,

that is, all the nations, will have been the object
of definitive studies, when India, China, Judea,
Egypt will be restored, when we will definitively possess a perfect comprehension of the
entire human development. Only then will the
reign of criticism [*la critique*] be inaugurated.
For criticism will proceed with perfect security
only when it will see open before it the field of
universal comparison. Comparison is the great
critical instrument.
—Ernest Renan, *L'Avenir de la science:*
  pensées de 1848

What is the time of comparison?
—Shelley Wong

The crucial moment when a comparative approach to scholarship developed by the Romantic theorist, especially J. G. von Herder and August
and Friedrich von Schlegel, becomes a comparative *method* occurs, according to Wellek around 1850, when "Romantic conceptions fell into discredit,
and ideals from the natural sciences became victorious, even in the writing
of literary history."[38] This inaugurates the reign of positivism thoroughly
discredited and later forgotten in the twentieth century. Among the more
extreme transfers of concepts from the natural sciences to the comparison of literature is Ferdinand Brunetière's application of Darwin's theory
of evolution directly to literature, with genres treated as species evolving
according to distinct laws and principles, including survival of the fittest.[39]
From the distance of our time, particularly in the wake of the concerted
critique of teleology over the last forty years or so, the distinction between
what one might call the humanist historicism of the early nineteenth century and the positivist evolutionism of the later nineteenth century can
seem blurred, and they do indeed share many general positions, not least
of which is the idea of a basic and temporally inflected unity underlying
human productions. But it is a distinction that is particularly crucial to the
practice of comparison precisely because most of the great postwar émigrés
would trace their intellectual descent from the former.

Scientific principles transferred from the social sciences inform the
first work on comparative literature to appear in English, Hutcheson Macaulay Posnett's *Comparative Literature* (1886). Widely read and translated,
this study exerted a powerful influence on Gayley, among others, who discusses Posnett alongside Hegel and Aristotle in his *Lectures*. Covering a

broad range of examples (the Hebrew, Greek, Indian, Chinese, French, and American, among others) Posnett interprets the development of literature according to the principles of Spencerian evolution and defines the discipline's task in the following manner: "We therefore adopt, with a modification hereafter to be noticed, the gradual expansion of social life, from clan to city, from city to nation, from both of these to cosmopolitan humanity, as the proper order of our studies in comparative literature."[40] Though he admits of regressions, stasis, and various indirections, the governing idea of his analysis is the "principle of growth," so central to Gayley's conception of the discipline in 1903. *Comparative Literature* treats literature primarily as a social phenomenon influenced by environmental factors, amenable to classification, and governed by large processes and general laws rather than as the product of individual genius. Curiously enough, comparison itself turns out to be a prominent measure of social progress: the more a society advances—that is, expands and specializes—the more it brings under the purview of comparison. As Posnett puts it, "the range of comparison widens from clan to national and even world-wide associations and sympathies" (Posnett, 77). Thus the ancient Greeks, despite the sophistication of their institutions, made "poor progress in comparative thinking," according to Posnett, because of their contempt for other languages (Posnett, 74). The civilizational activity of comparison is reproduced "consciously" at the yet more advanced stage where the critic, or student of literary science, himself undertakes to track these comparisons: "these external and internal evolutions of social life, take place often unconsciously, making comparisons and distinction without reflecting on their nature or limits; it is the business of reflective comparison, of the comparative method, to retrace this development *consciously*, and to seek the causes which have produced it" (Posnett, 78). The comparative method thus both recapitulates the progress of civilization and is its highest accomplishment. It follows that empires, including earlier empires (China, India, Macedonian Greece, Rome) but especially the contemporary British Empire, simply by virtue of the extent of their conquest and holdings, have entered into more extensive comparisons and have therefore advanced furthest toward cosmopolitan humanity. Comparison is indistinguishable from imperial progress.

The discovery of the New World brought this new European civilisation face to face with primitive life, and awakened men to contrasts with their own associations more striking than Byzantine or even Saracen could offer. Commerce, too, was now bringing the rising nations of Europe into rivalry with, and knowledge

of, each other. . . . Christian missionaries were bringing home the life and literature of China so vividly. . . . Then Englishmen in India learned of that ancient
language . . . and soon the points of resemblance between this language and the
languages of Greeks and Italians, Teutons and Celts were observed, and used like
so many stepping-stones upon which men passed in imagination over the flood
of time which separates the old Aryans from their modern offshoots in the West.
Since those days the method of comparison has been applied to many subjects
besides language; and many new influences have combined to make the mind of
Europe more ready to compare and to contrast than it ever was before. The steam-
engine, telegraph, daily press, now bring the local and central, the popular and the
cultured, life of each European country and the general actions of the entire world
face to face; and habits of comparison have arisen such as never before prevailed so
widely and so vigorously. . . . [We] may call *consciously* comparative thinking the
great glory of our nineteenth century. . . . (Posnett 76; emphasis in the original)

It is a bracing passage, not only for its vigorous faith in progress
but because it presents comparatism as an *ineluctable* consequence of the
great expansion of knowledge in history. Comparison as a "readiness" and
a "habit" seems involuntary, a condition deriving from material circumstance rather than the act or the practice of a subject. Until, of course, Posnett reaches the vanguard of modernity from which he writes and then that
comparison, at the apex of its glory, becomes "consciously comparative."
Imperialism prods "the mind of Europe" toward ever-expanding comparison and this historical movement, once it is grasped in the comparative
method, attains the consciousness needed for a privileged production of
knowledge. It is difficult to read a passage like this without noting an uncanny resemblance to the current discourse on globalization in its celebra-
tory mode, as it announces the great new age of the global village. A similar
emphasis obtains on technological advancement, on an explosive growth
of knowledge, on the transformative cross-cultural encounter, and perhaps
above all a narrative of cumulative ineluctability that interpellates its reader
into a condition rather than a possibility. There are differences, of course,
but what is striking is the persistence both of a kind of deterministic configuration of progress or change and, in tandem, the inordinate claim for
the novelty of the present. The euphoria of having achieved a telos, reached
an acme of development, accomplished in fact what was previously only
imagined, would seem to be a persistent trope of modernity. While I'm
digressing here, I may as well note another uncanny parallel, this time
with some comments by Homi Bhabha on the comparative method and
a "new" world literature for which we might well invert Posnett's phrase

and say that *unconsciously* comparative thinking is the great glory of the late twentieth century:

Goethe suggests that the "inner nature of the whole nation as well as the individual man works all unconsciously." When this is placed alongside his idea that the cultural life of the nation is "unconsciously" lived, then there may be a sense in which world literature could be an emergent, prefigurative category that is concerned with a form of cultural dissensus and alterity, where non-consensual terms of affiliation may be established on the grounds of historical trauma. . . . Where, once, the transmission of national traditions was the major theme of a world literature, perhaps we can now suggest that transnational histories of migrants, the colonized or political refugees—these border and frontier conditions—may be the terrains of world literature.[41]

For Posnett, comparison's expansion reaches its highest point in Western empires because these empires combine the greatest variety of cultural contact (one should of course write "conquest," but this aspect of empire is never mentioned in Posnett, just as those on the receiving end of conquest—precisely the dispossessed or "unhomely" who are Bhabha's new internationalists—are not counted amongst the "we" who have developed such vigorous habits of comparison) with the highest degree of individual autonomy or consciousness. Posnett's comparatism is imperial in various respects, but not as one might expect in the most obvious or instrumental sense as a pretext or justification for empire, whereby, for instance, Western literature and Western society, having reached the highest development, set out naturally as part of an impersonal process to civilize the world. His comparatism is imperial first of all conceptually in that it is intrinsically expansionist, but most important it is imperial because by definition it can only be available in its most evolved scientific or reflective form to a privileged denizen of empire. The authority to encompass comparatively all the literature in the world is thus reserved implicitly and without argument to the Western scholar because he represents comparison's highest development. It is this evolutionary, teleological unity that allows Posnett to locate all significant causes in a great impersonal evolutionary process and at the same time to gaze upon them from above.

The great innovation of the comparative method in the view of its practitioners was its subordination of the unruly and directionless similarities and differences generated by the table or chronological list of earlier attempts at universal literary histories to a meaningful and progressive temporality. Time is to such an extent the motor and frame of the comparative method that in Posnett's view the scientific comparatist's task is not so much to compare one object to another as to "retrace the development" of comparison's progress. It's unlikely that anyone would have thought to ask Posnett (though he would have welcomed the questions, especially as he claims—quite falsely—to have invented the discipline's name), "What exactly do you compare?" since the adjective "comparative" was ubiquitous at the time in the names of fields of inquiry. But if the question had arisen he might have answered, "I compare comparisons in time." The comparative method is not ultimately directed toward the objects under comparison, but to an invisible and impalpable entity manifested through them. Positivism imputes a transparent knowability to the empirical object and a corresponding capacity to know in the subject, but the objective of its knowledge is itself obscure, as Foucault reminds us: ". . . there is a whole layer of phenomena given to experience whose rationality and interconnection rest upon an objective foundation which it is not possible to bring to light; it is possible to know phenomena, but not substances; laws, but not essences; regularities, but not the beings that obey them."[42] This mode or condition of knowledge is peculiar to what Foucault calls the modern episteme, which is grounded in History. Foucault's definition of History helps situate the positivist dimensions of comparative literature in a broader modern epistemic field, particularly to the degree that it highlights the crucial link between empiricity and temporality: "History . . . is the fundamental mode of being of empiricities, upon the basis of which they are affirmed, posited, arranged, and distributed in the space of knowledge for the use of such disciplines or sciences as may arise" (Order, 219). The adjective "comparative" indexes precisely this temporal "mode of being of empiricities," the archaeological fragment of another era's positivity persisting in the discipline's name into the present.

Approached obliquely Foucault's seminal study can be read as an archaeology of comparison, since shifts in the modality of relations among objects of knowledge are crucial elements in the ruptures between the three epistemes he isolates, pre-Classical, Classical, and modern. What seems particularly useful in Foucault's almost clinical isolation of modes of knowledge from everything that might impinge on them is that it allows one to reflect on the structure of comparison itself as bounded but historically mutable. The pre-Classical world of knowledge Foucault evokes is to such an extent infused with resemblances that these can be divided into various dominant types. Foucault lists four: *convenientia*, in which sheer proximity in space signals a hidden resemblance; *aemulatio*, the ability of things to imitate each other over great distances; *analogy*, which Foucault defines as "subtle resemblances of relations"; and *sympathy*, the tendency of likeness to assimilate things into identity, a power counterbalanced by its opposite, *antipathy* (*Order*, 18–23). What makes these multifarious similitudes (between flowers and the sky, apoplexy and tempests, stars and plants, shells and moss) possible is the presupposition of a harmonious disposition in the world between microcosm and macrocosm. This provides all investigation with an assurance that "everything will find its mirror and its macrocosmic justification on another and larger scale, . . . [and], inversely, that the visible order of the highest spheres will be found reflected in the darkest depths of the earth" (*Order*, 31).

Thinkers in the Classical episteme will break utterly with this system of resemblance as a form of knowledge, consigning it to the realm of error, illusion, and the deception of the senses. Both Francis Bacon and René Descartes elaborate formal refutations of resemblance, which henceforth gives way to reason as a ground for knowledge. Comparison now emerges as the central function of thought, not in the service of tracking resemblances but rather of analyzing them "in terms of identity, difference, measurement, and order" (*Order*, 51–52). To know through comparison is thus no longer to draw things together, but to "discriminate." Measurement and ordering, and they are often indistinguishable, submit resemblance to proof by comparison, and at the same time open a new possibility for certainty based on enumeration and taxonomy. The form of Classical knowledge, as Foucault describes it in comparison with the modern episteme that follows it, is static in that it presents knowledge in its totality in the fixed form of taxonomic tables and series. But if resemblance is contained and submitted to comparative analysis in the Classical episteme, it almost vanishes altogether in Foucault's account of the modern episteme, in which "from now on the contemporaneous and simultaneously observable resemblances in space will be simply the fixed forms of a succession" (*Order*, 219) in what he calls a "mutation of Order into History." This mutation of knowledge's object from resemblances in space to successions in time underlies a crucial aspect of the idea of comparison for the comparative method of the positivist comparatists: comparison is not primarily a procedure for analyzing similarity and difference in order to determine individual units suitable to evaluation, but rather a means of determining the general laws of development ascertainable beyond objects of analysis. Comparability as such, a prominent concern in this epistemic schema for taxonomic comparison, does not emerge as a central problem for the positivists because a unified field or totality for knowledge is given in the comprehensive process of temporal development.

The Space of Comparison

[T]he logical consequences of our loosely
defined discipline were, surely, to include the
open-ended possibility of studying all literatures, with linguistic rigor and historical savvy.
A level playing field, so to speak.
—Gayatri Spivak, *Death of a Discipline*

In a brief and very influential essay, translated as "Of Other Spaces" and first delivered as a lecture in 1967 just a year after the publication of *The Order of Things*, Foucault writes: "The present epoch will perhaps be above all the epoch of space." He continues: "We are in the epoch of simultaneity: we are in the epoch of juxtaposition, the epoch of the near and the far, of the side-by-side, of the dispersed. We are at a moment, I believe, when our experience of the world is less that of a long life developing through time than that of a network that connects points and intersects with its own skein."[43] While this present "epoch of space" is clearly contrasted to a previous epoch of time, the governing terms of this essay differ sharply from those of *The Order of Things*. At issue here is space as an epoch, not an episteme; space is an object of experience, description, perception, emplacement, but not a modality for the formal production of knowledge. The simultaneity of juxtaposition or "heterochrony" emerges in "Of Other Spaces" as the primary modality of spatial comparison. To describe and analyze that spatial comparison, Foucault develops the concept of "heterotopia," which he defines in contrast to utopia as "real places . . . which are something like counter-sites, a kind of effectively enacted utopia in which the real sites, and the other real sites that can be found within the culture, are simultaneously represented, contested and inverted" (*Spaces*, 24). Including such diverse instances as psychiatric hospitals, boats, fairgrounds, cemeteries, gardens, brothels, libraries, colonies, Oriental carpets, vacation villages, theaters, prisons, and museums, the heterotopia is a site that can be construed as an "elsewhere" that produces the effect of dislocating one's fundamental sense of fully inhabiting a single space. It is a parcel of the world that at once brings the totality of the world into apprehension and destabilizes or contests its unity.

This experiential and representational emphasis of spatial heterotopia's comparative function contrasts starkly with Foucault's articulation of heterotopia in *The Order of Things*. Few readers can forget the extraordinary quotation from Jorge Luis Borges with which Foucault begins his preface to that text, the description of the Chinese encyclopedia, which reads, in part:

animals are divided into: a) belonging to the Emperor, b) embalmed, c) tame, d) sucking pigs, e) sirens, f) fabulous, g) stray dogs, h) included in the present classification, i) frenzied, j) innumerable, k) drawn with a very fine camelhair brush, l) *et cetera*, m) having just broken the water pitcher, n) that from a long way off look like flies (*Order*, xv).

For Foucault, the assortment of items on this list suggests there is "a worse disorder than that of the incongruous and of the inappropriate comparison; it would be the disorder that makes the fragments of a great number of possible orders sparkle in a single dimension, without law or geometry, the disorder of the heteroclite" (*Order*, xvii). Heterotopia appears in this epistemic and epistemological context as a figure for absolute incommensurability, which paralyzes the knower into aphasia if he looks too directly upon it. The taxonomic sites occupied by the disparate elements clash to the extent that it is impossible to "define beneath them a common ground [*lieu commun*]." Though the incommensurability of the heteroclite precedes and utterly confounds all the modes of knowing through comparison developed in the three epistemes, it nonetheless performs what one might call the foundational comparative function of revealing, negatively, that there *is* order. Heterotopic difference in the preface to *The Order of Things* is the other order at the limit of "our" own thought, for Foucault locates Borges' encyclopedia in a "real" place—China—at the limit of the Western imaginary. In presenting "the stark impossibility of thinking *that*," it reveals the "brute being of order," the very condition of possibility for an episteme—that is, for knowledge. In the spatial epoch sketched out in "Of Other Spaces," heterotopia, describable precisely as "fragments of a great number of possible orders [that] sparkle in a single dimension," no longer figures absolute incommensurability. The status of heterogeneity (the *hetero* in heterotopia) has shifted quite radically from that which exceeds and confounds the ordering function of comparison for knowledge to that which, on the contrary, generates relationality. Similarly, the status of place (the *topos* in heterotopia) has undergone a marked materialization from the metaphorical "site" of taxonomic categories to the actually existing common ground underlying disparate spaces. Borges' diverse elements become less forbidding and perhaps even partly intelligible if instead of seeking a conceptual common ground for them, we attempt to think of them spatially, using, for instance, the terms with which Foucault describes the spatial epoch: simultaneity, juxtaposition, the near and the far, the side-by-side, the dispersed.

Foucault's analysis of space has been celebrated as a pivotal critique of chronocentrism because it offers a historicization of space and sketches a framework for considering space not as a static backdrop to social meaning but as a dynamic constituent of it. I am more interested here, however, in exploring how it might illuminate the status of space as an epistemic (or epochal) ground for comparison in the realm of knowledge. The attempt to examine the epistemic frame within which one's own discourse might be taking place is indeed an abstract and markedly hypothetical exercise, but useful in order to defamiliarize what seems given about the comparative project. Several important studies of the relation of space to knowledge from theoretical vantage points different from Foucault's arrive at a paradox quite similar to that which one might read in the cleavage between his two elaborations of heterotopia. In the first and most thoroughgoing attempt to elaborate a materialist theory of space, *The Production of Space*, Henri Lefebvre insists on the analytical separation and disjunction between various registers of space: "logical-epistemological space, the space of social practice, the space occupied by sensory phenomena, including products of the imagination."[44] He formulates the paradox of this disjunction in the following terms: "it is not therefore as though one had global (or conceived) space to one side and fragmented (or directly experienced) space to the other—rather as one might have an intact glass here and a broken glass or mirror over there. For space 'is' whole and broken, global and fractured at one and the same time. Just as it is at once conceived, perceived and directly lived."[45] A similar disjunction attends Fredric Jameson's description of the totality of the world system in "knowable but unrepresentable."[46] Developing on the difficulties of this paradox for the aesthetic within the epochal framework of late capitalism, Fredric Jameson argues that the cultural dialectic that binds experience and knowledge is severed, detaching individuals from affective access to history. The knowability in question here is reducible to the apprehension of information: one can know that this extensive totality exists but one cannot grasp it affectively or through the medium of representation. He poses the consequences for this waning of historical consciousness and corresponding prominence of spatial consciousness in a particularly arresting way in the sequel to that essay, *The Seeds of Time*. Reflecting on the early years of the twentieth century he remarks that it is easier today to imagine the end of the physical world in ecological catastrophe than it is to imagine an end to the (historical) capitalist mode of production.[47] In these conditions, he argues, political agency requires a new epistemic pedagogy to orient the subject in space—something he calls "cognitive mapping," a notion he approaches from a radical, indeed hyperbolic, condition of unknowing.[48] At issue is not primarily space as an object of interpretation, a fundamental constituent of meaning, but rather space as a perplexing condition of knowledge in which there is a fundamental cleavage between the possibility of conceiving a spatial totality and the impossibility of experiencing or representing it as such.

To return to our initial juxtaposition between the Bernheimer report's articulation of the "space of comparison" and Shackford's paean to the comparative method a century earlier, one might propose the following observation. Temporalizing comparison encompassed a multiplicity of cultures as objects of knowledge because the evolutionary scale allowed that comparison to discriminate; it welcomed all the difference in the world, so long as all those differences could occupy fixed places on a hierarchical scale. The space of comparison, inclusive by virtue of its transversal extensiveness, would in a first moment negate the negation of this temporal unity and withdraw the discriminating evolutionary hierarchy from the geography of the globe as one might lift a distorting temporal veil in order to reveal space as such. All cultures would thus appear as Fabian would urge— coeval, or truly "simultaneous." Simultaneity, itself a temporal category, becomes a kind of degree zero of equivalence. Comparability, in the form of a ground or a space of comparison, remains, but without discrimination. The grounds of comparison today, thus, are in a first moment, literally *ground*— that is, in a rather bewildering way, potentially the globe itself. But if space provokes comparison, it also confounds its epistemological operations.

James Clifford's seminal 1992 essay "Traveling Cultures" offers one symptomatic instance of this problem. Clifford urges the idea of traveling cultures as a "spatial chronotope" that would dislodge anthropology from its constricted locations and lingering colonial vocation, and humanist disciplines from their national and canonical grounding. This concept is directed toward a disciplinary practice where it might help "to define a very large domain of comparative cultural studies: diverse, interconnected histories of travel and displacement in the late twentieth century."[49] The modifier "comparative" immediately undergoes a suggestive estrangement here in its association with the explicitly post- or even anti-disciplinary assemblage of "cultural studies" from its original role as the marker of "scientific" disciplinarity, *par excellence*. "Traveling Cultures" is shot through with "comparison" (the word occurs sixteen times in various grammatical guises), which points in a general way at once to the extensive scope of culture's possible travels and, as in the citation, to the diversity and interconnectedness of those itineraries. Clifford avers that "a comparative cultural studies needs to work, self-critically, with compromised, historically encumbered tools," but there is no mention of comparison's disciplinary history, though it often seems to haunt the text. The supreme teleology of the comparative method in early anthropology is implicitly reversed in a phrase like "genuinely comparative and nonteleological cultural studies" (Clifford, 29). Comparison no longer points to a method but rather to a scope and a disposition toward knowledge that clearly aims to displace the Archimedean view of the traditional comparatist with a transversal practice of comparison: "The comparative scope I'm struggling toward is not a form of overview. Rather, I'm working with a notion of comparative knowledge produced through an *itinerary*, always marked by a 'way in,' a history of locations and a location of histories. . . . The metaphor of travel, for me, has been a serious dream of mapping without going 'off earth'" (Clifford, 31). The term "comparative knowledge" suggests that comparison might not be the end or object of knowledge but intrinsic to its processes. Nonetheless, comparison persists implicitly as a perplexing problem of method, particularly in some of the examples. Clifford proposes a comparison between Alexander Von Humboldt's view of the "New World" and that of an indentured Asian laborer:

But although there is no ground of equivalence between the two "travelers," there is at least a basis for comparison and (problematic) translation. Von Humboldt became a canonical travel writer. The knowledge (predominantly scientific and aesthetic) produced in his American explorations has been enormously influential. The Asian laborer's view of the "New World," knowledge derived from displacement, was certainly quite different. I do not now, and may never, have access to it. But a comparative cultural studies would be very interested in such knowledge and in the ways it could potentially complement or critique Von Humboldt's. (Clifford, 35)

What this passage so presciently grazes but never quite brings into focus is a particular form of incommensurability. Incommensurability is precisely the problem comparison reveals here and Clifford phrases it with great accuracy: there is a "basis for comparison" between the laborer and Von Humboldt, presumably the space they have in common, but "no ground of equivalence" when it comes to the production, circulation, and analysis of their knowledge.[50] When Clifford does compare cultures in motion or travel, the comparison is of the classic taxonomic variety, in which a type or category is reinforced rather than dispersed or diversified. For example, his inclusion in the cultural category "Haitian" of both those Haitians residing in Haiti and those living in New York as a kind of comparative or traveling culture, can as one of his respondents remarks, easily essentialize the cultural identity and preclude analysis of the multiple relation into which Haitianness enters in New York, Haiti, or points in between. The normative powers of taxonomic comparison here overwhelm the very incommensurability the culture's "travel" has introduced it to in the first place. The ground of comparison has become a basis of equivalence.

"Incommensurability," which denotes literally, "that which cannot be measured by comparison" is, I propose, a useful term to name that tenuous space Clifford has briefly identified between a basis for comparison and a ground of equivalence because it suspends the relation between comparison and measure. I would reverse the terms here and propose "ground for comparison and basis of equivalence," since it is the spatial chronotope's ground that brings previously separated objects into comparison, even as that ground offers no given basis of equivalence. Incommensurability is probably more familiar in its maximal, epistemological sense, as the radical absence of common ground between different orders in Foucault's initial definition of heterotopia or as the rupture between paradigms in the history of science famously described by Thomas Kuhn. With Foucault's spatial heterotopology in mind we might propose a minimal form of incommensurability, which produces a generative dislocation without silencing discourse or marking the limit of knowledge. This minimal incommensurability instead opens up the possibility of an intelligible relation at the limits of comparison.

To say that the grounds of comparison today are literally "ground" is to speak heuristically, or within the quasi-figurative language of speculation, for in the realm of knowledge we know that there is no such thing as sheer ground and that our understanding of the globe derives from layers of overtly ideological designations for areas (East/West; North/South; West/Rest, etc.) determined by successive hegemonies and complex histories of domination that ceaselessly intertwine knowledge with power. It is also, however, to pause at an experience of estranging spatial dislocation or a disturbance of givenness in the knower's relation to a field or object of knowledge that is at once constitutive to knowledge and foreclosed in its production. The decade since the publication of "Traveling Cultures" has seen the consolidation of an important body of scholarship that elaborates a thoroughgoing critique of the disciplinary methodologies and presuppositions that divide the world's surface unevenly into areas of knowledge. On one side the European tradition in the general humanities holding the place of an exemplary, implicitly universal form from which theoretical models can be generated; on the other side all non-Western languages in the more specialized realm of area studies, holding the place of raw material, as it were, on which these theoretical models can be applied.[51] From the perspective of the discipline of comparative literature, the breaching of this division has far-reaching and as yet unforeseeable consequences.

Incommensurability: Postcoloniality and the Ends of Comparison

Before, the fetishes were subject to the law of equivalence. Now equivalence itself has become a fetish.
—Adorno and Horkheimer, *Dialectic of Enlightenment*

The application of this criterion to all of our games necessarily entails a certain level of terror, whether soft or hard: be operational (that is, commensurable) or disappear.
—Jean-François Lyotard, *The Postmodern Condition*

Les poétiques multipliées du monde ne se proposent qu'à ceux-là seuls qui tentent de les ramasser dans des équivalences qui n'unifient pas.
[The multiplied poetics of the world present themselves to those alone who attempt to gather them into equivalences that do not unify.]
—Édouard Glissant, *Le Discours Antillais*

Future scholars of comparative literature looking back at this time may well see in it a formative moment equal to if not surpassing the two periods examined in this chapter, the turn into the last century when Gayley was active in the initial consolidation of the discipline and the period of postwar expansion during the 1950s and 1960s. Over the turn into the twenty-first century, a remarkable number of innovative studies have addressed the problems of studying literature in an expanded geographical scope as well as, explicitly or implicitly, the question of comparison. Unlike the two previous formative moments, however, the present conversation does not emerge principally from within the discipline of comparative literature and its main thrust, therefore, is not necessarily to establish methods and approaches proper to a discipline nor is it primarily aimed at specific institutional change or consolidation.[52] Indeed all of these works are conspicuously transdisciplinary in various ways. One of the most startling developments is the reemergence of systematic approaches based on sociological and scientific models. Preeminent among these is a set of essays on world literature by Franco Moretti, which seek to apply various models from the social sciences and the natural sciences to the elaboration of a comprehensive theory of the novel on a world scale. Comprehensive and systematic, Moretti's approach is startlingly reminiscent of Gayley's, though by all appearances unknowingly. In the first of these essays, "Conjectures on World Literature," Moretti adapts Emanuel Wallerstein's world-systems theory with its uneven divisions between center and periphery to the worldwide dissemination of the novel. As a way of dealing with the enormous practical problem of the multiplicity of languages and traditions, he provocatively proposes a methodology of "distant reading," the abandonment of close textual analysis in favor of "a patchwork of other people's research . . . the ambition is now directly proportional *to the distance from the text*: the more ambitious the project, the greater must the distance be."[53] The vast collaborative endeavor thus required is uncannily close to the one envisioned in Gayley's call for a "Society of Literary Evolution." Though lacking Gayley's positivist certainty (for Moretti, world literature is a problem requiring conjecture and hypothesis, not a given requiring simple data collection), his exhaustive scope (the world-inclusive comprehensiveness is limited to one genre, the novel), and his primary temporal unity of development, Moretti shares the basic idea that study of the entirety of world literature can only be pursued as a collaborative project in which specialists in the various areas all contribute to elaborating literature's general laws.[54] Moretti's tone, particularly in the first of these essays, the shortest and the most ambitious of the series, is authoritative and provocational whereas the substance of the argument is tentative and conjectural (by the looks of it, the volume of text in the footnotes, occupied with qualifications and hesitations, is at least double that of the essay proper), a discrepancy that casts a distinct ambiguity on the transparency of the systematic application of the world systems model to the novel. Perhaps distant reading cannot quite overcome the estrangements of spatial dislocation, even as the impressive charts and graphs cannot completely occlude the inherent problems in determining comparable units for quantitative analysis from fictional forms over so vast and diverse a field. Another study that takes a systemic approach to world literature is Pascale Casanova's *La république mondiale des lettres*, where she undertakes a sociological analysis, inspired by Pierre Bourdieu's notion of structure rather than Wallerstein's of system, of the complex distribution of cultural capital in what she argues is a single, semi-autonomous "world republic of letters."[55]

Overlapping with Moretti's essays as they appeared in the *New Left Review* between 2000 and 2004, a sequence of essays by Benedict Anderson elaborates a contrasting, nonsystematic approach to world literature, or perhaps more accurately to the global network of literature in history. Digressive and narrative in form and method, these essays begin with the objective of elucidating a few specific puzzles in a single novel from the periphery, José Rizal's *El Filibusterismo*, and in the process they trace an astounding historical network of global intersections involving "Bismarck and Vera Zasulich, Yankee manipulations and Cuban insurrections, Meiji Japan and the British Museum, Huysmans and Mallarmé, Catalonia and the Carolines, Kropotkin and Salvador Santiago," to name but a few.[56] Considering that Rizal's other novel *Noli Me Tangere*, held a central place in Anderson's *Imagined Communities* as an example of the nation's investment in print culture, these essays, more than his intriguingly but ultimately deceptively titled book, *Specters of Comparison*, constitute a rigorous account of the comparative underpinnings of what would normally be categorized as national literature.[57] The disciplinary frame of these essays oscillates between history and literature; they offer a historical account of the late nineteenth century finely attuned to the fictional probabilities of historical narrative and a literary history of influence grounded in world-historical events. The method approaches that of ethnography's "thick description," but on a world scale. Extensive, but in no way comprehensive, the scope of the study takes the form of the intersecting itineraries of the kind Clifford describes. Comparison inheres on the one hand in the multiplicity of overlapping encounters, irreducible to any single organizing concept or national ground, and on the other hand in the world picture all the essays together produce, which is that of a specific period in world history as experienced and perceived from the perspective of the periphery and as rendered by a particular scholarly eye. For the scholar here is present as a singular persona throughout, a move that both underlines the stupefying erudition of this particular investigator and implicitly limits the generalizability of his stance into a model. In contrast to Moretti's abstract and hypothetical theoretical model for world literature as a "planetary system," Anderson describes a particular trajectory through, in his words, a "global landscape" at a particular moment in time. Both studies are fundamentally historical, but Moretti's on a "macro" register of a materialist formalism first developed in Georg Lukacs, and Anderson's on the "micro" register of a branching, open-ended narrative, dense with empirical detail. Another eclectic, nonsystematic, recent approach to world literature, David Damrosch's *What is World Literature?* offers a disarmingly pragmatic and democratic criterion for world literature (any work that has crossed the boundaries of its place of origin) with wide-ranging consequences.[58] To this brief sampling one would have to add the work of Naoki Sakai on translation and national "co-figuration," a crucial intervention on the comparative constitution of discrete and equivalent cultural units; that of Walter Mignolo on a postcolonial epistemology grounded in "border gnosis"; that of Emily Apter on the forgotten "global *translatio*" that some of the central figures for comparative literature undertook during their time of exile in WWII; that of Marcel Detienne in his brief manifesto, *Comparer l'incomparable* [Comparing the incomparable], which advocates the active construction of "comparabilities" as a dynamic and collaborative task for cross-disciplinary analysis; finally, that of Gayatri Spivak on a "planetary comparative literature" that would combine the linguistic breadth and rigor of area studies with philological close reading, and to which I shall return subsequently.[59] Other works could be added to this selective inventory, but I hope this will suffice to indicate that the central concerns of comparative literature have made a robust entrance into the twenty-first century.

The present study differs from these approaches without standing in antagonistic opposition to them. The challenges of reconceptualizing the comparative project for an expanded geographical scope are great and certainly cannot be met by a single method or a single set of presuppositions.

I seek to do so from the standpoint of postcolonial critique, which entails several distinct emphases. The first involves a particular inflection of the spatial ground of comparison, which, as Edward Said elaborates in *Culture and Imperialism*, corresponds in a first moment with the imperial geography of the world and hence with a history of domination and presumes, in its imperial form, the sovereign authority of a single perspective. Once a postcolonial literature emerges—that is, a body of texts that occupies sites of enunciation, to use Mignolo's term—outside the metropolitan centers, that unique perspective becomes untenable. This does not necessarily give onto a relativistic enclosure into particularism, but rather, as Glissant puts it, onto a relational and necessarily comparative "degeneralized universal," in which worldliness does not inhere in exemplary representativity; that is, in standing for the world, but rather in standing *in* the world, in multiple relation with its unsystematizable extensiveness. Glissant's elaboration of Relation and the *Tout-monde*, or world-totality, to which I will return in greater detail in chapter three, bears a striking affinity with the kind of epistemological disjuncture Lefebvre and Jameson associate with space, particularly in his insistence on the necessary imbrications of any given particular site with the whole, but he arrives at it from a different direction, that of the master narrative of colonial conquest. For Glissant the spatial imperative of imperial conquest necessarily gives onto an intrinsically incommensurable relationality.

The second emphasis is a critical stance with respect to disciplinary norms of legitimacy and authority, or, to put it another way, a stance that fully registers the disturbance of givenness in the knower's relation to a field or object of knowledge that the imbrications of knowledge in colonial domination implies. Comparison is overdetermined at both ends of colonialism's culture. Western supremacy was discursively consolidated in a binary and evaluative comparison in which the West produced itself as the standard and model of humankind. Archly asserting culture as a discriminating civilizational value, the coercive comparison of the colonial cultural project conflated the ground of comparison with the basis of equivalence. Just as it was in large part the immense wealth produced in the colonies that provided Western modernity's conditions of possibility, so too the formation of the exemplary autonomous subject of modern humanism both assumes as its other and disavows from its narrative the partial and insufficient figures of racial and gender difference. The widespread dissemination of Western modernity's principal forms, from the nation-state to the subject as individual and citizen to the predominance of the written word and a certain idea of literature itself, in turn produce their own multiple forms of comparatism in which these forms interact in various ways with local conditions or pre-colonial forms. A substantial body of scholarship explores many facets of this constellation. Postcolonial studies offer a great number of avenues toward an analysis of colonialism and comparison. I have chosen to focus my analysis on ideas or figures of comparison in a set of colonial and postcolonial texts. The advantage of this approach is that it doesn't presuppose a given unit or standard of comparison (genre, nation, gender, or period, to name the most obvious) but attends as closely as possible to how postcoloniality and comparison are construed in particular instances. Comparison is, in practice, a normative and generalizing activity, and through one medium or another, it nears what Rodolphe Gasché calls the "Hegelian temptation" of mediating or sublating contradiction, or of assimilating the singular.[60] Instead of actually comparing one text or region or theme to another, I seek to forestall this assimilatory tendency by foregrounding figures of comparison. As such, this study is a ground-clearing exercise that aims to investigate those forms of equivalence that do not unify, which Glissant suggests must underlie the "multiplied poetics of the world." The idea of postcoloniality subtending this analysis is ultimately beholden to his elaboration of Relation, in which, to put it briefly, the overarching commensuration of imperialism's cultural comparison is overturned and also relayed in the postcolonial condition as cultures come into constant contact without a unifying standard, thus engaging in ubiquitous processes of comparison that are no longer bound to commensuration.

Given the saturation of colonial others in discourses that purport to fix and decode them, my approach to postcolonial literary texts doesn't assume that they transparently represent a culture or can be reduced to a discernible chain of historical causes and effects or to a set of material conditions. I endeavor as far as possible to read texts off the page, as it were, presupposing them ultimately to ground their own authority and to possess the opacity, to use Glissant's term, expressive culture usually presumes. This approaches a formalism quite different from the materialist formalism that informs Moretti's planetary system of world literature, but also distinct, I want to argue from the radical high formalism we associate with the New Criticism, in which a work of art is approached in strict isolation from all its conditions of production. A postcolonial formalist criticism takes extrinsic conditions as its point of departure and as its analytical frame and thus, in the present case, locates its historical engagements most acutely in an attempt to trace the conditions of its own production. The history of the discipline of comparative literature and its practices of comparison are at least as important to framing the postcolonial incommensurability in, for instance, Derek Walcott's *Omeros*, as Derek Walcott's biography or the history of St. Lucia. This postcolonial formalism is also inflected by the particular history of the postcolonial literature under consideration here. The Caribbean islands of St. Lucia, Martinique, and Guadeloupe, from which the principal postcolonial authors in this study hail, are small places and nationalism played a very small part in their postcolonial trajectory, particularly for the latter two, which entered the postcolonial era as dependencies of the former colonial metropole. This alone complicates the task of locating this literature with respect to a discrete political-economic territory. It is a literature that could not meet any criteria for inclusion in Gayley's comprehensive list, since it will not slot into the categories of peoples, races, language groups, or nations, or in Moretti's planetary system, since it does not possess a longstanding and distinct history of the novel. These factors already detach it from any obvious conditions of production. In addition and perhaps most importantly, it is ultimately the privileged repository of slavery's violent history of dispossession so that its relation to history is not simply mimetic, or ascertainable as one aspect of a particular political project such as national liberation, but memorializing in its attempt to figure an erased collective history and utopian in its attempt to maintain emancipatory hopes.[61] In this sense the very autonomy of this expressive culture has intrinsically political ramifications similar to those Paul Gilroy claims for the diasporan modernity of the black Atlantic as a counterculture of Western modernity in which, paradoxically, "the bounds of politics are extended precisely because this tradition of expression refuses to accept that the political is a readily separable domain."[62] Despite its temptation to aesthetic fetishism and its tendency toward philosophical nominalism, close reading offers an important approach to cross-cultural engagement, because it points toward an open model of interlocution rather than mastery. Gayatri Spivak elaborates this point eloquently in *Death of a Discipline*. Opposing the "disciplinary politics of distant reading and the scopic ambitions of mapping the world's literature and bringing it under Euro-U.S. rational control," she advocates a notion of reading over distance, *teleopoiesis*, in which the aim is not to master or transcode a text as representative of a culture, but rather "to affect the distant in a *poiesis*—an imaginative making—without guarantees."[63] This ethic of reading foregrounds the "unverifiable" quality of literary textuality as a crucial, if unpredictable and unsystematic, access to collectivities.

The loose academic disciplinary assemblage of postcolonial studies, with its ambiguous and inadequate central term, "postcolonial," has been the object of concerted critique, the most stringent of which comes from sociologically minded critics who fault the discipline for an aesthetic depoliticization and deradicalization of political movements as well as for an occlusion of the discipline's own historical origins.[64] From the perspective of actually existing social movements and of a measurable effect upon the political and economic conditions they address, these judgments are certainly accurate. As an intellectual project, postcolonial studies is not organically linked to a social movement, nor is its entrance into the curriculum reflective of a broader historical mandate. But to dismiss the intellectual project of postcolonial studies as apolitical ignores the force and value of a specifically *cultural* politics within the restricted and separate sphere of the academic humanities. One aspect of this cultural politics is a concerted attention to the aesthetic value of postcolonized expressive culture within the remaining disciplinary frameworks that produce cultural capital. Another aspect of this cultural politics is the concerted transdisciplinary academic project of what Dipesh Chakrabarty calls the deprovincialization of the non-West, a disciplinary alignment that challenges the centrality of European forms as exclusive models of historical and aesthetic experience and scholarship.[65] Barely begun and of uncertain outcome, the colossal task of reducing European racio-cultural predominance and privilege in the forms of knowledge produced in the university remains a central project of postcolonial studies.[66] That this project should be undertaken with reference to colonial and anticolonial legacies that have an ambiguous and uncertain bearing upon the politics of the present is the patent paradox I take to be expressed in the ungainly term "postcoloniality" in this book's title. A certain hint of mustiness hangs about the term these days that cannot entirely be accounted for by the aura of inbuilt obsolescence that affects academic trends like anything else in consumer culture. David Scott makes a cogent argument for criticism's need to look toward what comes after the postcolonial on the grounds of a non-teleological periodization built around what he calls "problem spaces." The anticolonial moment culminating in the Bandung conference of 1955 was one such problem space centered on the urgency of developing a politics of liberation. The postcolonial problem space, which he interestingly locates not after colonialism, but after anticolonialism, is centered in the "North Atlantic academy," and addresses "the demand for the decolonization of representation, the decolonization of the West's theory of the non-West."[67] Partly for internal reasons (it has exhausted its capacity to produce new objects of knowledge) and partly in response to the exigencies of the post–cold war period, Scott argues, "the critical investigation of colonialism" in the present must open onto a new problem space, whose exact outlines are as yet uncertain. While sympathetic with the general tenor of his argument, I am wary of the strict demarcations he draws between the various problem spaces. These may hold for sociological investigations directed at empirically grounded objects, but it seems to me that postcolonial literature often articulates a more disjunctive relation to time in which what is at stake is precisely giving expression to all that is left over, forgotten, or unaccomplished in history's rapid march. In a subsequent study, Scott himself seems to come closer to articulating the contemporary problem space of colonialism precisely in a disjunctive refusal of the "normalization of the present."[68] Postcolonial studies has been successful in garnering intellectual prestige, and perhaps in normalizing a certain rhetoric of inclusion, but it has been far less successful in establishing new institutional forms and marshalling institutional resources. We thus inhabit institutional and disciplinary forms with a sense of their inadequacy but without any indication of the ways in which they might be changed or indeed if the historical circumstances obtain under which they will or can be changed. The danger of neutralization arises for postcolonial criticism also from conditions internal to the culture produced in the university.

Critiques of an instrumental or otherwise inadequate pluralist multiculturalism are perhaps broadly familiar by now,[69] but the problem arises most acutely for academic comparatism because of the conjuncture between the entrance of multiculturalism into the academy and the increasing hegemony of the commodity form in late capitalism. In his analysis of the impact of a generalized exchange value on the contemporary U.S. university, Bill Readings argues that, as an increasingly transnational economy no longer requires of the university the cultural function of forming national subjects, the university itself becomes corporatized and the culture it distributes therefore is increasingly "dereferentialized"—that is to say, indifferent as to content as long as, like the commodity, it can be successfully marketed.[70] This explains, Readings thinks, the rapid success during the 1980s and 1990s of a whole set of para- or interdisciplinary studies (women's studies, ethnic studies, cultural studies, postcolonial studies, etc) whose self-definition is overtly marginal and oppositional. The novel form of such disciplines can be exchanged for the value of status and renown, regardless of their oppositional content. Commentators have rightly drawn attention to the exaggerations and reductions in Readings' position.[71] All the same, the crux of Readings' argument, namely that in the corporate university the commodity form within a generalized model of exchange ultimately determines the value of academic humanities, seems to me largely accurate. It also suggests that the institutional considerations, which, I argued, largely informed comparative literature's exclusively European orientation in the postwar period, have, then, only become more acute after the end of the cold war. For the financial crisis provoked by the withdrawal of government funding only exacerbates competition among disciplines and intensifies the institutional determination of their intellectual orientation. An extreme institutional and disciplinary self-consciousness, however, curiously coexists with a marked lack of awareness of the disciplinary past. Even as constructivism or social and historical determination are everywhere emphasized, the possibilities that open up before the researcher and, implicitly, her capacity to master them seem boundless and at any moment exchangeable. From one point of view, one postcolonial view, this can amount to an extraordinary and salutary dismantling of the unitary construction of the object and the subject of knowledge. Ideally, this differentiation would reorient learning toward a kind of knowledge grounded in dissensual communities, to use Readings' term, or pursued as a collaborative endeavor rather than the supreme accomplishment of a single great mind's mastery. That this community of comparatists no longer has a general high culture in common, or reads the same books, or attends the same lectures is, from this point of view, an occasion for celebration, not lament, a welcome challenge to invent new forms of collaboration and interchange, to elaborate ways in which cultures that are not held in common can make a difference, and to forge links and cultivate affinities between the intellectual projects developed in the university and cognate endeavors in other institutional and political locations.

Comparison makes its comeback not as a method but as a space, where it signifies inclusiveness and a non-hierarchical transversality. But the age of multiculturalism's impulse not to discriminate easily verges into the indiscriminate and the spatial scope of comparison can open on a limitless horizon of interchangeable objects. In large part this particular temptation

to equivalence has to do with the increasing hegemony of the commodity form in our moment of late capitalism. Detached from the imbrications of context or what Marx called use value, the commodity is a *form*
theoretically amenable to any content because what determines its value is
an abstract equivalence derived from a system of exchange. There are no
limits to commensurability on this model insofar as it can hypothetically
bring all objects into relation on the basis of equivalence. The commensurability of the commodity is a comparison in which the comparability of
form is already given and the comparability of content is moot. In the exchange of commodities, equivalence is subordinated to commensuration.
As commodification increasingly permeates all aspects of social life, at the
extreme we approach what John Guillory calls "the condition of the absolute commensurability of everything" (Guillory, 322–323). A previous era's
normativity gives way to a generalized equivalence and the commodity
form subordinates normative comparison to its laws of exchange. A generalized basis of equivalence trumps the grounds of comparison. This is
something akin to what Spivak has in mind with the notion of the "global
commensurability of value" as a massive countervailing force to *teleopoiesis*,
a kind of pall expressed in the title, *Death of a Discipline*, which hangs over
the projection of a utopian hope for a planetary comparatism.[72]

This study is located in the perplexity between these two perspectives
on the renewed scope of comparison. On the one hand the space of comparison fulfills a postcolonial cultural promise in which the "fragments of
a great number of possible orders sparkle in a single dimension," a dimension that neither reduces those fragments to equivalent forms nor induces
a paralyzing incommensurability. It is a mode of cultural relation (if not an
inclusiveness) that contrasts with academic comparison's institutional past,
the one remembered and the one forgotten, the cosmopolitan discrimination of comparative European literatures, and the positivist discrimination
of an evolutionary hierarchy of races and nations. On the other hand, this
space coincides with what is variously called late capitalism or globalization whose generalization of exchange value neutralizes the ideological resistance and the political consequence claimed for the culture produced
and circulated in the university. I qualify this culture by its institutional
location, as I have throughout, for other forms of culture may well constitute sites of significant contestation in the global order, by no means an
even system whose forms therefore differ according to location.[73] But the
invitation or taunt, "Dare to Compare!" blares from the pages of computer

catalogs, from storefront roadside banners and drugstore windows, forming an inescapable backdrop for anyone musing on the modest resurgence
of comparison in academic inquiry. Perhaps the darkest evocation of this
generalization of commensurability is Jean-François Lyotard, who argues
in *The Différend* that capitalism and what he calls its "economic genre"
inflicts the ultimate injury upon the incommensurability produced in the
clash among heterogeneous genres because it subordinates all differends to
the genre of exchange in such a way as to render them indifferent. Ultimately for Lyotard it strikes the fatal blow both to culture and philosophy.[74] I do not attempt to resolve or conflate these discrepant contexts for
comparison; rather, I articulate figures of postcolonial incommensurability
in their ambiguous interaction.

  This sequence of chapters describes a postcolonial itinerary that proceeds from the breakdown of imperial comparison in the colonial narratives of Joseph Conrad, to the moment of postcolonial response or "writing
back," and from there to adumbrations of the possibility of intercultural
community beyond domination. This arc of the postcolonial comparatist's
desire for an emancipated comparatism is qualified and undercut by a focus
on the incursion of contrary and incommensurable forces upon it, especially the effects on culture, particularly literature, of the rapidly evolving
demands of globalization in its neocolonial dimensions and the disruptive
silence around the intercommunal difference of gender. Postcoloniality,
and comparison itself, both centrally involve a meditation on community
and collectivity as literature represents its aspirations, and often, indeed, its
failures. As will be clear by now this book does not develop a single continuous argument about postcolonial comparison. The texts addressed hail
from diverse traditions and have no necessary or intrinsic connection; the
point of postcolonial comparatism here, thus, is precisely to bring them into
relation over a ground of comparison that is in common but not unified.

Ungrounding Comparison:
Conrad and Colonial Narration

> The very ground on which I stood seemed to melt under my feet.
> —Joseph Conrad, *Lord Jim*

On the inside cover of Doubleday's 1929 "Malay Edition" of Joseph Conrad's *A Personal Record and the Shadow Line*, there is an artist's (William Kemp Starret's) rendition of a map of the world crisscrossed throughout with dotted lines in intersecting loops. The land masses bear the names of continents, but instead of cities and rivers the points of destination that link the dotted lines are titles of Conrad's fictions: *Heart of Darkness* in Africa, *Nostromo* in South America, *Lord Jim* on the Arabian Peninsula, *Almayer's Folly* in Southeast Asia, *Within the Tides* near Australia, and so on. At the bottom right, framed by palm trees, the legend reads, "The Voyages of Joseph Conrad, Master Seaman." Beyond the infamous dual career of seaman and writer spectacularly conflated here (a highly marketable quality that Conrad himself exploited for all it was worth), what this map makes visible is the obsessive geographical comprehensiveness of Conrad's oeuvre. Geographical reach was one of his trademarks, as it was for the other two prominent colonial writers of the time (Rudyard Kipling on India and Robert Louis Stevenson on the Pacific)—instances of geographical expansion in the world of letters all too rarely remarked upon—but he was to explore its consequences the furthest. The primary frame and the condition of possibility for Conrad's actual and verbal circumnavigations of the globe was the imperial order that partitioned and dominated it at the time. During the period between 1880 and 1914 colonial conquests were systematized and the greater part of the earth's surface was annexed and brought under direct administrative control of a handful of European nations, chiefly Britain and France. A veritable explosion in merchant shipping (its volume doubled from 1870–1914) kept Conrad employed, though not as consistently as he would have liked, from port to port across the globe.[1] Conrad's exceptional geographical and linguistic dislocations are partly a product of imperialism and they find a particularly rigorous and complex expression in his fiction. The emblem of imperialism for the center of its power might well be a single figure contemplating a map or a globe colored as a patchwork from end to end with different hues keyed to various European nations, with a preponderance of red (Britain) and blue (France). Conrad provides a memorable description of Marlow contemplating Africa on such a map in the office of the headquarters of the Company in Brussels: ". . . a vast amount of red—good to see at any time, because one knows that some real work is done in there, a deuce of a lot of blue, a little green, smears of orange, and on the East Coast, a purple patch, to show where the jolly pioneers of progress drink the jolly lager-beer."[2] The imperialist viewing subject possesses the whole of the world in his gaze, a world submitted to a single (if not always unconflictual) European standard whose governmental and economic realizations are accompanied by the ideology of the civilizing mission and its unified, evolutionary, civilizational scale.

Master Seaman Joseph Conrad's participation in empire did not, however, take the form of this map gazing, more proper to a national subject of the imperial nation who can identify his national person directly with imperial possession, for while he traversed the empire as an employee of the British Merchant Service, he could lay no stable claim to a national territorial identity, and as such he was in the fullest sense a *denizen* of empire. Just as his narrator Marlow is "going into the yellow," so too Conrad's work charts a restless movement rather than delimiting a particular position and what distinguishes the map of his fictions from its imperial counterpart is precisely the myriad dotted lines that connect title to title across the continents. In the early works (through *Lord Jim*), Conrad grapples with the particular problems imperialism presents for narration, for in the fictions the imperial world cannot be represented in a single impersonal narrative point of view, in part because the necessary presence of "natives" shadows the unity of character and plot such that the imperial narrative fails to consolidate a viable audience and assure its own transmission and reproduction. These two registers of narrative, the plot or diegesis with its ethical development of character on the one hand and the manner and the condition of its telling (discourse or extradiegesis) with its explicitly communal or public function on the other hand, occasion in Conrad's work a rich and paradoxical meditation in narrative on the contradictions surrounding colonialism's culture of comparison.

Imperial Comparison

Heart of Darkness is an extraordinary compendium of imperial themes because it is perhaps the most thoroughgoing literary critique of imperialism from the inside. Its exceptional and rather isolated canonical status (no other imperial fiction comes close to the kind of exposure and circulation *Heart of Darkness* enjoys), nonetheless, can easily occlude the existence at the time of an established literature of anti-imperialist critique.[3] Moreover, like many areas of life and thought in which an earlier optimism turned at century's end to gloomy pessimism, imperialist triumphalism gave way to what Patrick Brantlinger calls "imperial doubt," an attitude of suspicion toward the effectiveness of the civilizing mission and the evolutionary progress it indexed, in addition to more prosaic concerns about whether empire was in fact economically beneficial to the exploiting nations.[4] The catastrophic figure of Kurtz is in good company, for popular literature of the time was replete with fantastic tales both of reversion and degeneracy on the imperial frontiers and of atavism overtaking the metropolis. Herbert Spencer himself, a true believer in the certainty of progress and who was so instrumental to the translation of biological laws of evolution to the realm of social life, wrote in 1898, "we are in the course of rebarbarisation."[5] It is remarkable, as scholars have fully noted, how faithfully representative *Heart of Darkness* is of a broad scope of late-nineteenth-century ideas and attitudes. Because it explores the notion of progress and attends with such excruciating care to its devolution in the imperial sphere, the novella gives a very complex figuration of the aporias of imperial incommensurability to be read. But if *Heart of Darkness* takes the degeneracy or reversion that upsets the hierarchy of progress's comprehensive basis of comparison as its central concern, it also strenuously averts or diverts the consequences.

Heart of Darkness is an easily misremembered text. It contains a documentary narrative with a withering critique of imperial ideology told in elusive and subjective modernist style; it has a simple unilinear plot conveyed in a complex and intermittently retrospective narratorial discourse;

its frame tale complicates its substance by the manner of its telling. It is easiest to misremember the story as one that recounts the progress of disillusionment: a sailor sets out for the heart of Africa with the enthusiasm and belief of a civilizing explorer. He discovers instead a place managed by petty bureaucrats whose overwhelming greed is nowhere tempered by humanitarian aims. Setting out to find the lone imperialist with a strong sense of mission, he finds him gone unspeakably native in the depth of the wilderness. But if we read back carefully, no such clear and continuous motive binds the tale. What gives this impression is that, in increments, as Marlow nears Kurtz, his narration takes on the retrospective coloring of Kurtz's catastrophic reversion and becomes so powerfully imbued with the notion of progress that, I think, it transmits it to one's memory of the entire text. The most significant trace of this retrospective cast is what I will call the "rhetoric of darkness," that overblown, repetitive, and self-canceling abstraction with its portentous and inconclusive symbolism that intermittently characterizes Marlow's diction. British critics in particular have lamented this aspect of the novel's narrative discourse, with F. R. Leavis, for instance, faulting Conrad for an "addiction to the adjective" and for "making a virtue out of not knowing what he means."[6] Conrad's style, at least in the earlier works, tends toward abstraction and wordiness, but the rhetoric of darkness is too exaggerated and stylized to be a mere idiosyncrasy. It prominently features the word "darkness" (often in allusions to the story's title) and draws much of its repertoire from that word's wide and deep semantic field. In its many and bewildering symbolic reversals of such polar opposite as darkness and light, blackness and whiteness, lies and truth, the rhetoric of darkness translates the reversal of the civilizational scale into language even as it mimics the high-flown and hollow discourse of imperialist propaganda. This rhetoric intermittently characterizes Marlow's diction as he approaches Kurtz, but it is plainly a *product* of the encounter, not its starting point, since it reflects Marlow's response to the depredations of the civilizing mission he witnessed on the imperial frontier, a mission and a discourse in which he clearly has little interest at the point of his departure.

The word "darkness" intrudes into Marlow's very first sentence and its rhetoric inflects the preamble to his story (an imaginary account of a Roman colonist going mad in the dark, savage wilderness of Britannia), but there are few traces of the rhetoric of darkness in his account of his journey's origins. When he sets out to secure a job he is on a lark, not a mission. The high ambitions and moral motives of the civilizing mission are, in fact, the misty and feminine enthusiasms that he attempts vainly to dispel in the aunt who helps him secure his post:

There had been a lot of such rot let loose in print and talk just about that time, and the excellent woman, living right in the rush of all that humbug, got carried off her feet. She talked about "weaning those ignorant millions from their horrid ways," till, upon my word, she made me quite uncomfortable. I ventured to hint that the Company was run for profit. (*HD*, 12)

The clearest statement Marlow ever makes about his motives and expectations at the outset of his journey is the famous passage describing his boyhood dream of going to the blank space in the center of Africa. It is, and Marlow knows this, an anachronistic dream. He is a realist narrator, grounded in the world around him and observing it from a slight tilt of irony. Colloquial in a jaundiced sort of way, at times heavy-handedly jocular ("I have a lot of relations on the Continent, because it's cheap and not so nasty as it looks, they say."), alert to absurd detail (the secretaries, the phrenologist), Marlow's narrative presentation is quite solidly anchored to a realist here and now. This Marlow and his narrative discourse never entirely disappear in the course of the story, but they do noticeably recede, as though progressively overtaken by the rhetoric of darkness and its narrator (who is Marlow on the face of it, but increasingly a Marlow possessed by Kurtz). The figure of Kurtz exerts a seductive and coercive pull on this narrative that both draws its language into overblown symbolism, a kind of distorted mirror of Kurtz's infamously elevated diction, and, more importantly, scrambles the comparative logic of devolution. If we remember this story as a consistent narrative of disillusionment, it is in part owing to the diversionary tactic at its very heart that strains to contain the effects on the shape of this narrative and on its lesson, if one may say so, of Kurtz's reversal of the civilizational scale. By insisting on *Heart of Darkness'* narrative logic, I attempt here to read against the grain of this rhetoric of darkness, which, with its ontological and epistemological suggestiveness, also exerts a powerful seduction on criticism itself. With a symptomatic reading of one narrative crux, I aim also to show the intrinsic relation between colonialism and Conrad's "modernist" narrative technique, an argument developed more fully in the second half of this chapter.

Though Marlow's preamble sounds the note for the theme of the story to follow in a very general way—the effects of the wilderness on the colonizer at the imperial frontier—his actual narrative follows a linear temporal sequence with very little telegraphing ahead to the tale's climax. Indeed, Marlow's reliability and his power as a critic of imperialism depend on the impartiality conveyed by his lack of preconception; we believe that he doesn't know what he will find ahead of time. This impression is only reinforced by Marlow's particular quality as a marginal observer, for just as he seems to have no foreknowledge, he is never at the center of events. He just happens to stumble across the grove where sickly African slave laborers ("criminals") are sent to die at the Company Station, the outermost of the three stations he visits. At the Central Station he pieces together his impressions of petty and bureaucratic imperial rapaciousness from fragments of overheard conversations so that the text bristles with quotation marks within quotation marks.

The result of this narrative presentation's linear temporality is to make the figure of Kurtz—and the redemptive idea he embodies—internally necessary to the tale; that is to say, to the observer's experience of imperialism. Marlow charts quite clearly the initial progress of his interest in Kurtz. He first hears of him in the context of the absurdly competitive ambitions of various imperial bureaucrats when the fastidious clerk at the Outer Station informs him that Kurtz is "a first class agent," a "remarkable person" who will "be somebody in the Administration before long" (*HD*, 19–20). At this point Marlow evinces no interest whatsoever and Kurtz is simply another pointless detail in a stream of professional gossip. When on his next stop, at the Central Station, another imperial agent pronounces Kurtz a "prodigy . . . an emissary of pity, and science, and progress" (*HD*, 25), Marlow remarks, "[Kurtz] was just a word for me. I did not see the man in the name any more than you do" (*HD*, 27). A little later, he develops a vague curiosity about him: "I wasn't very interested in him. No. Still, I was curious to see whether this man who had come out equipped with moral ideas of some sort, would climb to the top after all, and how he would set about his work when there" (*HD*, 31). This faint progress in Marlow's interest is charted with realist explicitness, but this realism extends no further for we can only guess at the moment when Kurtz becomes Marlow's sole obsession in a sudden surge of the rhetoric of darkness that intervenes between this spike of curiosity and the full-blown obsession a handful of pages later. "For me [the steamer] crawled towards Kurtz—exclusively . . ." (*HD*, 35). It is a slight breach in the sequential account, a kind of mysterious rhetorical premonition that bursts upon Marlow when he overhears the Central

Station manager and his uncle gossiping about Kurtz. The uncle breaks off, commending his manager nephew on keeping in such good health in the bush:

"H'm. just so," grunted the uncle. "Ah! my boy, trust to this—I say, trust to this." I saw him extend his short flipper of an arm for a gesture that took in the forest, the creek, the mud, the river—seemed to beckon with a dishonouring flourish before the sunlit face of the land a treacherous appeal to the lurking death, to the hidden evil, to the profound darkness of its heart. It was so startling that I leaped to my feet and looked back at the edge of the forest, as though I had expected an answer of some sort to that black display of confidence. (*HD*, 33)

The rhetoric of darkness irrupts over the stutter of a dash into the simple, concrete evocation of visible features of the landscape (forest, creek, mud, and river) converting them suddenly and unaccountably into the huge, ominous, and ambiguous abstractions of "lurking death," "hidden evil," and "darkness of its heart." There is no manifest accounting for Marlow's reaction. He has already overheard several tawdry imperial conversations without leaping up at the call of darkness. The force that impels him toward the landscape (now becoming darkness, or Kurtz) seems to be beyond him and it overwhelms his practical realist account. It is at this specific moment and in this specific way that Kurtz suddenly, indeed catastrophically, becomes necessary to Marlow's narrative. The rhetoric of darkness exceeds Marlow's realist powers of explanation and circumvents his powers of observation, marking Kurtz's necessity as one of compulsion or perhaps even coercion rather than logic. And the narrative logic of realist plotting, the logic of humanly or socially probable cause and effect, absconds from *Heart of Darkness* from this point on, to be replaced by the sublime incomprehensibility of catastrophic turns. We need only think of Conrad's earlier account of a comparable breakdown of civilization at the imperial frontier—the short story "An Outpost of Progress," where devolution is presented in the spirit of psychological realism—to appreciate the particular coercion at work here.

This passage sets up Kurtz as the "answer" to the question posed by the hollow rapaciousness of all the imperialists encountered in Marlow's journey through the pointless and murderous bureaucracy of the first two stations. What Marlow found there were "hollow men," "flabby devils," and the "papier mache Mephistopheleses," so utterly engrossed in their petty ambitions as to be entirely insensible either to the murderousness of their endeavor, to its absurdity (the brick maker who makes no bricks, etc.), or to their dwarfish unreality amidst the hugeness of the wilderness around them. These garden variety imperialists are no hypocrites; quite to the contrary they seem to have not the faintest inkling that their exploitation requires any redemptive pretext. Hypocrisy, interestingly enough, only enters this text with the catastrophic failure of an exalted civilizational altruism. The accumulated tawdriness of the hollow imperialist's *lack* of hypocrisy calls out almost uncontrollably, as the earlier cited passage tells it, for an antidote, in this case, rather astonishingly, a genuine Mephistopheles, a true and sinewy devil, the previously unlooked-for imperialist with an idea and a mission to leaven his greed. In a strange but convincing way *Heart of Darkness* posits the necessity of imperial ideology *retroactively*. The narrative doesn't start with a civilizing ideology and then show it to be false; it starts without one, finds it—inductively—to be necessary, then encounters its ruin. This creates in *Heart of Darkness* a peculiarly self-contained, self-created, and self-indicting conceptual structure. This belatedly constructed belief in the civilizing mission and the ineluctability of disillusionment forecloses the consequences of ideological positions elsewhere underpinning the text. Compelled necessity not only diverts logical necessity, it overwhelms it.

The logical necessity at issue is the consequence for civilizational comparison of Kurtz's movement down the civilizational scale. The reversibility of "progress" prompts a crisis of comparison since the crucial element of temporal distance that underwrites the absolute separation between comparability and equivalence is precisely what becomes unstable. The obvious question made strangely impertinent if not impossible by the rhetoric of *Heart of Darkness* is simply: If an individual's position on the racial and civilizational scale is not fixed by the forward movement of time, then might there be other grounds of comparison between people besides its progressive hierarchy? To put this in the context of *Heart of Darkness*, one might be lead to ask: If the scion of civilization can revert to savagery, that is, enter into direct comparison with African natives, what is to guarantee his superior worth? Why is his life intrinsically more valuable or interesting than theirs? These are the kinds of questions *Heart of Darkness* explicitly raises and strenuously diverts. The idea of the comparative scale of civilizations, the classic anthropological spatialization of time, is brought up in Marlow's very first words and it provides the dominant framework for his perception of Africa all along his journey, until he reaches Kurtz. Marlow breaks into speech just as darkness descends over the Thames estuary where he and his companions await the turning of the tide: "And this . . . has been one of the dark places of the earth" (*HD*, 5). This statement reads the darkened landscape abstractly, associating the quality of darkness with a civilizational condition and tempers the primary narrator's musings on triumphal imperial progress a paragraph earlier. ("What greatness had not floated on the ebb of that river into the mystery of an unknown earth! . . . The dreams of men, the seed of commonwealth, the germs of empire" [*HD*, 5]). Marlow expands the primary narrator's temporal template to Roman colonialism, thus recalling the British Empire to its own origins in savagery. But if the Roman colonizers in the frigid wilderness of pre-Christian England are equivalent to the contemporary British imperialists in the torrid jungles of Africa, then it must follow that the "native" ancestors of British imperialists are equivalent to contemporary natives in Africa and that, therefore, those African natives may one day develop into civilizing missionaries themselves. What contains this spatial equivalence between the heart of Africa and the heart of Britain is a definitive temporal disparity ironically telescoped into an almost geological time scale in Marlow's comment: "darkness was here yesterday" (*HD*, 5). The equivalence suggested between African natives and British imperialists is strictly and crucially mediated by teleological time, the before and after of civilizational progress.

Marlow is by no means a cheerleader for progress but he relies on the stability of the evolutionary scale to frame his perception of the bewildering diversity of the imperial world. His journey into Africa is figured unambiguously as a journey in time: "Going up that river was like travelling back to the earliest beginning of the world (*HD*, 34). . . . We were wanderers on a prehistoric earth" (*HD*, 36). He sounds this note relentlessly throughout his journey upriver. On several occasions he remarks on the fundamental comparability between himself and those "prehistoric" natives: the faint sound of drumming is comparable to church bells, "the thought of heir humanity—like yours—the thought of your remote kinship with this wild and passionate uproar. Ugly" (*HD*, 37). He even provides some explanation for the distant kinship he experiences: just as ontogeny recapitulates philogeny, "the mind of man is capable of anything—because everything is in it, all the past as well as all the future" (*HD*, 37). This is the basis of Marlow's racism: Africans are not absolutely different; rather, they occupy the inferior position of an anterior time with respect to the European. This is a difference of degree, measurable by the remoteness of a kinship. The basis of equivalence (a common humanity) is thus coincident with an absence of comparison introduced by an absolute temporal lag. It is essential to the workings of this framework that differences be strictly maintained, that each temporal element or racio-cultural type keep to its taxonomic place on the civilizational scale. Marlow, for instance, comments on the cannibals hired as his crew: "fine fellows—cannibals—in their place" (*HD*, 35), but he reserves all his contempt for hybrid or "improved specimens," such as the fireman whom he characterizes as "a dog in a parody of breeches and a feather hat, walking on his hind legs" (*HD*, 37). It is true that Marlow repeatedly warns his internal audience, retired sailors now engaged in respectable bourgeois occupations in the capital, against civilizational self-satisfaction, evoking an idea of civilization that appears quite contrary to the evolutionary scale—not a teleological certainty, but a thin veneer maintained and policed by the external constraints of a disciplinary society ("with solid pavement under your feet, stepping delicately between the butcher and the policeman, in the holy terror of scandal and gallows and lunatic asylums . . ." [*HD*, 50]). Nonetheless, these two ideas—the comparative scale of civilization and civilization as veneer—are by no means mutually exclusive; temporal remoteness remains crucial to both, though less certain for the latter.

Civilizational comparison and civilizational veneer have an important point in common once the scale or the veneer become traversable in either direction. The possibility logically arises for both equally that the basis of equivalence may in fact coincide with a ground for comparison. Once the engine of ineluctable teleological progress stalls out, nothing any longer guarantees a judgment of value that would make the high end of the scale unquestionably superior to the low end: reversion raises the possibility of a sliding scale of civilization. I do not want to argue that reversion or devolution must simply give on to a full-blown civilizational relativism by some ineluctable internal necessity. But I do want to suggest that in the absence of the certainty of progress, the civilizational scale no longer provides a stable support to judgments of value; it becomes rather flimsy, vulnerable to the possibility of other kinds of comparison, other, unexplored horizons of judgment. At the very least it would seem to open the novelistic possibility that there might be more to African characters and African lives than is contained in cliché and stereotype. What is striking about the text of *Heart of Darkness* is that it does not repress or ignore this possibility; on the contrary, it raises the possibility quite directly, deploys considerable rhetorical power to obfuscate it, and finally forecloses it so successfully that it vanishes altogether. Most critics, particularly in the wake of Chinua Achebe's withering critique, concur that while *Heart of Darkness* presents a powerful critique of imperialism, imperialism is nonetheless a political and philosophical limit it cannot see beyond.[7] My reading here confirms this general position, but I suggest that the extraordinary rigor with which this text follows through on the contradictions in the imperial idea does in fact lead it toward an alternative to imperialism, particularly in terms of the comparative disposition of Africans and white Imperialists, and that, therefore, its ultimate consolidation of imperialism is contrived if not strained.

Marlow explicitly invites a comparison between the civilizational extremes of black and white when he draws a parallel between the death of his African helmsman and the death of Kurtz, the only two deaths formally announced in the narrative. The helmsman, unable to restrain himself (to use Marlow's key word) from shooting back at the natives showering the steamer with arrows just before it reaches the Inner Station, is speared through the open window of the pilot house. His death is witnessed by Marlow and one of the "pilgrims" on board:

We two whites stood over him, and his lustrous and inquiring glance enveloped us both. I declare it looked as though he would presently put to us some question in an understandable language; but he died without uttering a sound, without moving a limb, without twitching a muscle. Only in the very last moment, as though in response to some sign we could not see, to some whisper we could not hear, he frowned heavily, and that frown gave to his black death-mask an inconceivably sombre, brooding, and menacing expression. . . . "He is dead," murmured the fellow, immensely impressed. "No doubt about it," said I, tugging like mad at the shoelaces. "And by the way, I suppose Mr. Kurtz is dead as well by this time." (*HD*, 47)

The attention to the moment of death, the signifying finitude of a life, opens the possibility that this African occupies a temporality that exceeds the hierarchies of the civilizational scale, a temporality that may be coeval (to use Johannes Fabian's term) with Marlow's, and therefore that he may have something intelligible to say within this narrative, some experience of life that isn't already coded in his temporalized, anthropological taxonomy. This mere suggestion of coevalness contained in the description of the helmsman's moment of death (that it should be describable at all) represents a radical narrowing of the temporal remoteness through which Marlow consistently views Africans. "I don't think," he comments earlier, "a single one of them had any clear idea of time, as we at the end of countless ages have. They still belonged to the beginnings of time—had no inherited experience to teach them, as it were" (*HD*, 41). The singularity of the helmsman's final moment and the possibility that he may possess the words to sum up his individual life would seem to introduce him into some more or less "clear idea of time." But Marlow opens this door only to close it immediately upon the helmsman's silence, whereupon he assimilates his face in death back into the portentous wilderness, sombre, brooding, menacing, and dark, where the African "belongs." The haunting of this missed comparison returns, however, in the racially inverted death scene that is the very culminating point of the narrative—the death of Kurtz, witnessed by Marlow and announced by a black servant:

> Anything approaching the change that came over his features I have never seen before, and hope never to see again. . . . It was as though a veil had been rent. I saw on that ivory face the expression of sombre pride, of ruthless power, of craven terror—of an intense and hopeless despair. Did he live his life again in every detail of desire, temptation, and surrender during that supreme moment of complete knowledge? He cried in a whisper at some image, at some vision—he cried out twice, a cry that was no more than a breath:
>
> "The horror, the horror!"
>
> I blew out the candle and left the cabin. The pilgrims were dining in the mess-room, and I took my place opposite the manager. . . . Suddenly the manager's boy put his insolent black head in the doorway, and said in a tone of scathing contempt:
>
> "Mistah Kurtz—he dead." (*HD*, 71)

The structural similarities are unmistakable: a white face and a black face whose expression in death shares an adjective (sombre) drawn from the rhetoric of darkness, who at the very moment of death sees a vision utterly inaccessible to the witness, and whose death is announced by the other race, in its own particular accents. These are the kinds of narrative parallels that invite reflection on equivalence. In this case, these nearly symmetrical frames, however, sharpen differences, for the helmsman is denied the possibility of a life that he might live again in the instant before death, and more importantly he dies speechless. Achebe insists that this denial of coherent, meaningful speech to all the African characters in *Heart of Darkness* is the most damning sign of its insistence on denying them a recognizable humanity. "The horror, the horror!" are this story's most memorable words and probably its most famous. But the memorability of Kurtz's death, and indeed its commemorability, becomes contingent in the narrative, I will argue, on the forgettability of the helmsman's death. Marlow amply provides the basis of equivalence between these two deaths in the narrative, but at the same time he withdraws all possibility for comparison.

If we turn back to the helmsman's death scene, we note that it is followed by the only significant breach in the chronological sequence of Marlow's narrative in the text of *Heart of Darkness*, a six-page digression that intervenes between the moment Marlow witnesses the helmsman's death and the moment soon after when he throws his body overboard. The scene in sequential narrative time leaves off with the helmsman's muteness and the digression begins with an evocation of Kurtz's voice: "I couldn't have been more disgusted [at the thought of Kurtz's premature death] if I had travelled all this way for the sole purpose of talking with Mr. Kurtz. Talking with . . . I flung one shoe overboard [the shoes soiled with the helmsman's blood], and became aware that that was exactly what I had been looking forward to—a talk with Kurtz. . . . The man presented himself as a voice . . . of all of his gifts one stood out pre-eminently . . . the gift of expression, the bewildering, the illuminating, the most exalted and the most contemptible, the pulsating stream of light, or the deceitful flow from the heart of an impenetrable darkness" (*HD*, 48). The rhetoric of darkness once again intrudes upon a prosaic, realist detail, but this time it elicits an utterly disproportionate "extravagance of emotion" in Marlow: "I couldn't have felt more of lonely desolation somehow, had I been robbed of a belief or missed my destiny in life" (*HD*, 48). His narration suddenly veers wide off its course and takes on the extraordinary identification, the secret sharing with Kurtz that shapes the story's telling from this point on. Narrated before Marlow has actually reached Kurtz, this digression not only presents a preemptive summation of that spectacularly catastrophic life, it also sums up Marlow's entire story down to the encounter with the Intended. The digression is further extended by Marlow's own silence during two long pauses in his narrative, both of which are followed by aggressive comments to his audience.

This formal breakdown of linear narrative progress converges with its subject matter, the deregulation of civilization's progress, which comes to provide a kind of a model for how the narration diverts the bewildering comparisons it has raised. In the course of this digression, Kurtz is inflated to become the personification of imperialism itself: "'My ivory.' Oh yes, I heard him. 'My Intended, my ivory, my station, my river, my——' everything belonged to him" (*HD*, 49). It is also here that we learn of that paradigmatically damning document, the report Kurtz wrote for the Soci-

ety for the Suppression of Savage Customs. It is a "beautiful piece of writing" that begins with "the argument that we whites, from the point of development we had arrived at, 'must necessarily appear to them [savages] in
the nature of supernatural beings . . . our power for good is practically unbounded.' . . . This was the unbounded power of eloquence—of words—
of burning noble words" (*HD*, 51). Noble all, with the exception of four
words scrawled at the foot of the last page: "Exterminate all the brutes."
This document is important because it is in fact the only evidence the text
provides to explain Kurtz outside of Marlow's own words and it suggests a
distinct self-canceling logic precisely where the civilizing mission's evolutionary teleology conflicts with the requirements of colonial exploitation.
Kurtz comes to the heart of Africa prepared to lead the "savages" into the
light of civilization. But the actual work of extracting wealth (in the form
of ivory) from the territory engages him in a very different relation to the
natives, a relation dictated not by theoretical or ideological mission alone,
but by the necessity of direct control. Kurtz's actions upriver thus reveal
the instrumental aspect of the civilizing ideology (Kurtz sets himself up as
a "real" god in order to secure the extraordinary quantities of ivory he ships
downriver) and also expose a contradiction internal to the colonial project
whose result is a near conflation of inferiority and expendability that I will
call the paradox of necessary superfluousness. In order to elaborate this
paradox, I turn to the account of North African settler colonialism in a moment of crisis in two mid-twentieth-century anticolonial theorists, Albert
Memmi and Frantz Fanon. The history and social forms of settler colonialism and those of the brief, bloody imperial adventure in Africa are of
course very different, but they do have in common the self-cancelling logic
of the civilizing mission, one that stands out with particular sharpness at
the moment of its implosion. Citing a familiar colonial quip, "tout serait
parfait s'il n'y avait pas les indigènes" [everything would be perfect, if there
weren't the natives], Memmi shows that the impulse toward racial extermination is not aberrant, but integral to the ideology of colonial domination.[8]
This domination is legitimated by the assertion of the inferiority of the colonized and the superiority of the colonizer; the civilizing mission promises
ultimately to abolish this difference by raising the colonized to the level of
the superior civilization. But in practice, the colonialist "ne peut admettre
une telle adéquation, qui détruirait le principe de ses privilèges" [cannot
admit such an adequation for it would destroy the principle underlying his
privileges], that is to say that the ideology that legitimates colonial domina-

tion logically ultimately destroys itself. The asymmetry between colonizer and colonized is therefore internally incommensurable and maintains itself untenably. Frantz Fanon writes of the colonizer and the colonized as inhabiting two zones that oppose each other "non au service d'une unité supérieure" [not in the service of a superior unity] but in a condition of reciprocal exclusion: "il n'y a pas de conciliation possible, l'un des termes est de trop" [there is no conciliation possible; one of the terms is superfluous].[9] The paradox of colonial comparison, then, can be formulated as that comparison in which of the two terms (colonizer/colonized), the necessary one (colonized) is figured as superfluous. "Exterminate all the brutes" expresses the contradiction quite accurately, with the added twist that this scrawled outburst is itself testament to Kurtz's fall down the civilizational scale.

The result of Marlow's long digression about Kurtz is to seal the helmsman and his death into such superfluousness in narrative terms. Marlow by no means overwrites the helmsman's silence with a defense of Kurtz, or any other justification for the imperial endeavor. On the contrary, this preemptive eulogy of Kurtz is unsparing in the amplitude it gives to his breakdown. By endowing Kurtz with the rhetorical role of personifying imperialism, Marlow indeed inflates the magnitude of his failure; the real consequences of Kurtz's actions are, after all, if one reflects on it, quite paltry compared to those, for instance, of a Rhodes or a Kitchener. But the rhetorical process of articulating this magnitude—its unmotivated intervention into the moment of the helmsman's death— overwhelms the suggested comparison between Kurtz, the white imperialist gone awry, and the African helmsman who dies needlessly in the line of duty. When Marlow returns to the helmsman at the end of this digression with a rather extensive comparison of worth and of quality with Kurtz, one cannot but read the comparison ironically "Poor fool! If he had only left that shutter alone. He had no restraint, no restraint—just like Kurtz—a tree swayed in the wind" (HD, 52). Marlow grants the basis for equivalence and simultaneously withdraws the ground of comparison. When he asserts "No. I cannot forget him [Kurtz], though I am not prepared to affirm the fellow was exactly worth the life we lost in getting to him," it is impossible to imagine by what criteria of judgment this could be the case. Comparison has been locked into a disproportionate incommensurability so secure as to function almost implicitly. With Marlow's last words on the helmsman— "And the intimate profundity of that look he gave me when he received his hurt remains to this day in my memory—like a claim of distant kinship affirmed in a supreme moment" (*HD*, 52)—he returns the African to his proper place in the remoteness of kinship and the character of the helmsman becomes superfluous to the story. There can be no question of his having any claim upon Marlow's or any reader's memory equivalent to that of Kurtz. He is as forgettable as he is evidently expendable. The narrative has utterly diverted the possibilities it raised for his finitude, and in lieu of last words (his own or his eulogy) we have read of Marlow's seduction by the high cant of imperialism transmitted through Kurtz's voice and his fate; in the time between the departure of the helmsman's spirit and the disposal of his body, it is, narratively speaking, Kurtz who dies and is eulogized.

What is bewildering about this particular irony is not its inconclusiveness, but on the contrary the suspicion one has that it is utterly closed, a kind of conceptual and linguistic dead end. If irony can be defined as a negation combined with an unarticulated, or unarticulable, promise (not this, but . . .), this irony is incomplete: there is no virtual supplementary clause, no possible "but": *not that* Kurtz's life wasn't worth the helmsman's, *but* Kurtz's life is redeemable, worth something by potentially intelligible standards. Marlow's words may not say what they mean, but they do not point elsewhere in or beyond language. The text neither presents redeeming apologies for Kurtz nor draws any conclusions from his reversion. It stops at the negation as though to freeze the movement across the civilizational scale with his fall. His degeneracy will have no effect on our evaluation of any of the other lives he may have touched, intruded upon, or robbed. For all its unsparing critique, there is no outside to imperialism in *Heart of Darkness*. The text's extremity, indissociable from the uncompromising nature of Marlow's presentation of imperialism, is the project of writing an account of imperialism in a language debased by imperialism; that is, one in which there is not only the familiar discrepancy between word and thing, word and deed, but where the relation between them is one of outright negation. With his fraught ironies and overwrought abstractions, Marlow uses this language against itself, but at the cost of evacuating any alternative to imperialism. This exemplary critique of imperialism from within also functions as a strategy of containment that allows Marlow to evade his critique's consequences.

The radical closure of Marlow's narrative is repeated in the gesture of transmission with which it ends. Bette London, in an ingenious reading of Marlow's asides to his captive audience, argues that Marlow "carves out for himself a position of colonial authority" by projecting onto his listeners (through verbal echoes within the story) the degraded positions of natives and women within his narrative.[10] *Heart of Darkness*, she argues, shows or enacts the coercive construction of the voice of colonial authority in a particularly acute instance of the "coercive dialogue" Aaron Fogel considers the fundamental structuring device and mode of thought in Conrad's fiction.[11] Marlow's asides show him aggressively seeking to implicate his listeners, in a sense compelling rather than inviting the retelling of his tale and foreclosing the possibility of telling it differently. The listener can only retell the story by taking on Marlow's voice, as the novella's final sentence, spoken by the primary narrator, discloses:

I raised my head. The offing was barred by a black bank of clouds, and the tranquil waterway leading to the uttermost ends of the earth flowed sombre under an overcast sky—seemed to lead into the heart of an immense darkness. (*HD*, 79)

The faint asyndeton expressed in the grammatical stammer of a dash designates precisely the point where Marlow's rhetoric of darkness invades the next teller's and the tale begins anew and the same.

Marlow and the Rhetoric of Dissimilation

We take it for granted by now that time is the single determining necessity for narrative. The *locus classicus* of this principle for modern narratology is probably Gérard Genette's *Figures III*, where he writes:

By virtue of a dissymetry whose deeper causes escape us, but which is inscribed in the very structures of the language [*langue*] (or, at the very least in the great "languages of civilization" of Western culture), I can very well tell a story without specifying the place where it occurs, and whether this place is more or less distant from the place from which I tell the story, whereas it is almost impossible for me not to situate the story in time with respect to my act of narration.[12]

It is notable that a principle that has commanded so much certainty and generated so much discourse should be stated so hesitantly and amidst so many qualifications, and that these should converge on the "languages of civilization" of Western culture, in quotation marks within parentheses. Genette's tentativeness suggests the possibility that cultural boundaries may be involved in the siting of narration, in its grounding in a determining presence as well as a determining present. Indeed, for Homi Bhabha the ambivalence of colonial authority is predicated precisely on the problems surrounding its dislocation, the nature of what he calls its "split presence" in the colonial sphere.[13] The larger question that frames the argument that follows concerns the extent to which the colonial situation introduces a kind of necessity to the relation between a narrative and the place of narration and how this relation becomes a problem of transmission; that is, of the constitution of a coherent cultural community of listeners and readers.

Marlow, Conrad's unusual narrator, part Buddha, part chummy seaman, spinner of modernist yarns for his befuddled colleagues, enters the world of letters (in "Youth," 1898) with the following introduction: "Marlow (at least that is how I think he spelt his name) told the story." From the start his defining characteristic is presence: he tells his stories aloud to people who know him. His performances are always located in particular places and addressed to particular listeners: men of his "class," merchant seamen, and imperial servants. The conditions that led to Marlow's emergence, I will argue, suggest how for Conrad colonial narrative came to require a metonymic grounding in place.

In his early works, Conrad employs an omniscient narrative point of view modeled on the emotional *impassibilité* of Gustave Flaubert and the ironic distance of Guy de Maupassant. Critics normally account for the development of Marlow and the Marlowian scene of narration as the resolution for two problems this detached narrative stance presented for Conrad. The first is that Conrad's omniscient narrator neither intrudes fully enough into his characters' state of mind to provide a satisfying account of motivation nor keeps a sufficient distance to keep such motives mysterious.[14] Ian Watt suggests that Conrad was unable to view Almayer, for instance, with "consistent sympathy or resolute detachment" and produce the kind of authorial identification with the primary character that would make the novel convincing.[15] The second problem is Conrad's tendency to intrude on the action with ironic commentary that disrupts the fiction's self-sufficiency. Both of these problems must, I propose, also be considered in terms of the particular difficulties cultural difference presented for novels that aspired both to Flaubertian artistry and ethnographic accuracy. After all, with his first two novels, *Almayer's Folly* (1895) and *An Outcast of the Islands* (1896), Conrad was heralded both for his complexity and for being the first author to bring the Malay archipelago into English literature.[16]

The position Conrad took in his early omniscient narrations resembles the stance of ethnology's participant observation. While we can assume that this narrator has "been there," that is, has privileged knowledge about an exotic culture that his metropolitan readers do not share, he at the same time effaces himself as a figure from the text and observes from above or beyond. In effect, he participates by observing. The effacement of the mediating "I" in favor of the mediating "eye" yields a posture of horizontal relativism; that is, in its self-effacement the omniscient narrative voice must give the appearance of impartiality in order to produce the *style indirect libre* through which it renders incompatible positions. When these positions involve the incommensurability of different cultures in a relation of domination, as they do in Conrad's early novels, such a narrative device pushes language to the edge of plausibility. Two characters thinking in the same words mean completely different things. We see this in Nina and Almayer, and perhaps even more dramatically in the internal discourse of Willems and Aissa in *An Outcast of the Islands*:

(Willems) He was carried away by the flood of hate, disgust, and contempt of a white man for that blood which is not his blood, for that race which is not his race; for the brown skins; for the hearts false like the sea, blacker than night. This feeling of repulsion overmastered his reason in a clear conviction of the impossibility for him to live with her people.

(Aissa) . . . and her eyes looked fixedly, sombre and steady, at that man born in the land of violence and evil wherefrom nothing but misfortune comes to those who are not white. Instead of thinking of her caresses, instead of forgetting all the world in her embrace, he was thinking yet of his people; of that people that steals every land, masters every sea, that knows no mercy and no truth—knows nothing but its own strength.[17]

(Narration) Hate filled the world, filled the space between them—the hate of race, the hate of hopeless diversity, the hate of blood; the hate against the man born in the land of lies and of evil from which nothing but misfortune comes to those who are not white. And as she stood, maddened, she heard a whisper near her, the whisper of the dead Omar's voice saying in her ear: Kill![18]

These passages illustrate the weaknesses of Conrad's omniscient narration: inability to develop motive, intrusive pontification. But what is at issue here is something more than a vague subjective shortcoming in Conrad's ability to get inside his characters' minds. The need for didactic intrusion arises out of a concern to convey the degree to which the abyss that separates Willems and Aissa is as much cultural and political as it is psychological. The hatred that binds them, Conrad is anxious to emphasize, cannot be rendered merely as a product of their internal state. It is worth noting that what makes these passages awkward and lifeless is the repetitiveness of the language.

One feels that had Conrad found substantially different ways of expressing the substantially different hatred of Willems and Aissa he might have made them more convincing. But the omniscient narrator has only one neutral language through which to convey culturally incommensurable conditions.

Early critics saw in Conrad's narratorial intrusiveness an unfortunate lack of restraint, the manifestation of an overweening authorial desire to dictate the meaning of a story. In "An Outpost of Progress" (1898), a short story about the undoing of two clerks in a forgotten colonial outpost in Africa, Conrad is not content to let alone the irony of Carlier and Kayerts' feeble hypocrisy in affirming the evils of slavery even as they depend on it:

"Slavery is an awful thing," stammered out Kayerts in an unsteady voice.

"Frightful—the sufferings," grunted Carlier with conviction.

They believed their words. *Everybody* shows a respectful deference to certain sounds that he and his fellows can make. But about feelings people really know nothing. *We* talk with indignation or enthusiasm; we talk about oppression, cruelty, crime, devotion, self-sacrifice, virtue, and we know nothing real beyond the words. *Nobody* knows what suffering or sacrifice mean—except, perhaps, the victims of the mysterious purpose of these illusions.[19] (my emphasis)

Edward Garnett, Conrad's friend and early mentor, considered such commentary excessive and intrusive.[20] Ford Madox Ford put it this way: "If your yearning to amend the human race is so great that you can't possibly keep your fingers out of the watch-springs there is a device that you can adopt. . . . You must then invent, justify, and set going in your novel a character who can convincingly express your views."[21] It seems to me, however, that the faltering of the narrative point of view and the uncertainty of the narrative voice in passages like that from "An Outpost of Progress" betray less of a desire to dictate meaning than they do a distinct anxiety about the disposition of the audience. The commentary does not so much spell out the dialogue's irony as it diverts it into a more general register that both blunts the brutal edge of the two characters' particular hypocrisy and also implicates a collective entity, "we," that encompasses both omniscient narrator and readers and thus interrupts any facile dismissal or containment. The progress of pronouns is instructive in this regard: Conrad's authorial commentary moves from "They" [Carlier and Kayerts] to "Everybody" to "We" to "Nobody." The intrusive narrator here seems to be less concerned with amending the human race than with establishing it—not to say implicating it—or some less ambitious collectivity, as an audience for his text. The problem is not that the narrator is unable to remain sufficiently detached from his characters, but that he has difficulty maintaining faith in his readers. Conrad is anxious that the actions conditioned by a colonial context not be judged too hastily, that the cultural distance be preserved and maintained. What is remarkable is that the conflict of cultures that makes up the content of the story should be displaced onto the level of its transmission.

Ian Watt observes in passing that in Conrad's first novel, he "departed from the Victorian tradition of the intrusive author in favor of Flaubert's attitude of narrative impersonality."[22] As the telling choice of the word "depart" suggests, Conrad begins by deviating from his adopted tradition and enters the stage of English fiction in French guise. Once he abandons Flaubertian omniscience, however, Conrad does not "re"-enter the fold of Victorian narrators, but rather fashions an archaic oral participant-narrator, a seafaring spinner of yarns addressing his similars, thus restricting the compass of his audience. Whereas narratorial *impassibilité* maintains a rigorous detachment from its addressees, the Victorian narrator actively interpellates a community. Intrusive and semi-individuated as in *Vanity Fair*, or generalized into near omniscience as in *Middlemarch*, this narrator can be said in broad terms to occupy the position of, as J. Hillis Miller puts it, a "transindividual mind," the voice of the social organism. "The reader of a Victorian novel" Miller writes, "in his turn is invited by the words of the narrator to enter into complicity with a collective mind which pre-exists the first words of the novel and will continue when they end, though without the novel it might remain invisible."[23] The collectivity the Victorian narrator makes visible and thus consolidates is composed of social classes, and political and economic institutions that frame the progress of individual lives. Moreover, the identification offered through the medium of the transindividual narrator is clearly, if often implicitly, national. During the time we are under the sway of the narrator of *Vanity Fair*'s "rhetoric of assimilation," in Miller's apt phrase, we magically take the place of mid-nineteenth-century vaguely middle-class English citizens. While a fuller analysis of this rhetoric would have to modulate Miller's formulation in view of the complex systems of repression and discontinuity, recent critics of Victorian narrative have elaborated, one can say that this narratorial rhetoric aspires to assimilation; with an assurance that projects itself as implicit beyond question, it marks its readers as culturally and nationally specific and united. Conrad seems at once unable to trust this unified collectivity and reluctant to abandon it. He endows Marlow with a "noble sociability of vision," in Henry James's words,[24] a vision in which the aspiration toward an implicit social collectivity, toward speaking "for," survives in the restricted compass of sociability, the will to conversation, the insistence on speaking "to."

The ethnographic participant observer claims to speak as a cultural insider on the paradoxical authority of a scientifically *disinterested* participation that other participants in "primitive" cultures (imperialists, missionaries) cannot claim. In abandoning omniscient narration Conrad chiefly abandons any pretension to disinterested objectivity. Marlow is a participant narrator both in his claim to have partaken in the actions he describes and to belong to the class of his characters, but also and more particularly because his act of narration itself has a participatory structure. The emphasis thus shifts from speaking *as* to speaking *as* and *to*. The consequences of this deflection of cultural incommensurability from diegesis to extradiegesis will be most fully worked out in *Lord Jim*. For the moment it suffices to remark that Marlow replaces the participant observer's impartiality with the participant narrator's structure of address; instead of participating by observing, he participates by narrating. Marlow emerges at least in part to preserve a colonial authority for the possibility of speaking across cultures without losing the coherence or even dominance of the position of address, but despite the intimacy of its setting, his participant narration does not assimilate its readers to a coherent transindividual entity, not even to so rudimentary and homogeneous a grouping as the small group of his listeners. It has the result, rather, of separating them. Conrad counters the Victorian "rhetoric of assimilation" with what I will call Marlow's "rhetoric of dissimilation."

This attempt to cling to Victorian sociality by means of a modernism fashioned from an archaic scene of storytelling would be yet another odd twist in Conrad's ambiguous position in literary history.[25] My argument here is that those characteristics of Conrad's style that conventionally align him with European modernism are in many ways consequent upon his position as denizen of empire. This has important consequences for an attempt to interpret the relation of these novels to what Fredric Jameson calls a "political unconscious." The manifest content of Conrad's early work is so obviously concerned with the imperial world that the temptation for a mimetic reading of these narratives and the conditions they describe is great. Critics have, thus, tended to sunder the imperial content of the works from their modernist style, frequently setting the skeptical, discontinuous, and fragmentary sensibility of the style in a redemptive opposition to the realist expression of colonial biases. Fredric Jameson argues in his magisterial reading of *Lord Jim* that the "impressionist" style of the narrative functions at once as an expression of and an aesthetic compensation for a feature of industrial capitalism in the metropolis: rationalization. While an imperial contradiction does, at the very end of Jameson's lengthy analysis, rather improbably appear as the "real" contradiction the text attempts to contain, the mediating codes operating within it are entirely drawn from the European context. The notion of community so crucial to Jameson's elaborate anagogical scaffolding ("only the community, indeed, can dramatize that self-sufficient intelligible unity (or 'structure') of which the individual 'subject' is the decentered effect"[26]) is unquestioningly identified with Europe alone. Jameson thus skips over significant and historically signifying disjunctions and discontinuities in the constitution of communities that, in contexts like imperialism, which are defined by dislocation, problematize the very determination of a provisional *ground* that would lead back to a single geographically discernible historical necessity. Marlow's dissimilation seems in many ways to delimit the conditions of impossibility for a community capable of guaranteeing the imperial text's final social currency and intelligibility.

In the early works this rhetoric of dissimilation involves a number of displacements. It has often been remarked that Marlow is Conrad's projection of what sort of author he might have been had he been born English.[27] Furthermore, Marlow's emergence coincides with the first works Conrad published in *Blackwood's Magazine*, and thus inaugurates his legitimation as a serious English author. As critics have observed, *Blackwood's Magazine*'s readership corresponds in class and occupation quite precisely with the internal audience in Conrad's stories.[28] The cluster of Marlow stories culminating in *Lord Jim* thus occupies a representational tightrope in which the narrator speaks *as* the author might, were he to belong seamlessly and naturally to the nation, and the hearers are addressed *as* the readers might, were they to be present, in which, that is, the "real" is inscribed as a foil, an unsteady backdrop, to the fiction. What is striking here is that the cozy homogeneity achieved by these personations produces fictions that disjoin and disarticulate it. To return to the anthropological paradigm of participant observation, one might say that even as Conrad's introduction of a partial narrator evinces the impossibility of speaking as an insider, so it also distorts or displaces all positions of address with a marked personation.[29] Within this overdetermined frame, Conrad will deploy Marlow's act of narration on the borderland of given communities and fashion it as a test of the givenness of community.

The first story in which Marlow comes to narration begins auspiciously with the words: "This could have happened nowhere but in England, where men and sea interpenetrate, so to speak—the sea entering into the life of most men, and the men knowing something or everything about the sea, in the way of amusement, of travel, or of bread-winning." [30] Unlike the Victorian narrators, who launch us into the specificities of their tales with little explanation, the primary narrator of "Youth" (1898) begins not only by establishing the nation where the action presumably has occurred, but, in a sequence of specifications that protest all too much, explaining why the story would be uniquely English ("where men and the sea interpenetrate"), equivocating (well, "most men"), stumbling into near contradiction ("knowing something *or* everything"), and finally canceling out all remaining claims to an implicit identification by having to enumerate just how "most men" are bound together by the sea. The very tentativeness of such a start signals the extent to which the national grounds of narration are in question. The story goes on to establish its frame, minimally, by specifying the four listeners as former merchant seamen and the storyteller, Marlow. The anxiety about grounding the story in a national territory descends into further irony when it turns out that what could occur "nowhere but in England" refers not to the action of the story, but to the scene of its telling, that particular gathering of men. Marlow's story itself takes place on the transnational waters of harbors and the open sea between colonial ports. And surely it is more than disingenuous to claim that the telling of sea stories, the very currency of the transnational sea, expresses the uniqueness of any nation (they express the "uniqueness" of *all* seafaring nations). But "Youth" does not deploy these ironies as satirical critique; instead, it maintains the desire for identification in the unity of the nation even as all its elements work toward the dismantling of affirmations of solidarity. In a gratuitous and therefore all the more significant detail, Marlow extols the crew of the ill-fated *Judea*, whose exploits the story recounts:

No; it was something in [that crew of Liverpool hardcases], something inborn and everlasting. I don't say positively that the crew of a French or German merchantman wouldn't have done it, but I doubt whether it would have been done in the same way. There was a completeness in it, something solid like a principle, and masterful like an instinct—a disclosure of something secret—of that hidden something, that gift of good or evil that makes racial difference, that shapes the fate of nations. (*Y*, 32)

Among the discrepancies and exaggerations involved in the transformation of Conrad's actual experiences on the *Palestine* into Marlow's on the *Judea*, the most striking is that the *Palestine*'s crew included not a single Liverpudlian, being instead composed of English, Irish, Antillean, Dutch, Norwegian, and Australian nationals, the usual transnational hodgepodge of the imperial merchant marine.[31] What makes this detail as remarkable as the dramatic "national" opening is that absolutely nothing in the story bears it out. The Liverpudlian sailors earn this grandiose endorsement of their racial and national mettle for obeying Marlow's command to furl the sails on a ship that is being towed by another because, last along a string of mishaps, its cargo has exploded. That "gift" of racial difference, the givenness of national cohesion the story seems to insist upon, runs counter to its substance, a simple reminiscence about a jinxed voyage, an absurd comedy of errors. For "Youth" does not even unequivocally manage to complete its modest aim, that is, to bind its homogeneous audience together in the brief nostalgia of reminiscence. Marlow's language of romance and heroism is at all points ironically undercut by the patent absurdity of the events it describes. He thus offers the solace of community in the reminiscence of sea days even as he takes it away. And this seems to me a very particular Marlowian inflection: he does not unmask the pretensions of youth by measuring them against hard reality in the manner of satire. Rather, he offers the lie of illusion itself as the vehicle in which the community of his listeners can share so that they are in some sense united by the very acknowledgment of ironic disjunction. The story's final words carry the full weight of this ambivalence:

. . . our weary eyes looking still, looking always, looking anxiously for something out of life, that while it is expected is already gone—has passed unseen, in a sigh, in a flash—together with the youth, with the strength, with the romance of illusions. (*Y*, 48)

In these last words, spoken by the primary narrator, the first-person plural binds Marlow, the narrator who produced the irony, to his audience. The story that began with such a forceful appeal to national cohesion and particularity ends with a tenuous community of five whom the story has united by exposing their disjunctions, their separateness even from illusion. Marlow offers his narrative "I" as the mediation and catalyst for that peculiarly tenuous "us."

"Karain" (1897), Conrad's first story for *Blackwood's Magazine*, written less than a year before "Youth," marks Conrad's first use of the participant (though in this case anonymous) narrator. In "Karain" the foundation of the bond in separateness is a particular effect of cultural and imperial disjunction. The narrator, one of three English sailors illegally running arms in the Malay archipelago, tells the story of Karain, a heroic Bugis leader the sailors had known. "Karain's" climax takes shape on a certain night when a dispossessed and desperate Karain appears on his English friends' ship and tells them the story of a ghost from his past who has driven him from the heights of power and glory to the edge of despair. He ends his story by appealing to his powerful white friends for "your protection—or your strength. . . . A charm . . . a weapon."[32] Conrad quite explicitly expresses this demand in racial and cultural terms: "We three white men looking at the Malay, could not find one word to the purpose amongst us . . ." (*K*, 81), making of this extradiegetic exchange an instance of the white man's burden. "By Jove," says one of the sailors, "he seems to have a great idea of our power." This sailor is then struck with a brilliant idea that has worked so well for so many white men in the annals of colonialism, namely, to pacify the distraught native with a trinket. The trinket, or "lie" as the sailor calls it, is a Jubilee sixpence engraved with an image of Queen Victoria. The charm works but, like all cross-cultural lies, it is fraught in excessive, bewildering ironies. Money, the very material basis of colonial profit, is made to commemorate the reign of the conqueror; that is, turned from sign to symbol, its value sublimated from exchange into icon. Transported to the dark reaches of the colonial world it loses all reference to material value ("never was sixpence wasted to better advantage" [*K*, 89]) and enters into relation with other sign systems, in this case those operating around the fetish, the charm. In presenting the sixpence to Karain, Hollis compares Victoria to an Islamic figure: "This is the image of the Great Queen, and the most powerful thing the white men know. . . . She is more powerful than Suleiman the Wise, who commanded the genii . . ." (*K*, 85). Soon after, however, he addresses his fellow sailors, in English, in an attempt to ground the sign in their reckoning:

She commands a spirit, too—the spirit of her nation; a masterful, conscientious, unscrupulous, unconquerable devil . . . that does a lot of good—incidentally . . . a lot of good . . . at times—and wouldn't stand any fuss from the best ghost. . . . (*K*, 85; all except final ellipses Conrad's)

One might read this as a recuperation of the primacy of the white, English significance of Victoria from the danger of Karain's turning her into merely the most powerful among a whole collection of genii. In other words, white supremacy and wisdom might be consolidated and affirmed in the very power it has to deceive the native. The native meaning imposed on the coin would thus act not as a threatening comparative equivalent to European meanings, but as a foil, a backdrop that sets it off and consolidates it: Victoria is like the nation, not like Suleiman; Victoria commands a national spirit and principle, not genii. The story might thus provide itself as a vehicle for its readers to share in this triumph. Instead it remains on the fence between the two grounds for signification; that is, the Malay archipelago and London and retains the mark of estranging contiguity. As Karain exults in his new amulet among the Malays, the narrator muses, "I wondered what they thought; what he thought; . . . what the reader thinks" (*K*, 88; Conrad's ellipses). Though it does not stage its own transmission, "Karain," like "Youth," is presented as a reminiscence shared by a "we" referring to former men of the sea. The narrator's most decisive intrusion is precisely at the juncture of legitimating cultural truth. His insistence on turning the question back onto his readers interrupts any easy sharing and invites us to join the participating sailors in the event's disjunctions. The story ends with the narrator encountering one of the sailors back in London. Following a description of the bustling metropolis, the story's last words are as follows:

"Yes; I see it [the spirit of the metropolis]," said Jackson, slowly. "It is there; it pants, it runs, it rolls; it is strong and alive; it would smash you if you didn't look out; but I'll be hanged if it is yet as real to me as . . . as the other thing . . . say, Karain's story." I think that, decidedly, he had been too long away from home. (*K*, 91; Conrad's ellipses)

The narrator's participation in "Karain" does not amount to a mediating stance of cultural equivalence or relativism between the metropolis and the colonial outland, nor yet of the consolidation of the truth of European standards against the backdrop of native primitivism, but rather of a subtle disruption of the relation between foreground and background, between foil and subject. The power relation retains a marked asymmetry; what's no longer clearly fixable is which element is foil to the other, which, to keep with Conrad's comparative, is *more* real.

If to be "too long away from home" renders figuratively the disruption of the grounds for stable cultural reference and value, it also literally denotes the dispersal and dislocation that colonial work entails. As Homi Bhabha argues, in the colonial arena this displacement on the level of signification occurs simultaneously with and as a result of a literal dislocation in space.

Consequently, the moment of transparency, of meaning, is not produced by an original correspondence between signifier and signified, but by a "complementarity of meaning" based on the *differential* disposition of elements. The Western claim of power then, despite its appearance as universal, is in fact contingent at least in part because the objects of authority (the colonized) are by definition excluded from what Bhabha calls the "rules of recognition."[33] Marlow's difficulties in establishing a consistent position of address evince a kindred instability in the rules of narrative recognition. Whereas this colonial disposition of power results in myriad forms of subversive mimicry and hybridity for the colonized, it provokes for the colonizers, at least as Marlow represents them, a dissimilation that operates on the level of the community itself, the very enunciation of the first person plural. The rules of recognition, even in Conrad's earliest work are not given; once Marlow enters the scene they are constantly under construction in variously dislocated spaces. In associating Marlow with a scene of oral storytelling, Conrad leaps backward over the social text to a more rudimentary form of community. Francis Mulhern calls Conrad's insistence on "restoring the communicative guarantee" of orality in the written medium of the novel "hyperphasia" and argues that it arises from "an impulse to abolish the novelistic, or at least to outwit it" by withdrawing its particular claims to authority (Mulhern, 60). Not unlike Jameson, Mulhern sees the ultimate effect of the storytelling frame and the community it invokes in *Heart of Darkness* and *Lord Jim* as means to divert attention from, or disavow, the manifest content of imperialism. Keeping to a smaller segment of Conrad's work and reading the texts closer to the letter, I argue that the structure of address itself thematizes an important dimension of imperialism. When in *Lord Jim* Marlow takes up directly the problem of grounding the community of imperial servants, his oral narrative will fail precisely where its multivocality interrupts the metaphoric moment of closure in which, as Peter Brooks has it, "the claim to understanding is incorporate with the claim to transmissibility."[34]

Foiled Communities

Marlow's first three acts of narration chart a suggestive progression of locales. He tells "Youth" in a pub in England to former seamen now occupied in dreary, bourgeois pursuits; he tells *Heart of Darkness* on a cruising yawl waiting in the Thames estuary for the rising tide to the same audience of retired sailors; he tells part of *Lord Jim* on various occasions to a company of imperial servants in various and unspecified locations in the imperial outland and sends the conclusion of the tale as a letter to a single recipient in the unnamed metropolis. These tellings thus move from firm national ground to liminal national waters to unspecified imperial territories and finally end in the return of a written missive back to the metropolis. The progressive ungrounding of the scene of telling corresponds to a shifting focus in the narration from constituting a national community out of the experience of imperial servants to constituting a community of imperial servants on the borderlands. At the same time the entire process moves from an intimate scene of oral storytelling to writing, specifically in the form of a letter—that most private of all communications—sent back to a metropolitan center. I would suggest that Marlow's errant itinerary across these texts is significant both because it makes dislocation an integral problem for the conversion of imperial themes into narrative and because it maps out the consequent unrecoverability of that unified collectivity called forth in earlier narrators' "rhetoric of assimilation." Marlow's experiment in community and communication comes to an end with and within *Lord Jim*.

Conrad insisted that the collection of short stories that was to span from "Youth" to *Lord Jim* shared a "moral idea." He wrote to William Blackwood: "It [*Lord Jim*] has not been planned to stand alone. *H of D* was meant in my mind as a foil, and 'Youth' was supposed to give the note." [35] To my knowledge, critics have made little of this striking authorial prescription. Watt limits himself to suggesting, rather hesitantly, that Conrad "may have . . . turned *Lord Jim* into a dialogue between the two Marlows, with Jim as the voice of his earlier innocence, and Marlow confronting him with the disenchanted voice of later experience." [36] But "dialogue" is not the word Conrad chooses to name the kind of comparison he has in mind. He invokes instead the rather obscure term "foil," which suggests far less autonomy for the particular way these two tellings are "not meant to stand alone." It is difficult to fix the precise relation the term denotes: a foil, according to the Oxford English Dictionary, is a thin backing that sets something off "by contrast or quality." A foil does not answer back or reflect like a mirror image; rather, it is the technical name for the thin sheet of metal set behind the glass of a mirror to produce reflection. It is the vanishing ground (and the vanished ground) of reflection. And yet the more decisive and threatening sense of the verb "to foil" subtends its retiring nominal counterpart. The verb "to foil," according to the OED means "to frustrate the effort of a person, to parry, baulk, baffle." This last sense, "baffle," is closest to the verb's origin in hunting terminology. It comes from the French "*fouler* [fr. L. *fullare*]," which means to trample down, and appears originally in phrases like "to run the foil," meaning "to run over the same track a second time (with the effect of baffling the hounds)" or "to break her foil: to run out of the track after having doubled." "To foil," then, at its origin has the sense of baffling or frustrating by doubling back, and it is precisely in this double movement, this return, that it overlaps with the noun's virtual reflection, that is, with the necessarily comparative disposition of a foil.

I have taken a detour through this word because it seems to me an apt vehicle for pointing to the particular inflection of a mode of Conradian comparison in which what ought to resolve itself into equivalence or proper metaphorical subordination veers into comparison as a momentary oscillation between foreground and background in which the retiring foil threatens to baffle, parry, or balk instead of setting off. As participant narrator, Marlow is both the mediator and the catalyst of this effect. That this should be a sign of the particular pressure of colonialism on Conrad's style has to do not only with the clash of cultures of which he fashions the subject of his stories—imperialism as content—but also with the decisive importance of dislocation in the setting of the act of narration and the process of transmission. In this version of colonial narrative, Marlow's metonymic presence—the story's grounding in place—disrupts the metaphoric closure of its progress through time.

Colonialism marks *Lord Jim* with an excessive displacement from symbol to sign, which culminates in an association of metonymy with place itself. Displacement from symbol to sign and reversal between foreground and background are hallmarks of "impressionist" style that critics find Conrad raising to high modernist art in the *Patna* section of *Lord Jim*. One of many famous instances is the way the purely accidental intrusion of a dog occasions the meeting of Marlow and Jim. (Marlow, seeing the dog, says, "Look at that wretched cur." Jim overhears and, believing the remark is directed toward him, confronts Marlow.) Jameson aligns this "fragmentation," and "relative independence between foreground and background" with the modernist aesthetic of James Joyce and the Bloomsbury group (Jameson, 223) and finally sees in the "self generation of the text" of the first part of *Lord Jim* an instance of postmodern *écriture avant la lettre* (Jameson, 225).

But alongside the style wrought from arbitrary reversals of foreground and background and its attendant narrative device of what Watt has baptized "delayed decoding," in which events are reported out of sequence through a subjective prism, there is a displacement of symbol to sign in which language itself is insistently territorialized; that is, diverted from its generalizing capacity to its national ground, from its symbolic function to its location in space. This displacement duplicated from the texture of language to the novel's structure is of a piece with what I take to be the overt overarching motive for telling the tale in the first place: to construe from Jim's paradoxical faithfulness to the ideals of the merchant service despite his breach of its code of conduct, a principle that might bind the far-flung "heroic bureaucracy of imperial capitalism," to borrow Jameson's words. Jameson, as I pointed out earlier, seems to disavow this particular "manifest content," proclaiming, against all evidence, that "if this is what *Lord Jim* is really all about, then it only remains to ask why nobody thinks so, least of all Conrad himself. . . ." (Jameson, 265). Marlow thinks so, and lays his thought out unequivocally in the following passage where he describes himself on the verge of returning to an unspecified home:

We return to face our superiors, our kindred, our friends . . . even those who have neither . . . have to meet the spirit that dwells within the land, under its sky, in its air, in its valleys, and on its rises . . . I think it is the lonely . . . who return not to a dwelling but to the land itself, to meet its disembodied, eternal and unchangeable spirit . . . who understand best its severity, its saving power, the grace of its secular right to our fidelity, to our obedience. Yes! Few of us understand, but we all feel it though, and I say *all* without exception, because those who do not feel do not count . . . [Man] is rooted to the land from which he draws his faith together with his life. I don't know how much Jim understood; but I know he felt, he felt confusedly but powerfully, the demand of some such truth or some such illusion—I don't care how you call it, there is so little difference, and the difference means so little. The thing is that in virtue of his feeling he mattered.[37]

The stance of Marlow's participant narration here, that in speaking for "we all" he must embrace so many particular lands into one general spirit, causes the sense of this passage to strain against its expression: the spirit is in the land, but "disembodied"; it is attached to an absolutely particular place but shared by all. The absence of particularizing detail to describe the land that claims such profound fidelity in this passage, may also echo with the longings induced by Conrad's own multiple displacements, as critics have argued.[38]

Marlow punctuates his narrative with the refrain that Jim is "one of us." Marlow's attempt to redeem Jim and refashion his story as a medium for consolidating that community, in the *Patna* section, takes the form, as Benita Parry shows, of a multivalent interrogation of a utilitarian, institutional basis for codes of conduct rendered through various interviews and encounters with Jim along with discussions of his case with others. Perhaps the most celebrated of these is Marlow's encounter with the French officer who guided the *Patna* to safe harbor after she had been ignominiously abandoned by Jim and the rest of her crew. Critics have pointed out that the French officer is a crucial thematic figure because, though he is a paragon of understated courage and faithfulness to the code of conduct that Jim betrayed, he is also incapable of following Marlow in the finer psychological ambiguities of Jim's act. Furthermore, the passage's style has been claimed by critics as a prime example of Conrad's impressionistic device of diverting meaning from the verbal to the visual register. The "truth" of the two men's fundamentally adversarial position emerges not from the conversation between them, but from such observations as: ". . . trying to throw infinite politeness into our attitudes, we faced each other like two china dogs on a mantlepiece" (*LJ*, 90). Yet what's even more striking about the passage's style is the linguistic opacity of its surface, which is woven from a bewildering array of translations to and from the officer's French. Marlow moves inconsistently from unclarified mistranslation ("for make up your mind as much as you like") to humorous literal translations ("I have rolled my hump [*roulé ma bosse*]") to elegant nonliteral renditions ("Abominable funk [*un trac épouvantable*]") to happy exact correspondences between English and French that make it impossible to decide which language provides the ultimate reference ("'Pardon,' he said punctiliously. . . . 'Allow me . . .'" [*LJ*, 89–91]). Sometimes Marlow provides the French equivalent, sometimes he doesn't; sometimes this bewildering translation is framed in quotation marks as directly reported speech, sometimes as indirectly reported, not to say mimicked, so that in this instance participant narration withdraws any standard by which to measure the utterances. That the French officer who is so clearly presented as an ideal should be rendered in a language that insistently and in every possible direction draws attention to his national particularity would seem to unsettle the very generalizability of his stance.

Stein, who anchors the Patusan portion of the text both in terms of narrative motivation (since it is he who sends for Jim to work at his trading concession in Patusan, at Marlow's request) and in terms of governing ideas (since he embodies the spirit of idealism and romantic adventure that contrasts sharply with the French lieutenant's unadorned rationalism), is marked by similar opacity in translation. Conrad critics have burned much midnight oil trying to untangle the logic and genealogy of his famous dictum:

Yes! Very funny this terrible thing is. A man that is born falls into a dream like a man who falls into the sea. If he tries to climb out into the air as inexperienced people endeavour to do, he drowns—*nicht wahr?* . . . No! I tell you! The way is to the destructive element submit yourself, and with the exertions of your hands and feet in the water make the deep, deep sea keep you up. So if you ask me—how to be? (*LJ*, 130)

"A man that is born" . . . as opposed to what? What does the sea represent? Is the destructive element the "ideal" or the "real"? Many ingenious solutions have been proposed, but not one of them fully acknowledges that what brings the passage to the verge of unintelligibility, not to say comedy, is primarily its peculiarly broken English. It is precisely the displacement of language from a generalizing medium to a national, territorial sign that calls into question the power of any single articulation to be representative. Again, that Stein, who is so obviously positioned to ground the meaning of Jim's actions in Patusan, should be rendered in language that diverts attention to his national particularity even as he articulates general principles presents us with an oscillation between foreground and background that is not arbitrary. It enacts the paradox of claiming cohesion for the dislocated imperial endeavor. The displacement of value from symbol to sign in Marlow's narration disrupts any sharing in general principles precisely at the point of recognition. Marlow's rendition of figures who offer standards of unity produces first and foremost a bounded sense of cultural marking, an exposition of singularity. "All Europe went into the making of Kurtz," Marlow proclaims in *Heart of Darkness*. Kurtz's hypnotic eloquence, though never directly rendered in the text, clearly has the power to sway equally the Russian attendant, Belgian imperialists, and African natives. In *Lord Jim*, while all Europe clearly composes the "us" of imperial servants, what is in question is precisely how that "all" can be articulated as any kind of unity. In his pivotal encounters with the French officer and Stein, Marlow makes of their language a metonymic grounding in place, which runs counter to their discourse's generalizing intentions.

Oddly enough this process is reversed in Marlow's rendering of the speech of a half-caste Mr. Malaprop, the captain of the boat that is to take Jim toward Patusan. His English (seemingly "derived from a dictionary compiled by a lunatic" [*LJ*, 146]), manifestly absurd on its surface, points to more general truths, and even verges on the prophetic. Patusan, he tells Marlow, "is situated internally," as though preempting interpretations of Jim's adventure as a psychic journey.[39] He comments that Jim is "already 'in the similitude of a corpse" and specifies "like the body of one deported" (*LJ*, 147), with a few words foretelling Jim's death and linking it to his state as an outcast. The diversion here is insistently, if erratically, from sign to symbol, and endows the captain's utterances with an uncanny authority. Marlow reserves for him what is probably his only outburst of unalloyed, unironic nastiness: "that half-caste croaker . . . I could see that little wretch's face, the shape and colour of a ripe pumpkin" (*LJ*, 148). What is striking is that the distortion in the half-caste's language is ungrounded; it bears no marks of a particular place. He speaks in missed metaphors rather than in the metonymic variances of mistranslation. His speech is culled entirely from a dictionary, his usage conditioned by the pure and estranged presence of the book. One might argue that the speech of native speakers of English, particularly that of Marlow as the narrator of the story, stands out as the standard language and unifying principle in contrast to the varied instances of foreign-accented English. But the narrative is overwhelmingly composed of reported speech, so much so that Marlow's own voice is often difficult to isolate, and while the individual native-English-speaking characters' speech does not necessarily carry indications of regional origin, each is marked with individual idiosyncrasies. One thinks of Marlow's avuncular exclamations ("by Jove!") and of Jim's colloquial boyish stammering (". . . your room—jolly convenient—for a chap—badly hipped" (*LJ*, 108).

If the determining excess in *Heart of Darkness* has nearly unanimously been diagnosed as vague and superfluous speech, in *Lord Jim* the excess is located in structure; that is, in the text's rather abrupt division into the *Patna* and the Patusan sections. From Leavis to Jameson critics decry the novel's fall from virile modernism in the *Patna* portion of the text to reified romance in Patusan. Politically inflected readings almost invariably see the adventures in Patusan as an atavistic recuperation of all the certainties that had come under question in the course of Marlow's investigation of the *Patna*'s desertion. Yet the very excessiveness of the structural doubling, the way the narrative exceeds its own stylistic and thematic boundaries, partakes of the movement from symbol to sign. The names attached to each section—from *Patna* to Patusan—enact this passage. *Patna* (which convention dictates we distinguish from our discourse in italics or underlining like the title of fiction), the name of a city in India, is in *Lord Jim* the proper name of a ship, itself always already a symbol, the fabled "microcosm" we dutifully learn the first time we read *Billy Budd* in school. The *Patna* is a mobile site that defines the work of imperial servants and figures their dislocation from any necessarily determining national ground. Patusan, as the name of a place, is a sign that refers to a territory. Several critics have noted that the two names are virtual anagrams. It's striking that the syllable that prevents them from being an exact anagram, a mixed mirror image, is the "us" in Pat(us)an. The attempt to create an identity between the place and the imperial servants is thus quite literally foiled (baffled by doubling back—the doubling of the narrative) by the impossibility of constructing a stable reference for that community denoted in the text by "one of *us*." The relation between the names for the two incommensurate episodes that split the text thus enacts the failure or the collapse of correspondence, of mirroring identity, into the foil.

A crucial and surprising figure emerges in the Patusan episode as an agent of this effect. Marlow calls her "girl" and Jim calls her "Jewel"; as the damsel in distress and subsequently Jim's lover, she is central to the romance plot in Patusan. A half-caste whose mother and grandmother were native women who had been seduced and abandoned by white men, she might pass relatively unnoticed among the many colorful characters in this episode if her speech did not have such an unexpectedly notable effect on Marlow. She waylays him during his visit and passionately appeals to him for assurance that Jim will not abandon her at the call of his homeland. In her dialogue with Marlow, by sheer repetition, she deflects the value of his words. For example, Marlow affirms repeatedly, "nothing . . . there could be nothing in the unknown world . . . there was nothing . . . there was no face, no voice, no power that could tear Jim from her." In answer she sighs, "Nothing." A few sentences later Marlow again insists,

"No one wants him." "No one," she repeated in a tone of doubt. "No one," I affirmed, feeling myself swayed by some strange excitement.

Shortly after this Marlow addresses his audience:

"I felt I had done nothing. And what is it that I had wished to do? I am not sure now." (*LJ*, 193)

As the girl repeats Marlow's negative affirmations, his words seem to lose all persuasive signifying power so that, instead of marking the victory of Marlow's arguments, her final assent only seals their failure. Pushed to the limit, Marlow finally reveals to the girl the "world" would never take Jim back because "he is not good enough." She counters, "this is the very thing he said . . . You lie!" Marlow adds that she "cried out at him" the last two words in "the native dialect." At this point, we might expect Marlow to dismiss the girl's intransigence as a sign of her ignorance, or of the need for illusory assurances of fidelity the fair sex in Conrad seems always to require. But, surprisingly, he turns the lie back on himself. He falls silent after this exchange and one of the listeners prompts him,

"Well?" "Nothing," said Marlow. . . . He had told her—that's all. She did not be-lieve him—nothing more. . . . Both of us [Marlow and Jim] had said the very same thing. Did we both speak the truth—or one of us did—or neither? (*LJ*, 194)

The girl (unlike Kurtz's Intended) not only rejects the comfort and redemption Marlow's lie promises her, but by giving Marlow the lie in "the native dialect" she uses the territorializing capacity of language to turn her rejection into an act of contestation. Her discourse intervenes in a powerful and direct way into the text's territorialization of language. However, the effect in this case is not to leave signification open in a loose relativism as it was in "Karain." In fact the girl's most serious challenge to Marlow's attempt to ground the community of "us" in an abstract nation takes the form of a competing de-territorialization. In her appeal to Marlow, she counters his notion of the disembodied homeland with her own version of the imperial nation; a version that presents a competing meaning to Marlow's:

"What is it? What is it?" she put an extraordinary force of appeal into her suppli-cating tone. "He says he had been afraid. How can I believe this? You all remember something! You all go back to it. What is it? You tell me! What is this thing? Is it alive?—is it dead? I hate it. It is cruel. Has it got a face and a voice—this calamity? Will he see it—will he hear it? In his sleep perhaps when he cannot see me—and then arise and go. Ah! I shall never forgive him. My mother had forgiven—but I, never! Will it be a sign—a call?" (*LJ*, 191–192)

The sentiment that, in Marlow's elegiac peroration, had been a mea-sured tribute to the disembodied spirit of the homeland explodes in the girl's articulation into a series of questions that all aim at embodying or personifying this "spirit" as a direct rival to herself. Again, we might expect her impassioned words to go the usual route down female hysteria into irrelevance, but on the contrary they return in the form of repetition to create a marked difference in Marlow's last words on Jim in the novel's final paragraphs. I will juxtapose the two passages, with the girl's earlier speech marked in italics, to show the effect of the girl's words as a foil:

For it may well be that in the short moment of his last proud and unflinching glance, he had beheld the face of that opportunity which

has it got a face and a voice—this calamity?

like an Eastern Bride, had come veiled to his side. But we can see him, an obscure conqueror of fame, tearing himself out of the arms of a jealous love

in his sleep perhaps when he cannot see me

at the sign, at the call

Will it be a sign—a call?

of his exalted egoism. He goes away

—and then arise and go

from a living woman to celebrate his pitiless wedding with a shadowy ideal of conduct

What is this thing? Is it alive?—is it dead? I hate it. It is cruel.

Is he satisfied—quite, now, I wonder? We ought to know. He is one of us—

You all remember something! You all go back to it.

and have I not stood up once, like an evoked ghost, to answer for his eternal constancy?

What is it? You tell me!

Was I so very wrong after all? (*LJ*, 253)

   It seems to me that the girl's speech foils the closure of this summing up, this plot's *anagnorisis*, precisely by forcing via repetition a diversion from symbol to sign, to be exact, from the colonial metaphor of the Eastern Bride as heroic opportunity to the claims of a "living woman." Her effect can be described as a "strategic displacement of value through a process of the metonymy of presence" (Bhabha, 162). The metonymic quality of her presence within the diegesis calls into question the metaphoric currency; in this case chivalric colonial dedication to the ideals of the homeland, which it was the narrator's desire to transmit to his audience. Thus a relation of contiguity within the narrative space undoes the will of the symbol to cancel out the specificities of place and assimilate the colonial sign to the metaphorical ground of a universally adequate standard. The intrusion of the girl's speech in Marlow's final words indicates her passage from diegesis to extradiegesis, from story to discourse through the medium of participant narration. He does not render her words or her position independently as the omniscient narrator did Aissa's in *An Outcast of the Islands*. He is not speaking as an insider, but quite deliberately as one of the outsiders, one of the "us" to whom she is a "them."[40] For her words to shadow his summation for and about "us" alienates him from his own position: He is an outsider to his own outside. By foiling the metaphorical closure of Marlow's tale, the girl's language dissimilates him from the self-identity that his authority would seem to require in order to make his listeners/readers cohere. *Lord Jim* is still, of course, a novel about white imperialists, but the surprising, skeptical resonance of the half-caste woman's voice in the text's surface and in its narrative structure marks a subtle but distinct shift from the position of necessary superfluousness into which Marlow sealed the helmsman's mute appeal in *Heart of Darkness*. Geoffrey Galt Harpham eloquently argues that Conrad's overdetermined "Polish experience" made him singularly disposed to occupy the antithetical positions of dominating and dominated and that his multiple displacements made him "uneasy in any company," thus never fully one of "us" or one of "them."[41] Without denying the degree to which Conrad's exceptional life experience undoubtedly inflects his narratives, I want to argue that in the Marlow stories and novels the complex disarticulation of community emerges from within the specificity of the colonial situation.

Heart of Darkness is to such an extent imbricated in imperial coercion that it figures transmission as the repetition of the same. Oral storytelling also breaks down within the text of *Lord Jim*, but here transmission is not so much invaded as it is dispersed into silence. Marlow breaks off his spoken discourse with the report of his last glimpse of Jim—well before the latter's spectacular end:

Men drifted off the verandah in pairs or alone without loss of time, without offering a remark, as if the last image of that incomplete story, its incompleteness itself, and the very tone of the speaker, had made discussion vain and comment impossible. Each of them seemed to carry away his own impression, to carry it away with him like a secret. . . . (*LJ*, 204–205)

Instead of yielding negotiation or affirmations of solidarity, Marlow's story breaks up into the private reception of each listener. The narrative has not, thus, functioned as an *oeuvre* in which the community of imperial servants finds an immanent representation of itself, of itself as transcendent unity, transindividual voice. Each listener carries "his own impression" away "as a secret," something that is not public or social, but rather a mark of his singularity. The narrator's rhetoric, "the very tone of the speaker," has dissimilated him, divided him from his similars, or exposed him as similar to them but definitely not "the same." The story is what comes between the listeners, what separates them. Yet the effect is not coercive as in *Heart of Darkness* and is not figured as loss or nostalgia for communion as it is in "Youth."

Jim's story continues in writing to a singularly selected recipient, a member of the listeners who distinguished himself by clearly not being a reader of *Heart of Darkness*. This listener seems to have complained that Jim was not an adequate example of the white man's burden. Marlow writes:

You [the final recipient] prophesied for him the disaster of weariness and of disgust . . . with the self-appointed task. . . . You said also—I call to mind—that "giving up your life for them (*them* meaning all of mankind with skins brown, yellow or black in colour) was like selling your soul to a brute." You contended that "that kind of thing" was only endurable and enduring when based on a firm conviction in the truth of ideas racially our own, in whose name are established the order, the morality of an ethical progress. "We want its strength at our backs," you had said. "We want a belief in its necessity and its justice, to make a worthy and conscious sacrifice of our lives . . ." (*LJ*, 205–206)

The internal reader doesn't know that in *Heart of Darkness* Marlow had investigated just such an idea:

The conquest of the earth, which mostly means the taking it away from those who have a different complexion or slightly flatter noses than ourselves, is not a pretty thing when you look into it too much. What redeems it is the idea only. An idea at the back of it; not a sentimental pretence but an idea; and an unselfish belief in the idea—something you can set up, and bow down before, and offer sacrifice to . . . (*HD*, 7)

And we, Conradian critics, or faithful readers of *Blackwood's Magazine* from 1899 to 1901, cannot fail to hear the echo of Kurtz's brutal addendum to his eloquent civilizing report: "Exterminate the brutes!" as a foil to the reader's "selling your soul to a brute." If we had been resting comfortably on the idea that there was an exact correspondence between Conrad's "real" readers in *Blackwood's Magazine* and his internal audience, here we are once again exposed in our difference as we find the internal audience slipping in its relation to "us" from metaphor to foil. What is repeated on the extra-extra-diegetic level is a disjunction in the formation or projection of a community. And it might be, again, the shared experience of "our" separateness from the internal collectivity that paradoxically projects us onto a different horizon for what might constitute community.

In emphasizing community in Conrad's texts I am aligning myself with a range of critics who, in contrast with Jameson, find this to be a central and not merely diversionary narrative topos.[42] However, most of these critics seem to presume that this community rests on some notion of communion, in Watt's words an "intimacy of communication," which amounts to "a movement towards human solidarity" (Watt, 213–214). I would like to emphasize, however, the degree to which Conrad departs from such a consoling model of communion even as he invokes it. In the complex developments within and across Marlow's narrations, community as communion is clearly disrupted and finally foiled. But it may just be that in its place, in the spacing, the betweenness it exposes as it separates "us," there is an intimation of what Jean-Luc Nancy has in mind with community as an effect of *com-paraison*.

La communication consiste tout d'abord dans ce partage et dans cette comparution de la finitude: c'est à dire dans cette dislocation et dans cette interpellation qui se révèlent ainsi constitutives de l'être-en-commun—précisément en ce qu'il n'est pas un être commun.

[*Communication consists first of all in this sharing and this com-appearance of finitude: that is, in this dislocation and this interpellation which reveal themselves as constitutive of the being-in-common precisely to the degree that it is not a being held in common.*][43]

Empire's Loose Ends: Dissimilated Reading

> Conrad died fifty years ago. In those fifty years his work has pen-
> etrated to many corners of the world which he saw as dark. It is a
> subject for Conradian meditation; it tells us something about our
> new world.
> —V. S. Naipaul

> But why is this a matter of what to read and about where?
> —Edward Said

Dissimilation

After the announcement of the not-guilty verdict for the beating of
Rodney King on April 29, 1992, Los Angeles erupted in what, depending
on their racial and socioeconomic relation to the event, some called a riot,
others called a rebellion, and still others called a civil disturbance. This
rift in the social fabric was visible soon after the uprising in a notable
phenomenon in the editorial pages of the *Los Angeles Times*: a surprising
number of the letters to the editor included an identification of the writer's
race.[1] The rebellion disturbed the unity of civic identification: the concerned citizens were suddenly made aware of their racial difference, almost
always present to the minority, almost always absent to the white "majority" and expressed this difference as, at least with respect to this particular
event, insurmountable. Where the editorial page normally functions as a
medium that assimilates individuals to a common civic identity, here it set
them apart. By writing the letters they entered the civic space, but also expressed their sense of being in a relation of difference to it. Racial difference
here is a difference that inhibits the impartial sharing in the event. For Los
Angeles at this particular moment it was a difference that dissimilated.

The previous chapter outlined the dissimilation operated by Conrad's texts on his internal listeners and readers. Marlow in *Lord Jim*, I argue, could not tell a story around which imperial servants might cohere as a group. I would now like to extend the notion of dissimilation first as a problem for postimperial readings of Conrad, and, coextensively, as a problem for imagining a cultural community in the aftermath of imperial domination. The readerly and interpretive "we" that is problematic within Conrad's texts becomes a site of cultural marking in readings of the text itself when third world writers add their voices to canonical interpretations of Conrad. Chinua Achebe begins the process with a bang when he exposes the racism in *Heart of Darkness*.

"Conrad was a bloody racist," concludes Achebe in an essay entitled "An Image of Africa," originally delivered at the University of Massachusetts in 1975 and later disseminated widely in various publications.[2] But for the minor outburst of the word "bloody" the essay presents a highly reasoned and systematic argument for its proposition. Achebe's argument marks a turning point in Conrad criticism; few interpretations of *Heart of Darkness* written after its appearance have failed to take account of it. This has played a major role in shifting the grounds of criticism from canonical considerations—concerned with placing Conrad in the "Great Tradition" or evaluating the ethical import of his texts—to the intersection of aesthetics and politics. Beginning with his title, "An Image of Africa," what Achebe refuses are the grounds of *Heart of Darkness'* metaphoricity. The vague and ambiguously evocative metaphorical "Heart" of Conrad's title becomes an "Image," the fuzzy and metaphysical "Darkness" becomes the place "Africa." Achebe's argument keeps rigorously close to this reading of symbol back into sign. He evaluates the text's representation of Africa and Africans by the realistic criteria that critics normally reserve for Marlow's indictment of imperialism and finds this representation wanting. *Heart of Darkness'* Africa is shrouded in turgid vagueness, and "amounts to no more than a steady, ponderous, fake-ritualistic repetition of two sentences, one about silence and the other about frenzy" (Achebe, 3). Africa is the "antithesis of Europe and therefore civilization, a place where man's vaunted intelligence and refinement are finally mocked by triumphant bestiality" (Achebe, 4). Far more damaging than the occlusion of the landscape, however, is the representation of the people. When they are not collections of savage "limbs and rolling eyes" engaged in inscrutable rites, they are ridiculous pretenders. Africans are only vital "in their place" as energetic ornaments to a savage land. Above all Achebe points out "it is clearly not part of Conrad's purpose to confer language on the 'rudimentary souls' of Africa" (Achebe, 6). On the two occasions when Africans do speak, language damns them as caricatures: the "catch 'im . . . eat 'im" of the cannibals and the "Mistah Kurtz—he dead," as an ironic epitaph for Kurtz's degeneration. Achebe finds Conrad to be not the unveiler of truth about imperial Africa, but a "purveyor of comforting myths" (Achebe, 4).

Achebe accounts for the most obvious objections to his positions. The first is that Marlow is not Conrad. Achebe points out that if it had been Conrad's intent to draw a *"cordon sanitaire"* between himself and Marlow, "he neglects to hint however subtly or tentatively at an alternative frame of reference . . ." (Achebe, 7). Furthermore, however ironic and uncertain, Marlow is presented as "a witness of truth . . . holding those advanced and humane views appropriate to the English liberal tradition . . ." (ibid.). It is precisely this liberalism, Achebe argues, one that can show a sort of compassion even as it upholds racist myths, that "almost always managed to sidestep the ultimate question of equality between white people and black people." The most Conrad will allow, Achebe continues, is in Conrad's words a "distant kinship," or "the thought of their humanity like yours . . . Ugly."[3] To another possible objection—and this one is the most consistent in later responses to Achebe's view—that Conrad only reflected the biases of his time, Achebe responds with evidence external to *Heart of Darkness* that Conrad's views are clearly in excess of what was possible at the time. As to the related objection that Conrad does in fact represent the Congo as it was in 1890, Achebe points out that contemporary Europeans involved for instance in modernist art were able to appreciate the sculptures of the Fang people from this region, demonstrating that a broader vision of African culture was at least conceivable.

The most important objection Achebe anticipates, however, and one that turns on a point of interpretation, not facts, is that *Heart of Darkness* is not about Africa at all, but about Europe and imperialism. At its extreme this position sees Africa as "merely a setting for the disintegration of the mind of Mr. Kurtz" (Achebe, 9); that is, a backdrop for a critique of imperialism, or for the mind of Europe gone mad. Achebe's insistence on evaluating the image of Africa in the text might seem from this position a naïve reading that takes metaphor and symbolism literally. What's problematic, however, is the notion that the text could be a critique of imperialism in Africa and therefore, in a fundamental sense, documentary, and have nothing to do with Africa. It is an imperial contradiction that may be bearable for critics writing from and perhaps for the metropolis but not for Achebe who very specifically writes *from* Africa. This is not to say he writes for all Africans—Ngugi wa Thiongo, another notable African writer, does not share Achebe's views[4]—but that he locates his reading in precisely the place *Heart of Darkness* would deploy as metaphor. He recognizes a position for himself in the text that is not one the text avows, and he refuses it. In this sense Achebe is the colonial reader who refuses and cannot but refuse. As such he is also a reader dissimilated from the loose imagined community of readers and interpreters who accept the text's base metaphor.

Achebe ends his essay with an ethical argument, not unlike Jean-Paul Sartre's in "Why Write?," which famously proclaims that great literature cannot be anti-Semitic. Achebe argues that since great literature cannot promote evil, and *Heart of Darkness* promotes racism, it should be removed from the canon and the general circulation this position authorizes. It is a highly provocative assertion and I don't wish to dwell on it, except to point out that it seems to me to move too rapidly from a forceful exposure of the difficulties of postimperial reading to the simple solution of a purged and renewed canon. What I would like to emphasize is not so much Achebe's prescription as his diagnosis. More important ultimately than the regulatory impulse of Achebe's general equation between the aesthetic and the political is the specific historical disposition it indexes in which Achebe's critique in fact occurs, and in which *Heart of Darkness* must share the cultural field of English literature with a substantial body of modern African fiction, among which Achebe's own inaugural text, *Things Fall Apart*, takes pride of place. This is an extraordinary, epochal change that, with its multifarious and ongoing ramifications, exceeds more restricted questions such as whether Conrad could have authored an African novel Achebe would approve of.[5] It's worth noting in this regard that in the final version of his essay (included in the most recent Norton critical edition of *Heart of Darkness*) Achebe tempers some of the more severe aspects of his original critique.

It is notable that it should have taken Achebe to announce the greatest imperial fiction's new clothes. He attributes this to the blinders of racism: "That this simple truth [that Conrad was a bloody racist] is glossed over in criticisms of his work is due to the fact that white racism against Africa is such a normal way of thinking that its manifestations go completely undetected" (Achebe, 9). This charge has drawn heated responses from white critics. Most of them, however, simply repeat and elaborate the objections Achebe already accounted for, often duplicating the very racist positions he is at great pains to expose. Many point out disingenuously, for instance, that the Africans in *Heart of Darkness* are much more "vital" and "energetic" than the corrupt and hollow imperialist and that the text therefore presents a positive image of Africans.[6] Cedric Watts is perhaps alone among them to take on directly Achebe's most serious challenge, which is aimed at the objectivity of the Western critical stance itself.

After an introductory paragraph, Watts launches into his response to Achebe in "'A Bloody Racist': About Achebe's View of Conrad" with the stark assertion: "Achebe is black and I am white; he argues that whites have long overpraised *Heart of Darkness* precisely because it reflects their racial prejudice. . . . There seems to be an insinuation, as Achebe proceeds, that whites are disqualified on racial grounds from judging the text. However, I have taken heart from my acquaintance Lewis Nkosi, the black playwright and critic."[7] The first sentence registers an elemental acknowledgment of racial difference; it marks Watts' sudden dissimilation from his interpretive position. This difference, however, is almost immediately assimilated to absolute racial exclusion—whites cannot judge the text. First Watts ascribes to Achebe a total—one might say imperialistic—representativity (he speaks for all blacks), which Achebe nowhere arrogates to himself, and then divides and conquers it by producing a black writer with a different opinion. But the move is defensive since it issues from a sense of threatened authority. The essay's thrust will be to reassert that authority, the authority to discourse on literature and imperialism from a "neutral" or "objective" point of view, unmarked by race or location.

The main point of Watts' critique is to neutralize racial difference as a criterion, to suture the dissimilation of the initial assertion "Achebe is black and I am white." The substance of the argument is that Achebe on the one hand fails to make proper distinctions between degrees of racism, for instance between King Leopold and Conrad as racists, and on the other fails to attend to the similarities between the whites and blacks represented in the text, which, he argues, at once humanize the Africans and barbarize the Europeans. But this kind of comparative differentiation is precisely what Achebe refuses in his attack on liberalism: his point is that there is no such thing as being a little racist. This attack on liberalism is clearly what irks Watts most: "To sneer at liberalism is to sneer at democratic principles and to support racialism" (Watts, 202). What the text wants, Watts insists, is more liberalism, not less. Following this is a spirited defense of Conrad's anti-imperialism against Marxist critics who claim the balance of pro-imperialism cancels the anti-imperialism and poststructuralists who detect other sorts of undecidability. For the purpose of countering Achebe's argument, the essay should by all counts end here, or perhaps with the comments against ethical approaches to literature, but instead it veers into a rather detailed comparison of Achebe's *Things Fall Apart* and Conrad's *Heart of Darkness*, which, it need hardly be said, turn out to have a great deal in common. If Watts' avowed purpose with this comparison is to assert precisely the brotherhood that Achebe claims Conrad's liberalism withholds, its chief function is to reestablish Watts' own critical authority. The stance of the comparatist here removes the critic from the particularizing fray of cultural antagonism to a safe distance.[8] From this neutral authority he can designate the similarity and complementarity that imply a common standard, a transcendent concern, for instance with "man's inhumanity to man" (Watts, 206). It is a synthesis that would aim to overcome the dissimilating racial interpellation of the earlier "Achebe is black and I am white."

But it is precisely the position from which such comparison emanates that Achebe's charge of racism refuses. When he rejects the comparative disposition of Africa and Europe that underlies all metaphysical interpretation of the text, he is not merely objecting to this particular comparison but to the neutral and distant stance from which it is proposed. None of the responses to Achebe can counter the racism he points to in particular passages, they can only attempt to excuse or defuse it. But what they seem unwilling to envisage is the particularizing incommensurability that the fact of this racism introduces into readings of the text. A neutral or transcendent critical position is simply not tenable. Every reader is implicated in the racial differentiation into which *Heart of Darkness* and imperialism itself place her. In taking account of how that racism conditions our reading we are brought to a consciousness of culturally (in this case racially) bounded interpretation.[9]

I want to emphasize that Achebe's reading of racism in *Heart of Darkness* cannot simply take its place as one of a boundless variety of readings made possible by the text's polysemia or indeterminacy, but that it introduces a determining difference that exposes cultural boundaries to the act of reading. Insofar as one can historicize reader response on the basis of the expectations various genres assume at various times, this dissimilation is one of the characteristics of the initial moment of postcolonial reading.[10] Third world responses, and by this I mean critical response after Achebe that emanate from institutions outside metropolitan centers of power, have in common a distinctly local positionality as well as a partial and an almost intimate mode of identification. Through all the difference of opinion they exhibit, these readings share a disregard for the kind of magisterial critical stance Watts is so anxious to regain; what is at stake instead is the challenge of reading Conrad as the first writer of "half-made societies" in the context of those societies making themselves.

Wilson Harris, the Guyanese novelist and critic, is sympathetic to Achebe's response to the "biases that continue to reinforce themselves in post-imperial western establishments"[11] and to his charge of racism, but takes issue with his wholesale dismissal of *Heart of Darkness*. In striking contrast to Watts, this difference of opinion is nothing to be overcome or overwhelmed. He attributes it to the difference between Africa and South America. In Africa, he claims, "by and large, tradition tends towards homogeneous imperatives," whereas in South America constructing a community requires the bringing into "play [of] a complex wholeness inhabited by other confessing parts that may have once masqueraded themselves as monolithic absolutes or monolithic codes of behavior in the old worlds from which they emigrated by choice or by force" (Harris, 87). The stakes in reading Conrad therefore have little to do with guaranteeing his pristine position in a canon or with consolidating the authority of the critical establishment legitimated by that canon, but rather with his usefulness in articulating an aesthetic within a "heterogeneous asymmetric context." In Harris' view, "the pressures of form that engaged Conrad's imagination transform biases founded in homogeneous premises" (Harris, 87). Conrad stands on the "threshold" of this capacity. By hollowing out the imperial order through the distortion of imagery and stylistic excess, the parody in *Heart of Darkness*, according to Harris, points toward transformations to come. In keeping with his positioning of Conrad on a frontier rather than the boundary on which Achebe locates him, Harris sees in the vague and misty language of the text an openness to something unfinished rather than a foreclosure: "Marlow's bewilderment at the heart of the original forest he uneasily penetrated reveals unfinished sense within him and without him, unfinished perceptions that hang upon veils within veils" (Harris, 91).

If Wilson Harris reads Conrad from a distinctly South American or more precisely Caribbean location, V. S. Naipaul, disenchanted Caribbean author and avatar of colonial bad faith, reads Conrad as the very site of his own coming to consciousness as a colonial subject. The particularity here develops in the movement from a general, aesthetic (that is, supra-cultural and political) identification to a deeply ambivalent and particularized positioning in a betweenness, both on the map and in the colonial historical continuum. Naipaul's essay, "Conrad's Darkness," is about the impossibility of a colonial reading grounded in purely literary judgment. The essay begins with the disavowal of detachment: "It has taken me a long time to come round to Conrad. And if I begin with an account of his difficulty, it is because I have to be true to my experience of him. I would find it hard to be detached about Conrad."[12] Naipaul begins with an account of his earlier misreading of Conrad, whose stories he found "refined away by explicitness . . . there was something unbalanced, even unfinished about Conrad" (Naipaul, 212). He shared the Leavisean complaint about Conrad's overwriting ("the words got in the way"). Experience, however, leads him to revise this reading. His early judgment, he says, had been "only literary"(Naipaul, 215). For Naipaul a great deal rests on the possibility of the purely literary; it is the common high cultural ground that allows the Trinidadian of Indian descent to claim seamless belonging to metropolitan culture. But it is exactly what the new conditions of postcolonial independence make impossible. As Sara Suleri deftly argues, this essay shows Naipaul in his unique position at the crossroads of the colonial and the postcolonial "caught between the excessive novelty of postcolonial history and the excessive anachronism of the canon."[13] His narratives, she notes, "are forced to record the astonishment of the initiate. They cannot believe that there are no sacred texts—not even the vestigial grace of a canon—in a postcolonial context" (Suleri, 28). The realization and the articulation of this particular position take the shape of a re-reading of Conrad that foregrounds historical and experiential specificity.

To be a colonial was to know a kind of security; it was to inhabit a fixed world . . . I had seen myself coming to England as to some purely literary region, where untrammeled by the accidents of history or background, I could make a romantic career for myself as a writer. But in the new world I felt that ground move below me. The new politics . . . the simplicity of beliefs and the hideous simplicity of actions, the corruption of causes, half-made societies that seemed doomed to remain half-made: these were the things that began to preoccupy me. They were not things from which I could detach myself. And I found that Conrad . . . had been everywhere before me. (Naipaul, 216)

What Naipaul comes to realize is that while he assumed the great novelists could rely on a unified society at their backs, he could not "detach" himself from the half-madeness of his. What had been imagined as an abstract "literary" region now becomes a problematic geopolitical place. What an earlier romanticism imagined as a kind of sublime detachment turns in the light of experience into an irrevocable attachment (ironically, to something half-made and incomplete). This inability to reach a disinterested, universalizable position is part of what Naipaul calls his "political panic." Rethinking Conrad in the light, or darkness, of his own journey of disappointment to the metropolis, Naipaul becomes a colonial reader who can neither fully refuse nor fully accept. Conrad is the medium for Naipaul's recognition of his dissimilation from transcendental common ground.

The initial dissimilation—the recognition of the absence of common ground—is figured as a radical and alienating separateness, but at the same time paradoxically comes to characterize a very particular kind of attachment. In order to examine the call of dissimilation, I would like now to develop it in terms of a form of recognition it mirrors but from which it fundamentally differs: Althusserian interpellation. As Althusser develops it, interpellation is the "ideological recognition" that "'transforms' individuals into subjects."[14] The category of the subject here signifies an ethical, autonomous, "distinguishable and (naturally) irreplaceable subject" (ISA, 162), a subject who, therefore, would be free to choose. What we choose or recognize in the constant interpellations of ideology is the obviousness of our position as subjects, which is to say we acknowledge ourselves as subjects *in* ideology, embedded in the apparatuses that guarantee the fixity and continuance of existing social and economic relations: "It [ideology, in this example, religious] interpellates them in such a way that the subject responds: 'Yes, it really is me!' . . . it obtains from them the recognition that they really do occupy the place it designates for them as theirs in the world, a fixed residence . . ." (ISA, 166). This interpellation and the recognition it entails have the effect of setting the subject into a "fixed residence" within a system of relations. This ground is precisely what is to be recognized as the obvious, the unquestionable basis. For Althusser, moreover, *"individuals are always already subjects"* (ISA, 164; original emphasis); the temporal before and after transformation of individual into subject is a hypothetical presupposition or a heuristic fiction posited in order to express the workings of ideology. The distinction between concrete separate individuals and autonomous subjects is therefore not, for Althusser, an operative distinction.

It seems to me that the readings I have been calling "dissimilated" answer to a certain interpellation. There is a distinct "that is me" involved in all third world responses to Conrad, whether to reject the hailing or justify it.[15] But, and this is most visibly the case with V. S. Naipaul, the recognition involved does not assimilate the individual to the identity of a subject—on the contrary, it dissimilates him. What he "recognizes" is precisely not an identification or similarity with a position, but rather a difference, and more specifically a differential effect. As such, dissimilation is an interpellation from, to keep Althusser's terminology, subject to individual. Naipaul begins as a subject confident in the fixity of the colonial world, and is interpellated into the political panic of partial vision, of belonging to an unfixed world constantly making and unmaking itself. He experiences his separateness, his elemental distinction from whole and functioning societies, but this is not structured as a recognition that reinforces an obviousness, or the free choice of an identity. On the contrary, it is a separateness that takes the form of the recognition of a cultural and historical partiality, a state of incompleteness. Dissimilation is not an experience of pure difference, but of boundedness—a recognition of cultural and historical limits, precisely because these limits are uncertain or ambiguous. It is also a hailing away from fixed positions and their recognized obviousness and into particularized positions whose definition, whose obviousness is precisely never dependable or even ascertainable. Dissimilation is an interpellation into dislocation. Althusser's concrete individual is interpellated as a subject at which point he appears to assent freely to his place, his identity within a given system. The colonial subject is interpellated as a concrete individual; in that moment he can only acknowledge the uncertainty of his belonging to anything fixed. What he is called into is not a position of total identity corresponding to his place in a system of relations, but rather to an identity whose experience is one of dissimilation: that is me, but not like me. Interpellated as an autonomous subject, he recognizes himself as an implicated individual. Dissimilation is not misrecognition. Althusser mentions misrecognition in passing as, it seems, the inversion of recognition. In acknowledging a misrecognition the subject presumably can still share in the ideological effect, but simply through difference; that is to say the interpellation would still engage him in the affirmation of subjecthood. What I have in mind with dissimilation is an interpellation that instead of assimilating the subject to a social whole dissimilates him from it and provokes an experience of difference, of being outside. This outside, however, is not a position outside or beyond all specific localities. Rather it is differential; that is, it marks the individual as different and as such leads him or her to a position of attachment rather than detachment.

An aesthetic object or literary text is not absolutely equivalent in its mode of address to the ideology sustaining the state. I think, however, that reading and certainly interpretation assume or perhaps project some kind of collectivity even if it is only the *sensus communis* invoked in Kant's judgment of beauty in which, even as the beholder knows his judgment to be subjective, he feels it must be universal. The collectivity implied may be more narrowly defined as national, for instance; nonetheless when a reader deploys the first person plural it carries with it more than just rhetorical flourish or persuasion; it articulates the desire to be in company, to assimilate and be assimilated to a larger community. By developing the idea of dissimilation to characterize a certain mode of postcolonial reading, I want only to suggest the possibility of a reading that, in foregrounding the experience of cultural particularity, exposes cultural boundaries.

The aspect of dissimilation that separates and alienates is fairly apprehensible. What is more difficult to grasp is how dissimilation could indicate a sharing and implicate individuals into a form of commonality. Yet this is precisely the effect Naipaul will describe in his relation to Conrad. After having misread Conrad from a purely literary standpoint, Naipaul concludes that "to understand Conrad, then, it was necessary to begin to match his experience" (Naipaul, 217). On its face the prescription would seem impossible, since the postcolonial moment makes Conrad's historical experience unmatchable by definition, and since his personal experience is unique. But, abstracted slightly, it is a remarkable proposal, and one reflected, I think, in the third world readings I have pointed to. Naipaul does not suggest the duplication or repetition of Conrad's experience, but rather its "matching." To begin to match an experience almost ironically invokes two apparently incompatible meanings: measurement and partiality. This would seem to be a judgment or a comparison that grounds itself on something that cannot be consolidated from similarity, namely experience. It is impossible to match an experience exactly; at best you can approximate, or perhaps, allowing for deviations and adjustment, match against. We can surmise that Naipaul also means something rather ambiguous by experience, something both personal and sharable. Remarkably enough, especially for Naipaul who so often sets himself up as the bitter arbiter of cultural quality, he concludes "Conrad's Darkness" by suggesting that "perhaps it doesn't matter what we say about Conrad; it is enough that he is discussed" (Naipaul, 227). The essay ends with a citation of the famous passage in *Heart of Darkness* in which Marlow asserts that his tale's meaning is not "inside like a kernel but outside, enveloping the tale which brought it out only as a glow brings out a haze" (quoted in Naipaul, 227). Dangling here in the guise of a conclusion, dislocated from their original context on the cruising yawl on the Thames in Conrad's novella, these words become instructions for postcolonial reading. Instead of deep correspondence of meaning or value, the matching of cultural experience plays ambivalently on the outside of the tale. And the matching of experience, not the drawing room tussle over the place of his writing among the greats, is one of the modes of reading that makes the continuation of the Conradian conversation meaningful. The moment of dissimilation is perhaps quickly overstepped, but not fully overcome in comparisons that assimilate the new texts and the new reading to the old standards so that we restore order and discipline through preestablished categories like influence, debt, genre, etc. There is, for instance, a critical literature devoted to, in the words of one title, "Ngugi's debt to Conrad,"[16] or Naipaul's, but it has seemed to me worth focusing on the critical responses partly to highlight the dissimilation that I think necessarily precedes the "comparative" assimilation to preexisting categories. That is to say, I wish to stop at the peculiar demand the postcolonial condition makes upon us to read *from* a cultural site, and therefore to apprehend a text as readers dislocated from transcendent common ground.

Dissimilation and *Com-paraison*

Naipaul's reading of Conrad resonates with Edward Said's call "to rejoin experience and culture" by reading "texts from the metropolitan center and from the peripheries contrapuntally, neither according the privilege of objectivity to our side nor the encumbrance of subjectivity to theirs."[17] The splitting of what he calls "secular experience" from culture and scholarship "testifies to the achievement of an imperial structure of feeling that thought and acted as if the world were there for the dividing, the taking and the holding" (Said, 49). But if this division between culture and experience was an effect of imperialism, their conjunction in a mode of contrapuntal reading is "to reaffirm the experience of imperialism as a matter of interdependent histories, overlapping domains" (Said, 50). This critical project is, thus, part of the evolving history of imperialism and the move from fact to experience involves both a departure from claims of objectivity and a contextualization in both the historical moment of a text's production and of criticism itself. The themes articulated in this essay would find their full-est elaboration in Said's *Culture and Imperialism*, a sequel to his *Oriental-ism* that consolidated the field of postcolonial studies in the early 1990s. The contrapuntal reading of the varied, often antagonistic experiences of imperialism he develops is clearly positioned dialectically and perhaps cor-rectively to the predominant mode of critique developed in *Orientalism*. On the one hand, Said contextualizes the moment of his own writing in what he considers to be the continuation of imperialism's "structure of feeling" in the politics and cultural dominion of the United States, but on the other hand he also adumbrates a postimperial perspective that, indeed, constitutes the condition of his own writing.[18] This is perhaps expressed most directly in the essay that he ends by calling for a "scholarship and pol-itics from a world viewpoint, past domination, toward community" (Said, 50). Said doesn't elaborate upon it, nonetheless this evocation of commu-nity is arresting. What kind of community "past domination" might post-colonial criticism assume, imply, or project? In another set of essays crucial to articulating the postcolonial during this time, Homi Bhabha also alludes to the complexity of this problem when he asserts, for instance, that "the postcolonial forces us to rethink the profound limitations of a consensual and collusive 'liberal sense of cultural community.' "[19] But beyond point-ing to the necessity of "[founding] a form of social individuation where communality is *not predicated on a transcendent becoming*,"[20] he does not elaborate. The challenge postcoloniality poses is to conceive of commu-nity and communication across cultures in such a way that they do not rest on the shared ground of common humanity, or an unproblematic notion of cultural diversity that, taken to its particularizing extreme, would pre-clude any sort of communication whatsoever. If imperialism finally makes reading on purely literary grounds impossible and if it also disturbs the purity of cultural difference and therefore of a reading predicated on cul-tural identification, what basis for cross-cultural interpretive community remains?

To pursue this question, I would like to take a detour through a meditation on community that arises not out of imperialism but out of a critique of the subject—Jean-Luc Nancy's *La communauté désoeuvrée*.[21]

Community, according to Nancy, is the "great absent" of metaphys-ics because this metaphysics centers on the subject as an absolute; that is, "of 'being' as absolute, perfectly detached, distinct and closed, without re-lation" [de l'être comme ab-solu, parfaitement détaché, distinct et clos, *sans rapport*] (Nancy, 17–18). Community on the model of the subject is a site of fusion and communion in which individuals transcend their mortal finitude. Separate subjects give over their separateness in exchange for a more lasting identification that repeats the subject but writ large; single human beings together partake of the human. Community organizes itself around a common *oeuvre*, work, or project, and effectuates itself as an *oeuvre*, which is what gives it its quality of immanence. Communism itself—and the volume's eponymous essay emerges out of a critique of the lingering humanism in Marxism that prevented it from reconceiving community—works on this model, with labor functioning as the *oeuvre* of the community, the medium through which individual subjects rejoin the human:

> . . . [Il] n'y a aucun type d'opposition communiste . . . qui n'ait été ou qui ne soit toujours profondément soumis á la visée de la communauté *humaine*, c'est-á-dire a une visée de la communauté des êtres produisant par essence leur propre essence comme leur oeuvre, et qui plus est produisant précisément cette essence *comme communauté*. Une immanence absolue de l'homme à l'homme—un humanisme—et de la communaté à la communauté—un communisme—soustend obstinément . . . tous les communismes d'opposition. . . .

> [*There is no type of communist opposition which has not been or is not always deeply committed to the idea of the human community, that is the idea of a community of beings producing through essence their own essence as their* oeuvre, *and what is more, producing this essence precisely as community. An absolute immanence of man to man—a humanism—and of the community to the community—a communism—obstinately subtends . . . all oppositional communisms. . . .*] (Nancy, 14; original emphasis)

Community on the model of immanence is always a matter of melding and belonging, a denial or sublimation of estrangement and exteriority, or of any unrecuperable experience of difference.

Nancy proposes a version of community that, rather than fusing subjects, would expose singularities, the latter understood as separate beings—"one body, one face, one voice, one death, one writing, not indivisible by singular" (Nancy, 23). The distinction between an individual as subject and an individual as singularity is important. It allows a conception of separateness that is not at the same time self-enclosed or autonomous, that is, indivisible. Nancy's "singularity" is equivalent to Althusser's concrete individual since Nancy positions the encounter of singularities as a potentiality that precedes and perhaps parallels the constitution of subjects in fusion or identification with a community. For Althusser, we recall, there is in actuality no such position as that of the concrete individual. One might say, though Nancy makes no explicit reference to Althusser, that *La communauté désoeuvrée* is an attempt to open a space in which to theorize this concrete individual. From the point of view of the notion of dissimilation I am trying to develop here, Althusser's concrete individual would mark dissimilation's effect of sheer alienation or differentiation while Nancy's "singularity" extends that dissimilation into the basis for community, articulating that which links separateness and commonality.

The exposure of singularity is an *ekstasis*, an experience that is as constitutive of the individual as it is dependent on an experience outside of herself, on the experience of herself as an outside. For Nancy, community is that which allows for the appearance of singularity as such: "Community signifies that there is no singular being without another singular being" (Nancy, 71). As the exposure of this singularity, an instance of spacing rather than fusion, community cannot be a sublation or transcendence. What these singular beings share or divide up [both of these senses obtain equally in the French "partage"] is not a common work that exceeds them, but the differential experience of the other as finite being:

Mais ces êtres singuliers sont eux-mêmes constitués par le partage, ils sont distribués ou *plutôt espacés* par le partage qui les fait autres: autres l'un pour l'autre, et autres, infiniment autres pour le Sujet de leur fusion, qui s'abîme dans le partage. . . . Ces "lieux de communication" ne sont plus des lieux de fusion, bien qu'on y *passe* de l'un à l'autre; ils sont définis et exposés par leur dis-location.

[*But these singular beings are themselves constituted by the partaking; they are distributed or rather spaced by the partaking that makes them other: other one for the other and other, infinitely other with respect to the Subject of their fusion, which is ruined in their partaking. These sites of communication are no longer sites of fusion, though there is passage from one to the other; they are defined and exposed by their dislocation.*] (Nancy, 64–65)

The *partage* or dividing/partaking at the center of this community mutually differentiates singular beings rather than fusing them. In fact community is in essence a *resistance* to fusion: "without this resistance, we would never long be 'in common'; rapidly we would be 'realized' in a unique and total being" [sans cette resistance, nous ne serions jamais longtemps en commun, très vite nous serions "réalisés" dans un être unique et total] (Nancy, 54). Nancy's exposure of singularities very explicitly counters the specular, Hegelian notion of mutual recognition as the dialectical model of communal identity. The specular disposition involves, according to Nancy, a recognition of the self in the other and of the other in the self, which presupposes the subject. An individual knows only another individual "juxtaposed to him at once as identical to him and as a thing—as the identity of a thing" [juxtaposé à lui à la fois comme identique à lui et comme une chose—comme l'identité d'une chose] (Nancy, 81). Mutual recognition therefore is the affirmation of something already known, the perception of an enclosed, knowable thing that shares a base of sameness with the self. Singularities, on the contrary, are not the recognition of the same, in fact the singular properly knows or apprehends nothing, but rather "*experiences* her similar [*éprouve* son semblable]" (Nancy, 82; my emphasis).[22] On the one hand the partaking of singularities has neither a reified object of knowledge nor does it invoke the faculty of recognition, and on the other it necessarily also does not presuppose a priority in time.

If the moment of recognition between subjects is founded on a perception of identity and sameness, the exposure of singularity turns on a very particular notion of similitude contained in the French word "le semblable," the similar. The *semblable* does not hark to prior identity, to an original recognizable sameness; in the place of such an original identification there is the partaking of singularities in which similarity is constituted by the simultaneous experience of separateness: "the *semblable* resembles me insofar as I resemble her: we resemble [each other] together [Le semblable me ressemble en ce que moi-même je lui ressemble: nous nous ressemblons ensemble]" (Nancy, 83). What is crucial for a reconfiguration of comparison is that Nancy discards the notion of recognition to describe the apprehension of similarity. Where similarity is exposed rather than recognized it leads into alterity rather than assimilation. No longer the recognition of sameness nor the sublation of difference, similarity becomes differential, an effect of externalizing difference:

Le semblable n'est pas le pareil. Je ne *me* retrouve pas, ni ne *me* reconnais dans l'autre: j'y éprouve ou en n'éprouve l'altérité et l'altération qui 'en moi-même' met hors de moi ma singularité, et qui la finit infiniment. La communauté est le régime ontologique singulier dans lequel l'autre et le même sont le semblable: c'est-à-dire le partage de l'identité.

[*The "similar" is not the "same." I do not find myself, nor do I recognize* myself *in the other: I experience the alterity and alteration which "in myself" externalizes my singularity. The community is the singular ontological regime in which the other and the same are similar: that is to say, they are the sharing or dividing up of identity.*] (Nancy, 83–84)

Nancy calls the phenomenal process of the exposure of singularities "com-paraison." As with the term "similitude," so too comparison here undergoes a notable distortion if not a full transvaluation. Com-paraison signifies the simultaneous appearance of singularities, the prefix "com" meaning that even as it exposes what is most singular, this appearance is always presented to others and with others. Com-paraison is the singular and finite community's counterpart to the communion of total and unique notions of community. The process of comparison is no longer assimilation to a preexisting common ground since simultaneity replaces the priority of recognition; nor is comparison the constitution of such a common ground out of perceived similarities. Nancy initially derives the noun *com-paraison* from the verb *comparaître*, a legal term referring to the call to appear before a judge in the company of an advocate. Com-paraison arises as that without which, in a very elemental sense, no singularities would appear. The locus of Nancy's reconception is the rereading of "-par" in com*par*ison, an Indo-European root of somewhat uncertain origin that seems generally to convey the establishment of equivalence or equal worth as a way to measure and evaluate two things, a sense we associate with words like "parity." In Nancy's "com-paraison," the equalizing evaluative "par" leaves place to "paraître," meaning "to appear." Comparison thus becomes an exposure of the limit that separates rather than a judgment of value or an evaluation founded on equivalence. Nancy's term transposes the word comparison from the realm of judgment and value to the realm of the phenomenal.

In his use of the word "expose" where one might be more accustomed to "reveal" or "express," as well as in the very notion of *désoeuvrement*, whose English equivalent is "idleness" but which in French means literally the condition of having no *oeuvre* (work or task), Nancy is careful to emphasize that the community he envisages is not something individuals can make or produce, but rather something that individuals experience, something that happens to them, something given in the very disposition of things. "We do not produce community, we experience it (or, this experience makes us)" [On ne la (la communauté) produit pas, on en fait l'expérience (ou son expérience nous fait)] (Nancy, 78). Or again: "Community is given to us and is a given—or, we are given to and delivered according to the community: it is a gift to renew, to communicate, it is not a work to produce ... [La communauté nous est donnée—ou nous sommes donnés et abandonnés selon la communauté: c'est un don à renouveler, à communiquer, ce n'est pas une oeuvre à faire]" (Nancy, 88–89). This sense of experience as something

given, something that "approaches us" [qui nous arrive] and reveals what
there is between oneself and another chimes with Naipaul's reading Conrad
by "matching his experience." Nancy's re-vision of comparison would seem
also to fill a background against which matching is something that could
be brought upon or out of an experience. And this sense of experience as
the exposure of givenness would also help characterize a certain postcolonial encounter with the imperial moment as a binding and bounded past. I
realize Naipaul's little phrase is a very thin example upon which to rest the
weighty edifice of a theory of community, but it does help to crack open a
door on what kind of community is possible when total or given identification no longer operates, when people are bound by a single historical experience without having between them the common ground of consensus, or
indeed consent, or any other unobstructed channel of communication. I
want to suggest that, in the wake of imperialism, cultural difference can be
construed along the lines of Nancy's exposure of singularities. It is difficult
to move between an ontological level of abstraction and historical experience. The exposure of cultural difference (or even the exposure of culture
as something that is between people, a limit, not something they have and
hold) is in many respects an effect of imperialism. To describe this difference in Nancy's terms, that is, as something other than the dominance of
a single culture, is on the one hand to project forward into a future where
cultures might co-appear but also, I think, to point a condition always existing, but always obscured beneath imperialism's triumphalist claims.[23]

Dissimilation marks a breach in the wholeness and transcendence of
an imagined readerly community, an interpellation away from subject positions and into an unfixed particularity. It is the effect of a mode of reading
in which one does not fully recognize oneself in the text, or more particularly one does not find a comfortable, neutral, or sublimatable site from
which to read, and consequently from which to enunciate the critical "we."
To schematize, dissimilation is the experience of a cultural dislocation in
reading that results or can be understood in terms of an interpellation into
something other than an autonomous subject position. This position can
be illuminated through Nancy's elaboration of singularity, which in turn
gives onto a different version of community. Comparison reemerges as an
operative term on the basis of a perception of commonality that is not
based on a recognition of sameness or identity.

Central to the development of Nancy's argument is the notion of
finitude; that is, the individual's absolute determination by death. What is

most proper to an individual, Nancy argues, following Hegel, is his own death. That death, however, is also precisely what he can never be fully present to, for he can never say, "I am dead;" only others can pronounce these final words. Death as the determining end of a single life cannot be contained in a metaphysics of the subject since the *finis* of a singular being can only appear to others and through others: "Dividing/sharing addresses itself to this: what the community reveals when it presents to me my birth and my death is my existence outside of myself" [Le partage repond à ceci; ce que la communauté me révèle, en me présentant ma naissance et ma mort, c'est mon existence hors de moi.] (Nancy, 68). Finitude, therefore, can only co-appear.

The experience of culture as difference in the aftermath of imperial relations can be construed along the lines of the sort of ontological finitude Nancy assigns to death. To affect a translation from Nancy's community to cultural difference one might begin by substituting, or perhaps overlaying palimpsestically, culture for death. Culture then dramatically stands out as an experience of limits:

. . . je reconnais qu'il n'y a dans la mort [culture] d'autrui rien de reconnaissable. Et c'est ainsi que peut s'inscrire le partage—et la finitude . . . La similitude du semblable est faite de la rencontre des "êtres pour la fin" que cette fin [culture], *leur* fin [culture], chaque fois "mienne" (ou "tienne"), *assimile et sépare d'une même limite*, à laquelle ou sur laquelle ils com-paraissent.

[*I recognize that there is nothing recognizable in the death (culture) of another. And because of this, sharing or partaking—and finitude—can inscribe themselves. . . . The similitude of the* semblable *is formed by the encounter of "beings for the end" that this end (culture), their end (culture), each time mine (or thine), assimilates and separates with the same limit, at which or on which they com-pare.*] (Nancy, 83)

The first sentence here seems crucial since it offers a third path to the usual either/or of culture difference: either all cultures are variations of one identical human experience or all cultures are absolutely discrete and hence exist in mutual incomprehension and total relativism. The recognition that there is nothing recognizable in another culture reveals the limit between. Another culture is neither apprehended in a comparison in which it figures as a negativity (the *non-moi* of the dialectic through which I return to myself) nor something with which I can have no relation, but rather is the exposure of this relation itself. Homi Bhabha develops a similar idea when he distinguishes between cultural diversity and cultural difference.

Cultural diversity is "the recognition of pre-given cultural 'contents' and customs, held in a time-frame of relativism" and rests on "the separation of totalized cultures that live unsullied by the intertextuality of their historical locations." Not only cultural difference, but "the problem of cultural interaction," Bhabha points out, "emerges only at the significatory boundaries of cultures" (Bhabha, 34). The cultural becomes a problem or, to use Nancy's term, is exposed at the limits of culture. If culture is a limit that only appears when two entities come into contact, and a limit therefore that does not enclose cultures on the model of subjects but reciprocally marks them off as singular, then comparison as the appearing-in-common of that limit is conceivable as an act of enunciation from that limit, not from a magisterial and transcendent position beyond it. The position of such a comparatist is not separable from cultural limits and limitations.

Relation

> Penser la pensée revient le plus souvent à se retirer dans un lieu sans dimension où l'idée seule de la pensée s'obstine. Mais la pensée s'espace réellement au monde. Elle informe l'imaginaire des peuples, leur poétiques diversifiées, qu'à son tour elle transforme, c'est-à-dire, dans lesquels se réalise son risque.

> [Thinking thought most often comes down to withdrawing oneself to a place without dimensions where the idea of thought alone persists. But thought takes a real place in the world. It informs the imaginary of peoples, their diversified poetics, which in turn it transforms, that is to say, in which it realizes its risk.]
> —Édouard Glissant, *Poétique de la Relation*

> Peut-être éprouvons nous partout le même besoin d'expansion non conquérante?

> [Are we perhaps everywhere experiencing the same need for a non-conquering expansion?]
> —Édouard Glissant, *Le discours antillais*

Jean-Luc Nancy asserts that neither communism nor decolonization yielded a new thought of community; that is, a thought of community that is not based on sublation and melding of separate subjects into an *oeuvre*, or an identitarian project. Having argued that his notion of *com-paraison* has many affinities with the dissimilation that characterizes postimperial reading, I now want to extend this argument by examining the idea of Relation developed by Martinican writer Édouard Glissant, which posits that something like Nancy's inoperative community with its com-parative mode of relation is a necessary consequence of imperial domination and therefore the condition underlying the postcolonial world. Glissant's writings precede Nancy's, and the relation between them is one of affinity rather than influence. That affinity as well as the affinity between Glissant's thought and many of the dominant themes of postcolonial theory in the U.S. academy most probably derives in large part, as Celia Britton argues, from the fact that they share the general ethos of a multifarious critique of humanism in French thought of the postwar era.[24] Glissant begins articulating Relation in his theoretical writing at least as early as 1969 (*Intention Poétique*) and carries the notion through nearly thirty years in subsequent works, *Discours antillais* (1981), *Poétique de la Relation* (1990), *Vers une poétique du divers* (1994), *Traité du Tout-Monde* (1997) and *La cohée du Lamentin* (2005), to name only the major titles of his expository prose and not the poetry and novels where this idea finds another kind of articulation.[25] While I will want to argue that there is a shift of emphasis in the concept of Relation over the time marked by these texts, it doesn't yield to a simple progressive development, but proceeds in the creative, unpredictable repetition of "houles, ressacs" [wave, backwash] to use one of Glissant's own characterizations. Mobile and variegated, conveyed in a complex, sometimes impressionistic, sometimes aphoristic prose, the concept itself is not fixed to a stable truth, so any account of it is necessarily a reduction. With that in mind, one might as well start with a schematic grand narrative. Beginning with the conquest of the Americas, Western man was "du monde, l'irrésistible véhicule" [of the world the irresistible vehicle]. It is indeed only with his conquests that the world became present to itself as a single, empirical totality. His function then was "d'être le relayant du monde" [to be the one who relays the world as a whole], but he overreached and asserted his ambition to be "l'absolu du monde" [the absolute of the world]. Thus he thought he lived "'la vie du monde', la où il ne fit souvent que réduire le monde et en induire une globalité idéelle—qui n'était certes pas totalité du monde" ["the life of the world," when he often only reduced the world and induced from it an ideal globality—which was not the totality of the world] (*IP*, 27). Because it "relays" the world as a co-present totality, conquest is the initial instance of Relation. However, Relation at this stage is mainly a "plénitude negative" [negative plenitude] whose extensiveness is most clearly manifest in "les atermoiements, les erreurs, les dénis" [deferrals, errors, denials] (*IP*, 207). It doesn't begin to take its full dimensions until the rest of the world (especially during the period of decolonization but also before) contests Western hegemony and "prends le relais agissant" [actively relays], at which point it becomes possible to envisage a truly planetary civilization (*IP*, 28).

For Glissant, Relation does not begin with the com-parative encounter of subjects, but with the encounter of collectivities. The Diverse [*le Divers*] a term Glissant takes from Victor Segalen, and which I prefer to translate provisionally here as the "Differential," names the relation between "others" (not *l'Autre* but *autrui*), and the plural here is decisive for it indicates that Relation is always multiple—one might call it collectively comparative: "Comme le Même s'élève *dans* l'extase des individus, le Divers se repand *par* l'élan des communautés. Comme l'Autre est la tentation du Même, le Tout est l'exigence du Divers." [Just as the Same arises *in* the ecstasy of individuals, The Differential disseminates itself *through* the impetus of communities. As the Other is the temptation of the Same, so the Whole or the Totality is the exigency of the Differential] (*DA*, 190). One can debate Glissant's development of these terms in various ways,[26] but it is striking that he comes at a notion of a nonassimilatory and nonsublimating relation of cultural difference from a historical disposition between communities and the world rather than from a critique of the subject. Relation explicitly unfolds in com-parison or co-appearance with the whole of the world: "Le Divers à besoin de la présence des peuples, non plus comme objet à sublimer, mais comme projet à mettre en relation." [The Differential requires the presence of peoples, no longer as an object to sublimate, but as a project to set into relation] (*DA*, 190).

Glissant and Nancy overlap in important ways, particularly around the crucial node of what Nancy calls *le semblable*, the similar or the recognition that there is nothing recognizable in the other, which finds its analogue in Glissant's notion of "consensual opacities": "Dans le monde de la Relation, qui prend le relais du système unifiant de l'Être, consentir à l'opacité, c'est-à-dire, à la densité irréductible de l'autre, c'est accomplir véritablement, à travers le divers, l'humain. L'humain n'est peut être pas l' "image de l'homme" mais aujourd'hui la trame sans cesse recommencée de ces opacités consenties." [In the world of Relation, which relays the unifying system of Being, to consent to opacity, that is, to the irreducible density of the other, is truly to accomplish, by way of diversity, the human. The human is perhaps not the "image of man," but today the web always recommenced of these consensual opacities] (*DA*, 245). But there are also significant differences. Glissant allows us to appreciate first of all the degree to which Nancy's *com-paraison* depends on the I/thou structure of intersubjectivity even as it forswears the unicity and autonomy of the subject. More importantly, perhaps, Glissant's analysis brings out the degree to which Nancy conceives of community on the purely ontological register of a singularity radically detached from any determining relation to place. When Glissant, in a move that seems to drop out of his later writings, explicitly associates sublimating and universalizing generalization with the primacy of the individual's relation to private property over the individual's relation to a community, a whole dimension of communism and community occluded in Nancy's exclusive focus on work and the *oeuvre* inserts itself. Glissant links this identification with land as possession or property with the process of colonial depropriation: "L'universel généralisant est la prétention suffisante qui permet de sublimer la dignité de la personne a partir de la réalité de la propriété privée. C'est aussi l'arme la plus concluante dans le processus de dépersonnalisation d'un peuple démuni." [The generalizing universal is the sufficient pretension which permits the sublimation of the dignity of the person starting from the reality of private property. It is also the most conclusive weapon in the process of depersonalizing a dispossessed people] (*DA* 249). The conjunction of a collectivity and a place, a *lieu*, is crucial to Relation, for a "harsh will to remain in place" [volonté rêche de rester au lieu] is the first recourse against the generalizing universal. Though *Le discours antillais* strenuously argues for a reappropriation of the means of production and representation from the metropole, the identification it proposes is never simply nationalist, unless one could twist that word to the contours of a fundamentally relational identity. The indispensable *lieu* is at once more elemental and more extensive than the territorialization underlying the nation; it is not only the island itself but also a conjuncture of erased histories that link it to the Antillean archipelago and beyond it to the Americas. The *Antillanité*, which this work elaborates as a cultural and political alternative to what might be called *Francité* and *Africanité*, is, as Glissant calls it, a "multi-relation."

We have noted the ambiguous positionality of Nancy's *communauté désouevrée*; while he intends ultimately to provide a model or an ethos for a different kind of politics, he stays rigorously clear of any direct reference to the political or social world.[27] For Nancy, the *communauté désoeuvrée* is *à venir*, to come, both in the sense that it is not to be *made* and that it belongs to a potentiality that is in some sense of the future. Glissant, on the contrary, elaborates Relation in direct reference to the world of the time of his writing from the late 1960s to the late 1990s. But the exact nature of the reference—that is, of how his discourse relates to external conditions—is opaque and complex. To the extent that Relation describes a cultural world freed from the dominance of an imposed universality, it seems to be the fulfillment of emancipatory desires. How could one not welcome the "degeneralized universal" of Glissant's "Tout-monde" (world-as-a-totality) where the universal refers not to an idea or a quality but to the "realized quantity" of all existing particulars in relation (*PR*, 193)? The dimension of Relation that describes a com-parative relation that never measures value and an equivalence that is not unified articulates an emancipatory comparison. And yet, contrary to the exultation conveyed by the tone of such invocations of Relation, Glissant insists again and again that "Relation n'est pas vertueuse ni 'morale' et qu'une poétique de la Relation ne suppose pas immédiatement et de manière harmonieuse la fin des dominations" [that Relation is not virtuous or "moral" and that a poetics of relation does not presuppose the immediate and harmonious end of dominations] (*PD*, 78). The difficulty is that Relation expresses at one and the same time the realization of a cultural logic of decolonization and also the depropriating world of late capitalism in which that logic is apprehendable and describable. Economic globalization is the *Tout-monde*'s negative manifestation, doubling its diversity with a decentered standardization that perpetuates colonialism's domination in modes that resist direct anticolonial opposition. The double-articulation of Relation strains against the desires of a postcolonial discourse to progress smoothly "beyond domination, towards community." It is a tension that inhabits Glissant's text in a very peculiar way, especially when it takes the shape of a rupture between a rich and seductive articulation of Relation's multifariousness in the text and the brief and brusque reference to economic globalization in the footnotes as we will have occasion to examine at the end of this chapter. The referentiality of Glissant's theoretical writings presents a challenge of interpretation. While these texts contain concrete examples from literature or from contemporary life, they consistently steer clear of a discourse of historicization, that is, of pinning reflection causally to a particular account of history or a particular autobiographical trajectory through time.[28] For this reason, one must seek such insights in texts that record a dialogic exchange in the form of questions and answers, such as *La poétique du divers*, where he spells out a change in historical conditions from decolonization to postcolonial globality, one that clearly marks a distinct postcolonial disenchantment:

Je pense que dans le contexte de la mondialisation les manières de résister vont changer. Et on sera obligé de les changer parce que toutes les manières de résister que nous avons connues depuis cinquante ans—et Dieu sait si elles étaient héroïques, et Dieu sait si elles étaient sensationnelles—ont versé dans l'innommable, que ces soit en Algérie, en Afrique noire, en Asie ou ailleurs. [. . .] Mais elle a versé dans le même trouble et le même acharnement et le même enfermement que le colonisateur proposait. Il faudra trouver d'autres manières de résister, sans faire de l'idéalisme. Je ne veux pas faire de l'idéalisme. Il y a des résistance concrètes qu'il faut mener. Dans le lieu où on est.

Tout le reste est Relation: ouverture et relativité.

[*I think there will always be attempts at domination, but that the manner of resisting them will change. And we will have to change them because all the forms of resistance we have known over the last fifty years—and God knows they were heroic, and God knows they were sensational—have given onto the unnamable, whether in Algeria, in black Africa, in Asia or elsewhere. [. . .] But it [anticolonial resistance] gave onto the same turmoil and the same determination and the same enclosure that the colonizer proposed. It will be necessary to find other modes of resistance, without invoking idealism. I do not want to "do" idealism. There are concrete resistances one must carry through. In the place where one is.*

All the rest is Relation: opening and relativity.] (PD, 78–79)

While Glissant himself resists the reassurances of biographical correspondences even as his texts, especially the novels, both invite and thwart historical reference, it is important to consider, nonetheless, how closely he both observed and engaged in France's colonial and postcolonial itinerary. I want here briefly to insist on this location, not to constrict Glissant's texts as though they had no relevance or relations beyond it, but because it seems to me that his pronouncements issue, as this passage makes clear, is from a specific colonial history, one which in the last decades is particularly marked by the events in Algeria and the impenetrable pall they cast over any lingering commitment to a narrative of national liberation. Born in 1928, by just three years Frantz Fanon's junior, and active alongside him in the anticolonial ferment and the intellectual life of the 1950s in Paris, Glissant returns to Martinique in the mid-1960s where he develops the analysis of Martinique's "successful colonization" we read in *Discours antillais*, which indeed bears the traces of a discourse of disalienation and national liberation reminiscent of Fanon's, even as it necessarily articulates them from a distinctly post-liberationist theoretical stance.[29] He leaves Martinique to take up a post as editor of the *Courier de l'Unesco* in the early 1980s and at the end of that decade moves to the United States to take up various university teaching posts (first at the Louisiana State University in Baton Rouge, currently at City University of New York). His very movements thus trace a trajectory from the colonial metropolitan locus of international movements of decolonization back to the *lieu*, the locality of origin, and then to a global institution, and finally to the United States—if not the unique center, then the primary beneficiary of a new global order. This itinerary alone and the prolific writings that mark its way open the question of how to read the relation between the aspirations of postcoloniality and the conditions of the unfurling present. In a recent study, Chris Bongie argues that we can understand this in terms of the complex rupture and overlap between the modern and the postmodern. He poses a crucial question: "how does a Fanonesque politics of national identity and anticolonial resistance—an ideological position to which Glissant once seemed wholeheartedly committed—fit in with the anti-ideological poetics of *inter*national creolization that he has so productively pursued over the entirety of his career as a writer and especially over the last decade?"[30] Bongie goes on to suggest, in a nuanced reading of Glissant's entire novelistic production, that he develops a metafictive mechanism "for coming to grips with the inadequacy of the ideologies to which he once subscribed but that he finds himself in the uncomfortable position of having survived." And consequently that Glissant articulates a "transition from the *engagement*" (in Sartre's sense of the word) of modernist ideologies to the "(dis)engagement of the postmodern" (Bongie, 139). This transition is, in Bongie's complex analysis, no simple one-way street; nonetheless, he does claim that Glissant's conception of history becomes increasingly a matter of textuality. I am not convinced that Glissant can be fully assimilated to the paradigm of modern/postmodern, even in the nuanced version Bongie develops. But what I find striking is that in his formulation, the movement from decolonizing nationalism to a kind of *inter*nationalism, as outlined in Glissant's development of Relation, should centrally involve (dis)engagement; that is, a disjunction between discourse and praxis, between poetics and politics.

But where exactly can we locate this disjuncture in Glissant's theoretical texts? One would be hard pressed to find it in their manifest content, for Glissant is at pains to underline that Relation is not necessarily "moral" or good, that it must be understood in the present, as at once an expression of decolonization *and* of continued domination. There is the suggestion of a teleological necessity in Glissant's arguments, whereby the initial violence of world conquest sows the seed of a non-essentialist relationality that eventually sprouts and unfolds into full-blown Relation. But the end of that development is by no means necessarily emancipatory, so the teleology inheres only in the historical form of the argument, not in its content, which argues for quite the opposite of a transcendence toward a single, accomplished truth. It seems to me that the sense of rupture between discourse and reference, poetics and material conditions in Glissant's texts is most readily locatable in the rhetoric, whose affect sometimes runs counter to its manifest, expository sense. The question then shifts from apprehending the idea of this rupture, what is thinkable about it, to querying its actual articulation, what is sayable about it within the discursive parameters of Relation's postcoloniality. A footnote in *Le discours antillais* prompts these reflections. It is appended to a couple of sentences commenting on the resurgence of orality: "Je ne serai pas loin de croire que l'écrit est la trace universalisante du Même, là ou l'oral serait le geste organisé du Divers. Il y a aujourd'hui comme une revanche de tant de sociétés orales qui, du fait même de leur oralité, c'est-à-dire de leur non-inscription dans le champ de la transendance, ont subi sans pouvoir se défendre l'assaut du Même" [I am not far from believing that writing is the universalizing trace of the Same, where the oral would be the organized gesture of the Differential. There is today a kind of revenge of oral societies which, by the very fact of their orality, that is of their non-inscription in the field of transcendence, suffered the assault of the Same without being able to defend themselves] (*DA*, 192). The footnote comes very close to locating brute oppressive conditions underlying this hopeful, desired revenge of oral societies, in a kind of banal unspeakability: "Cette revanche au droit ne peut occulter l'écart grandissant qui en fait discrimine pays riches et peuples pauvres. Toute théorie du passage (du Même au Divers, de l'écrit a l'oral) serait naïve, qui occulterait si peu que ce soit l'effrayant pouvoir d'aliénation de domination mise en œuvre par les pays riches et leur émanation ultimes: les multinationales. Il est benêt de le dire, il le serait plus encore de l'oublier."

[This requital (of oral societies) cannot obscure the increasing gap which in fact separates rich countries and impoverished peoples. Every theory of the passage (from the Same to the Differential, from the written to the oral) would be naïve if it obscures, in the slightest way at all, the terrifying powers of alienation and domination worked by the wealthy countries and their ultimate emanations: the multinationals. It is stupid to say it, it would be even more so to forget it] (*DA*, 192n). Short of imputing a staggering arrogance or hypocritical naïvete to Glissant's text itself, one has to interpret a footnote like this as a complex and paradoxical comment on the text's own status and function. In what sense might relegating to a footnote the "terrifying" disparity between rich and poor that accompanies the *Divers* not constitute precisely the occlusion this footnote forbids so adamantly? The footnote provides an answer in the last sentence, which avers the "stupidity" or "foolishness" of putting the fact into words. The word *benêt* (deriving, oddly enough from *béni*, "blessed") in its nominal form means "simpleton" and thus implies a very strong and permanent sense of stupidity. It seals the uncharacteristically blunt finality of Glissant's pronouncement and pushes the sense of the last sentence into paradox. For with the same word (*benêt*), Glissant impatiently dismisses the idiocy of having to articulate the disparity between rich and poor and urges the absolute necessity of remembering it, whereas a common sense idea of language as communication would suggest the opposite: saying it will keep you from forgetting it. The initial sense of the idiocy of speaking of the disparity is that it is too obvious to merit mention, but beneath it is the suggestion that putting this disparity into words neutralizes or banalizes it (makes it idiotic). Presumably, then, the function of this text is to put us in mind of the disparity, to put us into relation with it, and to keep us from forgetting it in some other way. But how? There is no ready answer except in the very gesture of disruption that the footnote operates on the flight of rhetoric in the text above. The combination of the affirmation of the centrality of material conditions and the stark refusal to discourse on them installs a disjunction between the eloquent and voluble text of postcoloniality and the insipid reality of the continued domination of various neocolonialisms and, in so doing, positions that text as a failed or refused sublimation.

I have traced an arc from dissimilation to comparison to Relation in the conviction that it is important to make discursive space for modes of relation that are not hegemonic; to do otherwise would be to arrest imperialism's sequels before the good parts begin. At the same time, one cannot evade the conjuncture between the emergence and construction of a postcolonial cultural archive and the neocolonial conditions of globalization in which we read it. One must resist the totalizing temptations of so total a term as globalization, just as one must be cautious about drawing too absolute a boundary between the various phases of decolonization and postcolonization that precede it. Nonetheless, the extensive discourse of postcoloniality that has now accumulated can occlude the crucial ambiguity of its location past one form of domination and *toward* community, to re-invoke Said. I think that the literary and theoretical texts of postcoloniality possess their own positivity and cannot be dismissed as misguided mystification, as some critics argue. What seems important, however, is to read the manifest disjunction between the postcoloniality they articulate and the unequal condition of globalization they occupy as in some sense constitutive, precisely in the way that it is for Glissant's idea of Relation. This does not mean that the aspiration toward communities beyond domination they both embody and often advocate is delusory or false in view of their time, but rather that it is cut into by that time and hence at once ironized and deferred. The dizzying and unpredictable unfolding of Relation "change plus vite que l'idée qu'on peut s'en faire" [changes faster than the idea one can form about it] (*DA*, 31), and language itself cannot possibly keep pace:

C'est un paradoxe, que tant de violences partout ferment sur la même élémentarité de langage, quand ce n'est pas sur l'extinction de la parole. Le Chaos n'aurait-il pas de langage qui vaille? Ou bien n'en produirait-il que d'une sorte, réductrice et néantisante? Son écho s'amenuiserait-il dans un sabir des sabirs, a niveau de hurlement?

[*It is a paradox that so many acts of violence everywhere close down upon the same elementarity of language, when it isn't upon the extinction of the word. Is there no viable language for Chaos? Or does it produce only one kind of language, reductive and annihilating? Does its echo dwindle into a pidgin of pidgins, level with the scream?*] (*PR*, 138)

Ruined Metaphor: Epic Similitude and the Pedagogy of Poetic Space in Derek Walcott's *Omeros*

> Once the New World black had tried to prove that he was as good as his master, when he should have proven not his equality but his difference. It was this distance that could command attention without pleading for respect. My generation had looked at life with black skins and blue eyes, but only our painful strenuous looking, the learning of looking, could find meaning in the life around us, only our own strenuous hearing, the hearing of our hearing, could make sense of the sounds we made. And without comparisons.
> —Derek Walcott, "What the Twilight Says: An Overture"

"Comparison" in the sentence fragment "and without comparisons" from this epigraph distinctly signifies an equivalence that proves equality. Walcott attributes it to an earlier generation of New World black anticolonial writing and, though he doesn't spell this out, clearly points to negritude and its negation of the colonial negation through the assertion of the equivalent value of African culture. Walcott forswears the practice of comparison that measures value through equivalence, indeed properly speaking the grammatical comparative itself ("to prove that he was *as good as* his master"), but he represents his own generation of postcolonial writers as inhabiting or embodying another kind of comparison altogether, one that is not so much asserted or practiced but given in the experience of an inescapable doubleness at a certain point in time. This difference is not articulated as one of essence or quality (an ethnological anteriority or originality) but rather as distance or distanciation. It doesn't attempt to tear white masks from black skin but attends as closely as possible to the divided condition of black skin/blue eyes as itself constituting alternative grounds for creativity and cultural distinction. The first generation of postcolonial poets in the West Indies, born and bred in the fading twilight of the British Empire (Walcott and Brathwaite both are born in 1930), faces the curious combination of overdetermined European forms transmitted through colonial education and the open horizons for a new postcolonial poetry. "The writers of my generation," writes Walcott, "were natural assimilators. We knew the literature of Empires, Greek, Roman, British, through their essential classics; and both the patois of the street and the language of the classroom hid the elation of discovery. If there was nothing, there was everything to be made."[1] The paradox of the postcolonial writer, in Walcott's view, is to be an assimilator without being assimilated, to practice an art of mimicry in order to thwart comparison. Mimicry, as Rei Terada has so eloquently shown, is for Walcott at once an explicitly elaborated theory of culture and a polyvalent and highly honed principle in his poetics.[2] It is a risky procedure, without a doubt, but it offers a crucial way for a postcolonial literature in that it creates a new, original expression in the very gesture of asserting or acting out an illegitimate filiation to the tradition of the former colonial metropole. Mimesis as mimicry creates a distance between imitation and comparison and in that interstitial space a cultural density becomes possible that can "command attention without pleading for respect."

Walcott's aesthetic of mimicry is specifically postcolonial insofar as, first, it sets itself as the heir both to the anticolonial generation and to the colonial mimicry preceding it. Colonial cultural domination is not immediate in the postcolonial world of Walcott's maturity, but contained in a colonial past and in his relation to that past as it informs the project of creating a new Caribbean poetry. In a sense, his aesthetic project revaluates colonial mimicry's corrosive internalized inferiorization into a postcolonial mimicry whose hybridity would provide a viable and legitimate cultural identity. But to claim a precise coincidence between Walcott's cultural practice and the postcolonial moment necessarily means that that precision is overdetermined and opaque, for perhaps the only general comment one could make about so amoebic a term as "postcolonial" is that it involves a multilayered belatedness, a constitutive noncoincidence between the formulation of a cultural project—a concerted critique of colonial discourse—and the material conditions of its present—precisely, that is, *not* the historical colonial condition itself. Postcolonialism deploys its counter-discourse against that colonial discourse that no longer dominates in a colonialist form. This is not to say that colonial discourse has no afterlife, or has definitively entered into obsolescence, or that a critique has no impact on continued domination in the present, but rather that the engagement in the present takes the form of a critique directed toward the past.[3] To the extent that, as Chris Bongie argues, the postcolonial in its relation to the colonial, like the postmodern in its relation to the modern, is "not (simply) a matter of either/or but (also) of both/and," the postcolonial occupies the paradoxical duality of existing in the wake of something, the end of colonialism, that is never quite finished.[4] Walcott has maintained a remarkably consistent position in his theoretical writings from the late 1960s to the present, one that reveals the paradox of noncoincidence or belatedness in a particularly acute way. His insistence on traditional European forms and on the autonomy of the aesthetic in the very midst of militant critiques of Eurocentrism in the late 1960s and 1970s made him appear as a pre-postcolonial, an assimilationist Ariel figure, an Afro-Saxon seeking salvation on Prospero's terms or from within Prospero's order, rather than in the refusal of an oppositional Caliban.[5] Two decades later, however, in the efflorescence of a discourse of hybridity and multiculturalism, this position, with its claim for the legitimacy of a mulatto aesthetic and a hybrid cultural order, will make him appear premonitory rather than anachronistic, no longer a dépassé Ariel but a post-Caliban. This recursiveness takes a further and startling turn with Walcott's 1992 *magnum opus*, the book-length poem *Omeros*, which appears to assert a monumentality that affirms the elegiac relation between art and history so strenuously rejected in his previous work. The poem self-consciously does so, however, in the explicit setting of a material condition, the new global economic and political order for the Caribbean of tourism. Extending the interstitial space between imitation and comparison, *Omeros* parlays a colonial paradox of assimilation into a saving incommensurability that might stave off tourism's instrumentalization of indifferent and unlimited differentiation.

If a long or epic poem "invites comparison" in the words of one critic, "with an august tradition that extends from Nikos Kazantzakis all the way back to Homer and the very roots of Western literature,"[6] then Derek Walcott's book-length poem *Omeros* entitled with the proper name of the progenitor of the genre in the Western tradition would seem to go one step further and *compel* comparison. What has Homer to do with the postcolonial Caribbean?

The comparison has elicited two often overlapping forms of commensuration from U.S. critics: aesthetic and historical. On an aesthetic register the critic implicitly judges the worth of the poem against its precursors and the question of inviting comparison gives onto the question of deserving it. That worth constitutes a ground of equivalence that in turn legitimates the continuity of a tradition. *Omeros* has earned the last slot in the Great Books of Western Civilization courses in U.S. universities as the postcolonial legitimation of Homer and, by extension, the canon of his cultural progeny. However, the figure of filiation so crucial to articulating legitimacy as a *natural* continuity in the tradition is peculiarly vexed here. The *New York Times* Book Review paired its review of *Omeros* with the review of a new translation of the *Iliad* under the banner headline "Bringing Him Back Alive." The graphic of Homer separating the two reviews resolutely turns from the translation to the postcolonial version as though hopeful of new life. But the phrase "bringing him back alive" wraps its hopes for resurrection in the more sinister connotation of kidnapping, as though the transaction between original and postcolonial version had involved abduction, confinement, and the threat of death before resolving into a happy filiation.

The review itself plainly demonstrates that one desire this postcolonial epic can fulfill for combatants in the noisy culture wars of the 1980s and early 1990s is the seamless blending of aesthetic and historical commensuration where the apparent confirmation of the tradition's continuity translates into the possibility of historical absolution. The reviewer, Mary Lefkowitz, a classicist who led the charge against Martin Bernal's *Black Athena*, receives *Omeros* quite explicitly into the context of postcolonial challenges to the supremacy of the Western tradition (another reviewer, one associated with contemporary poetry and as such perhaps a more immediately obvious choice for reviewing a major new work by a contemporary poet of Walcott's stature, would no doubt have set an entirely different context for the poem). It is crucial to the logic of this review that Walcott should be on the receiving end of tradition, and have no claim to its beginnings. Equivalence must pass through analogy and this analogy, in the reviewer's presentation, takes two forms: transcendent and historical. The mere invocation of Homer endows the postcolonial subject matter with universality. However "insubstantial" the references to Homer in *Omeros*, they "suggest that their [Walcott's characters'] experiences, particular as they are to specific places and present times, are also timeless and universal."[7] In its historical or, more precisely, temporal form the Homeric analogy indexes a process of *translatio imperii*, that movement of empire across time as an abstracted form rather than a historical development. The passage bears extensive citation:

. . . the brutal attacks of the slavers on Achille's African forebears, of Europeans on Native Americans, of French warships against British when the Windward Islands were first colonized; of the impersonal, devastating shelling of armies in World War II. But Mr. Walcott recalls these scenes of death and suffering with the objective sympathy of a Homer, who tells what happened to Trojans as well as Greeks. *No loss, individual or collective, is felt more keenly than any other's.* The Romans enslaved the Greeks; the Southerners built Greek Revival houses and gave the slaves they mistreated Roman names. Sons are lost, or never born, alike to black and white. (Lefkowitz, 402; my emphasis)

Beginning with a catalogue (drawn from the text of *Omeros*) of the particular cruelties of colonial history and WWII, Lefkowitz ends with the analogical passage of imperial forms, particularly as these bear on slavery, through history—Greece, Rome, Plantation colonies. This analogical temporality translates with extraordinary ease into the commensuration of historical loss, or history as loss: "No loss, individual or collective, is felt more keenly that any other's." The phrase "no loss," so prominent in this sentence, sums up the desires of a certain reading of *Omeros* in which the poem might balance the accounts of history and silence postcolonial grievances once and for all. What mediates between the inventory of particular suffering and the absolution of analogical commensuration is "Homer's objective sympathy"; that is to say, the quality of epic distance, here attributed to Derek Walcott. The result of this analogy of authorial distance and sympathy is the astonishing feat of making the relation between Trojan and Greek, with their evenly matched armies, their patron gods, their cities, identical to the relation between colonizer and colonized or master and slave that otherwise would be sharply distinguished with its unremitting asymmetry. Thus, the review lays bare the direct conversion of comparability to commensuration: if Greeks and Trojans are comparable to masters and slaves, then their struggles can be measured with the same historical standard. The transfer of names across the Homeric analogy creates a field of equivalence that in turn legitimates the commensurability of historical loss. That loss, now countable, becomes the undifferentiated common denominator that can make black and white "alike." As generous with culture as it is rapacious with property, a paternalist neocolonialism happily extends its immaterial patrimony to all, no matter how degraded their origin: "[*Omeros*] is a significant and timely reminder that the past is not the property of those who first created it; it always matters to all of us, no matter who we are or where we were born" (Lefkowitz, 403).

History and the Place Without People: Amnesia and Analogy

> In this becalmed zone the sea has a smooth sur-
> face, the palm tree stirs gently in the breeze, the
> waves lap against the pebbles, and raw materials
> are ceaselessly transported . . . all the while the
> native, bent double, more dead than alive, exists
> interminably in an unchanging dream. The set-
> tler makes history; his life is an epoch, an Odys-
> sey. He is the absolute beginning: "the land was
> created by us"; he is the unceasing cause . . .
> —Frantz Fanon, *The Wretched of the Earth*

It is precisely against this reassuring view of world history as a remainderless system of equivalence, a system in which a pretense of accountability maintains unspoken preeminence and with it the privilege of commensuration and judgment, that Walcott positively rails in all his major essays. The problem of history is a major preoccupation, if not a kind of obsession, for postcolonial Caribbean intellectuals,[8] but Walcott stands out, I think, for his rigorous extremity. He articulates his position with dramatic hyperbole, but carries it through quite consistently. "History is irrelevant in the Caribbean," he writes point blank in "The Caribbean: Culture of Mimicry."[9] In "The Muse of History," the essay in which he elaborates his argument most fully, he explains himself in words that are no less provocative: "the truly tough aesthetic of the New World neither explains nor forgives history. It refuses to recognize it as a creative or culpable force."[10] This essay is perhaps the strongest and most complex intervention in a polemic against history that Walcott had been pursuing in other forms, most prominently in his first major work, the long autobiographical poem "Another Life." For Walcott, history is always "History" with a capital "H." It is the History countable in the number of possessions won, in the extent of power and visible in monuments—in short, the imperial history transmitted by a colonial education ("I saw history through the sea-washed eyes / of our choleric, ginger-haired headmaster").[11] Walcott mocks this obsessively comparative history of ranking by ordinals in "Another Life":

> "Boy! Name the great harbours of the world!"
> "Sydney! Sir."
> "San Fransceesco!"
> "Naples, sah!"
> "And what about Castries?"
> "Sah, Castries ees a coaling station and
> der twenty-seventh best harba in der worl'!
> In eet the entire Breetesh Navy can be heeden!"
> —(AL, 172)

It is the history that makes St. Lucia count for having "der twenty-seventh best harba in der worl'!" as a schoolboy recites by rote in the wrong accent. This history, both triumphalist and exculpatory for the colonizer is, Walcott writes, for the colonial "an almost inexpressible banality" ("Muse," 22).

In a first moment, then, Walcott addresses a specific strain of imperial history directly instrumental in mediating domination through the colonial classroom. It is a comparative and commensurative history that attributes value to people and places on the basis of world-historical "achievement" and judges the inhabitants of tiny colonial backwaters like St. Lucia unworthy. Indeed, in the words of a notorious sentence passed upon the Caribbean's people by imperial historian James Anthony Froude in 1888, this history hardly registers them on the scale of being, "There are no people there in the true sense of the word, with a character and purpose of their own. . . ."[12] As the Trinidadian schoolmaster and intellectual J. J. Thomas was the first to point out in a scathing response published just a year later, Froude's racial prejudice is so pronounced that he doesn't bother investigating the social and intellectual life of educated blacks in the Caribbean and that therefore his account in *The English in the West Indies; or The Bow of Ulysses* cannot be taken seriously as a historical record. Froude's sentence in its context is, however, instructive in terms of showing the mechanisms of evaluation at work in imperial history.

Spaniards, English and French, Dutch and Danes scrambled for them, fought for them, occupied them more or less with their own people, but it was not to found new nations, but to get gold or get something which could be changed for gold. Only occasionally, and as it were by accident, they became the theatre of any grander game. . . . France and England fought among the Antilles, and their names are connected with many a gallant action; but they fought for the sovereignty of the seas, not for the rights and liberties of the French or English inhabitants of the islands. Instead of occupying them with free inhabitants, the European nations filled them with slave gangs. *They were valued only for the wealth* which they yielded, and society there has never assumed any particularly noble aspect. There has been splendour and luxurious living, and there have been crimes and horrors, and revolts and massacres. There has been romance, but it has been the romance of pirates and outlaws. The natural graces of human life do not show themselves under such conditions. There has been no saint in the West Indies since Las Casas, no hero unless philonegro enthusiasm can make one out of Toussaint. There are no people there in the true sense of the word, with a character and purpose of their own, unless to some extent in Cuba, and therefore when the wind has changed and *the wealth for which the islands were alone valued* is no longer to be made among them, and slavery is no longer possible and would not pay if it were, there is nothing to fall back upon. (Froude, 346–347; my emphasis)

Froude's blithe and racist dismissal partakes of the broad polemical objective of his book; namely, to call for increased British imperial intervention in the region that he sees as having gone to waste after emancipation. While indentured labor imported from India and China came to replace lost slave labor, British commentators in the second half of the nineteenth century often worried over the loss of productivity, lamenting the return of once cultivated plantation land back to a state of wilderness.[13] Froude's denunciatory passage is particularly useful, however, for the clarity with which it lays bare the colonial contradiction wherein the monomania of economic exploitation, unmitigated as it was in the Caribbean by the political and social pressures of settler colonial societies, precludes civilizational progress, that favorite colonial alibi. The two kinds of value here, economic value in the form of the extraction of profit on the one hand and the political and civilizational value contained in the project of nation-building on the other, are mutually exclusive.

Froude's indictment rings through Walcott's writings often in conjunction with an equally notorious postcolonial sentence on the Caribbean (occasionally indeed conflated with Froude, as in *The Antilles*[14]) and that is V. S. Naipaul's comment in *The Middle Passage* (1962): "History is built around achievement and creation; and nothing was created in the West Indies."[15] For Naipaul the exclusively economic imperative still dominates the region's destiny, only now (1960), in the postindependence period, it reverses the itinerary of the triangular trade and labor itself, in the form of emigrants, replaces colonial commodities as the islands' chief export. This theme sounds throughout the book's eponymous essay, "The Middle Passage," which narrates Naipaul's journey to the West Indies on the *Francisco Bobadilla*, a Spanish "immigrant ship" whose main business is transporting emigrants from the West Indies to England. He actually makes the infamous comment twice. The first time it issues from a stark and depressing comparison between the original middle passage and his own journey: "Sometimes for as much as three months at a time a slave ship would move from anchorage to anchorage on the West African coast picking up its cargo. The *Francisco Bobadilla* would be only five days. It would go from St. Kitts to Grenada to Trinidad to Barbados: one journey answering another: the climax and futility of the West Indian adventure. For nothing was created in the British West Indies, no civilization as in Spanish America, no great revolution as in Haiti or the American colonies. There were only plantations, prosperity, decline, neglect: the size of the islands called for nothing else" ("Passage," 27). For Naipaul, the notion of "creation," coupled as it is with its opposite, an endlessly repeated circuit of exploitation, clearly signifies the possibility of historical redemption: the narrative climax that condenses a meaning and a purpose out of time's passage. It's interesting to note that he restricts this first formulation to the *British* West Indies; he provides examples of this historical "creation" elsewhere in the Caribbean—Haiti, Cuba, the United States. When he repeats the sentence a few pages later it has lost this specification, even as it now encompasses not only the possibility of meaningful historical action to redeem the futility of exploitation, but also the difficulty of *representing* the unmitigated brutality of colonial Caribbean history:

How can the history of this West Indian futility be written? What tone shall the historian adopt? Shall he be as academic as Sir Alan Burns, protesting from time to time at some brutality and setting West Indian brutality in the context of European brutality? Shall he, like Salvador de Madariaga, weigh one set of brutalities against another and conclude that one has not been described in all its foulness and that this is unfair to Spain? Shall he, like the West Indian historians, who can only now begin to face their history, be icily detached and tell the story of the slave trade as if it were just another aspect of mercantilism? The history of the islands can never satisfactorily be told. Brutality is not the only difficulty. History is built around achievement and creation; and nothing was created in the West Indies. ("Passage," 28–29)

Naipaul's postcolonial observation confirms Froude's imperial indictment (indeed, Naipaul uses the quote from Froude as an epigraph for his book), but with a significantly altered perspective since the stress is on the brutality of exploitation as the exploited suffered it, rather than on the absence of noble purpose in the exploiters. To Naipaul's dismally dispassionate eye, the historical futility blithely noted in Froude becomes an insuperable seal of failure, since economic dependence guarantees the repetition of the old pattern despite political independence. But unleavened brutality and the difficulty of representing it are only part of the problem for Naipaul; the absence of achievement looms much larger as a source of profound postcolonial shame. Naipaul's positioning within the postcolonial moment is entirely bound up in the kind of colonial comparison Walcott aims to overstep, for the Western model of accomplishment becomes the single measure of value, one against which every third world locale Naipaul visits and describes in his copious *oeuvre* falls short. In a sense, as Strachan details, Naipaul projects his own postcolonial striving for recognition onto the postcolonized world, submitting it in its entirety to a "plantation discourse."[16] History becomes a kind of code word for this endlessly predictable comparative judgment.

This idea of history as the record of a single teleological narrative of progress or regress has been roundly challenged in the forty some years since Naipaul's *Middle Passage* was published. The elaboration of epistemic ruptures rather than continuities, of the history of institutions and mechanisms of exclusion, of discursive formations pioneered in, for instance, the work of Michel Foucault in the late 1960s and early 1970s has provided very different possibilities for how history might be approached or written besides the old model of records of achievement. Similarly, social and cultural history have moved the emphasis of historical accounts from a narrative of world-historical "accomplishment" to the analysis of complex social and cultural developments that are by no means limited to the experience and glory of world-historical conquerors. The work of the subaltern historians is particularly notable in this respect since they attempt to read the colonial archive for traces of the colonized's insurgency. Postcolonial writers have countered the erasures of (non)history by elaborating histories that establish possible continuities in and amongst the depredations of colonial history by radically redefining what counts as social fact and cultural or political accomplishment. Edward Kamau Brathwaite anticipated this direction with his groundbreaking historical work, *The Development of Creole Society in Jamaica 1770–1820*, which narrates the formation of a viable and autonomous Creole society that, even if it failed at the time to rise to full self-consciousness and accede to political independence, nonetheless adumbrates the possibility of a mixed national culture that differs significantly from the unitary Western model. His work as a cultural historian and a professor of history complements his work as a poet.[17] Martinican novelist Patrick Chamoiseau defines his project in *Texaco* as the search "beneath History, for the histories/stories of which no book speaks,"[18] a task that takes him into the wealth of narratives conserved in the oral tradition. His epic intention in this novel is quite explicitly to "satisfactorily tell" a history of Martinique; that is, to fashion a mode of verbal expression conjoining the oral and the written through which a continuous history of survival can be narrated. Histories (small "h") in the form of the narratives in Chamoiseau's novel, or the figures in Brathwaite's poetry, attempt to represent a form of collective life that links the past to the present and seeks out the viability and value of modes of life and modes of survival entirely invisible within the strictures of imperial history. For all this, however, the problem of how the history of victims is to be told and in what context it can be received has by no means been resolved, and the writing of history—whether within a factual or fictional frame—remains intimately bound up with the question of value. It is precisely the possibility of value that Walcott aims to wrest from history for art.

Walcott's writings from as early as the late 1950s reveal an explicitly formalist aesthetic, reserving a particular value for the aesthetic as such, separate from its contexts and its engagements. As Naipaul perhaps best exemplifies, if negatively, pure formalism is ultimately inaccessible, perhaps impossible for the colonial, even as an illusion, since he cannot escape the origin of his striving for purely aesthetic value in a particularly colonial condition. Instead of disavowing the paradox of colonial division, Walcott's work straddles it and embraces its ambivalence. If he works toward aesthetic perfection, he does so from a base of illegitimacy and transgression:

> I had entered the house of literature as a houseboy,
> filched as the slum child stole,
> as the young slave appropriated
> those heirlooms temptingly left
> with the Victorian homilies of *Noli tangere*.
> —(AL, II 219)

Walcott's manifold articulation and thematization of intrinsically con-flicting identifications make him, as many critics have observed, compelling as a poet of and for the Caribbean, all the more so perhaps for his failure ever to resolve them. Too often the neat polarization between Brathwaite as the authentically revolutionary Caliban and Walcott as the assimilationist Ariel has obscured the complexity of Walcott's positions. His relation to Africa, for instance, is a far cry from Brathwaite's to the extent that he makes no claim to diasporic solidarity, but it is, nonetheless, determining as he memorably expresses it in a poem from 1962:

> I who am poisoned with the blood of both,
> Where shall I turn, divided to the vein?
> I who have cursed
> The Drunken officer of British rule, how choose
> Between this Africa and the English tongue I love?[19]

If Walcott's formalism is caught in a generative ambivalence in his earlier work, it comes to be inflected and perhaps exaggerated into a polar-izing opposition between art and history in the set of essays written in the early 1970s, as well as in the long autobiographical poem *Another Life* writ-ten between 1965 and 1972. The intense sharpening of this stance on the relation between aesthetics and politics is to some extent a direct response to the rise of the black power movement, particular in the revolutionary form it briefly took in Trinidad in 1970, which deeply affected Walcott who lived and worked there at the time.[20] The unresolved divisions that characterize and sustain Walcott's writing suddenly seem to rigidify and it is as though he is compelled to do the impossible thing: take sides. One might say that he switches the terrain to his advantage and projects the polarity onto a full-blown war between art and history in his essays. As uncompromising as Walcott's trenchantly eloquent rhetoric in the essays is, there are myriad inconsistencies, conflicts, and indirections between these and the practice of his writing.[21] Tejumola Olaniyan shows, for instance, the degree to which Walcott's plays (*Pantomime* in particular) engage the substance of colonial history directly and in a nuanced and critical manner that would seem to belie his strident rejection of history. In a sustained analysis of Walcott's *oeuvre*, Paul Breslin traces out the paradoxical coexis-tence of a celebration of historylessness on the one hand and a clear project to retrieve West Indian history on the other.[22]

It is also important to distinguish between the various modes and

platforms of expression in Walcott's work because of his polyvalent relation—like many Caribbean writers—to the region. Until recently, all
of his plays premiered in Trinidad, in the venue of the Trinidad Theater
Workshop, which he founded in 1959, and thus address a specifically Caribbean audience, though not perhaps in any unproblematic way a national
one. His poetry on the other hand tends to focus quite particularly on his
home island of St. Lucia, even as it was (necessarily, given the econom-
ics of publication and distribution) published first in England and more
recently in the United States and thus addresses a much broader Anglophone audience. In the poetry, thus, Walcott mediates between a very small
(238 square miles), neglected postcolonial backwater and the "world" of the
former colonial metropolises. The stakes and practice of Walcott's postcoloniality differ markedly between these two genres in accordance with the
sharp divide between the two audiences they address. Walcott's biographical itinerary is distinctly American: from an exclusively Caribbean education (he studied at the University of the West Indies at Mona) to a career
in regional theater and finally, after some years of occasional visits to the
United States where he established strong relations with many well-known
poets (Joseph Brodsky, Seamus Heaney), to a life lived shuttling between
the American mainland and St. Lucia. This distinguishes him from many
writers of his generation, notably Kamau Brathwaite who developed his
diasporic perspective on the Caribbean in part through his education in
England and his tenure as a teacher in Ghana (a reversal of the triangular
trade several Caribbean intellectuals have undertaken). For Walcott, the
idea of a specifically American new world identification offers a viable third
way between the dream of returning to native lands lost or never won:
"I would no longer wish to visit Europe as if I could repossess it than I
wish to visit Africa for that purpose. What survives in the slave is nostalgia
for imperial modes, Europe or Africa" ("Muse," 26). Though it seeks to
escape the filiative logic of colonial cultural domination, "The Muse of
History" (first delivered as a lecture to a U.S. audience at Columbia University in 1971) is nonetheless very much a counter-discourse, only instead
of opposing the substance of historical negation with the affirmation of
occluded histories, this essay proposes a poetics that inverts and transvalues
the *form* of imperial history. My interest here is to follow out the analogical
logic of this transvaluation and trace out its particular foundering in the
text of *Omeros*.

For the Walcott of the essays, there is no alternative history to the history of ordinals and monuments; a victim's history can only be subsidiary to it and take a stance of recrimination and revenge. In his polemic, history is an unrelieved nightmare from which art must separate itself absolutely in order to awake, to use the words of Stephen Dedalus' famous plaint in Joyce's *Ulysses* that hang over the "The Muse of History" as an epigraph.[23] In rejecting history Walcott abjures not only a simple deterministic relation between culture and economic conditions, but the concept of continuity itself. In "Muse" he castigates militant anticolonial writing for its "shame and awe" of history, its "masochistic recollection"("Muse," 8), and its "oceanic nostalgia" for ruins. Walcott mixes a rhetoric of condescension ("manic," "inferior," "belligerent naïveté," etc.) with one of disease and injury ("malaria of nostalgia," "delirium of revenge," "morbidity," "wounded sensibility") for his opponents and contrasts this with a rhetoric of strength and virile health for those he champions ("tough," "exuberant," "elemental," "supple," "grandeur"). Behind the almost Nietzschean polarization of abject victim and resilient survivor is the charge that the oppositionality of this "victim's literature" is a "filial impulse" that holds fast to the oppression of the colonial cultural father over his colonized mongrel son. The search for pure origins is not, according to Walcott (in an argument that has become dominant in the wake of academic postcolonial studies), a means of breaking out of the imperial framework, but on the contrary merely an inversion of the constraining structure of a "nineteenth-century ideal," the "simplification of choosing to play Indian instead of cowboy"("Muse," 22). Filiation and its Oedipal overtones become for Walcott the master trope for the collusion of historical continuity and commensuration. It is in terms of paternity that he phrases his absolute rejection of continuity in an extraordinary passage toward the end of the essay:

I accept this archipelago of the Americas. I say to the ancestor who sold me and the ancestor who bought me I have no father, I want no such father, although I can understand you, black ghost, white ghost, when you both whisper "history," for if I attempt to forgive you both I am falling into your idea of history which justifies and explains and expiates, and it is not mine to forgive, my memory cannot summon any filial love, since your features are anonymous and erased and I have no wish and no power to pardon. ("Muse," 27)

With this figure of the half-breed, elaborated elsewhere in his poetry (most memorably perhaps with the figure of Shabine in "The Schooner

Flight," 1979), Walcott definitively rejects legitimation through the historical comparison of filiation. Far from seeking in a legitimate paternity the line of memory between the historical past and the present, he celebrates the anonymity of the bastard son and seizes amnesia as his rightful inheritance. It should be noted that Walcott here figures the illegitimacy of miscegenation uniquely in terms of a paternal line. Edward Baugh points out that in Walcott's own case, both grandfathers were white and well-to-do and both grandmothers black and poor, and notes that Walcott may be inspired in his figure of the grandfathers by Nicolás Guillén's "The Ballad of Two Grandfathers."[24] Walcott sidesteps the question of gender in the process of filial legitimation or delegitimation, though it figures in Shabine's genealogy[25] and may be said to haunt *Omeros* in the childless grandmotherly character of Ma Kilman and in the character of pregnant Helen herself, who carries a child of uncertain paternity. Though setting up the black ghost and white ghost as fathers allows Walcott to underline his equal rejection of both, it also endows the ancestors with a great deal more equivalence in power and symmetry in influence than the gendered figure might convey, even as it indexes once again the difficulty of accommodating the black woman in postcolonialism's residual manicheisms.

"Amnesia," Walcott proclaims, for the slave at least, is the "true history of the New World" ("Muse," 4). In "The Caribbean: Culture or Mimicry" he explains that "in the Caribbean history is irrelevant, not because it is not being created, or because it was sordid; but because it has never mattered. What has mattered is the loss of history, the amnesia of the races, what has become necessary is imagination, imagination as necessity, as invention" ("Mimicry," 53). The crucial move here is the transfer of necessity ("what matters") from a historical modality to an aesthetic or imaginative modality. If what matters about history is loss then the creation and achievement that possess the capacity to give meaning to a Caribbean people's presence in the world is displaced onto art and art can mediate that presence without invoking temporal commensuration or narratives of redemption. In rejecting history, Walcott lays a claim to a historical function for art, in the sense that art asserts the presence of a people to and in the world. One might call this a distinctly postcolonial formalism, particularly to the extent that, paradoxically, it is precisely art's autonomy, its separation from other spheres, that constitutes its political function.

Amnesia is precisely the inverse of monumental history: "an absence of ruins," which is also the *presence* of "a green nothing." This "Adamic" space of "wonder" opens up the "staggering elation in possibility" of new beginnings ("Muse," 17). The figure of an absence of ruins conveys a paradoxical wholeness (the full presence of nothing) in which amnesia compensates for fragmentation precisely by failing to recall fully or clearly (Walcott insists on the "*partial* recall of the race") either the original catastrophe or the inexorable work of time. The virtues of such an amnesia are perhaps best appreciated when viewed against a poetic disposition located at the very opposite end from St. Lucia on the spectrum of history as ruins, modern Greece. This is a landscape crowded with ruins whose very antique remoteness and fragmentary greatness seem to strike with futility all thought of monumental creation in the present. As George Seferis puts it in a marvelously inverted expression of modernist belatedness:

> Really, those statues are not
> the fragments. You yourself are the relic;
> they haunt you with a strange virginity
> at home, at the office, at receptions for the celebrated,
> in the unconfessed terror of sleep;
> they speak of things you wish didn't exist
> or would exist years after your death.[26]

This is also an anguish that bypasses filial *agons* because it addresses itself directly to an ancient and unreachable monumentality, a general patrimony rather than an immediate inheritance. For the modern Greek poet, ruins are not merely elegiac traces of history's passage or evocative fragments of transient human endeavors; they are insuperable obstacles, fragments that are more complete and uncorrupted ("a strange virginity") than anything in modernity's present. And one might well speculate that Seferis here articulates a material relation to ruins and ruination for an emergent Greek modernism that echoes but is also distinct from those figured in dominant European modernism (one thinks of the lines in T. S. Eliot's *The Wasteland*: "These fragments have I shored against my ruins"). Belatedness is absolute, but it is also fundamentally discontinuous. The modern Greek poet's contact with tradition is at once extraordinarily proximate through the obtrusive presence of ruins in his immediate landscape and extraor-dinarily remote because of the very long time that these very ruins so accurately measure. The distant patrimony is, however, no less castrating for its materialization as shattered marble. Seferis, in a poem to which Walcott responds and that stands as a kind of backdrop to the marmoreality of Omeros in *Omeros*, gives us a powerful account of trying to awake from the nightmare of a tradition that is indistinguishable from history:

> I woke with this marble head in my hands;
> it exhausts my elbows and I don't know where to put it down.
> It was falling into the dream as I was coming out of the dream
> so our life became one and it will be very difficult for it to
>   separate again.
>
> I look at the eyes: neither open nor closed
> I speak to the mouth which keeps trying to speak
> I hold the cheeks which have broken through the skin
> I haven't got any more strength
>
> My hands disappear and come toward me
>   mutilated.[27]

This terribly intimate and yet mutely remote relation to ruins stands as a contrast and corrective to the "yearning for ruins" and the envy of elegy Walcott sees as symptoms of a postcolonial desire for historical filiation. Armed with an inheritance of amnesia, Walcott exchanges the family resemblances of filial continuity for the unrooted affinities of analogy. New world comparability is not, according to Walcott, repetition, but a re-beginning where history is a "simultaneity" rather than a burdensome sequence in time: "So the death of a gaucho does not merely repeat, but is, the death of Caesar. Fact evaporates into myth. This is . . . an elation which sees everything as renewed" ("Muse," 3). A temporal order of commensuration here very clearly gives way to a spatial order of likeness mobilized through a circuit of analogies that cross space but defy time. Analogy is a form of resemblance that starts from the assumption that the objects under comparison have no relation other than the one the analogy's own logic develops. Aside from that logic, which is always contingent and therefore contestable, the elements are radically autonomous or singular. Walcott here transfers these qualities onto the field evacuated by history so that amnesia legitimates a broad array of cultural comparisons without thereby asserting intrinsic or substantive relations of priority or worth. Discontinuity makes likeness detachable. The similarities posited in amnesia's analogy do not reveal an underlying necessity, and so they function like accidental and fortuitous coincidences.

Walcott's rhetoric in "The Muse of History" is archly culturalist, perhaps even provocatively conservative, both in its language of greatness, race, tradition, inferior and superior talent and in some of its major references, particularly to the Matthew Arnold of *Culture and Anarchy* whose argument for culture's transcendent autonomy from politics is as much in evidence here as is his successor in matters of English cultural arbitration, T. S. Eliot, whose "Tradition and the Individual Talent" also echoes loudly through these pages.[28] Walcott, however, gives Eliot's notion a significantly new world inflection, for instead of assimilating new world poets to Eliot's universal "mind of Europe," he elaborates a separate canon based on the "shared sensibility of walking to a New World" (16). That sensibility's denial of history does not give onto a purely transcendent or immaterial realm, but rather to the place itself. Walcott announces a poetic project oriented toward the landscape in an arresting phrase from *Another Life*: "For no one had yet written of this landscape / that it was possible" (AL, 195). In the logic Walcott develops in the essays, the translation of historical loss into an elated amnesia discloses the horizon of an unappropriated space. From Walcott's particular postcolonial point of view, the fact Froude laments, that colonizers occupied the islands to "get something which could be changed for gold" and not to "found new nations," becomes an inspiring possibility, for the final collapse of empire leaves in its wake a pristine *uncolonized* space. This unpossessed space requires none of the violent and manichean strategies or the laborious reeducation of decolonization, for it remains free of colonialism's discursive traces: an absence of ruins. Walcott writes of the colonialist's "infection" of the landscape with the malaise of history in *The Antilles*:

A century looked at a landscape furious with vegetation in the wrong light and with the wrong eye. It is such pictures that are saddening rather than the tropics themselves. History can alter the eye and the moving hand to conform a view of itself; it can rename places for the nostalgia in an echo; it can temper the glare of tropical light to elegiac monotony in prose, the tone of judgment in Conrad, in the travel journals of Froude.

These travellers carried with them the infection of their own malaise, and their prose reduced even the landscape to melancholia and self-contempt. (*The Antilles*, unpaginated)

The colonizer's melancholy gaze prompted not by ruined fragments of lost greatness but by its opposite, a riotous vegetation, indexes a very particular kind of malaise, for what is unassimilable is not loss or lack but, on the contrary, surfeit. It is perhaps another version of the paradox of colonialism we have elaborated for Conrad's *Heart of Darkness* in chapter 2 under the name "necessary superfluousness," only here it expresses at once the malaise of absolute dominion in the absence of all resistance, as well as a projection of the colonized's abjection onto the entirety of imperial space. Walcott quotes a stanza from William Cowper's "The Solitude of Alexander Selkirk" that articulates this melancholy quite precisely:

> I am monarch of all I survey,
>   My right there is none to dispute;
> From the centre all round to the sea
>   I am lord of the fowl and the brute.
> Oh, solitude! where are the charms
>   That sages have seen in thy face?
> Better dwell in the midst of alarms,
>   Than reign in this horrible place . . .
> —(*The Antilles*)

It is this unassimilated space that Walcott reappropriates from the "wrong eye" of history's discourse with the homonymic transvaluation of "mourning" as a temporal affliction into "morning" as a landscape's possibility: "For every poet it is always morning in the world. History a forgotten, insomniac night; . . . because the fate of poetry is to fall in love with the world in spite of History" (*The Antilles*).

Forgettable Vacations and Metaphor in Ruins

> But in our tourist brochures the Caribbean is
> a blue pool into which the republic dangles
> the extended foot of Florida as inflated rubber
> islands bob and drinks with umbrellas float
> toward her on a raft. This is how the islands
> from the shame of necessity sell themselves;
> this is the seasonal erosion of their identity, that
> high-pitched repetition of the same images of
> service that cannot distinguish one island from
> the other, with a future of polluted marinas,

land deals negotiated by the ministers, and all
of this conducted to the music of Happy Hour
and the rictus of a smile.
—Derek Walcott, *The Antilles*

All-inclusive tax elusives
And truth is
They're sucking up we juices
Buying up every strip of beach
Every treasured spot they reach.

Like an alien
In we own land
I feel like a stranger
And I sensing danger
We can't sell out whole country
To please the foreign lobby
What's the point of progress
Is it really success
If we gain ten billion
But lose the land we live on?
—"Alien," written by Rohan Seon, performed
    by the Mighty Pep, winning calypso of the
    1994 Carnival King competition in St. Lucia

It is difficult to take up Derek Walcott's book-length poem *Omeros* without saying of it, as critics regularly do, that it is a monumental achievement. One can propose a catalogue of features that earn it this distinction: its virtuosic versification combining a kind of hexameter with a Dantesque *terza rima*; its complex narrative; its subtle and polyvalent reflexiveness; the sheer variety of its registers of diction and plot; the wealth and resonance of its imagery, etc. But in what relation does this monument stand to Walcott's postcolonial aesthetic of amnesia and to his practice of mimicry? The former would seem to resist, if not actively oppose, conventional notions of monumentality, posed as these are in a redemptive relation to history and the latter would seem to preclude the foundational formation and sacralization of the community, which is the epic's function. In *Another Life* (1965–1973), a long autobiographical poem that records the early phase of Walcott's career and stands in a dialogic relation to *Omeros* (1990), Walcott warns against the epic genre ("Provincialism loves the pseudo-epic") on the grounds of scale: the disproportion between the bombast of the genre and the smallness of provincial life is a recipe for mock epic. He even provides a demonstration through a witty catalogue of vignettes of local characters presented under the names of heroes from Greek mythology. How is it then that he attempts just such an epic twenty years later and avoids parody? One way to approach the question is to look in the text for the techniques Walcott develops to carve out a space for "an epic of the dispossessed," in Robert Hamner's words. *Omeros* is, for instance, highly reflexive for it stages the conditions of its own writing in two authorial figures and prominently features a metadiscourse on its own operations. If self-consciousness creates a distance from parody, other rhetorical strategies preempt it, such as the elaborate "rhetoric of disavowal" Gregson Davis outlines in which Walcott secures legitimation for the work's epic scope in the very gesture of disavowing any epic intention or pretension.[29] Another approach to *Omeros'* evasion of parody is to look at the text's context, its broader conditions of possibility. St. Lucia itself is no longer as provincial as it was in the twilight of empire; it has gone, along with so much of the region, from a backwater of colonial history to a tourist Mecca. The island that was once a forgettable speck on the fringe of empire has become an objectless destination and it is now the place itself—not its products or its people—that has become the commodity. This circumstance shifts the grounds of Walcott's aesthetic and his art of mimicry that averred itself "without comparison" now faces equivalences of a very different kind.

Tourism can resemble imperialism in many respects, particularly in the Caribbean where it wears uncannily similar faces, with relatively wealthy white visitors (though there is also an increase in black middle class heritage tourism[30]) served by black natives. But there are also important differences and these, as we will develop further, pose an extraordinary challenge to the very foundation of Walcott's aesthetics. History, for one thing, is irrelevant to tourism, not because it isn't manipulable or marketable but because, to echo Walcott's sentence, it isn't what matters. There is no *cultural* necessity involved in tourism's domination and economic exploitation, for these require neither the alibi of civilizational superiority and its arch and banal commensuration nor the ethical accounting of injury and guilt. Necessary continuities are alien to tourists, for their incursions are eminently transitory and their relation to the people who inhabit their destinations are, to use Dean MacCannell's words, "temporary and unequal."[31] Colonialism's historical relations subsist as vacant markers, often appearing accidental to the point of eluding even irony. There is, for instance, an all-inclusive (what the sociologists refer to as "plantation tourism," a resort in which all the tourist's needs are met on the premises so that s/he need never venture beyond its well secured boundaries, which locals, on their side, are forbidden to cross unless they are employed there) located between the two distinctive peaks named the Pitons in St. Lucia and built on the grounds of a former estate, Jalousie plantation, a name the resort apparently adopted without hesitation. Derek Walcott was a vocal opponent of the project, writing in the local paper that "[t]o sell any part of the Pitons is to sell the whole idea and body of the Pitons, to sell a metaphor, to make a fast buck off a shrine." You might as well, he adds, install "a casino in the Vatican" or "a take-away concession inside Stonehenge."[32] Despite the opposition, Jalousie Plantation Resort and Spa opened in 1992, the year of the quincentennial, which is also the year Walcott was awarded the Nobel Prize.

Unlike imperialism with its pomp and finery, its haughty monarchs, and popular jubilees, tourism is faceless and decentered. Its most visible subject, the one who bears its name and consumes its diversions, is precisely not the one who profits from it, who, in turn, is for all practical purposes unlocatable, since the majority of the tourist industry in the Caribbean (and elsewhere) is a multinational venture. Jalousie Plantation Resort and Spa, formerly a copra plantation owned by an English aristocrat, now belongs to a Swiss-based corporation, headed by an Iranian-born businessman, and managed by an Ohio-based subsidiary (Resorts 3). It is little wonder that a distinct nostalgia hangs about the remorseful imperialist inhabitant of St. Lucia in *Omeros*, Dennis Plunkett, an authorial figure within the poem who is, along with his wife, perhaps its most elaborately developed character and stands as the historian to Walcott/narrator's poet. To him at least the Walcott persona can direct a properly postcolonial outburst, "O Christ! I swore, I'm tired of their fucking guilt, and our fucking envy!" (*Omeros*, 269). This de-banalization of the imperialist historian is all the more noteworthy when we consider that Plunkett is another version of the schoolmaster who imperiously prompted the schoolchild's recitation in "Another Life." Plunkett offers the nexus for a rich array of colonial discourses and as the white resident alien in the poem he is as eminently given to representation in the ample and measured mood of valediction as the tourist, an alien in transit, seems to resist representation in Walcott's poetic lexicon. Tourists never appear as full characters or even complete human figures (they appear as body parts, as shrimp, as grilled or frozen meat, and once as corpses) and only speak once. Plunkett has the imperialist's long memory, exacerbated by an old head wound that leads him to hallucinate or relive the trauma of WWII and to catalogue obsessively the loss of imperial possessions. Tourists, on the other hand, travel light and manifest the occupational amnesia proper to leisure, for vacations are, as Walcott phrases it, eminently "forgettable."[33] The tourist precisely does not integrate leisure time into an individual or collective attempt to link past and present; s/he brings back clichés in the form of souvenirs and photographs that, in the words of a ubiquitous advertisement, "preserve the memories," that is to say, seal them off for display as transportable vestiges of the otherwise immaterial consumption of place. The imperial historian's ultimate condemnation, "there are no people there in the true sense of the word, with a character and purpose of their own" today would apply most readily not to locals but to the tourists who, for their part, have come to seek local "color" and count among themselves a good number of "people lovers." Crass, happily undifferentiated, blithely inauthentic, amnesic but always, ultimately, blameless, the tourist is a transient occupier who comes bearing gold and seeks only gratification. But then, the tourist is always already a stock figure, a type, a cheap shot, but a futile throw since tourism itself is a dispersed and invisible target. To indulge in deprecating the tourist is, as commentators point out, an intrinsic part of tourism.[34] This is not the strategy Walcott adopts when he takes on the thorny problem of the mode of address for/to tourists and tourism in *Omeros*.

In an extended and complex passage toward the middle of *Omeros*, Walcott/narrator confronts tourist development and in the process counterposes his art not to history but to poverty. Looking out onto "the cinder-blocks // of hotel development" as a transport takes him to his hotel, Walcott asks:

> . . . Didn't I want the poor
> to stay in the same light so that I could transfix
> them in amber, the afterglow of an empire,
>
> preferring a shed of palm-thatch with tilted sticks
> to that blue bus-stop? Didn't I prefer a road
> from which tracks climbed into the thickening syntax
>
> of colonial travellers, the measured prose I read
> as a schoolboy?
> —(*Omeros*, 227)

Faced with the exigencies of a new era, the postcolonial poet is suddenly haunted in a particularly acute and complicit way by the colonial past, in which he recognizes above all the power of its language in the formation of his poetry. That art, which promised to make a landscape possible, now must ask itself if it is not also a sublimation of poverty. Walcott's unstinting self-examination—["Why hallow that pretence / of preserving what they left, the hypocrisy / of loving them from hotels(?)"]—leads him to a staggering reversal of the opposition between Adamic Art and nostalgic History posed in the essays: "Art" Walcott writes in *Omeros*, "is History's nostalgia, it prefers a thatched // roof to a concrete factory" (*Omeros*, 228). The phrasing here is complex and revealing, for Art is not nostalgia *for* History, it is nostalgia *of* History. For Art to be History's nostalgia relegates the aesthetic not only to a derivative and compounded obsolescence (it gazes longingly backward from the point where History's backward look leaves off), but it also makes it static, a process of representation that "transfixes in amber," that preserves what the people have already left behind. It is an art inimical to change. Comparing his craft to that of skilled manual craftsmen whose labor is no longer needed in the era of cinderblocks, Walcott quite openly poses his virtuosic epic poem of the tourist era as a manifest anachronism.

Following this confessional moment, Walcott/narrator digresses on tourism in a rhetoric that expresses and indeed performs the collapse of clear opposites, the radical indifferentiation that tourism operates on colonial categories. In the passage in question, the third person plural subject "they" is to such an extent indeterminately conflated with the authorial "I" that the two perspectives enter into a resemblance verging on identity. We find the familiar purist's indictment of Caribbean culture's hybrid inauthenticity now displayed in souvenirs ". . . their dried calabashes of fake African masks for a fake Achilles / rattled with the seed that came from other men's minds" (*Omeros*, 228). This is followed by the equally familiar retort of the people's intrinsic beauty: "So let them think that. Who needed art in this place / where even the old women strode with stiff-backed spines and the fishermen had such adept thumbs, such grace // these people had, but what they envied most in them / was the calypso part, the Caribbean lilt (*Omeros*, 229)." Up to the hackneyed outsider's typing of "these people," the passage is vintage Walcott and could indeed belong to many of his characterizations in *Omeros* (of Ma Kilman and Achille, for instance) but this "poetic" rhetoric merges, over the silent distancing of a stanza break, right into the graceless platitude of the tourist's language ("the Calypso part"). By the end the passage's very obscurity makes it hard to distinguish tourist from expatriate poet from locals:

. . . the gold sea

flat as a credit-card, extending its line
to a beach that now looked just like everywhere else,
Greece or Hawaii. Now the goddamn souvenir

felt absurd, excessive. The painted gourds, the shells.
Their own faces brown as gourds. Mine felt as strange as
those at the counter feeling their bodies change.
—(*Omeros*, 229)

The interchangeability characteristic of tourist destinations, an equivalence that requires no other criterion of comparability than the money form, as extensive in the scope of its exchange as the sea itself, infects the next stanza with a contagious undifferentiation. To whom does the souvenir feel excessive, to the visiting poet who has earlier shopped at Helen's trinket stall in the market or to the tourists suddenly overtaken by self-disgust? Whose faces are brown as gourds, the tanned tourist, the black locals whose African origins are banalized in the fake masks, the visiting Afro–St. Lucian poet? What are the faces at the counter (what counter?), the masks for sale, the tourists buying them, the employees selling them and what change comes over whose bodies? Across the white space that separates the two stanzas, Walcott absorbs into his language a very different comparatism from that developed in his theoretical essays. His mode of cultural analogy in which correspondence is mediated by a sheer resemblance neither motivated by nor recuperable in any normative structure of commensuration outside the aesthetic is no longer posed against imperialism's historical commensuration, but against exchange, a sheer equivalence mediated by no fixed norm or standard and amenable to any content. Against such an uncanny double, Walcott's comparatism for a brief moment experiences its own incapacity to make strong distinctions. The interchangeability that tourism's commodification of place endows upon St. Lucia, Greece, and Hawaii, equivalent for marketing purposes as islands offering the leisure of sun, sea, and sand (rather than, say, the touring of monuments in European capitals), in the first stanza bleeds over into the formerly fixed positions of colonial domination (colonizer/colonized; victimizer/victim;

history/art; postcolonial artist/postcolonial space), blurring distinctions to the point where tourist, poet, local, and souvenir merge into a composite syntactical mass.

Tourism's marketing and consumption of leisure space, by some counts the world's largest industry during the last decade of the twentieth century, is an exemplary form of a new phase of capitalism, variously named neo-capitalism, late capitalism, and global capitalism.[35] An illuminating theoretical investigation of the dilemma that Walcott confronts in *Omeros* is Henri Lefebvre's elaboration of this phase of capitalism in terms of an extension of the mechanisms of capitalism to space itself:

The entirety of space must be endowed with *exchange value*. And exchange implies interchangeability, the exchangeability of a good makes that good into a commodity, just like a quantity of sugar or coal; to be exchangeable, it must be comparable with other goods, and indeed with all goods of the same type. The "commodity world" and its characteristics, which formerly encompassed only goods and things produced in space, their circulation and flow, now govern space as a whole, which thus attains the autonomous (or seemingly autonomous) reality of things, of money.[36]

Lefebvre goes on to specify that capitalism roughly divides the world into two kinds of regions, "regions exploited for the purpose of and by means of *production* (of consumer goods), and regions exploited for the purpose of and by means of the *consumption of space*" (Lefebvre, 353), of which tourist destinations, or leisure spaces, are primary examples. Space then is divided and reified; that is, detached from any larger context or process so that, as a commodity, it can be bought and sold or, rather, produced (in the narrow sense) and consumed. Its value is determined in relation to other commodities on the basis of an abstract equivalence alone. Tourism's space of consumption neither conforms to the appropriative strategy of private property nor of colonial domination and exploitation. Colonialism's production of space, which took the form of conquest and control, involved an assertion of sovereignty and the establishment of the governmental apparatus and institutions of cultural assimilation needed to secure it; its economic value depended upon the exploitation of labor and the extraction of raw materials. In the order of tourism, no one, no particular power and no particular discourse, lays a strong, appropriative claim to the land; rather, it is packaged and marketed for profit as a leisure space to be consumed. Tourism is not new in the Caribbean,[37] but it grew dramatically with the advent of the jet plane in the 1960s and the consequent expansion of mass vacation travel, until it became for most islands the economic mainstay by the 1980s and 1990s. The total population of St. Lucia in 1992, for example, was about 135,000. That same year, 341,282 people visited the island, of which about 160,000 were cruise ship passengers.[38] This disproportion alone is of epic proportions. Walcott, one might say, awakens from the postcolonial nightmare of history to the global or neocolonial daydream of tourism. The elaborate postcolonial aesthetic he developed in his essays no longer articulates a distinct resistance because the target has changed. And the irony or (more optimistically) the paradox I am suggesting here is that tourism's production of the space of consumption in many ways doubles Walcott's analogical poetics. The autonomy of the aesthetic and its power to detach representation from historical commensuration here confront the autonomy of the commodity form in its circuit of exchange.

Tourism can seem a negligible aspect of *Omeros* because it hovers almost exclusively in the poem's far background. It is, however, crucial to the poem's frame for it is precisely the tourist's presence and particularly his/her depropriating gaze that makes the epic form necessary to commemorate a disappearing life in a place that is on the brink of forgettability, in the true sense of the word. Tourism may be almost invulnerable to direct opposition because it can always change places, but Walcott has built his poetry from an art of mimicry that doubles the very thing it dissimilates. In *Omeros* he will continue to develop this strategy by transforming the accidental nature of tourism, its apparent disjunction from the continuities of historical necessity, into a poetic contingency. The epic form in *Omeros* is ultimately articulated in terms of a spatial problematic rather than a historical one; that is to say, its foundational aim is to endow a cultural viability to a people's existence in a place rather than to a people's unity and destiny in historical time. The epic distance created in *Omeros*, thus, does not deploy the conventions of heroism or depend on the ennobling aesthetic of mythical action. It takes the form of a wide-ranging metaphorical ruination of monumentality that dislocates the place from the platitude of tourist images through an extension of accidental similitudes. In the process the poem instantiates a figurative pedagogy of space.

Tourists may not crowd *Omeros*, but you do not have to look far to find them. The poem begins with the click of a camera:

> "This is how, one sunrise, we cut down them canoes."
> Philoctete smiles for the tourists, who try taking
> his soul with their cameras. "Once wind bring the news

*

to the *laurier-cannelles*, their leaves start shaking
the minute the axe of sunlight hit the cedars,
because they could see the axes in our eyes."
—(*Omeros*, 3)

For a few extra bucks he will show them his scar. But "he does not
explain its cure. // 'It have some things'—he smiles—'worth more than a
dollar.'" Tourists occupy the very place of a classical epic's invocation to
the muse. Homer's *Odyssey*, for instance, opens with the line: "Sing in me
Muse of the polytropic one, who wandered much after he sacked the
holy city of Troy." Unlike Homer's muse, tourists are invoked not as transcendent tellers, the ultimate authorities for the poem's representation of
the distant past, but rather as listeners called forth with a curiously didactic line ("This is how . . ."). The muse of tourism presents itself as an
elusive audience or a position of address. *Omeros'* inaugural gesture is also
a transaction between tourist and local that turns a story and a scar to
profit. It is perhaps tempting to say that Philoctete is positioned here as
the victim of tourism, but the phrase "taking his soul with their camera," a tired cliché among so many others in the richly futile lexicon of
tourist insult, warns us against any uncomplicated oppositional roles. The
scene is an instance of commodification in action, but a highly ambiguous one in many respects, not least of which is that the story Philoctete
won't tell (how the wound was cured) is precisely his story as it unfolds
in the poem, for *Omeros* begins at the end of its plot, not in the middle.
Philoctete, that is, reveals to the tourists his scar (a healed wound) and addresses them precisely as a recovered victim. It is important too that the
first speaker in the poem should be the fisherman Philoctete, for he represents the most conspicuous reversal of Walcott's censure of the militantly
"wounded sensibilities" of history's postcolonial elegists. Philoctete is an
uncannily exact personification of those militant writers, "who peel, from
their own leprous flesh, their names / who chafe and nurture the scars of
rusted chains, / like primates favouring scabs, those who charge tickets /
for another free ride on the middle passage" excoriated in "Another Life"
(AL, 270).

He bears the wound of slavery on his shin and throughout the poem
explicitly personifies the pain of a history of dispossession. He occasions
the following lines, for instance, with their overt allusion to Césaire's *Notebook of a Return to the Native Land*:

who set out to found no cities; they were the found
who were bound for no victories; they were the bound,
who levelled nothing before them; they were the ground.
—(*Omeros*, 22)

The tourist gaze thus quite directly calls forth the injury of colonial history, even if, or perhaps because, ultimately that gaze remains immune to ethical commensuration or the rhetoric of revenge.

Many critics have noted the sharp departure in the poem's plot and thematics from the stance of the essays, particularly concerning the African dimension of St. Lucian culture and the trauma of history. Of course, times have changed and Walcott is no longer compelled by the polarities of a polemic that pitted militant black indigenism against the divided consciousness of his mulatto style. The puzzle, however, is in the relation of the prominent trope of the wound of history to, on the one hand, the flaunted hellenic analogies and allusions and, on the other hand, the muse of tourism, or at least the phantom audience of tourists. In my reading, this last is determining for it fundamentally alters the nature and the stakes of representation and especially of cultural comparability and equivalence. Interpretations of the poem that do not take central account of tourism will tend to read the politics of comparison in the poem in terms of an overcoming of a simple colonial/anticolonial opposition. In an important essay, Jahan Ramazani, for instance, examines the figure of Philoctete as a "de-indigenized" Caliban.[39] The Greek name, belonging to a relatively minor figure in the mythology surrounding the Trojan War functions, Ramazani argues, to legitimize black suffering so that while "granting cultural authority to Europe, Walcott also reclaims it for Caribbean blacks" (Ramazani, 54). High European culture here is positioned in its colonial guise as a medium of cultural authority and legitimacy that endows value upon its subjects. Walcott, Ramazani argues, both avows and undercuts this authority. At stake in the comparison of Greece to the Caribbean is thus a politics of influence and cultural assimilation that pits dominant against subordinated cultures. Hellenism is a classic topos of colonial cultural assimilation, of which Sartre gives a memorable account in his preface to Frantz Fanon's *Les damnés de la terre*: ". . . from Paris, from London, from Amsterdam we hurled forth words 'Parthenon! Fraternity!' and, somewhere in Africa, in Asia, mouths opened: . . . thenon! . . . nity! And European humanism could congratulate itself on having 'hellenized the Asiatics,

created a new species, Greco-Latin negroes.'"[40] The operative questions
for Ramazani's postcolonial reading are: "Is Walcott recolonizing Caribbean literature for Europeans by using this and other Greek types? Or is he
decolonizing it by representing Caribbean agony? Does the poet reenslave
the descendant of slaves by shackling him with a European name and pro-
totype? Or does he liberate the AfroCaribbean by stealing from former
slavers and making it signify their brutality?" (Ramazani, 63). Ramazani's
answer turns out to be that Walcott overcomes this reductive opposition,
"becoming neither a Eurocentric nor an Afrocentric poet but an ever more
multicentric poet of the contemporary world." (Ramazani, 64). Ramazani
defends Walcott's hybrid practice both from the charge of "Greco-Latin
negro" assimilation (in effect the gist of Lefkowitz's paleocolonial reading) and from the nativist charge that it violates the integrity of discreet
cultures.

The poem's addressees are taken to be either the Eurocentric establishment or its Afrocentric opposition. If we add tourists to the mix then
the poem's postcolonial cultural politics can be seen to unfold on a post-
cultural stage, a context in which culture no longer primarily functions according to the colonial paradigm of assimilation where it forms or deforms
colonial subjects, but circulates instead through the export of mass culture
on the one hand and in the homogenizing representations of an increasingly centralized media on the other. The muse of tourism can hardly be
expected to remember the assimilatory imperative of the civilizing mission
whose Greco-Latin negroes would register in her framework as interrup-
tions of the necessary backdrop of recognizably authentic local color, simu-
lated or not. Most readers of *Omeros* are also potential tourists, wittingly
or unwittingly consumers of Caribbean leisure space or of the inescapable
and seductive representations of the area in advertisements, with their re-
deployment of the familiar tropes of a colonial imaginary[41]—enchanted
island, pre-lapsarian paradise, Robinsonnade and the romance of the ship-
wreck, the plantation fantasy of complete dominion, the racial fantasy of
complete mastery. This is not to say that the problem of colonial cultural
assimilation has been superseded in much of the Anglophone Caribbean.
High school students are, for instance, not generally exposed to much,
if any, literature of the Caribbean in their literature curricula.[42] Nor is
tourism an inescapable context or theme in much of the poetry written in
the Caribbean, which addresses other social and aesthetic problems much
more prominently and, indeed, very rarely takes up tourism at all. Tourism

is, nonetheless, a determining context for U.S. critics and for Walcott himself whose poetry like his person shuttles between the United States and the Caribbean and who, therefore, is particularly attuned to perceptions and representations of his native land abroad. This sensitivity pervades his Nobel speech entitled as a guidebook might be, *The Antilles* and incommensurably subtitled, as no guidebook is likely to be, *Fragments of Epic Memory*. In this text, Walcott contrasts the discourse of colonial travelers with that of tourism and ends on an acutely ambivalent note regarding his own inevitable participation in the process: "The fear of selfishness that, here on this podium with the world paying attention not to them but to me, I should like to keep these simple joys inviolate. . . ." (*The Antilles*).

On *Omeros*' manifest level, there is little trace of the danger of colonial assimilation around the figure of Homer. Homer's main role is ultimately to rescue Walcott from the "love of poverty" that implicates him by analogy with those who have sold out the island to tourism. In one of the poem's most baroque fabulations, an extended scene that begins the last of its seven books, Walcott/narrator hallucinates an encounter between himself and Omeros. From his hotel balcony he sees an object floating up on the beach that manifests itself alternately as the marble or plaster classical portrait, an ebony figure of an old African griot, and Seven Seas, the local storyteller. Far from mutilating the modern poet's hands, as the marble head did in Seferis' "Mythistorema 3," this head, metamorphosed into a full protean body, grips the poet's hand strongly to save him; it is in addition a light, comical, and shifting vision and (much unlike Seferis) all too voluble, at least to this reader's taste. The gap between these two evocations of the marble head leave to be seen the distinct advantages of Walcott's poetics of the new world, "with nothing so old / that it could not be invented" (AL, 294).

This composite Omeros leads Walcott by the hand as Virgil had Dante but this time through a St. Lucian version of the inferno with two main circles, one reserved for tourism's speculators and the other for self-serving poets. The "Pool of Speculation" brims with the "souls who have sold out their race, . . . saw the land as views / for hotels and elevated into waiters / the sons of others" (*Omeros*, 289). The demonic speculators try to pull Walcott/narrator down, but Omeros leads him "along the right path. . . ." Walcott, however, almost falls into the next pit, the "backbiting circle" of poets. "Selfish phantoms with eyes . . . who saw only surfaces in nature and men, and smiled at their similes" (*Omeros*, 293). Walcott recognizes himself in the dwellers of this pit and, but for Omeros, *Omeros* might have ended here:

> And that was where I had come from. Pride in my craft.
> Elevating myself. I slid, and kept falling
>
> toward the shit they stewed in; all the poets laughed,
> jeering with dripping fingers; then Omeros gripped
> my hand in enclosing marble . . .
> —(*Omeros*, 293)

The rhetoric of disavowal finds a particularly robust and comical incarnation here in the hyperbolically monumental hand that lifts the poet from his "slide" into self-elevation. Nonetheless, an equivalent relation to the island obtains between the pride of poets who elevate themselves and sublimate poverty and the greed of speculators who "elevate into waiters the sons of others." The carnivalesque hyperbole that surrounds the figure of Omeros turns serious when, in the form of Seven Seas, he lectures the transatlantic poet: "You ain't been nowhere, you have seen / nothing no matter how far you may have traveled / you have learnt no more than if you stood on that beach" (*Omeros*, 291). At the end of their little journey, Omeros drives this lesson home with a direct link to poverty in stern words that echo Walcott's self questioning in the passage discussed earlier in this chapter:

> . . . "You tried to render
> their lives as you could, but that is never enough;
> now in the sulphur's stench ask yourself this question,
>
> whether a love of poverty helped you
> to use other eyes, like those of that sightless stone?"
> —(*Omeros*, 294)

Walcott reflects on the relation of art to poverty in several of his prose works. In "What the Twilight Says," for instance, speaking of the arduous labor of his early theatrical work, he writes about the "gilded hallucinations of poverty . . . as if the destitute, in their orange-tinted backyards, under their dusty trees, or climbing to their favelas, were all natural scene designers and poverty was not a condition but an art" ("Twilight," 3). But he warns unequivocally that "the last thing which the poor needed was the idealisation of their poverty," because "the empire of hunger includes work that is aimed only at necessities. [. . .] Hunger induces its delirium, and it is this fever for heroic examples that can produce the glorification of revenge" ("Twilight," 19). But the stakes in *Omeros* have changed considerably since the enemies consigned in Michelangelo fashion to the pit of hell are no longer the militant intellectuals who prey on the people's deprivation but tourism's speculators and their promises of progress out of poverty. So Omeros' question is one that is in large measure aimed at this poem itself, with its explicit aim to commemorate a disappearing mode of life with the use of other eyes—most especially, those of the great blind bard himself. "When," Walcott/narrator laments shortly before his encounter with Omeros, "would I not hear the Trojan War / in two fishermen cursing in Ma Kilman's shop? / When would my head shake off its echoes like a horse // shaking off a wreath of flies? When would it stop, / the echo in the throat, insisting, 'Omeros'; / when would I enter that light beyond metaphor?" (*Omeros*, 271). The answer is, of course, never, or at least not until the last line of the poem, but the encounter with Omeros allows Walcott to have his metaphor and disavow it too, for by the end of the chapter, "the nightmare was gone. The bust became its own past." And by the start of the next chapter the poet can speak of this "homage to Omeros my exorcism" (*Omeros*, 294). The answer to Omeros' challenge to the poem—that is, whether it has used his "other eyes" to sublimate poverty and conserve it in monumental marble—hinges on how successfully Walcott can make Omeros disappear.

Omeros, like its namesake the bust, is a self-effacing monument. It constructs an elaborate verbal edifice made up of many narratives told or perceived by two major narrators and several minor ones and an extravagant web of imagery, metaphor, and allusion only to undo much of it at the end, leaving only a kind of poetic memory, or, more precisely, instructions or clues for a different and differential forgetting. Critics have often remarked on Walcott/narrator's confession to Omeros during their encounter that he never read his books "all the way through," a claim Walcott himself has repeated in interviews.[43] This may well be, as Gregson Davis argues, another instance of the rhetoric of disavowal; nonetheless, it is hard to deny that the Homeric poems inform the text of *Omeros* only in the most general way. The theme of the journey, particularly a filial journey of homecoming that reconciles fathers and sons, recalls the *Odyssey*, as does the island itself and its seafaring ways. The *Iliad* echoes through the central diegesis, the conflict between two fishermen, Hector and Achille, over a beautiful woman named Helen. The explicitness and contingency of the Homeric template, however, distinguish *Omeros* most strikingly from its modernist precursors. Homer's *Odyssey* is to Joyce's *Ulysses* the hidden epic code; however ambivalent the cultural filiation, the text's operations are unintelligible without knowledge of the ancient precursor. In *Omeros*, Homer is much more detachable; his indispensability lies, paradoxically, in the very incidental nature of his connection to the Caribbean. It is possible to write a great deal about *Omeros* without ever referring to Homer in any thoroughgoing way, or indeed mentioning him at all. In part this has to do with the fact that the Homeric aspect of *Omeros* is overwhelmingly associated with the metafictional operations of its two primary authorial figures, poet and historian, and also because, as such, the Homeric dimension of the text is overwhelming tropological. If one engages in the thought experiment of removing Homeric allusion from *Omeros*, one finds that most of the narrative remains unchanged. What disappears, however, is the text's manifest monumentality, which this little experiment reveals to be largely a product of metaphor. Homeric epic subsists in *Omeros* not so much as a precursory exemplum, of which this is a postcolonial or postmodern or Caribbean version (the way one could say that *Ulysses* or self-evidently, Kazantzakis' *The Odyssey: A Modern Sequel* are versions of Homer), but rather as a font of metaphor. Homer and *Omeros* unleash a copious lexicon for relations and affinities that mobilize accidental and incomplete similitudes. Critics have found this proliferating metaphoricity excessive and uncontrolled. Paul Breslin suggests that the poem doesn't consistently sustain the "critique of its own analogical method" and that the overwhelming Homeric comparison "might be seen as a lingering wound of colonized consciousness, motivated by an insecure longing to claim the founding authority of the European canon."[44] I cannot say that the reading I propose derives from the poet's conscious intention, but I will argue that whether or not the Homeric analogy betrays the unconscious vestiges of colonial comparison, it can also be seen to work instrumentally as a textual effect deployed in resistance to tourism's representational economy. Omeric comparisons are modes of metaphorical interchangeability that, in contrast to the system of exchange that brokers commodified space, detour around equivalence. In the very distances this metaphoricity and the mirage-like immanence of its disappearance establish between vehicle and tenor, we learn to read for an ontologically resistant depth in the place. This resistance is constituted from a differential effect of metaphor. Forced and excessive, these comparisons play across a spectrum defined by sameness and difference and marshall the extraordinary array of metaphor's gradations against the flatness of commodified space.

From its very title on, a slightly skewed rendition of the modern Greek pronunciation of Homer (Ομηρος, pronounced "O-meeros" in modern Greek) that is estranging enough so that most people are unsure exactly how to pronounce it, *Omeros* announces an incommensurability at the core of its flaunted comparisons to the classical model. The first book, substantially the longest of the seven, functions as an extended invocation or prelude that introduces all the characters and provides a multiple etiology of the poem's title and its comparative relation to the classical reference. Omeric incommensurability as it is developed here occupies a spectrum defined by minimal and maximal differentiation. Omeros enters the poem via a minimal differentiation at the end of Walcott's introduction of the local blind bard, old St. Omere, also knows as Seven Seas, occupied with his morning ritual:

> The dog scratched at the kitchen door for him to open
> but he made it wait. He drummed the kitchen table
> with his fingers. Two blackbirds quarrelled at breakfast.
>
> Except for one hand he sat as still as marble,
> with his egg-white eyes, fingers recounting the past
> of another sea, measured by the stroking oars.
>
> O open this day with the conch's moan, Omeros.
> —(*Omeros*, 12)

The plainness of the first stanza is leavened in the second stanza's first line with a single simile comparing Seven Seas' stillness to marble, and though by association his fingers now recount *another* sea, the entire stanza could still easily refer uniquely to the diegetic character of Seven Seas. By the opening of the third stanza, however, he has retroactively *become* Omeros. Cloaked in a simile that brings this flesh and blood figure into relation with a "blind bust," the moment of difference at which one could pinpoint precisely where Seven Seas leaves off and his classical or archaic analogue begins is obscure.

Leading into the much-quoted scene where Walcott/narrator first hears the word "Omeros," there is a passage that elaborates an analogy between Homer's time "across centuries / of the sea's parchment atlas" and the St. Lucian present: "Then the canoes were galleys / over which a frigate sawed its scythed wings slowly" (*Omeros*, 13). The analogy between prehistorical (taken broadly) Greece and ahistorical or posthistorical St. Lucia is one that Walcott draws fondly upon in his commentary on *Omeros*,[45] but while it figures at various points in the poem, it tends, as in this passage, to be elaborated in terms of metaphorical associations and not in the syllogistic form of an analogical argument. The analogy between the Mediterranean and the Caribbean is not uncommon in writing on the Caribbean where the two seas and the regions they define are compared as the crucibles of two great phases of world history, the first running from classical antiquity to the late middle ages and the second encompassing the era of global modernity initiated by Columbus' voyage. The parallel has its pejorative valuation in Naipaul, for instance, who sees the Caribbean as the Mediterranean in negative, and measures its depredation against the glory of Greek civilization. And it has its positive valuation in C. L. R. James, for instance, as a figure for new world historical possibilities. Walcott himself was partial to it at various points in his career, particularly like many other Anglophone Caribbean intellectuals around the hope for the West Indian federation.[46] In *Omeros* he alludes to the world historical dimensions of the parallel (see *Omeros* 37–38, inter alia), but keeps his poetic project well clear of it, preferring instead the stark discontinuities of an immediate juxtaposition of archaic Greece and the contemporary Caribbean. As though to exaggerate disjunction over a potentially explanatory historical analogy, at the end of this passage Walcott segues into the origin of the title "Omeros," which is accidental to the highest degree, as much from a historical as from a literary perspective:

> A wind turns the harbour's pages back to the voice
> that hummed in the vase of a girl's throat: "Omeros"

> III

> "O-meros," she laughed. "That's what we call him in Greek,"
> stroking the small bust with its boxer's broken nose,
> and I thought of Seven Seas sitting near the reek

> of drying fishnets, listening to the shallows' noise.
> I said: "Homer and Virg are New England farmers,
> and the winged horse guards their gas-station, you're right"

*

I felt the foam head watching as I stroked an arm, as
cold as its marble, then the shoulders in winter light
in the studio attic. I said, "Omeros,"

and *O* was the conch-shell's invocation, *mer* was
both mother and sea in our Antillean patois,
os, a gray bone, and the white surf as it crashes

and spreads its sibilant collar on a lace shore.
Omeros was the crunch of dry leaves, and the washes
that echoed from a cave-mouth when the tide has ebbed.

The name stayed in my mouth.
—(*Omeros*, 13–14)

The dissimilitude here is maximal for the figure of Homer insistently
diverts all abstract likeness in its relation to the Caribbean. The simile
that just a few pages earlier merged Omeros with Seven Seas here disag-
gregates into the thought of a particular subject contemplating not a bard
or a text or a landscape but a mundane object, a reproduction of a portrait. Detached from the immateriality of language (not to speak of history
or tradition), the Homer-object is at once territorialized by its proprietor
(and, contra Lefkowitz, he is very much, indeed hyperbolically, the property of a particular person—a modern Greek woman) as a transportable
souvenir of a particular place, Greece.[47] As an object, the bust of Omeros
is, strictly speaking, not susceptible to the usual dangers of poetic cultural
assimilation. Instead it circumvents the legitimacy of cultural traditions by
circulating in the contingency of "real" empirical space—St. Lucia, New
England. The connection between Homer and the St. Lucian bard Seven
Seas, or the New England farmers Homer and Virg occurs on the mode of
free association. The work of this crucial passage is to transform the purely
accidental nature of Homer's appearance to the poet in the form of a plaster
bust in the possession of one of his lovers into a contingent foundation for
the poem. Homer in the shape of Omeros comes (h)ome to the Caribbean by passing through the accidents of space rather than the necessity
of time. The dislocation that will bring the name into St. Lucian patois
adds an extra turn to this insistent materialization since it is transmitted in
the oral materiality of language rather than its written universality ("The
name stayed in my mouth"). And if this multiple dissimilation of Homer
through Omeros' materiality did not suffice, the transfer of the name from

Greek to patois also takes a carnal form since it coincides with Walcott/
narrator's sexual encounter with the bearer of the Omeros-object. Indeed as
the caresses of the Greek woman's marmoreal body begin, the precise moment when Walcott seizes the name "Omeros" for his poem, it is difficult
to distinguish between the Homer-object and the flesh and blood woman:

> I felt the foam head watching as I stroked an arm, as
> cold as its marble, then the shoulders in winter light
> in the studio attic. I said, "Omeros."

The bust's momentary incarnation in the woman's body coincides
with its etymological metamorphosis into creole, so that the passage's manifest creolization of "Omeros" into "O," "mer," "os" also distinctly lets an
homme's eros be heard. And this peculiarly carnal and incarnated translation allows an immediate contact between discrepant historical moments.
No longer mediated by the absolutions of tradition's continuity, Homer
directly confronts slavery. In its incarnated form, antiquity's "inculpable
marble" might be seen to widen its mouth to a scream:

> But if it could read between the lines of her floor
> like a white-hot deck uncalked by Antillean heat,
> to the shadows in its hold, its nostrils might flare
>
> at the stench from manacled ankles, the coffled feet
> scraping like leaves, and perhaps the inculpable marble
> would have turned its white seeds away, to widen
>
> the bow of its mouth at the horror under her table
> —(*Omeros*, 15)

In maximal differentiation likeness is evacuated as a form of cultural
mediation. The name "Omeros" is so radically detached from any original
or authentic high-cultural referent that it becomes available to a new etymological appropriation in which no claim to comparison with the original adheres. "O-mer-os," shattered like a word-object into fragments enters
into metaphorical relation with the Caribbean landscape alone. Shorn of
analogy or any temporal reference, the (re)naming of "Omeros" is perhaps
as close as a reader can get to seeing new world "Adamic naming" in action.
    The radical contingency behind the origin of the poem's title also
informs the origin of its plot. The scene, reminiscent of the multiple and
chance intersections of various characters in a single topography in mod-

ernist narrative (*Mrs. Dalloway*'s London, *Ulysses*' Dublin), unfolds on that
ultimate space of consumption, the beach. Walcott/narrator sits at a hotel
terrace "waiting for the cheque," while Major Plunkett and his wife Maud
enjoy a weekly drink at a different locale, "their Saturday place," and "the
tourists revolved, grilling their backs in the noon barbecue," when suddenly
the waiter frowns into the distance. Walcott/narrator turns around and

> . . . now the mirage
>
> dissolved to a woman with a madras head-tie,
> but the head proud, although it was looking for work.
> I felt like standing in homage to a beauty
>
> that left, like a ship, widening eyes in its wake.
> "Who the hell is that?" a tourist near my table
> asked a waitress. The waitress said, "She? She too proud!"
>
> As the carved lids of the unimaginable
> ebony mask unwrapped from its cotton-wool cloud,
> the waitress sneered, "Helen." And all the rest followed.
> —(*Omeros*, 23–24)

The poem's conceit is thus born of accident and formed through contingency as the poet's singular mirage-like vision of a woman is amalgamated
contingently with the voices of worker and tourist in leisure space ("Who
the hell is that?" "She? She too proud!" "Helen."). All three speakers see the
same woman, but they all see her differently, and Walcott's fellow gazers
are clearly cut off from "all the rest that followed"; that is, from the poem
itself. Meanwhile, from another side of the beach, Plunkett, his mind as so
often addled with memories of war, sees Helen and suddenly "smiled at the
mythical hallucination / that went with the name's shadow" and remembers
that the island was once known as the "Helen of the West Indies" because
the French and the English fought more than a dozen battles over it in the
eighteenth and early nineteenth centuries, including the glorious Battle of
the Saints when Sir Rodney routed the Comte de Grasse and sealed his
triumph in the Treaty of Paris.[48] These "Homeric associations" and "Homeric coincidences" will prompt Plunkett to undertake his "remorseful
research" to "give Helen a history." For the poet, however, this moment
of vision is much more elaborate and it extends into a very particular turn
of metaphor. He watches Helen walk down the beach singing "Yesterday,

all my troubles seemed so far away." There is smoke up ahead of her. She must decide whether to go through it or around it and "in that pause / that divides the smoke with a sword, white Helen died." Suddenly a boy on a horse gallops down the beach:

> . . . the stallion's sounds
>
> scalded her scalp with memory. A battle broke
> out. Lances of sunlight hurled themselves into sand,
> the horse hardened to wood, Troy burned, and a soundless
>
> wrestling of smoke-plumed warriors was spun
> from the blowing veils, while she dangles her sandals
> and passed through that door of black smoke into the sun.
>
> And yesterday these shallows were the Scamander,
> and armed shadows leapt from the horse, and the bronze nuts
> were helmets, Agamemnon was the commander
>
> of weed-bearded captains. . . .
> —(Omeros, 34–35)

The tourist sees a beautiful local woman (we know she quit her last waitressing job because she wouldn't put up with their groping) with a common name. His/her apparently incidental presence is pivotal because s/he is the one who asks her name and sees nothing in it (as far as we can tell) beyond the beauty already manifest in her person, a beauty that is part of the leisure space s/he consumes. The recovering imperialist sees in "Helen" the people in need of a history. The poet, on his side, makes the smoke a door revolving from white Helen to black Helen and hallucinates the Trojan War on the beach before him. The metaphors in this passage are nowhere subtended by the kind of correspondences that induce recognition by uncovering hidden similarities. Nothing about the sunlight brings it into similitude with a lance or the smoke with warrior plumes, much less a door. The passage verges on hallucination or fabulation because the metaphors are so sharply detached from the literal things they render. The Homeric association is at once supremely accidental since it partakes fully in the chance convergence of elements that bring it to the poet's mind and at the same time forced by a single perspective, willed, envisioned, and as such rather than beholding likeness one has the sense of witnessing a metamorphosis: sunlight becoming lances, smoke becoming warriors or a door.

The perception of resemblance is, for Aristotle, a gift of nature [*euphuias*] and as such it links philosopher and poet on an unbroken chain toward the truth.[49] Because Aristotle's ontology is grounded in a concept of truth, the knowledge available through resemblance is ultimately the recognition of an underlying sameness. The point is all the more apparent in ancient Greek, which signifies similarity and sameness with the same word: *homoiôsis* or *to homoion*. But of course resemblance *is* not sameness but rather the *recognition* of sameness. This detour to the same through resemblance occasions a paradox for the chain of being, for, as Derrida points out in his analysis of the status of metaphor in philosophy, the pleasure of mimesis depends on "giving us to see in action that which nonetheless is not to be seen in action, but only in its very resembling double, its *mimêma.*"[50] The imitation, in this case the resemblance, in fact precedes or even replaces the perception of truth in a paradox Derrida will develop most fully in "The Double Session." Even when metaphor is not explicitly associated with metaphysical truth, its workings and its recognition are thought, by anthropologists, for instance, both to uncover and depend upon a common culture, or by linguists and critics to plumb the depths of a single language. A cross-cultural metaphor is, thus, from a certain perspective, an oxymoron since it cannot draw on a system of shared commonplaces. Because Walcott's Homeric associations and hallucinations neither proceed from a perceived resemblance nor result in the recognition of similarity, they expose cultural boundedness and work on its limit. The Omeric metaphor extends the paradox of the *mimêma*, for rather than giving to be seen a resemblance that precedes the same, or the true object of knowledge, Walcott's metaphor reveals a lone resemblance neither followed nor preceded by a legitimately "true" original. He gives to be seen, culturally speaking, precisely what could never be seen because it makes no further claim to truth. Dislocation here is forced into artifice, just as accident becomes contingency.

Helen diverts equivalence but calls forth both minimal and maximal differentiation. The name Helen is nearly identical to the Homeric original; the comparison, linguistically, does not pass through resemblance but through the minimal difference of translation's repetition. But if the name is the same, the substantive difference in time and space and cultural context is vast to the point of complete disjunction. The comparison remains in tension between the collapse into near-identity and the absolute distinction of cultural difference. In Walcott/narrator's eyes, black Helen and white Helen merge through the mirage of a revolving door of smoke, and mirage is a crucial word for it suggests a complete and illusory materialization of desire. The mirage appears with absolute clarity and identity (no verisimilitude here: the scene in the distant desert does not *look like* an oasis, it *is* an oasis) and then, just as absolutely, disappears. At the same time however, the passage keeps Helen the figure of speech utterly distinct from Helen the human figure, who walks down the beach singing a Beatles song utterly heedless of the metaphors painting her into a Trojan landscape.

This radical distinction between a metaphorical epic magnitude and the daily doings of the St. Lucian characters obtains throughout the poem. We have, for instance, the poet's elevated epic presentation of the pirogues as fateful objects destined for heroes: "one would serve Hector and another, Achilles." We note in passing that Achilles occurs here with an "s," indicating we pronounce his name in thought exactly like that of his epic namesake. But the next line, across a chapter heading, presents us with an ordinary fisherman performing an ordinary bodily function we wouldn't dream of witnessing for his Homeric counterpart: "Achille peed in the dark, then bolted the half-door shut" (*Omeros*, 8).

Homeric Similes and Omeric Similitude: A Contingent Excursus

[W]e no longer have much use for Homeric comparisons, and the semantic concentration of the trope ensures its almost obvious esthetic superiority over the developed form of the figure. [Stéphane] Mallarmé congratulated himself on having banished the words "like" and "as" from his vocabulary.
—Gérard Genette, *Figures of Literary Discourse*

In order to insure that a reader or hearer will thus fully appreciate his metaphors a poet must be certain that his audience understands clearly and precisely the meaning of words as he uses them. . . . in the infancy of poetry and in the earliest days of a fixed literary diction this problem of accurate communication was a major difficulty for the poet. . . . because words lacked

precise definitions in Homer's time Homer
could not, even if he had so wished, have used
daring metaphors . . . So Homer had to educate
his own audience before they could fully appreciate his lays.
—W. B. Stanford, *Greek Metaphor*

Walcott's Omeric metaphor brings to the mind of this reader the extended Homeric simile, particularly as it occurs in the *Iliad*, where it ex-
hibits a similarly radical disjunction between tenor and vehicle, or between
the epic heroes and the particular magnitude made of them. Here we join
Odysseus in the midst of battle as he barely escapes the encircling Trojans:

> . . . They found Odysseus beloved of Zeus, and around him
> the Trojans crowded, as bloody scavengers in the mountains
> crowd on a horned stag who is stricken, one whom a hunter
> shot with an arrow from the string, and the stag has escaped him,
>   running
> with his feet, while the blood stayed warm, and his knees were
>   springing beneath him.
> But when the pain of the flying arrow has beaten him, then
> the rending scavengers begin to feast on him in the mountains
> and the shaded glen. But some spirit leads that way a dangerous
> lion, and the scavengers run in terror, and the lion eats it;
> so about wise much-devising Odysseus the Trojans
> crowded now, valiant and numerous, but the hero
> with rapid play of his spear beat off the pitiless death-day.
> Now Aias came near him, carrying like a wall his shield,
> and stood forth beside him, and the Trojans fled one way and
>   another.
> —(*Iliad*, XI. 473–486)[51]

The Homeric simile establishes a point of correspondence (or, as the
scholars call it, a *Vergleichspunkt*) here between Odysseus encircled by Trojans and a wounded stag encircled by scavengers, and then extends upon it.
The extensions, however, instead of clarifying the grounds of comparison,
develop into small narratives that, more often than not, wander far from
the tenor or subject they purport to qualify. The example here is particularly striking because the simile's initial correspondence, Odysseus/stag:
Trojans/scavengers picks up an extra element, the lion, in the process of
its narrative extension. This lion in turn comes to correspond to Aias in
the narrative. The simile's narrative develops to the point of contradict-

ing the scene it illustrates: a lion scatters the scavengers and eats the stag, whereas Aias scatters the Trojans but rescues Odysseus. If we focus on the correspondence Odysseus/stag we find that one survives while the other succumbs; if we focus on the unarticulated correspondence Aias/lion we find that one rescues and the other devours.[52] By simile's end the original equivalence that would subsume the stag's dire circumstances to Odysseus' predicament falls apart and each element moves on with a life of its own. The context—with its own contingencies and accidents—from which the metaphorical vehicle is plucked seems to overwhelm the similitude through which it entered the epic.

While the Homeric simile has generally been admired and widely imitated in the epic tradition, it has occasioned various degrees of consternation among critics who have proposed many explanations for these curious verbal artifacts, including hypothetical accounts as to the relative antiquity of the similes compared to other epic elements and various arguments for interpolation.[53] It wasn't until fairly recently, particularly in the wake of the "discovery" of the oral nature of Homeric epic, that critics came to interpret the similes as integral components of the poem's aesthetics and thematics.[54] In a challenging analysis of the ideology of figure in epic, Susanne Wofford suggests an interpretation of the radical disjunction between the narrated action in the *Iliad* and the tropes that qualify it.[55] The similes, according to her, endow aesthetic and ideological value to the action of the narrative by asserting metaphorical equivalence even as they allow for a critique of that very operation by virtue of the abruptness with which they are presented and the divergent narratives into which they extend. When blood from Menelaos' wound (*Iliad*, IV. 141–147), for instance, is compared to the exquisite dye a Maionian woman applies to ivory to make a cheekpiece for horses, the text emphasizes that Menelaos and his companions in the narrated action know the wound as pain and dread alone; the aesthetic perspective of the simile is available only to an audience, the observer of the poetry. The similes, then, magnify epic distance through the "transformation of violence into art—a transformation that occurs at the moment of seeing a connection between . . . dissimilar scenes" (Choice, 31). The epic distance, that great gap between the heroic world of epic narrative and the present of its telling, is expressed through many other generic conventions, such as the invocation of the muses and the ubiquitous presence of gods among the heroes. If the direct participation of gods in heroic action marks the greatest distance between the epic and its post-heroic audience then the substance of the similes, or their "vehicles," almost entirely drawn from nature and ordinary life (herding, hunting, carpentry, etc.), marks the closest proximity. Epic distance is crucial to the epic's authority to represent the past, which it conveys, across that distance, with a startling immediacy. Jean-Pierre Vernant argues that the epic poet does not so much recount the past from memory as bring his audience into its presence—a gesture uncannily similar to Walcott's initial encounter with the bust of Omeros.[56]

One of the peculiarities of the *Iliad*, in marked contrast to the *Odyssey*, is that the stage on which the action develops is nearly devoid of natural detail. There is no weather to speak of; when the Trojan plain unfolds before us it is from a general's strategic view (even if that perspective is adopted by a woman, as it is by Andromache in book VI): vast groupings of men engaged in battle or preparing for it with two rivers and a few trees as landmarks.[57] On the other hand, among the roughly three hundred and fifty extended similes punctuating this bleak narrative, every conceivable face of nature and pastoral life seems to make an appearance, from storms to childbirth to dolphins to donkeys in the field to flies crowding over a pail of milk to wounded stags escaping scavengers only to succumb to lions. Wolfgang Schadewalt fills up the first three pages of an essay with a selected catalogue of these natural elements and then argues that they seem so exhaustive and precise that they amount to a world on their own, a *Gleichniswelt* (simile world).[58] Furthermore, for all the specificity with which the similes are extended they rarely include references to particular places, so that while the minuteness of detail gives them vivid completeness they are not exclusively linked to any actual place outside the epic.[59] The stag is not on the run in Thrace particularly or in Pylos, nor is the chariot-maker hardening fallen poplars near a Euboean marsh; instead, these actions are available to Panhellenic signification.

As Gregory Nagy has forcefully argued, Homeric epic is among the cultural institutions of the time (other examples include the Delphic oracle and colonization) that aimed to define a translocal Panhellenic totality.[60] Epic, Nagy argues, suppresses or submerges all direct reference to hero cult, even as it appropriates many of its ritual structures toward the end of constituting its own competing version of immortality. Whereas the cult hero's immortality is linked to a specific locale, the epic hero's immortality is entirely contained in the renown that epic itself generates by virtue of its circulation among all Greeks. Thus, while one of the effects of the disjunction between simile and action may be to both make ideological links and expose this making, another is to create the illusion of independence for the ordinary cultural and natural world the similes allude to. The importance of the stag in our initial example, thus, may not be its problematic identification with Odysseus but rather that its brief race into the epic should, by means of its very disjunctive extension, make the poem appear to partake in the extensive and unlimited relations of an ordinary or "real" but translocal Panhellenic totality. Analogy or metaphor thus surprisingly emerges as the pretext for metonymy. It may be the Homeric *tour de force* to divert attention onto modes of resemblance while the simile surreptitiously and metonymically alludes to the totality of an imaginary world *as though* this world were already existing, even as the epic itself brings it into existence.

There are no extended similes on the Homeric model in Walcott's *Omeros*, but it seems to me that the incommensurable Omeric similitude he develops, one that systematically diverts equivalence, can be said to perform a similar function.[61] In *Omeros*, however, the tables are turned and it is the similes that carry epic magnitude while the narrative unfurls in ordinary life. The disjunction between the two, which, we remember, can take the form both of maximal and minimal differentiation, makes an epic monumentality appear and disappear in such a way that the ordinary life it shadows becomes aesthetically apprehendable, or apprehendable as an aesthetic object. Homer's similes create the illusion that the highly wrought epic, with its elevated style, its highly conventional structures, and its ideology, encompasses the whole world of nature—potentially extending in a metonymic way, that is, contingently, into the ordinariness of Panhellenic life. Omeric similitude interposes the ontological density and perceptual opacity of a metaphorical and therefore disappearing monumentality into the flatness or interchangeability of commodified space. Whereas the Homeric simile cannily separates specificity from locality, Omeric similitude delocalizes tourism's reified caricature of local type. Homer or Omeros thus provides Walcott with epic distance, or rather epicality as distance. Walcott has insisted again and again in published interviews that *Omeros* is not an epic. I want to suggest that we take his disavowal at its word and think of the poem as epical precisely in the way that it figures its *non*epicality.

If it is true, as Genette suggests in his essay "Rhetoric Restrained," that a high modernist poetics could banish the words "like" and "as" from its vocabulary as relics of an archaic past in a gesture that proclaims a distinct tropological progress of modernity, then perhaps Walcott's Omeric similitude bespeaks a postmodern and postcolonial use for comparison on the Homeric model. Few scholars now are likely to countenance W. B. Stanford's argument that it is the "infancy of poetry" and the "absence of a fixed literary diction" that made Homer's extended similes necessary, but I find his insight that there is a pedagogical dimension to the similes very suggestive. For Stanford, that pedagogy inheres in the extended explication of the similitude within the simile. I have suggested here a more ideological function for that pedagogy, one that derives both from the similes' extensive but unlocal specificity and from their disjunction from the narrative. The similes, I argue, educate or interpellate the epic's audience into a particular geographical and political identification. Omeric similitudes also suggest a function for poetic comparison besides cross-cultural analogy where the content or substance of one culture is measured against or superimposed upon that of another. Walcott shifts the emphasis from the content of cultural comparison to the mechanisms of poetic similitude, which, in turn, suggests a pedagogy of tourism's space of consumption.

Pedagogy of Poetic Space ("Our Last Resort as Much as Yours, Omeros")

Lord Jesus Christ, Son of God, have mercy
on the cities, the islands and the villages of
this Orthodox Fatherland, as well as the holy
monasteries which are scourged by the worldly
touristic wave.
— Greek Orthodox prayer

. . . and though the words "I must get away"
do not actually pass across your lips, you make
a leap from being that nice blob just sitting
like a boob in your amniotic sac of the modern
experience to being a person visiting heaps of
death and ruin and feeling alive and inspired at
the sight of it; to being a person lying on some
faraway beach, your stilled body stinking and
glistening in the sand, looking like something
first forgotten, then remembered, then not
important enough to go back for, to being a
person marvelling at the harmony (ordinarily,
what you would say is the backwardness) and

the union these other people (and they are other
people) have with nature. . . . and since you
are being an ugly person this ugly but joyful
thought will swell inside you: their ancestors
were not clever in the way yours were and not
ruthless in the way yours were, for then would
it not be you who would be in harmony with
nature and backwards in that charming way?
—Jamaica Kincaid, *A Small Place*

He is similar, not similar to something, but just
similar. And he invents spaces of which he is the
convulsive possession.
—Roger Caillois

Toward the end of *The Production of Space*, Henri Lefebvre makes
a startling suggestion: "In and through the space of leisure a pedagogy of
space and time is beginning to take shape" (Lefebvre, 385). He admits this
is as yet a "virtuality" and does not develop what he has in mind with this
pedagogy in any detail, but one gathers a general outline. Fully cognizant
of leisure space's neocolonial dimensions, Lefebvre warns against any notion that it is a "counter-space" outside "the control of the established
order" (Lefebvre, 383). Nonetheless, he suggests that its given role as a space
of pleasure for the body induces an experience of contradictory space, in
this case of the contradiction between the expansive pleasure of the body
in leisure space and the constriction of the fragmented, economized, and
rationalized "home" space of production. The space of leisure indeed epit-
omizes contradictory space because it "bridges the gap between traditional
spaces with their monumentality and their localizations based on work and
its demands and potential spaces of enjoyment and joy" (Lefebvre, 385).
Lefebvre insists on the materiality of space; it performs a bridging function between work and pleasure through the body rather than the mind.
Leisure thus cultivates the "body's differential tendency," its desire to be
"generative" rather than dominated (Lefebvre, 384). Tourism's pedagogy of
space and time seems, then, in a first moment to involve the undisciplining
of the body. It is an enigmatically optimistic pronouncement, perhaps even
a utopian hope, since for Lefebvre differential space is space emancipated
from the dominance of what he calls "abstract space" with its standard-
izing drive to evacuate all difference. It is striking, nonetheless, that this
pedagogy of space seems completely to neglect the plight of those very
numerous terminal locals, those "other people" who labor in leisure's space

of consumption and lack the means to buy into a leisure of their own or benefit from the schooling of its space.

It is from the point of view of those locals that Jamaica Kincaid directs her tourist diatribe in *A Small Place*, which, as much as it mocks and controverts an idea like Lefebvre's, has the unmistakable rhetoric and design of a stern, if not sadistic, pedagogy. What is it about tourists that seems to provoke mockery and pious instruction in equal measure? Is it their inert and self-satisfied physicality? Is it the wide and happy gaps in their cultural memory? Kincaid collars the tourist and shows him the ugliness of his/her body, to let him/her know what s/he looks like to the locals whose gaze s/he effaces in a haze of consumption. Then, she disenchants him/her utterly with a lesson in global capitalism, local corruption, and the harsh realities of poverty. The first section of her book reads like an insider's guide to Antigua intent on defacing every charm promised in the brochures. She explains exactly why the quaint roads are in such lousy shape, and where the sewage goes (straight into the turquoise sea), and where the local food really comes from (Miami). Having thus punctured the enchanted cliché, she abandons her direct address to the ugly tourist "you" replacing it, by degrees, with a generalized post-colonizer first world addressee, and proceeds to what seems her main task and that is to deliver a lesson in colonial history. This furious lesson is clearly meant to recall the stilled and stinking tourist body to its position as a privileged subject of history, the beneficiary of extraordinary violence and depropriation, a history that Kincaid is intent on holding accountable for the island's sorry contemporary condition. But the lesson in *A Small Place* falters when, having restored the historical divisions of colonizer/colonized to the tourist landscape, it hits a kind of dead end with a discrepant and improbable final appeal to a simple humanity in its final lines: "Of course, the whole thing is, once you cease to be a master, once you throw off your master's yoke, you are no longer human rubbish, you are just a human being, and all the things that adds up to. So, too, with the slaves. Once they are no longer slaves, once they are free, they are no longer noble and exalted; they are just human beings."[62] The idea that the tourist could cease to be a master or a "post-colonizer" and the "touristed" cease to be slave or a "post-colonized"[63] in any uncomplicated way contradicts the unstinting and demystifying analysis of the whole text, which demonstrates unambiguously that the forces that link the tourist to the colonial master and the local with his naïve enthusiasm for the new "Hotel Training School" to the plantation slave are far beyond the control of any ordinary human. Kincaid's ending betrays a desire to restore the tourist wrapped in her "hospitality industry" to a full historical subject of colonialism so that she might come out the other end as a human being, a true stranger, whom the author, herself divested of the victim's nobility and rage, might greet with the hospitality implicit to the text's dialogic structure, with whom, that is to say, she might enter into some kind of dialectic of recognition between human beings.[64] The stern pedagogy quite unexpectedly attempts to resolve itself into a dialogue.

Battered but toughened, the (white, U.S.) reader of *A Small Place* can only marvel with disappointment at this prematurely happy ending, since by page 8 or so she has already been thoroughly disabused of any longing for such a resolution. One suspects the sudden turn at the end has something to do with a breakdown of the strict polarization between tourist and local. For in the book's last section, the author herself gazes upon the island from the point of view of an outsider, in lines that are starkly reminiscent of Walcott's in "What the Twilight Says": "Antigua is beautiful. Antigua is too beautiful. Sometimes the beauty of it seems unreal. Sometimes the beauty of it seems as if it were stage sets for a play, for no real sunset could look like that . . ." (Kincaid, 77). And we are reminded that while Kincaid speaks out righteously *for* that small place, as an intellectual and an expatriate she is not in any simple way *of* it and she too is implicated in bewildering ways in the circulation of representation around the consumption of space (you will find a brief analysis of *A Small Place*, for instance, in the *1994 Caribbean Islands Handbook*, previously cited, in the chapter devoted to Antigua, in a subsection devoted to "The Economy," wedged between "Government" and "Flora and Fauna").

A desire like Kincaid's to address the tourist, to show him/her a truth, also animates *Omeros*, but the representation of bare human beings doesn't appear as a possibility for the poem even in Walcott's most hyperbolic disavowal, when toward the end of *Omeros* he seems to recant the poem's entire project: "there was no real need for the historian's remorse / nor for literature's. Why not see Helen // as the sun saw her, with no Homeric shadow, / swinging her plastic sandals on that beach alone, / as fresh as the sea-wind? / Why make the smoke a door?" (*Omeros*, 271). If it were a matter of viewing Helen from the sun's extraterrestrial and Archimedean objectivity then surely there would be no need for the historian's metaphors or the poet's fabulations, but as we well know beside these two authorial figures on that beach sits an anonymous tourist, and behind him a numberless

crowd of seasonal invaders. When subjects are to such an extent determined by space it is hard to imagine where the encounter between human
and human could take *place*. Even Walcott/narrator's rhetorical question
participates in the particular pedagogy he develops in *Omeros*, for the local
beauty herself is highly mediated, negatively, by the Omeric similitudes.
Walcott's pedagogy of poetic space aims to cultivate poetry's "differential
tendency" in order to make the St. Lucian landscape possible by giving it,
as it were, the verbal opacity of a Homeric shadow. While this pedagogy is
directed toward a certain kind of subject or nonsubject (the potential tourist and also the potential local), its object is not a body but a place.

   Omeros is an aesthetic "appropriation of space." The phrase is Lefebvre's and he develops it in a context unrelated to his remarks on tourism's space of consumption, but it seems relevant to an understanding of
that space from the point of view of those who inhabit it and work in it.
Lefebvre's sense of appropriated space is modified from Marx's notion of
appropriation, which signifies the elemental human domination of nature
through labor:

> It may be said of a natural space modified in order to serve the needs and pos-
> sibilities of a group that it has been appropriated by that group. Property in the
> sense of possession is at best a necessary precondition, and most often merely an
> epiphenomenon, of 'appropriative' activity, the highest expression of which is the
> work of art. An appropriated space *resembles* a work of art, which is not to say that
> it is in any sense an *imitation* of a work of art. Often such a space is a structure—a
> monument or building—but this is not always the case: a site, a square or a street
> may also be legitimately described as an appropriated space. (Lefebvre, 165)

   If the "highest expression" of appropriative activity is the work of art
then clearly the needs that appropriated space serves extend to symbolic as
well as material functions. The monument, Lefebvre's primary example,
is a structure that has both a practical function and a symbolic function
since it commemorates an event or an idea that unifies a group. An appropriated space resembles a work of art presumably in the sense that it
is *created* and that the meaning of the modification it creates inheres in
artifice. *Omeros* is, to reverse Lefebvre's formulation, *a work of art that resembles an appropriated space*. Colonialism failed, in Walcott's view, to appropriate St. Lucian space, but tourism imposes its constructions on the
landscape and marks the place for a marketable local specificity; it does not
modify space in order to *appropriate* it but in order to consume it. To sell
enjoyment in a place requires enhancing local specificity, and in that sense,

tourism appropriates a place as itself, as what is most proper to it. The work of art, in this circumstance, cannot function like a monument or a building since anything proper to the place can be assimilated seamlessly into tourist consumption, but it can, as *Omeros* does, alter a place through resemblance. *Omeros* is an appropriation of space that takes the form of a poetic dissimilation. Omeric metaphor draws a resemblance that is precisely *not* proper to the thing compared performing a gesture of appropriation that runs counter to the logic of "property in the sense of possession." Thus, similitude functions within the poem like ruins in a landscape; it marks through inequivalent resemblance the trace of an impossible or broken appropriation.

Like Kincaid's, Walcott's pedagogical project in *Omeros* involves a lesson in history, but the function of that history is not, ultimately, to restore a subject capable of dialectical recognition. Even as the poem markedly reverses Walcott's earlier disavowal of history, it does not do so in order to reveal and value alternative forms of a collective continuity in time for the extensive historical meditations all end in a return to place. In the middle books of *Omeros* we follow Achille on a dream or sunstroke-induced journey to Africa in the time of slavery—Plunkett through his research into St. Lucia's colonial history, Walcott/narrator's through the great capitals of the former empires as well as to the United States in the midst of the genocide of Native Americans, Ma Kilman's through the back hills of the island in search of the medicinal herb transplanted from Africa that will heal the wound of slavery on Philoctete's shin. But in the end most of these historical journeys, except for Ma Kilman's, change little in the daily life of the island except insofar as they have exorcised or appeased the desires and the longing for the elsewhere that prompted them in the first place.

After the Omeric exorcism, in the last book of *Omeros*, the poet takes leave of the poem. It is on the first few readings a notably repetitive ending. Chapter by chapter, in each subsection Walcott/narrator revisits a character or an aspect of *Omeros*, adjusting his lens from a wide to a narrow angle and allowing us to see again the whole panoply of the narrative. We find little changed since the poem's beginning (and we remember that it began at the end). Achille, who has given up on finding new fishing grounds away from tourist development, chafes at becoming part of a quaint local scene, rages at the tourists, and "howls at their clacking cameras" (*Omeros*, 288). Plunkett converses with his dead wife through the medium of the obeah woman,

Ma Kilman, and slowly overcomes his grief along with his wounded historian's obsession. In one section we are even given the tourist's isle-view:
"[The village's] life adjusted to the lenses of // cameras that, perniciously
elegiac, / took shots of passing things, [it] imitated the hotel brochure //
with photogenic poverty, with atmosphere" (*Omeros*, 311). And this is followed by a summary of the events narrated in *Omeros* as they are reproduced
in the tourist's snapshots: Philoctete showing his shin, Hector's grave piled
with shells, the rest stop at Ma Kilman's joint, the *No Pain Café*, the visit
to the local museum where they learn of the battle that earned St. Lucia
the name "Helen of the West Indies." In the wake of the tourist section,
we are not surprised, perhaps, to find a meditation on the poem's Omeric
conceit ("These Helens are different creatures, // one marble, one ebony"),
this time delivered in a prosopopoeic address voiced by a lizard, the emblem
of St. Lucia's aboriginal past, excoriating the poet one last time "to make
all those parallels pointless." There is a final scene for Seven Seas and Ma
Kilman chatting in the rum shop, interrupted by pregnant Helen coming
in to buy a tub of margarine. All of this leads up to the very last leave-taking
in the poem's final chapter.

   This epilogue is divided into three sections. The first is a measured and
almost formal bardic valediction, which looks ahead beyond the poet's own
funeral ("let the deep hymn // of the Caribbean continue my epilogue; /
may waves remove their shawls as my mourners walk home" *Omeros*, 321).
The second begins by addressing the reader directly, "You can see Helen
at the Halcyon, She is dressed / in the national costume: white, low-cut
bodice, . . . // . . . you might recall that battle / for which they named
an island or the heaving wreck / of the *Ville de Paris* in her foam-frilled
bodice, // or just think, "What a fine local woman!" (*Omeros*, 322). If the
poem was set off by an anonymous tourist's exclamation at the sight of a
local beauty ("Who the hell is that?"), here we find a final and quite astonishing reply from a convivial author, gracious host, or precursor who
addresses his readers as tourists and offers us explicit directions on where to
find the "local wonder" around whom he has woven the last 322 pages of
verse. No longer sharply distinguished by our very reading from the crass
tourist at the beach, we have merged with him/her. Walcott leaves little
doubt about the minimal differentiation between tourist and reader when
he makes no distinction between the addressees directed to local sites in
this passage and the intimate "phantom hearers" addressed on the next

page where he provides in his own voice the very last summary of *Omeros*, in which the Omeric conceit becomes an elaborate metaphor for the process of writing itself:

> But the name of Helen had gripped my wrist in its vise
>
> to plunge it into the foaming page. For three years,
> phantom hearer, I kept wandering to a voice
> hoarse as a winter's echo in the throat of a vase!
>
> Like Philoctete's wound, this language carries its cure,
> its radiant affliction; reluctantly now,
> like Achille's, my craft slips the chain of its anchor
> —(*Omeros*, 232)

What is so remarkable about Walcott's concluding identification of reader and tourist is that it so explicitly foreswears the neutral cultural space tacitly offered by a long poem that is in so many ways a monumental achievement on the model of high-cultural tradition. The poem does not attempt to redeem the brutality of history or to redress the corrupted and commodified social relations that frame its cross-cultural endeavor or to carve out a privileged transcendence for the aesthetic. In a sense, the poem marks out the opposite trajectory for its readers from the one Kincaid attempts: instead of developing from tourists into just human beings we move from (high) cultural subjects to tourists. At the end of the poem the readers are called forth in a spatial rather than a historical relation to St. Lucia. The "radiant affliction" of Walcott's language (and Philoctete's wound) that bears its own "cure" speaks at once for the injury of colonial history and the poetic appropriation of commodified space accomplished in *Omeros* itself.

One must ask why the poem ends with an almost obsessive repetition of its plot and its paradoxical Omeric conceit. It is, I propose, a pedagogical repetition whose aim is the opposite of the schoolmaster's in *Another Life* ("Boy! Name the great harbours of the world!"), where the schoolboy is called upon to reproduce the history lesson from memory. These repetitions are instructions to the tourist-reader for a haunted or partial forgetting. It is the pedagogy of Omeric similitude in which the *mimema* or double stands by itself, half of a mimesis whose other half is not the original but a contingency wrought from accident so that it gives us precisely nothing to remember. The test comes in the very last section of *Omeros*, its final two pages. *Omeros* leaves us with Achille on the beach gutting his day's catch. The first part of the passage is dense with metaphors ("scales of snappers faded like sunset," "unstitched the entrails," "hands gloved in blood"), not one of them drawn from the poem's Omeric vocabulary though the action is figured as a "slaughter." The last three stanzas, more closely focalized on Achilles, are much plainer, with one metaphor each, so that one has the sense of a progression into a more elemental simplicity, a movement underscored by the poem's ending in a sequence of minimal declarative sentences:

> He scraped dry scales off his hands. He liked the odours
>
> of the sea in him. Night was fanning its coalpot
> from one catching star. The No Pain lit its doors
> in the village. Achille put the wedge of dolphin
>
> that he'd saved for Helen in Hector's tin.
> A full moon shone like a slice of raw onion.
> When he left the beach the sea was still going on.

On a first reading, one feels Omeros and his army of metaphors has vanished without a trace and that the end of *Omeros* is to read the names Achille, Hector, and Helen without his shadow, exactly as they are. The immense artifice of the poem disappears so that we may see these characters as the moon does. But if this is the case, it would be difficult to distinguish *Omeros*' final scene from the ultimate fantasy of touristic voyeurism: to see *them* exactly as they would be in the tourist's absence, to confirm the very platitude promised in the brochure. A single letter disturbs this pictorial fantasy, like the ruin of a Homeric shadow. For the name Achille occurs twice in the middle of this section with an "s" as "Achilles." The first time in a sentence that provokes the Omeric mirage since it could apply equally to the Homeric hero in the midst of his staggering death-dealing blows in *Iliad* XX–XXI and to the St. Lucian fisherman contemplating his catch: "A triumphant Achilles // his hands gloved in blood" (324). "Achilles" with an "s" occurs a second time in a context more proper to Achille, though the offhand reference to the proverbial heel might make us look twice: "In the standpipe's sandy trough aching Achilles / washed sand from his heels." At the beginning and the end of the section, Achille is just Achille. The differential in the appearance and disappearance of the "s" lies somewhere between the minimal repetition of Helen and the maximal appropriation of the alternate spelling of Omeros. It is a cross-linguistic effect that mines St. Lucia's transfer from England to France throughout its colonial history, for the "s" only makes an oral difference in English since it wouldn't be pronounced in French, but the name's spelling without an "s" is in fact the accepted spelling of this once not uncommon French proper name. We have noted earlier in passing Walcott's use of the alternative spelling to draw a subtle distinction between the St. Lucian fisherman and his Homeric namesake. In *Omeros*' final pages, however, this minimal differentiation works like a cross-linguistic, postcolonial *différance*, a slippage that is imperceptible unless one is attuned to the right medium but that nonetheless makes all the difference in the world. It introduces a comparative opacity, the shadow of the disavowed possibility of Achille(s)' heroic magnitude and transiently suggests the full sense in which the poem has elaborated the way Achille is like Achilles and *not* like Achilles. The doubletake this lexical variance induces seems to me to endow this character and this scene with a very particularly memorable forgettability. The poem does not leave us with Achille in some unencumbered, original condition, apprehensible in his totality as "just a human being," for this would still make him indistinguishable from a local "type," a human figure of a piece with a landscape and interchangeable with it, and so ultimately forgettable like all vacations. Achille instead emerges here, to borrow Caillois's words, "similar, not similar to something, but just *similar*."[65]

Envoi

It is no doubt inevitable, especially after the Nobel Prize, that tourists should now travel to St. Lucia packing *Omeros* as guide. A full-page story in the *LA Times* travel section,[66] written by a professor of classics, recounts such a visit and oddly functions as publicity for the island and the poem at once. Predictably, the poem is converted for the tourist into a kind of catalogue of sites so that in addition to the usual destinations marked in run-of-the-mill guidebooks, this writer, John B. Van Sickle, seeks out the lighthouse that figures in the poem, the docking place of cruise ships where Walcott/narrator encountered the ghost of his own father, the top of the Morne where the Plunketts lived, etc. There are many ironies to what Van Sickle calls his "Walcott heritage tour," not the least of which is what it might mean to "recognize" a landmark from a poem or what sense exactly "heritage" has for a poem not quite eight years old built on an auto-effacing allusion to an oral poet who may or may not have existed nearly three thousand years ago at the other end of the earth. What drew my eye, however, is a picture of "Hector's Place," an eatery serving beer and fried fish. It's a perfectly ordinary place that figures as a stop on Van Sickle's itinerary for no other reason than the establishment's name itself.[67] Hector's place stands out as an Omeric incommensurability in this otherwise ordinary travel article, a name that subsists as a fragment of epic memory in the guide book just long enough for a differential distance to appear and disappear like a mirage.

The Gift of Belittling All Things: Catastrophic Miniaturization in Aimé Césaire and Simone Schwarz-Bart

—Et dites-moi encore, que peut bien faire une Bête aussi puissante
à la Guadeloupe, une motte de terre, une miette qui ne figurait
même pas sur la carte du monde a l'école de la Ramée? Et surtout:
Qu'avait-elle à faire de Fond-Zombi, notre petit Fond-Zombi de trois
pieds six pouces, qui n'était même pas connu de toutes les bonnes
gens de Guadeloupe? . . . vrai, tout cela est-il bien raisonnable? . . .
— . . . voici l'envers de ta question: le crâne de l'homme est a peine
plus gros qu'un noix de coco et ne contient-il pas des mondes, lui
aussi?
[—And tell me again, what could such a powerful Beast be doing
here in Guadeloupe, a clod of earth, a crumb that doesn't even figure
on the map of the world at La Ramée school? And especially: What
did she have to do with Fond-Zombi, our little Fond-Zombi three
feet and two thumbs long, which isn't even known to the good
people of Guadeloupe? . . . Seriously, is all this quite reasonable?
—here's your question turned inside out: the skull of man is barely
bigger than a coconut and doesn't it too contain worlds?]
—Simone Schwarz-Bart, *Ti Jean L'horizon*, 117

It is a commonplace to remark on the disproportion between the
size of the "vielles colonies" in the Antilles and the extraordinary wealth
they produced for France through the eighteenth century. Saint Domingue
alone, at 10,714 square miles (somewhat smaller than Rhode Island) and
occupying only a third of the island of Hispaniola, became by 1789 France's
most lucrative colony, accounting for up to 40 percent of the metropole's

foreign trade. Voltaire writes in 1772: "La petite île de la Martinique, la Guadeloupe, que les Français cultivèrent en 1735, fournirent les mêmes denrées que Saint Domingue. Ce sont des points sur la carte, et des événements qui se perdent dans l'histoire de l'univers; mais enfin ces pays, qu'on peut à peine appercevoir sur une mappemonde, produisirent en France une circulation annuelle d'environ soixante millions de marchandises. Ce commerce . . . n'est pas sans doute un vrai bien; mais les hommes s'étant fait des nécessités nouvelles, il empêche que la France n'achète chèrement de l'étranger un superflu devenu nécessaire. [The little island of Martinique, of Guadeloupe, which the French cultivated in 1735, furnished the same commodities as Saint Domingue. These are dots on the map and events lost in the history of the universe, but finally these countries that one can barely discern on a world map produced for France an annual circulation of around sixty million in merchandise. This commerce . . . is no doubt not a real good; but, men having created new necessities for themselves, it prevents France from having to purchase from foreigners a superfluity become necessary.] [1] Slave labor, intensive agriculture, the surge in European sugar consumption over the eighteenth century, and the prestidigitations of mercantilism account for this particular disproportion, even as capitalism's evolution toward other kinds of production and other commodities have in the meantime reversed the scale, reducing the Antilles to poverty and geopolitical insignificance. Haiti, one hardly needs reminding, is now the poorest country in the Western hemisphere; since the mid-twentieth century, Martinique and Guadeloupe subsist on subventions as Overseas Departments and therefore dependencies of France, with a local production so minimal that, by some counts, Martinique, for instance, possesses only enough food *in situ* to survive for a week, should it be severed from French imports. Some two hundred years after Voltaire's remark, well after the definitive abolition of slavery and after Martinique and Guadeloupe's change of status from French colonies to French *départements d'outre mer*, their smallness alone contributes to a particular tropology of colonial denigration, as instanced in an oft-repeated cartographic insult attributed to Charles de Gaulle on the occasion of a visit to Martinique in 1964: "Entre l'Europe et l'Amérique, je ne vois que des poussières." [Between Europe and America I see only specks of dust.] [2] Proposed from an Archimedean geographical perspective, the French president's statement takes the form of an apparently objective comparison based on relative size, but its effect is to negate the islands by reducing them to the sheer inconsequence of dust. Smallness here figures inferiority as an insignificance verging on immateriality.

Scale as a figure and a problem takes a prominent place in the anti-colonial literature of the Antilles, by which I mean here Martinique and Guadeloupe, and distinguishes that literature's geographical element, an element postcolonial critics have identified as a central feature of anticolonial writing. Imperialism's "geographic violence," Edward Said argues, provokes anticolonial literatures to the task of recovering the land in imagination as both prelude and postlude to regaining political control.[3] This is a struggle over representation wherein the hegemony of a denigrating and exoticist colonial discourse about a colonized place is countered and corrected by an opposing discourse articulated from the perspective of its "native" inhabitants. Chinua Achebe's *Things Fall Apart*, for instance, offers a representation of colonial Africa deliberately posed against imperial representations of Africa and Africans, particularly those of Joyce Cary's *Mister Johnson* and Joseph Conrad's *Heart of Darkness*.[4] The postcolonial critic, in a now familiar response to the inaugural challenge of Said's *Orientalism*, produces a catalogue or a schema of the representation of a colonized place or region in colonial discourse and tracks the counterrepresentation in the anticolonial or postcolonial text. The dyadic or dialectical structure of writing against or writing back puts into play a claim of equivalence grounded on a reality occluded in the misrepresentations of colonial discourse and carries with it, though often implicitly or at the level of desire, the distinct telos of parity.

From its beginnings in Césaire's *Notebook of a Return to the Native Land* (1939), the anticolonial literature of the Antilles articulates its particular colonial condition as precisely the *lack* of the primary ground for a counterdiscourse, namely a rooted, "native" claim to representation. The islands' indigenous people were annihilated early in the process of colonial exploitation, and the remaining inhabitants, having arrived under extreme coercion (slavery and indenture), can lay no precolonial cultural claim to the place. The absence of what Glissant calls an "arrière-pays culturel" or "cultural hinterland" and the problems this presents for grounding an anticolonial collectivity are further exacerbated by the "postcolonial" political fate of the islands that departed from the norm for decolonization of national independence and took the form instead of assimilation to the metropole as overseas departments. A space that is not possessed, indeed a nonplace, provides no given position from which to meet the colonizer's gaze and constitute a counterdiscourse. For this reason, the geographical impulse of anticolonial literature for the Antilles, beginning with Césaire, is primarily ontological rather than discursive; that is, it attempts to assert a claim of existence from within the negation of colonial discourse rather than establishing a counterdiscourse from outside of it (however tenuous and problematic the claims to such an outside may be). In this regard, it is significant that this literature begins under the sign of *poiesis* with an outsized, explosive poem rather than under the sign of *mimesis* with a realist narrative. Postcolonial criticism has tended overwhelmingly to privilege a power/knowledge matrix as the ground of its analysis and epistemology as the object of its critique and therefore has been less attentive to the ontological dimensions of anticolonial writing, by which I understand here not an assertion of identity but a claim of existence.

What are the ramifications of scale for the logic of colonial comparison in its geographical figuration? I propose the figure of catastrophic miniaturization as a starting point. Exemplified in the distant gaze of the colonizing "other" upon the islands, miniaturization is catastrophic when the reduction in scale is not reversible, a condition that obtains when there is no given countervailing perspective. Smallness is then fixed as signifying an irrefutable stigma. The adjective "catastrophic" suggests itself for two reasons. First because it associates reduction in size with the temporal configuration of a single sudden change, and second because catastrophe, in its Greek tragic sense, results specifically in *irreparable* loss. Though overlayed on the earlier extermination of the indigenous inhabitants, the originary catastrophe for the Antilles is slavery, the violent uprooting from the native land, and the resulting total dispossession. From the perspective of those transborded to the Antilles, cartographic belittling like De Gaulle's or Voltaire's where insignificance verges on immateriality finds a reference in the negation of slavery. In this context, the figurative step from belittling to nonexistence is almost inappreciable. "Antilleans have no proper value," writes Frantz Fanon in *Peau noire, masques blacs* [*Black Skin, White Masks*]; "they are always tributary to the appearance of the 'Other.'"[5] For the *évolué* or educated black Antillean, the reduction of racialization is unmitigated because it has no exit, no potential exterior or alternative provided by a separate, anterior cultural or psycho-social value. The black man, Fanon argues, lacks "ontological resistance in the eyes of the white man" (Fanon, 108). This lack of ontological resistance means also that smallness cannot easily figure an enclosed interiority—whether psychic or domestic—because it derives comparatively from an external gaze.

In the celebrated chapter entitled "L'Expérience vécue du noir" [The Lived Experience of the Black (man)] in *Black Skin White Masks,* Fanon attempts an elaboration of the phenomenology of race and presents us with a description of the racialized body as one incapable of orienting itself in the world. This text clarifies precisely how the problem of scale is linked to a crisis of subjectivity. The black man's lack of "ontological resistance" manifests itself in the dialectical or intersubjective encounter with the other that ought to constitutes a subject, but in which the black man is instead constituted as object, because the white other always receives him first as black, that is, as some predetermined thing. Consequently, for the black man the corporal schema whose given unity constitutes the phenomenological body (that body capable of perception, of worlding) "crumble[s], ceding its place to a racial epidermic schema" (Fanon, 110).[6] As a black man, Fanon writes of himself: "Je suis sur-déterminé de l'extérieur. Je ne suis pas l'esclave de l'idée que les autres ont de moi, mais de mon apparaître." [I am over-determined from the outside. I am not the slave of the "idea" that others have of me, but of my mode of appearance] (Fanon, 113). Particularly illuminating in this formulation is the distinction between the determinations of discourse (imposed "ideas") and their ontological and phenomenological effect; that is, between the cognitive understanding of racist discourse and the experience of racism. A preexisting racial typology intervenes before the body can establish its primary orientation as a being in space:

> Où me situez? Ou, si vous préférez, où me fourrer?
> —Martinicais, originaire de "nos" vielles colonies.
> Où me cacher?
> —Regarde le nègre! . . . Maman, un nègre! . . . Chut! Il va se
>   fâcher . . . Ne faites pas attention, monsieur, il ne sait pas que
>   vous êtes aussi civilisé que nous . . .
> Mon corps me revenait étalé, disjoint, rétamé, tout endeuillé dans ce
>   jour blanc d'hiver. Le nègre est une bête, le nègre est mauvais, le
>   nègre est méchant, le nègre est laid [. . .]
> Alentour le Blanc, en haut le ciel s'arrache le nombril, la terre crisse
>   sous mes pieds et un chant blanc, blanc. Toute cette blancheur
>   qui me calcine . . .

> [Where to situate myself? Or, if you prefer, where to stuff myself?
> —Martinican, originating from "our" old colonies.
> Where to hide myself?

—Look at the negro! . . . Mama, a negro! Shush!—he'll get
angry . . . Pay no attention, sir; he doesn't know you are as
civilized as we are . . .

My body returned to me sprawled, disjointed, refracted, clothed in
mourning this white day of winter. The negro is an animal, the
negro is bad, the negro is mean, the negro is ugly [. . .]

All around, Whites, above the sky tears out its navel, the earth grates
under my feet and a white, white song. All this whiteness that
chars me . . .]

—(Fanon, 111–112)

Fanon here describes, or rhetorically performs the disarticulation of the racialized body as its mode of appearance fixes or "confines and shrinks" it into preexistent categories. The lack of ontological resistance translates into a catastrophic spatial dislocation in which, along with the logical measures of syntax, the first person subject disappears, persisting between earth and sky only as a pair of feet in a stultifying landscape painted shut with racialized metaphors. All that remains of the phenomenological body as a vehicle of experience and movement toward the world is the cloak of mourning. The process of reduction, of shrinking to type, paradoxically blows all proportion apart.

The attempt to think colonial and postcolonial comparison through the spatial optic of scale fundamentally alters the terms of comparison because similarity or resemblance are not centrally in play. The principal issue here is not a direct comparison of one culture to another or the analysis of similarities and differences among variously defined cultural contents. It involves, rather, the response in a set of Antillean texts to a schema of inferiorization and, correlatively, the articulation of the grounds for a collective response to it. The tropology of scale mobilizes comparison in terms of proportion, particularly the dialectic of the small and the large. And the interpretation or evaluation of proportion rests on a system of equivalence anchored to some posited standard of measure that defines a given perspective. The notion of scale entails a more immediate or literal sense of perspective than that of the subject's abstract capacity for judgment and for formulating an opinion or a point of view, for both the perception and the representation of scale crucially involve the body. It is through the body that a subject establishes spatial relations and proportionality. Cultural, social, and economic determinations inflect the body and define it, but it is also the site and the sign of lived experience. Beginning with an analysis of the geographical dimensions of Aimé Césaire's *Notebook of a Return to the Native Land,* this chapter will trace the transmutations of catastrophic miniaturization in the subsequent generation of Antillean writers through a consideration of two novels by Simone Schwarz-Bart. The aim here is not to produce a comprehensive literary genealogy of this figure so much as to explore some of its ramifications across time. Because perspective and the body are crucial to the spatial comparison of scale, the question of gender will occupy a fair part of this analysis, if obliquely. Schwarz-Bart's novels, taken together, can be read, I propose, as a com-parison or co-appearance of an imagined Antillean collectivity fissured along gendered lines.

Theorists of the miniature in European literature draw a sharp dividing line between miniaturization and belittling. Susan Stewart, for instance, in her study *On Longing: Narratives of the Miniature, the Gigantic, the Souvenir, the Collection,* insists that "a reduction in dimensions does not produce a corresponding reduction in significance."[7] Miniaturization functions as an expression of interiority, a form for possessing the world and condensing values through imagination. "Smallness," writes Gaston Bachelard in his seminal work, *The Poetics of Space,* "is not ridiculous, but wonderful."[8] Stewart specifies that in order to avert the risk of the grotesque or of mockery, the miniature must meet a set of conditions. First it must establish an equivalence correlated to another scale. One might think of Ezra Pound's line from Canto LXXXI, "the ant's a centaur in his dragon world," as an example, for to merely call the ant a centaur would be to mock his diminutive size by comparison, whereas to call him a centaur in his dragon world encloses him in the heroism of a scale defined around his own size and set off through a comparison of equivalence to the centaur in the scale of the human world. Bachelard offers the important qualification that this equivalence is not absolutely relative and therefore convertible across scales. Convertibility characterizes the rationalized space of the geometrician in which scale is neutral and there is no operative difference between the large and the small. A map drawn to various scales represents exactly the same space, just as a scale model is an exact equivalent to the full-sized object. "Of course, we should lose all sense of real values," writes Bachelard, "if we interpreted miniatures from the standpoint of the simple relativism of large and small. A bit of moss may well be a pine, but a pine will never be a bit of moss. The imagination does not function with the same conviction in both directions" (Bachelard, 163). Similarly, the ant in Pound's comparison is not interchangeable with the centaur, but rather correlated with it in a structure that establishes the ant in its separate world.

Second, correlative to this equivalence, the miniature must be delimited by boundaries to prevent direct contamination with another scale. This is why, Stewart remarks, a miniature world is often placed on an island, as in the case of Swift's Lilliput. These conditions are fundamental for the miniature to function as a microcosmic model; its signifying properties rest on the combination of an enclosed autonomy with a particular form of transcendence or generalizability, just as its ontological properties of concentrating and centering the subject's imagination require the sense of wonder at what Bachelard calls the "plenitude of smallness" (Bachelard, 163). For both Bachelard and Stewart, this plenitude assumes the consciousness of a distinct perceiving subject, one that Stewart specifically limits to a range of subjectivity associated with modern bourgeois experience.

Belittling inverts all these conditions, beginning with the first one, for here reduction in scale corresponds exactly to a reduction in significance. In derision or revilement, smallness is always measured comparatively as lesser: lesser in value, lesser in significance, lesser in power. Since its object is diminishment, belittling imposes a single scale and necessarily denies smallness its own proportions, locking it into inferiority. Smallness thus indicates lack not plenitude. When miniaturization belittles it can be difficult, if not impossible, to distinguish between a diminutive of endearment and a diminutive of inferiority. Stewart remarks that diminutives of endearment are "especially reserved for children, pets, servants, and women" (Stewart, 124); that is to say, for beings belonging to the intimate realm of the domestic and defined by various kinds of lack with respect to the single adult (white) male standard of full humanity. As Ashis Nandy has shown, colonial discourse deployed many of these positions, particularly the child, the female, the servile, in its elaborate tropology of the inferiority of the colonized.[9] The colonial context, indeed, is one in which endearment and inferiority cannot easily be distinguished and one might say that the discourse of exoticism in most of its manifestations turns on a combination of the two into an endearing inferiority. The cliché of the Antilles as paradisiacal islands peopled with welcoming, gaily clad mulatta beauties, the *doudous*, would be an example of this as would an expression like "petit nègre," "little Negro-speak" for Creole. The smallness of the endearing diminutive always implies the measure of another scale, just as its separateness implies that the inferiority is fixed, unbridgeable. Miniaturization as endearing inferiority is the obverse of what Bachelard has in mind when he writes: "Je suis plus à mon aise dans les mondes de la miniature. Ce sont pour moi des mondes dominés. En les vivant je sens partir de mon être rêvant des ondes mondificatrice." [I feel more comfortable in miniature worlds, which, for me, are dominated worlds. And when I live them I feel waves of worldification emanating from my dreaming self.] [10] The belittling diminution at work in actual colonial domination (as opposed to Bachelard's imaginary domination of the subject) in the discourse of exoticism, on the contrary, seals the dominated space off from the generality of worlding.

The initial topographical movement of Aimé Césaire's *Notebook of a Return to the Native Land* turns on a sharp distinction between the diminutive of endearment and the diminutive of inferiority. The poem opens with a long and relentlessly disparaging account of Martinique, initially set up to counter colonial exoticist clichés of the tropical paradise briefly alluded to in the poem's first paragraph. From the very first lines about them, the islands are presented in language that is the precise opposite of the quaintness and sentimentality of exoticism's endearing inferiority; this is the language of affliction, starvation, disease, contagion, addiction, calamity, and disgust:

Au bout du petit matin bourgeonnant d'anses frêles, les Antilles qui on faim, les Antilles grêlées de petite vérole, les Antilles dynamitées d'alcool, échouées dans la boue de cette baie, dans la poussière de cette ville sinistrement échouées.

[*At the end of morning's small hours, burgeoning with feeble coves, the Antilles of hunger, the Antilles pitted with smallpox, dynamited with alcohol, wrecked in the mud of this bay, in the dust of this city sinisterly wrecked.*] [11]

Césaire turns the endearing inferiority of exoticism to the catastrophic miniaturization of misery and devastation. The landscape of the islands, familiar to us perhaps from woodcuts and photographs of graceful coves and picturesque towns overhanging bright turquoise bays, is rendered here as shipwrecked [*échoués*] in the mud, disposed in space by catastrophic accident not by the harmony of preserved nature. We are as far here as possible from the calm and alluring picture of order and pleasure that entices the Western traveler to exotic lands, such as the lulling refrain from Baudelaire's "Invitation au voyage:" "Là, tout n'est qu'ordre et beauté / Luxe, calme et volupté." [There all is but order and beauty / Luxury, calm and delectation.] The first quarter or so of the *Notebook* is a ferocious and hyperbolic demystification that reveals the abject poverty, exploitation, and powerlessness underlying this idyllic picture, conditions that are, indeed, in complete "rupture with flora and fauna." The overarching tropes in this passage are of prostration and diminution. The island and its capital city are heaped with adjectives of deflation, "prostrate, inert, sprawled flat;" constraint: "embarrassed, abridged, reduced, in breach of fauna and flora;" (Césaire, 34–35) nouns for baseness and ignominy of all kinds: "The prostitutions, the hypocrisies, the lubricities, the treasons, the lies, the frauds, the concussions—[. . .] the greeds, the hysterias, the perversions, the clownings of poverty" (Césaire, 36–37); and everywhere disease and degeneration: "The cripplings, the itchings, the hives, the tepid hammocks of degeneracy. Right here the parade of laughable and scrofulous buboes, the forced feedings of very strange microbes, the poisons without known alexins, the sanies of really ancient sores, the unforeseeable fermentations of putrescible species" (Césaire, 38–39). The adjective small, "petit," is repeated regularly throughout the poem almost always as a pejorative indicating spatial confinement, constraint, and the infinite pettiness of insignificance. The paradoxical effect of this expansive, indeed excessive, evocation of smallness is that the very force of hyperbole aggrandizes it. The inflations of Césaire's language here infuse the diminution of the Antilles with the breadth of catastrophe and thus produce a very precise articulation of a paradox at the heart of colonial inferiorization; namely, the enormity of the ontological calamity that underlies its diminutions. Smallness becomes "dazzling" [*éclatante*]:

De nouveau cette vie clopinante devant moi, non pas cette vie, cette mort, cette mort sans sens ni piété, cette mort où la grandeur piteusement échoue, l'éclatante petitesse de cette mort, cette mort qui clopine de petitesses en petitesses; ces pelletées de petites avidités sur le conquistador; ces pelletées de petits larbins sur le grand sauvage, ces pelletées de petites âmes sur le Caraïbe aux trois âmes.

[*Again this limping life before me, no, not this life, this death, this death without sense or piety, this death where greatness pitifully runs aground, the dazzling smallness of this death; this death that limps from smallness to smallness; the heaps of little avidities on the conquistador, heaps of little servilities on the great savage, these heaps of little souls on the three-souled Carib.*] (Césaire, 44)

Hyperbole alone carries this passage far beyond its original negation of exoticist discourse and it takes on its own generic, (anti)foundational force, inaugurating the poem's geographical dimension with the evocation of a reviled native land, an extreme *misotopia* or *topophobia*, to offer an awkward coinage as an antonym to *topophilia* or loved space, that space that, for Bachelard, provides an ontological dwelling for the imagination.[12] One hesitates on the terms that are both inadequate, for the native land in the *Notebook* is not hated or feared as such but reproved as unlivable because it bears its misery without protest. There is a long and august poetic tradition of eulogy or panegyric that extols native lands and home cities, and while there are certainly poems that evoke stultifying or corrupt cities (William Blake's "London" comes to mind as well as T. S. Eliot's "the Waste Land" and several poems of Baudelaire), there is little that compares with Césaire's hyperbolic inversion of the genre here. Unlike the poetic images of pristine natural and built forms that Bachelard takes up in his analysis, the space of Martinique as rendered in catastrophic miniaturization—that is, in the conditions underlying flora and fauna—is already entirely dominated by forces external to the speaker, not only by oppressive social and economic conditions but also by a repressed history of extraordinary violence and dispossession. The speaker finds no dwelling in this place—the first person pronoun as subject or object (along with active verbs) is extraordinarily scant throughout, even in the explicitly autobiographical passages. The crucial phenomenological dimension of a poetics of space—the conditions necessary for the constitution of a unified dreaming and speaking subject—is lacking and with it any stable sense of perspective and scale. This voice is dislocated, disembodied. What obtains through the poetics of revilement is the precise delimitation of a *non*-subject, for revilement concentrates the subject in the negative, through revolt.

The *Notebook*'s initial gesture of demystifying endearing inferiority by drawing out its catastrophic dimensions blasts smallness out of all proportion. But there is a consequent reversal, for if the native land catastrophically repels and revolts the speaker, it propels him outward to the larger world, whose immensity welcomes him into an intimate exaltation. It is, paradoxically, immensity, not smallness, that harbors this voice. The speaker moves first to the metropole where he discovers the cosmopolitan solidarity of oppression ("I would be a jew-man / a Kaffir-man / a Hindu-man-from-Calcutta. a Harlem-man-who-doesn't-vote" [*Notebook*, 42]) and to the motherland, unnamed as Africa, that land "a thousand times more native," even as his language, with the sudden eruption of a gigantic, heroically redemptive first person singular, moves from exaggerated smallness to great immensity: "I would rediscover the secret of great communications and great combustions . . . I would have words vast enough to contain you earth . . ." (Césaire, 44–46). A short passage marks the shift in the speaker's perspective from planing over the topography of the island to articulating a diasporan geography:

—Encore une objection! une seule, mais de grâce une seule: je n'ai pas le droit de calculer la vie à mon empan fuligineux; de me réduire à ce petit rien ellipsoïdal qui tremble à quatre doigts au-dessus de la ligne, moi homme, d'ainsi boulverser la création, que je me comprenne entre latitude et longitude.

[—*One more objection! one only, but please just one! I do not have the right to calculate life by my soot-colored finger span; to reduce myself to this little ellipsoidal nothing trembling four fingers above the line, me a man, to thus overturn creation, that I should contain and comprehend myself between latitude and longitude!*] (*Notebook*, 44)

What is striking here is the congruence between abstract cartographic measures and measures of the body. The "empan," the span between the thumb and little finger of the outstretched hand, a basic and archaic standard of measurement, here colored and therefore racialized (obliquely, through an arcane technical term, "fuligineux," that requires a detour through the dictionary for all but specialists), is positioned as a measure to calculate life. In the next lines, the speaker's perspective on the island has drastically broadened as he takes up the position of gazing on a world map divided into the spatial abstractions of longitude and latitude on which the island is a tiny geometrical form, the ellipsoid (a three-dimensional ellipse), whose placement can be measured with the human hand ("four fingers above the line"). The island's smallness, hyperbolically affective in the earlier passage, now becomes rationalized or objectified on the scale of a printed map of the world. Indeed it is rationalized space's objectivity (and not subjective emplacement) that allows the speaker to proclaim his humanity and aver that he has no right to calculate life by the epidermal quality of his race, or to be contained by the strictures of his place of birth. This is a crucial declaration for the narrative and the argument of the poem, for it sets the terms for the assertion of the racialized, diasporan identification of negritude just a few lines later.

Geometries of Blood

There will be no more from me about bodies
and trajectories, sky and earth, I don't know
what it all is. They have told me, explained
to me, described to me, what it all is, what it

looks like, what it's all for, one after the other,
thousands of times, as if I understood. Who
would ever think, to hear me, that I've never
seen anything, never heard anything but their
voices? And man, the lectures they gave me on
men, before they even began trying to assimilate me to him! What I speak of, what I speak
with, all comes from them. . . . It's of me now
I must speak, even if I have to do it with their
language, it will be a start, a step towards silence
and the end of madness, the madness of having
to speak and not being able to, except of things
that don't concern me, that don't count, that I
don't believe, that they have crammed me full
of to prevent me from saying who I am, where
I am, and from doing what I have to do in the
only way that can put an end to it, from doing
what I have to do.
—Samuel Beckett, *The Unnamable*

The lack of ontological resistance as a problem of emplacement and enunciation informs the poetics of Césaire's *Notebook* in a particularly novel form. By all accounts the poem grew out of a profound crisis in which the poet encountered the fundamental inadequacy of existing poetic forms in French to what he found himself under the necessity of expressing, namely, in his words from an interview, "my belonging to the unique condition of the Negro."[13] In another interview, Césaire recounts: "At the beginning, it was necessary to break everything, create from scratch and whole cloth, an Antillean literature. This presupposed a cannibal violence."[14] The para-dox of this originality, however, is that it fashions a poetics from within the very negation (linguistic, discursive, ontological) that determines such creation impossible. In an elegant formulation, Jacques Coursil suggests we think of the speaker of the *Notebook* as the voice of Caliban.[15] There are many possible ramifications to taking Caliban's voice as a premise for reading the *Notebook* and these await a full elaboration. I invoke Caliban here in order to highlight the doubled or self-canceling nature of the poetic voice in the poem. Caliban's is a voice of revolt that lacks its own inde-pendent subject position; it is tributary to the master's voice, in Fanon's sense, and locked, one might say, in an incomplete, agonistic comparison in which the master's standards, precisely those that deem the slave without value, are undercut from within. A similar internal dynamic attends the idea of negritude itself, which, as many early critics charged, works from within the binary standards of established racial discourse but inverts their value. The *Notebook's* overarching thematic progression from the account of alienation to the assertion of revolt to the intimation of some kind of emancipation and integration is at many points interrupted by turns and counterturns in which language seems to betray the speaker and his discourse is invaded by contrary or divergent voices. Abiola Irele draws attention to the various oral dimensions of the poem and suggests we read it as a series of dramatic monologues whose sequence does not follow a linear progression but "comprises a succession of *affects* rather than episodes."[16] The sheer multiplicity of these voices complicates and indeed destabilizes interpretation of the poem, particularly because it is difficult to gauge who or what may be the agent of language's betrayal or which modulation of the voice articulates a stable truth or a reliable intention, for the speaker's truth can just as well be found in affirmation as in self-contempt. Language turns on him and he betrays himself in it, as he does, for example, when he interrupts an ecstatic, utopian litany in full flight ("et les jours sans nuisance / et les nuits sans offense / et les étoiles de confidences" [and the days without injury / and the nights without offense / and the stars of trust]).

> Mais qui tourne ma voix? qui écorche
> ma voix? Me fourrant dans la
> gorge mille crocs de bambou. Mille
> pieux d'oursin. C'est toi sale bout
> de monde. Sale bout de petit matin.
> C'est toi sale haine. C'est toi poids d'insulte et cent ans de coups
> de fouet. C'est toi cent ans de ma
> patience, cent ans de mes soins
> juste à ne pas mourir.

> [But who turns my voice? who flays
> my voice? stuffing my throat with a thousand splintered bamboos.
>   A thousand
> sea urchin spikes. It's you dirty bit of
> the world. Dirty end of the small hours.
> It's you, dirty hate. It's you load of insults and a hundred years of
>   whippings, It's you a hundred years of my
> patience, a hundred years of my effort
> just to not die.]

—(*Notebook*, 54–55)

Several different modulations of voice or even several different voices inhabit the poem; motile, often contradictory they clearly issue from a single being, but not from a stable or self-possessed subject speaking for itself. It is difficult to pin down the inflection of intention, to answer in any definitive way the question of irony (does he mean what he says?). Césaire's poetics develop with extraordinary rigor from the speaking position of those deemed to lack cultural value. The principle of *démesure*, or inordinateness, is intrinsic to the Calibanic voice—the sustained poetics developed from the speaking position of the oppressed in all its contradictions—to the extent that the internal challenge to norms and standards produces a discourse that is in excess of proportion. The poem exceeds authorized sense at all its registers, from its outsized and unclassifiable form to its scrambled genres, to its wildly mixed diction, to its incongruous metaphors, to its neologisms, to its abrupt modulations of voice and its foregrounding of sheer sound.

Readings of the *Notebook*'s epic of consciousness tend to emphasize that consciousness's struggle with its historical determinations, for obvious reasons. In many cases, however, these historical determinations are not separable from geographical dimensions. Irele writes of the *Notebook*'s initial movement that is an "act of recognizance," which reveals "the concrete geography of [the speaker's] intimate self, the bounded horizons of a landscape that . . . resonates for him with the echoes of a tragic history" (Irele, l). Our analysis of catastrophic miniaturization opened onto a striking paradox whereby the speaker proclaims his humanity not through subjective emplacement, but through the technological, abstract mediation of the rationalized space of a map. A certain irony may cling to this particular manifestation of the voice, which of course has no more grounded claim to articulate the poem's truth than any other, nonetheless this is a claim to universality that contrasts starkly with the organic, irrationalist authenticity that grounds the affirmation of negritude later in the poem ["who abandon themselves, captivated, to the essence of all things / ignorant of surfaces but captivated, by the movement of all things" (*Notebook*, 68)]. While these passages describe a primal relation to the earth, they do not specify geographical location at all and so do not in any immediate sense participate in the poem's geographical dimension.

The figure of the map takes another turn in an extraordinary sequence of stanzas that presents us with a Calibanic map-gazer's inversion of the imperialist domination of space. The two stanzas are divided as a schoolchild's geography lesson might be between the cartographic exercise of identifying the continents and the recitation of the great harbors and cities of the world. The speaker fashions the map explicitly to begin the inventory of *what* is his, not *where* he is. And the irony laid out with awful bluntness is that everywhere is his, but, as it were, from below—through his absolute dispossession.

Ce qui est à moi, ces quelques milliers de mortiférés qui tournent en rond dans la calebasse d'une île et ce qui est à moi aussi, l'archipel arqué comme le désir inquiet de se nier, on dirait une anxiété maternelle pour protéger la ténuité plus délicate qui sépare l'une de l'autre Amérique; et ses flancs qui sécrètent pour l'Europe la bonne liqueur d'un Gulf Stream, et l'un des deux versants d'incandescence entre quoi l'Equateur funambule vers l'Afrique. Et mon île non-clôture, sa claire audace debout à l'arrière de cette polynésie, devant elle, la Guadeloupe fendue en deux de sa raie dorsale et de même misère que nous, Haïti où la négritude se mit debout pour la première fois et dit qu'elle croyait à son humanité et la comique petite queue de la Floride où d'un nègre s'achève la strangulation, et l'Afrique gigantesquement chenillant jusqu'au pied hispanique de l'Europe, sa nudité où la mort fauche à larges andains.

[*What is mine, these few thousand deathbearers who pace round and round in the calabash of an island and mine too the archipelago arched like the uneasy desire to negate itself, as if from a maternal anxiety to protect this impossibly delicate tenuity separating one America from another; and these loins which secrete for Europe the hearty liquor of a Gulf Stream, and one of the two slopes of incandescence between which the Equator tightrope walks toward Europe. And my non-bounded island its brave audacity standing at the stern of this Polynesia, before it, Guadeloupe, split in two down its dorsal line and equal in poverty to us, Haiti where negritude rose for the first time and said that it believed in its humanity and the funny little tail of Florida where the strangulation of a Negro is just ending, and Africa gigantically caterpillaring up to the Hispanic foot of Europe its nakedness where Death scythes widely.*] (Césaire, 46)

Neither the obscenely prostrated native land nor the crushingly objective map, this world map begins by presenting an abstract space grasped subjectively. With de Gaulle's cartographic dismissal in mind ("Between Europe and America I see only specks of dust"), one is struck by the way this passage subjectivizes scale without yielding to sheer invention. On a map of the world drawn objectively to a scale in which the continents of the Americas and of Africa are both visible, the windward islands of the Caribbean would indeed appear as indistinguishable specks in comparison. For the Calibanic map-gazer, on the contrary, it is only in the historical context encompassing these two continents that the native land is, as it were, deminiaturized and given subjective form; no longer just a single stultifying enclosure, but unbounded it bravely gazes north as part of an archipelagic procession toward Florida. The larger geographical sequence is then read or narrativized in terms of its links with black struggle and suffering in the Atlantic world. If the prose stanza subjectivizes the map by personifying, more precisely feminizing, the arbitrary forms of great continental masses, the lyric stanza following it grounds the possibility of this tenderness antithetically in a brutal history of suffering and revolt. This is indeed the world according to negritude, a neologism that makes its first appearance in the poem (and in published language more generally) in this passage, notably not as a racial essence but as a unifying historico-geographical term. The lyric stanza proceeds with a recitation of cities.

> Et je me dis Bordeaux, et Nantes et Liverpool et New York et San
>   Francisco.
>
> pas un bout de ce monde qui ne porte mon empreinte digitale
> et mon calcanéum sur le dos des gratte-ciel et ma crasse dans le
>   scintillement des gemmes!
> Qui peut se vanter d'avoir mieux que moi? Virginie.
> Tennessee. Géorgie. Alabama
> putréfactrions monstrueuses de révoltes
> inopérantes
> marais de sang putrides
> trompettes absurdement bouchées
> terres rouges, terres sanguines, terres consanguines.
>
> [And I say myself Bordeaux and Nantes and Liverpool and New
>   York and San Francisco
>
> not one bit of this world that doesn't carry my fingerprint
> and my calcaneum on the backs of skyscrapers and my filth in the
>   glitter of gems
> Who can boast of having it better than I? Virginia
> Tennessee. Georgia. Alabama
> Monstrous putrefactions of inoperative
> revolts
> marshes of putrid blood
> trumpets absurdly clogged
> red lands, sanguine lands, consanguine lands.]
> —(Notebook, 46)

The relation to space is doubly mediated, first by an interpretive gaze on an abstract visible form, then by history. As such, the passage provides no instance of spatial emplacement in the ontological sense. Without a doubt it produces, in Bachelard's wonderful phrase, "waves of worldification," but these do not emanate from subjective emplacement but its opposite, collective dispossession and displacement. The larger the scale, the greater the historical affect, the more a single subject as such disappears, leaving way to a collective configuration of space in which a certain kind of "objective" universality or worldliness is claimed for "objects," that is, non-subjects. In the second stanza, the speaker lays claim to the totality of world space in the name of centuries of invisible, coerced labor and failed resistance. The figure of the hand that previously acted as a measure (the handspan, the four fingers of space on a map), now returns in the form of a fingerprint that functions as a metonymic trace of labor on space. The body, therefore, is no longer positioned abstractly as a standard or a measure of scale, but rather as something that cumulatively occupies space. The fingerprint, joined by the trace of a heel (named by a technical anatomical term for a bone, the calcaneum), alerts us to a turn of *démesure*: the unit of measure and proportion is replaced with unbounded traces of the body over space. There is a further twist of irony here, for the fingerprint also indexes the modern policing technology used to identify criminals, a technology that exploits the uniqueness of fingerprints to each individual in order to identify those individuals who have failed to conform to the state's model of proper citizen-subjects.[17] The fingerprint here ascribed to a single representative speaker ironically underlines the anonymity of modernity's exploited laborers. One might also glimpse through this image a picture of the entire world as a crime scene covered over with fingerprints.

This breaching of the order of proportionality in which the body acts as a comparative measure in space is further intensified toward the end of the stanza when the fingerprint as a trace ultimately gives way to a fluid figure of diffusion, the body's substance ("sanguine lands"), a flood of blood dispersed over the world map. If no longer a unit of measure, the fingerprint maintains a reference to an individual body; blood, on the other hand, is the undifferentiated substance of bodies, here loosed from the containment of form. Re-invoking this passage differently later in the poem, the speaker will describe "my original geography also: a world map made for my own use, not tinted according to the arbitrary colors of scholars, but according to the geometry of my spilled blood . . . and negritude, no longer a cephalic index, or a plasma or a soma, but measured by the compass of suffering" [mon originale géographie aussi: la carte du monde faite à mon usage, non pas teinte aux arbitraires couleurs des savants, mais à la géométrie de mon sang répandu . . . et la négritude, non plus un indice céphalique, ou un plasma, ou un soma, mais mesurée au compas de la souffrance] (*Notebook*, 76–77). Blood is perhaps the poem's central element and the object of its most elaborate figurations. One might think of its spatial diffusion as the effect and trace of the violent breaching of individual bodies as integral forms in and measures of the world. In the later passage it is notable that the poet gives dispersed blood a *geometrical* force ("the geometry of my dispersed blood"), which is to say that it functions geometrically as a relational measure of the earth (unlike the arbitrary tints of scholars) rather than geographically as the tracing or writing on the earth effected by the fingerprints. The two geometrical figures here, "the geometry of my dispersed blood" and "negritude . . . measured by the compass of suffering" powerfully combine the inordinate historical consequence of suffering with the value-neutral objectivity of spatial measure.

The geographical dimensions of the *Notebook* partake of the complexity of the poem's formal fragmented unity and of the interruptive or dialectical movement that propels it, a movement intrinsic to the premise whereby the voice seeks freedom from within its very determination by slavery.[18] While a "universal thirst" for liberation propels the poem in an arc of progress and ascension, an antithetical movement of regression and self-negation pulls it back. A synthesis or an *Aufhebung*, which might be something like achieved freedom or perhaps a collectivized autonomy, projected and desired, indeed perhaps intrinsic to negation as a desire, is never accomplished and the ending of the poem, triumphant in its rhetoric and its rhythms, still articulates an opaque and open-ended contradiction. This ambiguously incomplete resolution in which failure and accomplishment are repeated by turns and finally coexist and interpenetrate, characterizes many works of Antillean anticolonial literature. It may mark, as Nick Nesbitt argues, the particular intimacy of that literature as an engaged literature, with the depredations of history that no ideological resolution in fiction can adequately contain, and whose pain and failure therefore must remain to fuel a hope projected onto the world of the future.[19] In the spatial tropology of the *Notebook*, the movement from the horizontal to the vertical, from prostration to standing erect, progresses through the countervailing interruption of repetitive turns and returns to the poem's inaugural topography of the native land. However definitive and grandiloquent the speaker's leave-taking from the native land appears in the first section of the poem, pages later he sinks back into identification with its smallness: "Ma lâcheté retrouvée! / Je salue les trois siècles qui soutiennent mes droits civiques et mon sang minimisé. / Mon héroïsme, quelle farce! / Cette ville est à ma taille. / Et mon âme est couchée. Comme cette ville dans la crasse et dans la boue couchée. Cette ville, ma face de boue" [My cowardice rediscovered! / I salute three centuries that sustain my civil rights and my minimized blood. / My heroism, what a joke! / This town is cut to my size. / And my soul is lying flat. Like this town in the filth and the mud lying flat. / This town, my face of mud] (*Notebook*, 62–63). The final movement of the poem, an ascension orchestrated around the repetition of "debout" or "upright" begins with a last topographical return to the native land that takes the form of a fabulous sexual union between heroic poet and native land. The poem's triadic structure and the breathless rhythm with which it abruptly rushes toward its culmination inexorably lead the critic to read for a culmination of the trope she has been tracing and indeed, the final geographical passage does suggest a reversal of catastrophic miniaturization, a sudden righting of proportions. But it also fundamentally differs from previous passages under consideration because it so decisively departs from any reference to phenomenological experience centered on an embodied consciousness implicit (in the negative) in the initial movement of recognizance and the subsequent Calibanic geography lesson. The geographical impulse presents itself in this final passage as a demiurgic *poiesis* giving the reader witness to a metamorphic topographical fabulation in action.

The passage leading into the finale revisits many of the themes and moods of the poem (negritude's cartography, biological racism, the violent history of slavery, self-abasement and disgust, exaltation) in the mode of a fragmentary summation punctuated by the assertion "j'accepte" [I accept]. Here the speaker returns to the topography of the native land, but this time with a declaration of love that endows the insular space with the topophilia so excessively lacking in the opening pages of the *Notebook*, though in a manner unimagined in Bachelard's analysis. The initial perspective gives us the islands in miniature, seen from far above, from what would be called in French a *regard surplombant*, in the form of a litany of insularity. While this diminution recapitulates the colonizer's view of the islands' formlessness and insignificance (like the one expressed in De Gaulle's dismissive comment), it does so with a vow of defiance and metaphors that recall historical injury.

Iles cicatrices des eaux
Iles évidences de blessures
Iles miettes
Iles informes

Iles mauvais papier déchiré sur les eaux
Iles tronçons côte à côte fichés sur l'épée flambée du Soleil
Raison rétive tu ne m'émpêcheras pas de lancer absurde sur les
    eaux au gré des courants de ma soif
votre forme, iles difformes,
votre fin, mon défi.

[Islands scar of the waters
Islands evidence of wounds
Crumb islands
Formless islands

Islands bad paper ripped up over the water
Islands stumps side by side driven onto the flaming sword
    of the Sun
Restive reason you will not prevent me from hurling absurd
    on the waters at the whim of the currents of my thirst
your form, deformed islands
your end, my provocation.]
—(*Notebook*, 74)

The perspective established by rational geographical scale, belonging to "restive reason," gives way in the next stanza to a perspective, if we can still call it that, deriving from desire and the voice is suddenly manifested in a gigantic erotic personification of natural forces.

Iles annelées, unique carène belle
Et je te caresse de mes mains d'océan. Et je te vire
de mes paroles alizées. Et je te lèche de mes langues d'algues.
Et je te cingle hors-flibuste.

[Ringed islands, single beautiful hull
And I caress you with my ocean hands. And I turn you
with my tradewind words. And I lick you with my seaweed tongues
And I sail you out of piracy.]
—(*Notebook*, 74)

Bursting out of realistic human proportion, the voice materializes itself in a tongue of seaweed, words of trade winds, and immense "ocean hands." Considered alongside earlier figurations of the hand (the hand span and the fingers measuring distance on a map, the fingerprint as the trace of labor on the world) these ocean hands no longer belong to the body as a figure of measure, but to the idea of the body as an agent of desire. The image scrambles proportion altogether for it at once gigantically inflates the speaker and drastically shrinks and domesticates the vastness of the ocean. This passage is, in this sense, the precise counterpart and corrective to the catastrophic miniaturization of the *Notebook*'s first pages whose description of the native land issues from a markedly disembodied, un-located, and ultimately untenable perspective. Moreover the direct address to the island here marks a clear arc of fulfillment from the lack of address in the first passage to the conditional that follows it [Je viendrais à ce pays mien et je lui dirais: "Embrassez-moi sans crainte . . . Et si je ne sais que parler, c'est pour vous que je parlerai" (I would come to this land of mine and say: "Embrace me without fear . . . And if I only know how to speak, it is for you that I would speak") (*Notebook*, 44)] to the direct address in the present tense here. In this highly allegorical and erotic topophilia there is no poetics of space that would concentrate the subject by providing an ontological refuge. Emplacement is lacking here as much as it was in the opening passage, but for the opposite reason. Where the land had previously presented the speaker with a catastrophic lack of a site for subjective enunciation, here on the contrary the poet invests the land with an excess of subjectification. For the lover of the island is figured also as its demiurgic creator:

> merveilleusement couché le corps de mon pays dans le désespoir
> de mes bras, ses os ébranlés et, dans ses veines, le sang qui
> hésite comme la goutte de lait végétal à la pointe blessée du
> bulbe . . .

> Et voici soudain que force et vie m'assaillent comme un taureau et
> l'onde de vie circonvient la papille du morne, et voilà toutes les
> veines et veinules qui s'affairent au sang neuf et l'énorme poumon
> des cyclones qui respire et le feu thésaurisé des volcans et le gigan-
> tesque pouls sismique qui bat maintenant la mesure d'un corps
> vivant en mon ferme embrasement.

> Et nous sommes debout maintenant, mon pays et moi, les cheveux
> dans le vent, ma main petite maintenant dans son poing
> énorme . . .

[marvelously lying down the body of my country in the despair of
    my arms, its bones shaken and, in its veins, the blood hesitating
    like the drop of vegetal milk on the wounded tip of a bulb . . .

And now suddenly strength and life assail me like a bull and the
    wave of life circumventing the nipples of the cliffs, and now all
    the veins and veinlets busy with new blood and the enormous
    breathing lung of cyclones and the fire hoarded in volcanoes and
    the gigantic seismic pulse which now beats the measure of a living
    body, steady in my firm incendiary embrace.

And we are standing upright now, my country and I, hair in the
    wind, my hand now little in its enormous fist . . .]
—(Notebook, 76)

Conveyed in an ecstatic, precipitous parataxis, the sexual union of
masculine poet and female land expresses the desired adequation of man
and country and accomplishes a magical resurrection or restoration of the
entire space as a living body. This marks the sudden turning point into
the poem's final movement when it gathers into triumphant uprightness.
The gendering of the speaker's relation to space in this final union is overwhelming, though it is worth pointing out that it was more emphatically
sexualized in earlier versions of the poem that included an additional sentence after "comme un taureau" [like a bull]: "et je renouvelle ONAN qui
confia son sperme à la terre féconde" [and I renew ONAN who entrusted
his sperm to the fecund earth].[20] By removing the figure of Onan, the
biblical masturbator, Césaire makes the act of ejaculation more ambiguous
and vague, since it no longer clearly issues forth from a single, lone male
figure; this ultimately blurs the distinction between the land and the poet
who does not appear as the mastering, grammatical subject of the action
in the stanza, but as the direct object of "force and life" and the indirect
object ("in my firm embrace") of the "seismic pulse." This is one of those
instances in the Notebook in which what appears on first reading as an
emphatically phallic or masculine tropology turns out, on second reading,
to be more ambiguous. In a deft and careful interpretation of gender and
geography in the poem, Hedy Kalikoff shows how the male/female bina-
ries in the poem's imagery (moon/sun, prostrate/erect, passive/active) are
all subjected to strategic reversals in which they exchange their gendered
connotation. She extends her reading of the instability of gender demarcations in the poem to those moments when the speaker overtly proclaims

his masculinity, such as, most pointedly, when he utters his "virile prayer" that he might be the father, the brother, the son, and the lover of his people (*Notebook*, 70). Kalikoff argues in effect that the speaker protests his masculinity too much, marking it not as a given but rather as precariously constituted and constructed in the process of the poem like other dimensions of subjectivity.[21] Many commentators pass over the gender of the *Notebook*'s speaker in silence, perhaps because it seems so obvious, while others underline the degree to which the phallic dimension of negritude's assertion compensates for racial denigration figured as castration.[22] Reading the poem with an emphasis on the affect and instability of the Calibanic voice, my sense is that this voice is indeed emphatically marked by race, gender, and the gamut of affect (revolt, recrimination, exaltation, denunciation, despair) and that the very excess of emphasis betrays the underlying precariousness of all these identifications, which are never fully, legitimately possessed, or possessible, since the subject capable of claiming them is in the very process of emerging within the poem. The poem shifts abruptly and unpredictably from one mode to another with equal emphasis. The stanza that follows the union of land and poet is a case in point, because it abruptly drops sexual difference altogether and reverses the proportion and the distribution of power between speaker and native land.

If we continue to read the next stanza sequentially, as the connective "and" ("*And* we are standing upright now, my country and I") would suggest, the movement ends by decisively separating speaker and native land as two distinct bodies, in a pairing whose upright stance overcomes prostration and whose dimensions would seem to correct the massive disproportion of catastrophic miniaturization. With the country restored to symbolic size as protector of the miniaturized poet as they head valiantly into the future hand in hand, this figuration installs something that looks like proper proportions between speaker and native land. In a final modulation, the hand once again takes the function of a measure of scale according to the body, as the poet's hand is "now little in the enormous fist" [ma main petite maintenant dans son poing énorme] of the native land, but the hand also loses its bodily specificity through the dizzying homonymic redundancy that dissolves this image into the decisive present of "maintenant" [now] which is also "main tenant" [hand holding]. With this final image a distinct transformation is accomplished, a righting of proportions that leaves us not with the mimetic scene of a man inhabiting a landscape but with two full allegorical personifications, hand in hand. Reminiscent, as

Nesbitt observes, of nationalist public statuary of the 1930s, this peculiar allegorical pair is a strangely anticlimactic outcome for the thrilling stanzas of transformation preceding it. One cannot help but read it as something of a counter turn whose manifest intent, the victorious uplifting of country and race, is conveyed in a starkly inadequate form, suggesting that the process of restoration remains unresolved and incomplete.[23] As the outcome of the poem's geographical discourse, this final allegory detours around a final return to the native land as such, in favor of a purely symbolic uplifting. The island itself, as a place, a site of emplacement, drops out altogether.

Césaire's *Notebook of a Return to the Native Land* is among the first works in the literature of decolonization and perhaps the most ambitious. Once it reached a broader public after WWII it enjoyed enormous influence throughout Africa, the African diaspora, and beyond, where it stood at the center of liberation struggles and debates over the ideology of negritude. It is perhaps the only work of its kind, modern and anticolonial, to have achieved uncontested canonical status in the nebulous arena of world literature, a status it invites by every measure: its originality, its universalizing aspiration, and its transnational influence. The *Notebook* is also, as Abiola Irele so aptly puts it, "a poem of circumstance." Begun in late 1936, first published in August of 1939 on the eve of WWII, revised and published in two separate and different editions in 1947, revised again for the more or less definitive edition of 1956, the poem cannot be fixed to one discrete period but rather registers a response to (and a premonition of) shifting conditions over a time of intensifying anticolonial movement.[24] Indeed the poem spans the political shift from anticolonialism in the prewar years to incipient decolonization in the years following the war. For France's colonial dominions, this would be marked by two major wars of independence, the war of Indochina from 1946 to 1954 and, hard on its heels, the Algerian war from 1956 to 1962. Elected on the communist ticket as a Martinican deputy to the postwar French National Assembly in 1946 (within the time span of the poem's revisions, in 1956, he will also resign from the communist party), Césaire was an active participant in political debates surrounding these critical struggles, distinguishing himself early on as a powerful orator.[25] He was also instrumental in forging the statute that determined the postcolonial political status of France's American colonies (Guadeloupe, Martinique, French Guyana) and Réunion as overseas departments. Unable to secure the equal application of French law to the overseas departments or, somewhat later, self-rule, Césaire was to struggle for decades, as a politician, a poet, and a playwright with the obdurate and multifarious persistence of colonial structures of domination into the nominally postcolonial world. These are some of the poem's historical and topical resonances; they help, I hope, to convey its improvisatory open-endedness, that quality of notes jotted in a notebook easily overwhelmed in the process of canonization.

The *Notebook* also founded modern Antillean literature, not only by placing it, with a single work, prominently on the world map of culture, but more importantly perhaps by establishing the very possibility of its discourse. The term "influence" is entirely inadequate to describe the *Notebook*'s shaping power on the two subsequent generations of writers, for the poem often reverberates through their works, manifestly or not, as though it were the hidden lexicon of their literary language, the touchstone of their impulse toward writing. Even the second of these, the créolistes, who evolved an anti-diasporan cultural ideology around local culture and the Creole language, carry the poem within them like a literary unconscious. Raphaël Confiant, for example, even in the midst of a long critique of Césaire for ignoring the richness of Martinique's local culture and language and for having failed to pursue national independence, testifies to the power of his poem: "For a long time I carried within me your *Notebook of a Return to the Native Land*, like a body-guard or a talisman" and, "by the grace of your word, you lived inside me, you lived in each of us and your place was that of the founding ancestor. That of the Fundamental Negro." [26] Césaire is the object of mighty literary *agons* for the brilliant male writers who follow him, and it is in no small part owing to his towering stature as precursor and his early identification with the cultural theory of negritude that the literature of Martinique in the twentieth century has been marked by a succession of powerful male writers associated with their own strongly articulated cultural theories. [27]

One cannot escape noting the pronounced masculinism that subtends these anticolonial theories, for they assume without question that decolonization is a contest between dominating and dominated men and that, subsequent to that contest, cultural emancipation can be extrapolated from the perspective and the experience of a single gendered subject. Woman, if she figures at all in oppositional discourses, as Mireille Rosello notes, is "often described as she who does not revolt," [28] that is, at best as a passive bystander to real historical action or, at worst, as a passive betrayer. One might argue that in a moment of acute historical crisis gendered interests give way to the common object of collective struggle, or that the extreme polarity of colonial Manicheism, as Fanon describes it in *Les damnés de la terre* [*The Wretched of the Earth*], leaves little room for a third term (an argument or an alibi that Algerian women, for instance, have since had occasion bitterly to lament). One might note that the double oppression of colonized women—the patriarchal oppression of the precolonial order and the oppression of the colonial condition—makes it harder to generalize women's experience of colonialism cross-culturally or to reduce it to a single exemplary type, because the double oppression produces a differential. One might proffer various explanations, historical or sociological, but that stark, unremarked absence of gender (even as doubt or hesitation) remains so blatant as to seem natural and unintended, an accidental oversight, that in itself is a testament to the continuing ideological givenness of male authority over the public, collective word in all its forms, even when the word in question is the cry of the oppression.

One can attempt to fill the lack: to seek women's cultural theory, to examine women's writing of and in negritude, or to examine women's writing of and in Glissantian *Antillanité*, or of and in *Créolité.* The problem here is that in doing so one posits precisely the equivalence that is under question, thus assuming as given the very standard and norm one set out to investigate. Of course, to some extent, the problem already inheres in the very category of "woman," whether as essence or construct, which, once deployed, will tend to draw some things into its set and keep others out. This then becomes the province of women, not a world exactly since it is predetermined and particularized, but a kind of subsidiary subdivision that you can elect to visit if you have special interests there. Gender itself drops out as a question. The relationship of the work of Maryse Condé and Simone Schwarz-Bart, the two most prominent Antillean women writers of the second generation, to that of Césaire cannot be described in terms of Oedipal *agons*, or anxieties of influence, but neither could one say in any clear way that theirs is a specifically feminine or feminist response, by which I mean that they do not seem to read the *Notebook*, for instance, in a consistently specifiable way *as* women. This does not mean that gender does not enter into their response to this text, but rather that it does so in complex and unpredictable ways. Maryse Condé's expository analysis of negritude takes a Marxian position, offering an analysis of the ramifications of the class background of Césaire and Léopold Senghor and concluding

that negritude is a moment of consciousness on the path to a larger liberation struggle.[29] Her first novel, however, *Heremakhonon* (1976), is in
constant dialogue with Césaire's *Notebook*. Negritude is the indispensable
ground of the protagonist-narrator's rebellion against the assimilationism
of her Guadeloupean black bourgeois family and the motive for her journey to Africa. The masculinism of the *Notebook*'s speaker does not figure
directly in this, or in her withering demystification of an ideal Africanity
that she contrasts with what she actually sees in Africa. Where gender most
clearly imposes itself as a question and a problem is in her own diasporan
attempt, as it were, to seek ancestors through sex, but perforce, as an Antillean woman in relation to an African man.

Criticism on Schwarz-Bart concerned with gender has overwhelmingly focused on her first Antillean novel, *Pluie et vent sur Télumée Miracle* (1972), which, with its female protagonist-narrator whose discourse is
forged from local folk forms, offers a powerfully direct representation of
an Antillean woman's experience. Much less attention—gender specific or
not—has been given to the other Antillean novel she authored, *Ti Jean
L'horizon* (1979), set in the same fictional place as *Pluie et vent sur Télumée
Miracle*, Fond-Zombi, but centered on a male protagonist and squarely
addressed to the diasporan problematic of negritude. I will devote the remainder of this chapter to an analysis of these novels not only because of
their Césairean intertext, but because they both develop insular scale as an
important dimension of their narrative premises and they do so in a way
that conjoins it with gender. Schwarz-Bart's two Antillean novels reposi-
tion the figure of catastrophic miniaturization in a different cultural context for the literary projection of Antillean collectivity. For what is striking
is that both novels prominently feature a failure of coupling early in their
stories, so that each novel ends with its protaganist conspicuously alone
and with the narrative conspicuously unable to integrate the opposite sex
into its resolution. Each novel, thus, produces the opposite sex as a "special
case" it cannot accommodate. If we look at these two works in tandem,
they allow us to understand the embodied perspective of the postcolonial
subject in insular space as a perplexing, open-ended question. Gender thus
emerges, I will argue in the pages that follow, not as the particular problem
of women or of women's exclusion, but rather as an unresolved, comparative question of Antillean collectivity.

Simone Schwarz-Bart's novels emerge from the colonial cultural crisis of the 1960s and 1970s: the rapid loss of local cultural forms and identi-

fications resulting from the first decades of Martinique's and Guadeloupe's absorption into the French polity as overseas departments. Perhaps most powerfully formulated in Édouard Glissant's *Le discours antillais* [*Caribbean Discourse*] (1981), the result of this phase of cultural assimilation and total economic dependence is the imminent "depersonalization" of Martinique and Guadeloupe, the danger of a "liquidation by absurdity, in the horror without horrors of an accomplished colonization."[30] During this period of rapid modernization under the social, political, and economic administration of the metropole, Martinique and Guadeloupe became welfare dependencies of France. For lack of an autonomous economic production and a national discourse to mediate this rapid change, the Martinican polity, as Glissant describes it, fell into a rupture with its past and indeed with itself as a collectivity, even as its cultural practices, particularly the Creole language, dissipated for lack of reference or relevance to lived experience. In the process, what was forgotten or repressed, specifically, is the history of slavery. In *Le discours antillais*, Glissant traces the resultant pathologies across a large number of areas (labor, the family, language, history, space), arguing that the condition of assimilation under departmentalization is an unconscious and unacknowledged extension of the pathologies of slave society. The writer thus still confronts the fundamental lack of ontological resistance that called forth Césaire's negritude, but it is no longer primarily caused by general racial oppression, but by the de-propriation of the island's cultural and historical specificity. The project of disalienation involves a turn away from the anticolonial critique of Eurocentrism and its prominent polarization of colonizer and colonized, and a turn inward to the excavation and reinvention of the specificity of localized resistance and cultural expression on the island. The writer's daunting ontological charge is directed at the specificity of place. Glissant writes, "Parce que le temps antillais fut stabilisé dans le néant d'une non-histoire imposée, l'écrivain doit contribuer à rétablir sa chronologie tourmentée, c'est-à-dire à dévoiler la vivacité féconde d'une dialectique réamorcée entre nature et culture antillaises" [Because Antillean time was stabilized in the nothingness of an imposed non-history, the writer must contribute to reestablishing its tormented chronology, that is to say, to unveil the fecund vivacity of a reignited dialectic between Antillean nature and culture] (*DA*, 133). Such a practice requires what Glissant calls "the risk of enclosure," an attentiveness to the native land in its Antillean context that is very clearly set in opposition to negritude's assertion of Africanity and to the vast reaches of diasporic humanism in Césaire's *Notebook*. The magisterial scope of Glissant's *Le discours antillais* is a testament to his belief in the "future of small countries." Simone Schwarz-Bart's novel, *Pluie et vent sur Telumée Miracle* (1972), though less sanguine perhaps about the future, avers a similar ontological sufficiency for the island. Schwarz-Bart has not authored a cultural theory that one might cite alongside Glissant's, but we do know from an interview that she was driven to write *Pluie et vent sur Télumée Miracle* out of a similar sense of urgency concerning the imminent loss of local culture. The novel is based on the life of a woman, Stéphanie Priccin, known to the author. Indeed she decided to write the novel the day she heard of Priccin's death. "I tried," she tells an interviewer, "to put into some kind of form—the novel—a whole Antillean universe I saw falling into ruin, a part of our capital. . . ." She asserts unequivocally that in her mind Télumée (and Stéphanie Priccin, her model) is exemplary for Antillean culture: "Ce n'est pas seulement sa vie, mais aussi le symbole de toute une génération de femmes connues, ici, à qui je dois d'être antillaise, de me sentir comme je me sens. Télumée c'est, pour moi, une espèce de permanence de l'être antillais, de certaines valeurs." [It is not only her life, but also the symbol of a whole generation of well-known women here, to whom I owe it that I am Antillean, and to feel the way I do. Télumée is for me a kind of permanence of Antillean being, of certain values.] [31]

The Plenitude of Smallness

The very first words Télumée, the narrator and protagonist of *Pluie et vent sur Télumée Miracle*, speaks about herself in the novel's prologue announce an adequation between the measure of her life and the size of the island: "I have never suffered from the exiguity of my country." The prologue offers a direct rejoinder to the figure in Césaire's *Notebook*, with his finger on a map, refusing "to reduce myself to this little ellipsoidal nothing trembling four fingers above the line, me a man, to thus overturn creation, that I should contain myself between latitude and longitude!"

Le pays dépend bien souvent du coeur de l'homme: il est minuscule si le coeur est petit, et immense si le coeur est grand. Je n'ai jamais souffert de l'exiguïté de mon pays, sans pour autant prétendre que j'aie un grand coeur. Si on m'en donnait le pouvoir, c'est ici même, en Guadeloupe, que je choisirais de renaître, souffrir et mourir. Pourtant, il n'y a guère, mes ancêtres furent esclaves en cette île à volcans, à cyclones et moustiques, à mauvaise mentalité. Mais je ne suis pas venue sur terre pour soupeser toute la tristesse du monde. A cela, je préfère rêver, encore et encore, debout au milieu de mon jardin, comme le font toutes les vieilles de mon age, jusqu'à ce que la mort me prenne dans mon rêve, avec toute ma joie . . .

[*The country often depends on the heart of man: it is tiny if the heart is tiny and immense if the heart is big. I have never suffered from the exiguity of my country, without thereby claiming to have a big heart. If I were given the power, it's exactly here, in Guadeloupe, that I would choose to be reborn, suffer, and die. Yet, not so long ago, my ancestors were slaves on this island of volcanoes, cyclones, and bad mentality. But I didn't come to this earth to weigh all the sadness of the world. I prefer to dream, again and again, standing upright in the middle of my garden, as do all the old women of my age, until death takes me in my dream, with all my joy . . .*][32]

The passage is laced through with verbal echoes of the *Notebook*. In the first sentence the antithesis of the very large and the very small and the assertion of a direct proportion between the heart of man and the size of the country recalls not only the *Notebook*'s prominent dialectic of small and large but also Césaire's own invocation of big hearts ("Partir. Mon coeur bruissait de générosités emphatiques" [To leave. My heart was rustling with emphatic generosities] [*Notebook*, 44]. More striking yet, as critics have noted, is the occurrence of *debout*, standing upright, Césaire's triumphant refrain at the end of the *Notebook*, here in the modest and restricted context of the last sentence where Télumée is *debout*, standing upright awaiting death in the middle of her garden. The garden in this context cannot fail to invoke the famous last lines of Voltaire's *Candide* ("We must cultivate our garden") and with them the ethic of the small place and of staying put. The novel thus declares as its premise the island's sufficiency and adequacy to calculating the life of those living on it. *Pluie et vent sur Télumée Miracle* stays rigorously close to the perspective and the experience of its first-person narrator, a peasant woman from the rural hinterlands of Guadeloupe. Télumée's is very much a perspective on the island from the inside; with two important exceptions (the prologue and a passage we will analyze later), she never perceives it from an external perspective as a figure gazing on the rationalized space of the map as the *Notebook*'s complainant does. The tragedy of the Calibanic voice, its internalization of colonial inferiority—that is of colonial culture's denigration—signals the perspective of the *evolué*, the assimilated and educated Antillean, who experiences catastrophic miniaturization precisely because he cannot separate the Archimedean colonial view from his own experience. Télumée instead confronts colonial denigration indirectly through the legacies of slavery that permeate her environment and shape the development of her life. With its premise of re-valuing smallness, the novel thus begins by separating catastrophe from miniaturization and part of the figurative labor of the displacements in Télumée's life is to produce insular space as multidimensional, even in its determination by the history of slavery.

To revalue smallness and posit a depth and sufficiency to the island's culture requires a revaluation of the popular culture of slavery, for it is this culture, not an anterior Africanness, that, in Glissant's words "founds today our 'depth,' that which it is ours to discover. It is starting from it [that culture] that we persist" [qui fonde aujourd'hui notre "profondeur," le ça qui nous est à découvrir. C'est à partir d'elle que nous persistons] (*DA*, 180). Two problems immediately present themselves to the modern Antillean writer, however. The first is that, as a culture of resistant survival and accommodation to nearly absolute domination, the culture of slavery is in no simple sense affirmative or, paradoxically, only affirmative through failed negation. As such, it offers no heroes and no obvious models of redemption and overcoming and hence only intimates the contours of a collectivity in the negative. The second is that the vestiges of this oral culture in the assimilated, literate present risk the fatal banality of folklorization in quaint popular stories and songs that have no expressive relation to social conditions or lived experience in the present. The rupture between the oral tradition and writing is particularly decisive here, for without a relay between them the desired cultural continuity is elusive.

Schwarz-Bart ingeniously addresses this second problem in *Pluie et vent sur Télumée Miracle* by creating a narrative discourse that blends the Creole language into written, novelistic French and transmutes Creole folk forms, particularly proverbs, into narrative topoi. Her language thus creates a bridge between oral and written expression and adjusts the form of the novel's narrative discourse to accommodate folk idioms. In an essay that is particularly illuminating for non-Creolophone readers, linguist Jean Bernabé provides a compendium of examples of what he calls Schwarz-Bart's "literary diglossia," a creative interpenetration of French and Creole that he presents as a compelling solution to the problem of Creole, which, as a dominated language, was at the time of *Pluie et vent sur Télumée Miracle*'s writing "still incapable of generating a universe adequate to elucidating the real (as *lived*, as *unthought* at once) of Creolophones."[33] The phrase "the bellies ballooned out" [*les ventres ballonaient*] (Bernabé, 82), for instance,

can seem simply a graceful metaphor for pregnancy, but "ballooned" resonates with the Creole term "*bolo*," signifying big (pregnant) stomach resulting from illegitimate sexual relations, according to Bernabé, thus trans-
mitting a whole other set of connotations from within the French word
(Bernabé, 119). Schwarz-Bart performs a particularly important form of
translation on the Creole proverbs and proverbial expressions that pervade
the text. She inscribes them into her text as crucial elements of narrative
unity and thematic development, but she does so, according to Bernabé, by
"deconstructing" them, that is by "an erasure of their proverbial characteristics," especially peremptory concision (Bernabé, 125–126). For example,
the Creole proverb "*Tété pa janmen two lou pou lèstomak*," or "Breasts are
never too heavy for the chest," repeated across the text as an emblem of
women's art of survival, occurs in the narrative in measured French syntax:
"Si lourds que soient les seins d'une femme, sa poitrine est toujours assez
forte pour les supporter" [However heavy the breasts of a woman, her chest
is always strong enough to bear them] (*Télumée*, 24–25). Translated into
formal syntax with the addition of the adverbial phrase, the proverb loses
something of its self-enclosure and becomes a sentence in a sequence of
sentences. On the other hand, the proverbial content sets the sentence off
from the expository sequence and interrupts the forward movement. This
produces at once a dilation of the proverb as a verbal miniature, thus avert-
ing folkloric banalization, and a condensation of the dilatory signification
of measured prose. At the level of rhetoric, this gesture distends the con-
traction and abbreviation of the folk form, endowing it with a new legibil-
ity and opening its enclosed form to unsuspected associations.

Irreducibility

As for woman, she is place. Does she have to
locate herself in bigger and bigger places? But
also to find, situate, in herself the place that
she is. If she is unable to constitute, within herself, the place that she is, she passes ceaselessly
through the child in order to return to herself.
She turns around an object in order to return
to herself. And this captures the other in her
interiority. For this not to occur she has to
assume the passage between the *infinitely large
and the infinitely small.*
—Luce Irigaray, *An Ethics of Sexual Difference*

If the novel takes as its premise the island's sufficiency, the plenitude of this smallness rests not on a positive integrated totality but rather on the underlying totality of a *néant* or nothingness, a foundational void of violent dispossession against which survival stands out in relief. Schwarz-Bart addresses the negativity of slavery's culture of survival by thematizing the Negro's nullity as an existential problem throughout the novel. It can intrude at any moment; here, for instance Télumée joins women at the river for the routine of laundering: "quand l'heure était à la dérision et à la nullité de la vie du nègre . . . et soudain l'ombre descendait sur moi et je me demandais si je n'étais pas venue sur la terre par erreur . . ." [when the hour went to derision and the nullity of the Negro's life . . . and suddenly the shadow descended upon me and I asked myself if I hadn't come to earth by mistake . . .] (*Télumée*, 50). The legacy of slavery is a catastrophic ontological dislocation in which the negation of value estranges everything, endowing life itself with the quality of error. This void underlies the text and shadows the struggles of the various characters with a distinct philosophical weight. The terms in which the novel sets this problematic, as well as the form through which it attempts to resolve it, recall aspects of Césaire's *Notebook*. Kathleen Gyssels has observed that while focused on the loss of local culture, Schwarz-Bart straddles negritude and Antillanité, for "a positive transgression, a transition towards a new identitarian vision" is still doubled in her work by the negational gesture of negritude.[34] In *Pluie et vent sur Télumée Miracle* Schwarz-Bart transposes the ontological problematic of the Negro directly onto the scale of insular space and therefore sets it within the legacy of slavery as it persists in the narrative present.

How does the ontological dimension of catastrophic miniaturization work itself out in this novel? I will pursue two linked manifestations here, the gendered intersubjective constitution of the couple and Télumée's movement through the island in the course of her life's development; both of these constitute insular space and insular scale around the emerging figure of *Télumée* as a subject. To begin with the former, it is important to emphasize that the first catastrophe of Télumée's life and therefore her first experience of slavery's negation does not come to her from her encounter with the descendants of white planters, but rather indirectly, through her intimate relation with her man, Élie. Her brief stint as a servant in a plantation house leaves her unscathed: "congratulating myself that I am on earth an irreducible little negress, a real drum with two skins . . . I left her the first side so that she could amuse herself, the boss, that she could beat on it, and I myself, from underneath, I remained intact, as intact as could be" [me felicitant d'être sur terre une petite negresse irréductible, un vrai tambour à deux peaux . . . je lui abandonnais la premiere face afin qu'elle s'amuse, la patronne, qu'elle cogne dessus, et moi-même par en dessous je restais intacte, et plus intacte il n'y a pas] (*Télumée*, 94). In a transvaluation of a pejorative Creole expression [*tambou a dé bonda* (drum with two asses) (Bernabé, 118)] indicating duplicity into an affirmation of a resistant, protective doubleness, Schwarz-Bart here indicates that Télumée resists the ontological negation of the white gaze by preserving herself from it, that is, by not seeking affirmation for her existence in that gaze. Her intactness does not, however, survive the beatings and recriminations of her man Élie when he is driven to despair and madness by the disappointment of all his hopes of earning a suitable living. Begun in the Edenic enchantment of childhood, the relationship between Élie and Télumée is wrecked under the pressures of social conditions a few months after they set up house together. In the brief time before this fall, however, Télumée puts before the reader an ideal of emplacement that, while short-lived, remains as a touchstone for the narrative. She wakes up after her first night in the shack she shares with Élie "with the impression of following my destiny as a negress, of no longer being a stranger on earth. [. . .] I looked at Fond-Zombi in relation to my shack, at my shack in relation to Fond-Zombi and I felt myself occupying my exact place in existence" [avec l'impression de suivre ma destinée de négresse, de ne plus être étrangère à la terre. [. . .] Je regardai Fond-Zombi par rapport à ma case, ma case par rapport a Fond-Zombi et je me sentis ma place exacte dans l'existence] (*Télumée*, 125). This passage concisely presents a picture of disalienation wherein the estrangement of slavery's foundational void is overcome by the perfect proportionality of an emplacement in the community that begins with the emplacement of the couple in the house. This accomplished relational possession of a place proceeds from the intersubjective recognition between man and woman, as Télumée spells out: "When Élie looked at me, then only did I exist, and I felt clearly that if one day he turned away from me, I would melt back into nothingness" [Lorsqu'Élie me regardait, alors seulement j'existais, et je sentais bien que s'il venait un jour à se détourner de moi, je m'evanouirais à nouveau dans le néant] (*Télumée*, 141). The initial and decisive sign of slavery's continuing depredation in the present is, for *Pluie et vent sur Télumée Miracle*, the failure of coupling. It falls upon Télumée catastrophically; when Élie does turn away from her, she describes it as death-in-life, the master trope of slavery itself: ". . . it was as if I were already rotting under the earth and I would say to myself internally . . . see how one deceives one's world, they think I am alive but I am dead" [. . . c'était comme si je pourrissais déjà sous terre et je me disais en moi-même . . . voilà comme on trompe son monde, on me croit vivante et je suis morte] (*Télumée*, 155). And this extreme reduction disarticulates Télumée's bodily schema in a way that is strikingly reminiscent of Fanon's description cited at the beginning of this chapter, except that it is transposed from the streets of Paris to the topography of Guadeloupe. Loosed from her "place in existence" in the couple, in the shack, Télumée floats above her inert body, escaping while remaining in place, upward, into a perspective in which Fond-Zombi disappears.

Alors je m'alongeais a même le sol et m'efforçais de dissoudre ma chair, je m'emplissais de bulles et tout à coup je me sentais légère, une jambe m'abandonnait puis un bras, ma tête et mon corps entier se dissipaient dans l'air et je planais, je survolais Fond-Zombi de si haut qu'il ne m'apparaissait plus que comme un grain de pollen dans l'espace.

[*And so I lay down on the bare ground and endeavored to dissolve my flesh, I filled myself with bubbles and suddenly I felt light, one leg abandoned me, then an arm, my head and my entire body dissipated in the air and I floated, I flew over Fond-Zombi from very high above until it appeared like a grain of pollen in space.*] (*Télumée*, 153)

In sharp contrast to the speaker in Césaire's *Notebook* whose dimensions exceed the island from the start, here the exterior perspective is achieved, before the reader's eyes, quite dramatically at the cost of the body, which literally remains behind on the ground in pieces. This passage underlines a fundamental opposition between Télumée's perspective, her quest to arrive at "her exact place in existence" on the island and the distant, objective perspective on the island in the rationalized space of the world map. Embodiment is crucial to her quest, but it is by no means given. Indeed this passage clearly marks it and with it the hope of emplacement, as the paradoxical lack the narrative will attempt to address.

Télumée's own story, her *Bildung*, if one can call it that, or development into adulthood, begins with the premature failure of the conventional marriage plot, in which the end of a woman's development is to enter the social realm through a successful marriage. The protocols of European bourgeois social relations and their sharp distinction between public and private spaces do not obtain in this context for all sorts of reason, as we will have occasion to discuss in somewhat more detail further in the analysis.

What is notable, nonetheless, is how the conventionally gendered scale of the domestic, private sphere as the small interior proper to women is so definitively precluded in the novel. Once Télumée has overcome the loss of her household, the prospect of a settled "place in existence" on the island becomes steadily more remote and Télumée drifts further and further into the hinterlands. She stops for a while in a place called "Madness Hills" [Morne de la Folie] inhabited by "disparate, errant Negroes rejected from the thirty-three communes of the island" and who call themselves "the brotherhood of the displaced" [*la confrérie des Déplacés*] (*Télumée*, 187). Her trajectory presents displacement as an additive series, for the Morne de la Folie is a site of displacement within a land of the displaced. One of its inhabitants indeed asks Télumée if this is her first "*dépaysement*," or spatial estrangement, implying that there could be many. A crucial word in this context, and one without exact equivalent in English, *dépaysement* combines the negative prefix "dé" and the verbal form of the noun "*pays*," or country, denoting literally something like "un-countrification." Originally meaning a state of exile, *dépaysement* in its modern sense signifies the estranging effect of a change of place, particularly associated with travel to foreign lands. While usually endowed with a negative affect of discomfort, dread, or disorientation, it can also indicate the salutary effects of a change of scenery. Schwarz-Bart's use of the word here calls forth both connotations. On the one hand it names and concretizes the vague sense of being a "stranger to the earth" [étrangère à la terre] that Télumée associates with slavery and the existential nullity of the Negro. On the other hand it suggests that even within this general condition of *dépaysement* further *dépaysements* are possible, in both the disorienting and salutary sense, perhaps indeed indistinguishably. The brotherhood of the displaced on the Morne de la Folie is a twentieth-century variant on the maroons during the time of slavery, communities of escaped slaves who founded renegade settlements in the most inaccessible parts of the island, thus establishing freedom in the midst of the place of bondage. The negative plenitude of smallness takes shape here as a multiple estrangement configured in space as the possibility of fleeing without leaving the island, of escaping in place.

Another term developed in the novel for this negative plenitude of smallness is irreducibility, which, like spatial estrangement, undergoes a distinct transformation in the course of the narrative. When, early in the narrative, Télumée describes herself as an "irreducible little negress" because of her ability to resist the abasing scorn of the plantation household, irreducibility refers to the invulnerable wholeness ("as intact as could be") of something that cannot be reduced. Later in the narrative, when she encounters a settlement at yet one further remove of displacement from the Morne de la Folie, she once again calls herself "irreducible," but the irreducibility in question is no longer that of the intact whole but rather that of the fragment, that is to say, of what is left over when everything is broken.[35] Seeing the inhabitants of that place, named the "Égarés" [the strayed or lost ones], "a tenderness weakened my bones and without knowing why, I felt myself to be just like them, rejected, irreducible" [une douceur alanguissait mes os et sans savoir pouquoi, je me sentais pareille à eux, rejetée, irréductible] (*Télumée*, 187). There is a fundamental paradox to the irreducibility of the fragment because what is irreducible in it is not a result of *resistance* to reduction, but of reduction itself: the fragment is, therefore, never intrinsically intact but accidentally left over. Because the fragment is always subject to further fragmentation, at the furthest extreme its irreducibility partakes of the irreducibility of infinite divisibility in which what is irreducible is not the thing in its intactness, but the process of reduction itself that, in turn, produces an infinity of smallness. At this degree, scale ceases to function as a measure of value since the small and the great rejoin each other in infinity. The central conceit of Jack Arnold's 1957 film, *The Incredible Shrinking Man*, offers an example.[36] Exposure to a mysterious atomic substance causes the main character progressively to shrink in size. In the first stages, when he goes from the size of a man to the size of a child, scale is a measure of social standing and his diminution amounts to a loss of influence and autonomy. In the next stages, as he shrinks from the size of a mouse to the size of a fly, scale is a measure of sheer physical power and in his diminution he becomes a prey, vulnerable to everything (cats, mice, spiders). In the final stage, however, when he shrinks to the size of a particle invisible to the naked eye, he escapes through a small crack in the basement where he was confined and the movie ends with a shot of the starry firmament. The logic—if not the neutral, cosmic symmetry—of such an irreducibility attends Télumée's movement over the island. She proceeds from one misfortune to another, discovering that after one site of displacement there is another, with its own community of the displaced. The ontological void that inscribed the condition of the Negro into the landscape as an abyss is replaced by this cumulative possibility of displacement in which irreducibility creates a paradoxical plenitude, a something instead of a nothing. This is what differentiates Télumée's wandering from Élie's demonic drifting, his succumbing to the "folie antillaise" [Antillean madness]. Élie's drifting generalizes displacement to the point of making space as such infinitely reduced. His own father makes the following pronouncement upon him when he begins his downward spiral:

Ainsi allant, il acquit le titre de Poursuivit définitf et le père Abel lui-même disait: Je revendique la tête d'Élie, son corps, ses membres, et même la flûte de roseau qu'il a entre les jambes, mais je ne revendique pas son coeur . . . ah, l'abîme des poursuivis est en lui et tel qu'il est lancé, il passera les trente deux communes de Guadeloupe et leurs hameaux et bientôt la terre entière lui paraîtra trop petite pour serrer son corps!

[*In this way he acquired the definitive title of "The One Pursued" and father Abel himself would say: I claim responsibility for the head of Élie, for his body, his limbs, and even for the reed flute between his legs, but I do not claim responsibility for his heart . . . ah, the abyss of the pursued ones is in him and the way he's set off, he will pass through the thirty-two communes of Guadeloupe and their hamlets and soon the entire earth will seem too small to hold his body!*] (*Télumée*, 150)

That "the entire earth will seem too small to hold his body" encapsulates a version of that catastrophic miniaturization in which smallness is blasted out of proportion and presents a very precise contrast for the intimations of infinite irreducibility that Télumée's trajectory suggests. While the more obvious contrast may be between Élie's wandering and Télumée's ultimately settled emplacement as an old woman upright in her garden, I want to stress the ramifications of her wandering and of what remains unsettled about her subject position throughout the novel. Critics have overwhelmingly read *Pluie et vent sur Télumée Miracle* as a triumphant affirmation of this black Antillean woman's capacity to endure extraordinary adversity and to constitute an integrated and autonomous autobiographical self within the frame of a family chronicle of enduring women.[37] But there is also a countercurrent to this affirmative positing of the female subject. The praise of female endurance that punctuates the narrative in the repeated proverbial expressions does not reliably gloss the actual episodes of Télumée's singular life; there is no guarantee as to how, when, or for how long their free-floating collective wisdom will come to correspond to her actual experience. It turns out, for instance, that her sense of irreducibility as "a real drum with two skins" was short-lived after all. Télumée's grandmother Reine Sans Nom's loving education conflicts with the blows she received from Élie as he vows to teach her "what the word woman signifies on this earth" [ce que signifie le mot femme sur la terre] (*Télumée*, 158), and here more than halfway through the novel, she declares that she would have to discover much before "I would know what this means exactly: to be a woman on the earth" [je sache ce que signifie exactement cela: être une femme sur la terre] (*Télumée*, 159). But how exact is the meaning of being a woman that she comes to know in the course of her own story? Her life experience seems rather to strip her progressively of precisely those social relations that demarcate the gender difference of womanhood. The failure of her attempt to set up house with Élie withdraws the complementary (and unequal) heterosexual differentiation of masculinity from her, together with the social web that sanctions the bond between the married or encoupled woman and the community. With the death of her grandmother and Man Cia, the obeah woman, she loses the gendering relation of kinship and gains a relation to the spirit world. For Man Cia continues to keep her company in the form of a big dog into which she definitively transforms herself and on this plane, where the distinction between human and animal has been breached, gender differentiation hardly figures at all. As Télumée moves further into the extreme poverty of the hinterlands, she is compelled to take up work in the "malediction" of the cane fields and there she directly experiences, or relives, the inhuman conditions of slavery. An important dimension of this reliving of the original labor of slavery is precisely the dissolution of gender differentiation, for in the fields there is little distinction between man's work and woman's work. She takes to drinking rum and smoking a pipe and joins the band of rough canecutting women who taunt respectable people outside church on Sundays. In one striking formulation, Télumée, who so often refers to herself and her forbearers in the feminine gender as "negresses" in the earlier part of the narrative, blends herself seamlessly into the masculine gender of the "nègre" in the canefield: "Et je me disais, c'est là, au milieu des piquant de la canne, c'est là qu'un nègre doit se trouver" [And I said to myself, it's there, in the middle of the spikes of the cane fields, it is there that a Negro must find himself] (*Télumée*, 200).

In this episode particularly Schwarz-Bart indexes the de-propriation of gender in the condition of slavery so rigorously described by Hortense Spillers, wherein "we lose at least *gender* difference in the outcome, and the female body and the male body become a territory of cultural and political maneuver, not at all gender-related, gender-specific."[38] Gender differentiation is reasserted later in this episode through the courtship and cohabitation with Amboise but this idyll of the couple is cut short by his assassination during a strike and so the determining gender differentiation instituted by heterosexual coupling turns out to be transitory, once again. Télumée also briefly takes the place of a mother when she raises an adoptive child, Sonore, but this female identification is also broken off before it can attain any kind of permanence and this bond of kinship falls away. Her final trial, the one that earns her the name "Miracle" from the community, is her encounter with a malevolent being, l'ange Médard, the epitome of slavery's depredation, of, in Beverley Ormerod's words, "the orphaned, alienated, godforsaken Negro whose soul has been shaped by 'enemy hands' to be 'at war with itself.'"[39] Though he clearly recalls other male characters beset with Antillean madness, most notably Élie, he is explicitly rendered as neither fully male, nor fully human. Thus, the crowning struggle of Télumée's life, her ultimate symbolic victory over slavery's negation, is not one that calls her forth or consolidates her as a specifically gendered subject. My point here is that in the course of her life's development the exact meaning of "woman" seems precisely and almost systematically to be withdrawn. That she is a woman, that she carries forth the legacy of generations of Lougandor women, this is not in question. What is in question is in what sense exactly, to recall Simone de Beauvoir's famous phrase, she *becomes* a woman in the course of life. This is important because it undercuts the conventional adequation between the embodied, gendered perspective of woman with smallness and insular space. The feminization of insular space is a familiar trope and can also be found in Césaire's poetry, most memorably perhaps in "Dit d'errance" [lay of errantry]:

> Corps féminin île retournée
> corps féminin bien nolisé
> corps féminin écume-né
> corps féminin île retrouvée
>
> [Woman's body island on its back
> woman's body full freighted
> woman's body foam born
> woman's body recovered island][40]

With its reference to the mythical birth of Aphrodite from sea foam, this stanza draws a precise parallel between the autonomy of insular space and the eroticism of the desiring and desired female body (though the peculiarity of the French word for island, "île," which is gendered feminine, but pronounced exactly like the masculine pronoun, "il," haunts with a bewildering linguistic doubt any definitive gendered equation a critic or poet might propose). From the title of the novel to Télumée's own asserted identification with Guadeloupe ("les jeudis faisaient de moi la Guadeloupe entière" [Thursdays made of me the entirety of Guadeloupe] *Télumée*, 73), Schwarz-Bart asserts an equation between her heroine and the island, but if she appears thereby to repeat the trope of feminine insularity, the particularities of this personification also hollow it out. Télumée's itinerary demonstrates the narrative's inaugural proposition of revaluing smallness ("I have never suffered from the exiguity of my country"), but also unsettles the fixity of this perspective's gendering.

With this in mind the return of Élie at the very end of Télumée's story is somewhat less surprising. Most readers will have entirely forgotten him at the end of the long sequence of misfortunes overcome that seem unequivocally to affirm Télumée as, in Condé's words, a "victorious victim," alone, self-sufficient, and autonomous.[41] But there he is, stalking the perimeter of her garden and disturbing the peace of her old age with a request for words of comfort that she proves unable to utter. This failure is, she declares, "the sole and only regret of my life" [le seul et unique regret de ma vie] (*Télumée*, 247). She tells the last words of her narrative literally against the backdrop of Élie's funeral bells and, indeed, reading the telling of the novel as a circular form, one critic tentatively suggests that the entire narrative is in fact told at this moment, with this funeral as its background.[42] This deliberate interruption of narrative closure with the specter of the failed couple has the effect of making Télumée seem solitary and incomplete and with her the literary task of representing the historical experience of slavery in a single subject.

When *Pluie et vent sur Télumée Miracle* appeared in 1972 it was criticized for the fatalism of its heroine, for the absence of historical content, and for what was felt to be the apolitical representation of social relations in the novel's drive to represent endurance and survival at all costs.[43] In short, it was thought to provide an entirely inadequate representation of the culture's collective being. Not all critics shared this view, and generally the novel's reception changed later in the decade when literary opinion turned decisively toward the preservation of vanishing traditions and privileged histories of survival over revolt. In a spirited critique of the plethora of "commands," "decrees," and detailed prescriptions regularly issuing from the Antillean intelligentsia as to what function Antillean literature should perform and how, Maryse Condé argues that women's experiences and their writing often fail to conform to these models because they tend to stress less conventionally "public" themes.[44] Schwarz-Bart's second Antillean novel, *Ti Jean L'horizon*, can be read as a response to such criticism against *Pluie et vent sur Télumée Miracle*, because it so clearly and explicitly deploys the terms set by the (male) public debate on the disalienating function of Antillean literature. Few critics have interpreted the two novels in tandem, though in a brief and suggestive discussion Clarisse Zimra argues that the difference between them is ultimately "less matter of kind than of degree," particularly on the subject of how the conditions of the island reproduce slavery.[45] I will argue along similar lines that the work of the two novels together is to inscribe a paradoxical parallelism in the place of binary oppositions. *Ti Jean L'horizon* presents a diametrical contrast to *Pluie et vent sur Télumée Miracle* in premise and form, an opposition that disposes itself with great ease along the conventional gender distinction of public/private or large/small. *Pluie et vent sur Télumée Miracle* posits the island's self-sufficient smallness as its starting point while *Ti Jean L'horizon* posits a world-historical framework that links the island to the continents of Europe and Africa. *Pluie et vent sur Télumée Miracle* is the autobiographical narrative of a particular woman who has lived out her whole life in one corner of Guadeloupe while *Ti Jean L'horizon* is the omniscient narrative of a folk/mythical hero who undertakes fantastic journeys across worlds and even through death in search of a means to rescue the world from catastrophe. The manner in which the narratives unravel or complicate these gendered topoi, however, makes the worlds they render neither antithetical nor mutually exclusive, but paradoxically parallel. Between them, these novels unsettle assumptions about what counts as public space or political speech and, more importantly perhaps, what is foreclosed in the allegorization of a collectivity.

The first and most immediate difference between the perspectives developed in the novels centers on catastrophic miniaturization. Renounced in *Pluie et vent sur Télumée Miracle*, the figure determines *Ti Jean L'horizon*, which begins with the belittling De Gaullian gaze of the other:

L'île où se déroule cette histoire n'est pas très connue. Elle flotte dans le golfe du Mexique, à la dérive, en quelque sorte, et seules quelques mappemondes particulièrement sévères la signalent. Si vous prenez un globe terrestre, vous aurez beau regarder, scruter et examiner, user la prunelle de vos yeux, il vous sera difficile de la percevoir sans l'aide d'une loupe. Elle a surgi tout récemment de la mer, à peine un ou deux petits millions d'années. Et le bruit court qu'elle risque de s'en aller comme venue, de couler sans crier gare, soudain, emportant avec elle ses montagnes et son petit volcan de soufre, ses vertes collines ou s'accrochent des cases rapiécés, comme suspendue dans le vide et ses mille rivières si fantasques et ensoleillées que le premiers habitants la baptisèrent ainsi: l' Île-aux-belles-eaux . . .

[*The island where this story unfolds is not very well known. It floats in the Gulf of Mexico, adrift, as it were, and only a few world maps, the especially scrupulous ones, mark it. If you take a globe, you can look and look, scrutinize and examine, wear out the lenses of your eyes, you will have difficulty making it out without the aid of a magnifying glass. It emerged just recently from the sea, barely one or two scant million years ago. And rumor has it that she risks going back to where she came from, to sink without yelling out a warning, suddenly, taking along her mountains and her little sulfurous volcano, her green hills to which cobbled shacks cling as though suspended over the void and her thousand rivers, so whimsical and sun-drenched that her first inhabitants baptized her thus: The-isle-of-the-beautiful-waters . . .*][46]

Comically exaggerating the minuteness of the island by stressing the great difficulty of locating it with the naked eye, the initial perspective on the island is distant, exterior, and Archimedean. This miniaturization is further accentuated by the island's catastrophic precarity: not only is it barely there, but on the temporal scale of a geological perspective it is ephemeral; only recently emerged from the sea, it already risks imminent disappearance. It might as well already have disappeared, for "it is a spit of land without importance and its history has been judged once and for all insignificant by the specialists" [c'est une lèche de terre sans importance et son histoire a été jugée une fois pour toutes insignifiante par les spécialistes.][47] The island's inhabitants echo this view, believing that "nothing happens there, nothing has happened there and nothing will happen there." The view from within repeats with self-abasing mockery the authoritatively belittling perspective of the view from without:

Ils ont pris l'habitude de cacher le ciel de la paume de leurs mains. Ils disent que la vie est ailleurs, prétendent même que cette poussière d'île à le don de rapetisser toutes choses; à telle enseigne que si le bon Dieu y descendait en personne, il finirait par tomber dans le rhum et la négresse, tout comme un autre, ouaye . . .

[*They've gotten in the habit of hiding the sky with the palm of their hands. They say that life is elsewhere, even maintaining that this dust particle of an island has the gift of belittling all things; to such a point that if the good Lord came down in person, he would end up falling into rum and negresses, just like anybody else, yeah . . .*] (*TJ*, 10)

If the island possesses gift of "belittling" all things, the reference in this passage to De Gaulle's infamous comment about French Caribbean possessions ("Between Europe and America I see only specks of dust") leaves little doubt that this miniaturization is colonialism's poisoned gift of internalized inferiorization, a self-indicting appropriation of the colonizer's view from on high in which the narrator extends the self-denigration so pervasive in Antillean proverbs. In *Pluie et vent sur Télumée Miracle*'s first person narration, the alienation of slavery is conveyed from within the protagonist's experience; here it is laid out in expository form as a repression of history. A distinct allegorical didacticism weaves through the narration. The topography of Fond-Zombi in *Ti Jean L'horizon* is divided, indeed polarized, between the people of "En-bas" down below, descendants of slaves, "cultivators of forgetfulness," and those "En-haut," up above in the hills, the dwindling and wizened, remnants of heroic maroons, who, in addition to a history of resistance and freedom in Guadeloupe, maintain an unbroken link to African traditions. The latter might be seen as a didactic gloss on the "brotherhood of the displaced" in *Pluie et vent sur Télumée Miracle* in that they inform us not only about the historical origins of such hill dwellers in maroon communities but also function to interpret the maroons as living links with the lost land of origin. The narrative presentation thus is inflected with the narrator's overt historical and political interpretation and aims determinedly to correct the alienation so blatantly laid out in the opening paragraphs.

In keeping with this procedure of corrective externalization, slavery in this novel is not so much indirectly experienced as fully reestablished and definitively overcome through the novel's central fable of the white cow who devours the world. A hero is fashioned for this purpose ("*nostr'homme*" [our man], as the folksy chapter headings call him), Ti Jean, who, born to Awa—baptized Heloise, last and only descendant of Wademba, the "immortal" leader of the people above—and to Jean L'horizon—a man from below—bridges Fond-Zombi's two worlds. When he is just an adolescent, the novel's plot and Ti Jean's heroic quest are set off by the appearance on Guadeloupe of a gigantic, languorous, blue-eyed, white cow, "devourer of worlds," who swallows everything in her path, until she gulps down the sun itself setting darkness upon the earth. As the catastrophe settles on the great capitals and Paris, Lyon, and Bordeaux burn, slowly, but inexorably, slavery is reestablished in Fond-Zombi. The whites force the blacks back to work on the plantations, erecting forbidding perimeter fences around their domains and transporting whole villages onto their holdings. After the death of his mother and the loss of his pregnant lover, Égée Kaya, to the beast, Ti Jean steps into her maw. He lands in Africa where he eventually finds himself following his father/grandfather's deathbed instructions to return to his native village, Obanishé ("you need only say your ancestor's name was Wademba and you'll be welcomed like brothers . . . I am of a weighty blood, a blood of very long memory and which forgets nothing" [*TJ*, 65–66]).

Catastrophe and Finitude

Enfin, et ce n'est pas le moindre aspect de cette contre-poétique, un vécu de l'histoire, à quoi nous introduisent le combat sans témoins, l'impossibilité de la datation même inconsciente, conséqence du raturage de la mémoire en tours. Car l'histoire n'est pas seulement pour nous une absence, c'est un vertige. Ce temps que nous n'avons jamais eu, il nous faut le reconquérir.

[Last, but not the least aspect of this counter-poetics, an experience of history which introduces us to the combat without witnesses (slavery), the impossibility of a periodization, even an unconscious one, consequent upon the erasure of memory by turns. For history is not only for us an absence, it is a vertigo. This time which we never had, we must reconquer it.]
— Édouard Glissant, *Le discours antillais*, 278

The fable of the cow restores the historical crime of slavery to the full world-historical dimensions of catastrophe: instead of being an unaccounted event affecting a handful of people on a few distant, tiny islands, it extinguishes the sun and plunges the whole world into darkness. The inordinate inflation of proportions here provides the antidote to belittling miniaturization and the novel patiently works this incommensurability through a variety of studied discontinuities in its narrative, scrambling generic registers of verisimilitude and leaving the reader without her customary literary orientations. The immediate account of the catastrophe combines the realistic with the fabulous in such a way that it becomes extremely difficult to fix the rhetorical coordinates of the text's proportions. By setting its hero in search of deliverance from this catastrophe on a quest through Africa, *Ti Jean L'horizon* invokes negritude's saving narrative of return to origins, but only in order to end it once and for all. The plot's line of motivation is irremediably broken by Wademba's fateful misremembrance of the conditions of his departure from Africa and his mistaken belief that the generation of his progeny would be welcomed back there in perpetuity. Ti Jean discovers that Wademba's people had in fact cursed him and sold him into slavery, and instead of welcoming his son, they kill him. Ti Jean L'horizon's original narrative motivation hits a dead-end and, with the exception of his contact with the spirit world and his ability—inherited from his father— to transform himself into a bird, none of the heroic qualities so memorably developed in his childhood figure in his quest; indeed they are almost never mentioned again. The plot's initial orientation pays homage to the cultural ideology of negritude and then abandons it as what Clarisse Zimra calls the history of "false fathers."[48] Once the road indicated by Wademba stops, the narrative goes adrift and Ti Jean L'horizon's journey takes on a dream-like horizontality in which it is difficult to mark consequential cruxes. Like episodes in dreams or folktales, the journey's events bear little direct relation to the outcome of the quest, so that they seem at once predestined and random. The narrative logic thus detours around motivating the relation between past and present or between Africa and the Antilles because it does not establish a *necessary* continuity through the agency of decisive heroic action. The temporality it posits is unhistorical in the sense that the figure of the hero in no way masters or represents time. While the novel draws relations between the Antilles and Africa, they are relations of analogy and correspondence, not relations of temporal continuity.

But if the narrative's development is fatally interrupted, it has a dead center that acts as a thematic touchstone and a philosophical counterpart to the restored world-historical proportions of the catastrophe of slavery figured in the fable of the white cow, and that is the reversal of the master/ slave dialectic. This theme is announced explicitly when Ti Jean and his compère Ananzé assert themselves as heroes of a new generation in the midst of one of those "eternal conversations" about the Negro, "his insignificance and his madness, the unfathomable mystery he represents to his own eyes" (*TJ*, 49), held by the older generation under man Vitaline's veranda. Père Filao reflects: "We are what we are and the disaster is bare, without the slightest pomp: but that is because we were struck down, struck down . . . Yes we were men long ago . . . but they struck us down, crushed us, until we didn't know any more if we belonged to the world of men or that of the winds, of vacancy, and of the void." This is the agonistic story for the origins of slavery, one that ties it to a masculine warrior ethos of physical strength and direct combat. The "men" in Père Filao's statement, "we were men long ago," thus clearly refers to the male gender and cannot transparently accommodate the generically human. Ti Jean breaks the melancholy silence that descends after this peroration to ask why this was done to them and Père Filao responds, "no one can say, my little flute, for those who hit us have kept the dagger in hand and their reasons locked in their hearts." And then in a fateful moment imbued with destiny, "strange words fell from his [Ti Jean's] lips, words he could not recognize though pronounced with his voice," and these are the words of the slave in rebellion who says "yes" to death: "Father Filao, with all due respect: *there are no more birds in last year's nest and I am not afraid of death; that dagger, I will withdraw it from their hands* (*TJ*, 51; italics in the original).

Schwarz-Bart operates a very peculiar kind of reversal of the master/slave dialectic, that mortal struggle Hegel imagines between two subjects in which the one who fears death most exchanges his freedom for life and becomes the slave of the other, now master, and which subsequent commentators have elaborated into the very origin of history in class struggle.[49] Ti Jean's reversal lacks a dialectical resolution. In conquering his fear and saying yes to death, he does not thereby accede to the *Aufhebung* or sublation of a life in which he benefits from the possession of the other subject's labor. On the contrary, Ti Jean remains in the moment of negativity and says "yes" to death not to overcome death, but to choose it. Ultimately, Ti Jean's saying yes to death also means saying yes to slavery in the broadest sense, but once and for all, that is, in such a way as to make it a thing of the past. I invoke Hegel's master/slave dialectic here not to claim it as a source for the novel but as a conceptual paradigm for a logic of slavery. Given the centrality of this dialectic and of Hegelian recognition in the anticolonial writings of Fanon and of Sartre, for instance, it seems likely that Schwarz-Bart would be familiar with it. But the direct reference is not necessary for the understanding of slavery as death cuts across many periods and regions, according to Orlando Patterson, who develops a wide-ranging analysis of, in the words of his title, slavery and social death.[50] Though he positions himself squarely in the masculine warrior ethos of exacting revenge by reversing aggression and seizing the knife, this hero is in fact perfectly unresisting. He proceeds through his journey with extraordinary delicacy and passivity, a hero walking on eggshells, "overcome by the fragility of this universe which might dissipate at the merest breeze, like a bubble of water" [envahi par le sentiment de la fragilité de cet univers, qui pouvait s'évanouir au moindre souffle, tell une bulle d'eau] (*TJ*, 187).

We must bear all this in mind in order to understand how it is that once Ti Jean enters the belly of the beast he receives death from Africans, for to accept the history of slavery must entail willingly undergoing the loss of origins. Ti Jean meets death first at the hands of the very elders who had sold his father/grandfather Wademba into slavery, and in doing so he takes possession of the finitude denied Wademba when he was condemned to the social death of slavery. The moment of death is overdetermined to such an extent by a long anticipated and long denied fatality that it doesn't even take place in a narrative present but in the conditional mood, that laden projection of an event that has already happened in thought:

—Non, ma route s'arrête ici, et je veux seulement voir ce que vous allez faire, dit Ti Jean en un sourire.

Le vieux dignitaire demeura en attente, une minute, une éternité, puis une lueur traversa son œil candide de perdrix: un éclair de tristesse infinie. Et, soulevant son arme, il la dirigea tranquillement vers Ti Jean, sans hâte, sans précipitation aucune, comme s'il savait que le jeune homme aux yeux dessillés ne bougerait pas non, au contraire: redresserait les épaules et ferait saillir le mitan de son ventre, afin que la lance l'atteigne en plein . . .

[*"No, my road stops here, and I only want to see what you are going to do," said Ti Jean with a smile.*

The old dignitary waited, one minute, an eternity, then a light crossed his candid bird's eye: the flash of an infinite sadness. And, lifting his arm, he directed it slowly toward Ti Jean, without haste, without any precipitation, as though he knew already that the young man with eyes wide open wouldn't move, no, on the contrary: would lift his shoulders back and extend the middle of his stomach, so that the lance would reach him full on . . .] (*TJ*, 150; ellipsis in the original)

Ti Jean magically survives this death, which earns him his first African name from the Ba'Sonanqués among whom he will dwell until his next death: Ifu'umwââmi, which means in the ancient tongue, "he-who-says-yes-to-death-and-no-to-life" (*TJ*, 162), and quite accurately details the diversion of the master-slave dialectic outlined earlier, namely that saying yes to death does not give on to the synthesis or *Aufhebung* of more life. Ti Jean dies again and for good, at least as time is counted in the beast, and as he journeys, an exile in the land of the dead, he takes the full liminal amplitude of his destiny as the deliverer of worlds, the diverter of dialectic: "living and dead at once, he belonged to both worlds and was a stranger to each, as displaced on the earth, incongruous, as if he had just fallen from a high star . . ." (*TJ*, 224). His great and perhaps only true struggle and test before returning to Guadeloupe is a final and passive contest against death that unfolds in an apartment in the Metropole in a rite guided by one of the ancients from En-haut.

The Horizon's Hero: Monocosm to Microcosm

Cet horizon trop sûr tréssaille comme un geôlier.
[This too secure horizon shudders like a jailer.]
—Aimé Césaire, *Notebook of a Return to the Native Land*

Ti Jean is the name of an Antillean folk hero. Schwarz-Bart deposits this folk hero in a complex mythic narrative, a world rendered in densely poetic language and saturated with forms and allusions that bind it to a broad array of mythological traditions, to which he is a complete generic stranger.[51] In a strong reading of this novel, Bernadette Cailler aligns this gesture with Glissant's notion of an irruptive Antillean modernity, which, in its compression of many stages of development into one moment, requires that Antillean narrative perform at once the countervailing functions of traditional foundational epic on the one hand, which is to "sacralize" a community, and that of modernity on the other, which is to de-sacralize, demystify, and open on to a political consciousness.[52] Cailler argues that *Ti Jean L'horizon* "succeeds, in a superb paradox, in making the presence of African cultures felt in an Antillean discourse (sacralization), to shatter the myth of a miraculous union both with the land of the ancestors and the land of the Conquerors (desacralization), and to outline, finally, the powerful lines of a new epic, without, all the while, having ever fully possessed ancient epic in its origins nor the development of its discourse in time."[53] Schwarz-Bart, Cailler continues, alters the "place and the role of the traditional text with respect to the society that inspires it," and she does so by passing, in Glissantian terms, from the "transparent lesson" of the folktale to the "non-clarity" of myth (Cailler, 293). In Glissant's thinking, this is a crucial movement toward the potential of a verbal art to locate and express a collectivity in historical time. The folktale, Glissant writes, is a "stylized reading of the real" but its "continuation is uncertain; it does not intervene in the history of the community as a patent and decisive factor" (*DA*, 150). While it invokes a "participatory ritual," in, for instance, its stylized structure of audience response (*Et cric! et crac!*), it "carefully excludes sacralization" so that instead of putting language to the work of foundational legitimation it "installs it in a militant derision" (*DA*, 243). This is precisely that problem laid out in the brief prefatorial text to *Ti Jean L'horizon*: "Les paroles du nègre n'entament pas sa langue, elles n'usent, elles ne font saigner que son coeur. Il parle et se retrouve vide avec sa langue intact dans sa bouche et ses paroles sont allées rejoindre le vent." [The words (*paroles*) of the Negro do not cut into his tongue or initiate a language (*langue*), they only wear away and bleed his heart. He speaks and finds himself empty, with his tongue intact in his mouth and his words have gone to rejoin the wind] (*TJ*, unpaginated frontmatter). The folktale is a negativity, for it delimits in a thoroughgoing fashion the absence of a functional collectivity. As Glissant puts it: "Le Conte nous a donné le Nous, en exprimant de manière implicite que nous avons à le conquérir" [The folktale has given us the "Us," by expressing implicitly the need we have for appropriating it] (*DA*, 152).

The transformation of the trickster folktale hero into the hero of a new epic hinges on the name, Ti-Jean l'horizon. In what follows, I will explore the ramifications of this transformation, which can ultimately be read as a de-miniaturization. For the folktale character, the first name is a diminutive that distinguishes him from an older brother, Gros-Jean, who is slow and dumb while Ti-Jean is small and wily.[54] He doesn't ever seem to have a father and his stories often begin with the death of his mother. There is, however, a well-known story about how he got his last name, l'horizon.[55] Ti-Jean may have no legitimate father, but he has a wealthy godfather, the master of a plantation, named Beaufond-Béké (which roughly translates into "white master of the beautiful depths"). One day, Beaufond-Béké journeys to the metropole and he gives Ti-Jean various small jobs to do while he's away. He asks him to tend a flock of mules. Ti-Jean instead sells them, but cuts off their tails and their manes and sets these out in a little pond so that when the godfather returns, he tells him they drowned when he brought them there to drink. He repeats the trick when Beaufond-Béké puts him in charge of a flock of sheep, but the godfather wises up and exclaims, "I'm going to drown you at the horizon!" [je vais aller te noyer a l'horizon!] And off he goes to the bluff carrying Ti-Jean in a big sack

weighed down with rocks. Ti-Jean escapes without Beaufond-Béké notic-
ing, and while the godfather is off throwing the sack of rocks far into the
sea, Ti-Jean steals a huge herd of cattle. On his return, Beaufond-Béké is
shocked to encounter Ti-Jean on the road with such a great herd and asks,
"didn't I just drown you at the horizon?" Ti-Jean answers him, "Yes, but
you threw me in too close to the shore; if you had thrown me out further, I
would have brought back much more than a herd of cattle!" And Beaufond-
Béké, his rapaciousness wetted, requests that Ti-Jean bring him to the horizon. Ti-Jean happily complies, wraps him in a great sack weighed down
with rocks, and escorts him far out to sea in a boat. Beaufond-Béké is never
heard from again and Ti-Jean inherits his vast estate.

For the Ti-Jean of this folktale, the horizon is the limit of the closed
world of the plantation. He draws no hope of riches or salvation from
beyond that limit, as his foolish master-godfather did; instead he masters
the subaltern arts of dodge, subterfuge, ruse, in a concert of improbable
survival. Ti-Jean l'horizon earns his last name by eradicating the master,
the false father, making "l'horizon" a provisional patronymic since it names
precisely the absence of legitimate paternity. Insofar as the horizon figures
the absolute limit of death in this story, the story reads like a parable of the
master/slave dialectic wrapped in the fantasy of its reversal. Ti-Jean says the
absolute "no" to death that seals the condition of the slave, and he exacts
a "yes" to death from the master, which, instead of securing the master's
supremacy, leads to his actual death and with it the slave's triumphant
and militantly derisive "legitimate" inheritance of the master's goods. But
where death disappears as finitude, it proliferates in an unlimited series
of repetitions. Like so many Antillean folk characters, Ti-Jean's powers of
resuscitation are limitless; he cannot seem to stop surviving. The Ti-Jean
stories elaborate ever more outlandish forms of annihilation, destruction,
disarticulation, atomization from which the hero is always and again reas-
sembled. The survival of the trickster Ti-Jean takes the opposite form of that
of the maroon Wademba, whose near immortality gives him a life without
limit and whose memory (though faulty in one fateful detail) stretches back
without interruption to the place of origin. The novel, I think, aims to put
an end to both of these forms of survival, the expansive, organic continuity
of the heroic maroon or slave who revolts and the radically miniaturized
seriality of slavery's anti- or counter-hero, the slave who survives.

The word "horizon" undergoes a violent figuration in the folktale
where it signifies at once the finality of death and the insurmountability of
the world of the plantation. By conflating a spatial, geographical reference

with the perimeter fence around the plantation, it makes the sea-girt island as a *place* absolutely and inescapably coincident with the plantation as the only (im)possible world. To refuse the horizon is also to foreclose all possibility of escape so that the horizon marks the very absence of an elsewhere, that line beyond which there are no other worlds. The world of Ti-Jean l'horizon is radically off the map, irremediably cut off from any possible correspondence. It is the microcosm of nothing: a monocosm. This radical withdrawal of all measure and the consequent erasure of location and proportionality, also reflected in the folktale's catastrophically precipitous plot, articulates the impossible paradox of survival: to refuse without revolting, to negate precisely what defines one, to evade death by affirming it. Social death is perhaps only survivable, it suggests, if it is figured as an unlivable life in a monocosm, a bare space no longer properly the world since it is stripped of horizons. Glissant remarks that in the folktale "excess and lack complete each other to underline the same impossibility. Thus the folktale plants its décor in a non-country, all exaggeration or void, which while exceeding the real country, nonetheless isolates its structure exactly." [L'exceès et le manque se complètent pour souligner un même impossible, Le conte plante ainsi son decor dans un non-pays, tout outrance ou néant, qui excède le pays réel et en fixe pourtant la plus exacte structure] (*DA*, 244).

The Ti-Jean of folktale (whom we will distinguish by the dash in his name) is *precisely* that hero who would never travel beyond the horizon of the island to Africa. Schwarz-Bart starts on her transformation of Ti-Jean l'horizon first by asserting the legitimacy of the patronymic and thereby initially occluding the word's reference. L'horizon (always capitalized in the novel) happens to be the last name of a perfectly ordinary fellow named Jean, with a son, a novelistic circumstance that translates "Ti" from a literal diminutive indicating size or birth order to a generational diminutive indicating legitimate paternity, a paternity that the novel goes on to overdetermine in a repetition of the gesture of incommensurable inflation, as Ti Jean receives at least four different names in the course of the narrative from at least three different father figures, all of them legitimate in one way or another. This translation of size into lineage encapsulates the project of that negritude that would seek to remedy the island's cultural inconsequentiality by tracing that culture back to a unitary, integral root. But it is ultimately not Ti Jean's inherited patronymics that reverse the figuration of his folk counterpart, but rather the two names he *earns* during his journey. The first, which he earns in Africa, "he-who-says-yes-to-death-and-no-to-life," converts the horizon from survival's insurmountable limit to that of a dialectical finitude. Ti Jean's horizon is an expanded or liminal limit and therefore a kind of threshold, for Ti Jean is, as the title of the English translation conveys quite exactly, *between* worlds. The second, which he earns over the novel as a whole, returns the horizon to its primary spatial and geographical reference as the circular line where the sky and the earth seem to meet that plots a subject's location in space. To the degree that he personifies this horizon, especially in overcoming the limit of slavery's impossible modes of survival, Schwarz-Bart's Ti Jean detaches the island's perimeter from its association with the limits of the monocosm of the plantation. Guadeloupe then can take its place on the map as a distinct and habitable location offering the site for a stable perspective where a subject might stand in the middle of a hypothetical center that delimits the reach of his vision along that line where the sky and the earth meet and separate. The horizon might then not only offer a vista onto possible relations and orientations but figure possible futures, an orientation for the hero who "went on ahead of the new story/history that awaited him" [s'en aller au-devant de la nouvelle histoire qui l'attendait] (*TJ*, 256).

There are many references to the horizon in this narrative, particularly in Africa where Ti Jean often scrutinizes it, but perhaps the most striking reference occurs when Ti Jean finally touches down on the native land of birth [*natif natal*] (255) and recapitulates his fall into the beast, only this time it is a horizontal fall in which the varied cultural landscapes of the island appear to him in their relation to the two great elsewheres that frame the Antilles' cultural geography, Africa and France. Restoring proportions and points of reference, Ti Jean's horizontal fall carefully undoes the folktale's monocosmic complementarity of lack and excess. Guadeloupe appears to him upon his return as a place rather than the décor of a noncountry:

un trou obscur qui venait de s'ouvrir sous son abri et se creusait dans les profondeurs de la terre, avec des sortes d'échappées lumineuses sur des paysages que frôlait dans sa chute, mais sans pouvoir s'y accrocher; petites cases rondes du plateau d'En-haut, qui se découpaient étrangement sur la plaine infinie des Ba'Sonanqués, termitières du village de l'Hippopotame, hautes falaises trouées de regards et c'était la ville des blancs qui fuyait déjà par-dessus sa tête, disparaissait en fumée, tandis qu'il tombait a l'horizontale, bras écartés et les joues parcourues d'un léger vent noir, frais, dans le gouffre qui l'attendait au cœur de la Bête . . .

[*a dark hole that had just opened in his shelter and dug itself into the depths of the earth, with luminous glimpses of landscapes which he grazed in his fall without being able to grab hold of them; little round huts on the plateau of up above, which strangely cut a figure on the infinite plain of the Ba'Sonanqués, the anthills of the village of Hippopotamus, high cliffs punctuated with glances and it was the city of the whites which already raced on above his head, while he fell horizontally, arms stretched out and his cheeks caressed by a light black wind, fresh, in the abyss that awaited him in the heart of the beast . . .]* (*TJ*, 255; ellipsis in original)

Having written the trickster-survivor of folktale out of her protagonist, Schwarz-Bart does not replace him with a heroic agent of history or an exemplar of heroic Antillanité unfurling through time, but fashions a traveler instead, adrift in the ancestral land, who stands for nothing in particular, but like a mythical prospector rather than a mythical hero, brings back the possibility of spatial location. The crushing standards of Africanity (the lost land of origin) and Francity (the always superior metropole) that erased the proper value of the Antillean and reduced him to a "société comparaison" without proper value have taken on the distance and incommensurable density of heterotopias, other spaces, at once "real" and amenable to a cultural imaginary. In this sense, Guadeloupe is made up of a plurality of worlds. In the passage these other spaces correlate with Guadeloupe's topography without obscuring it; they share a ground of comparison without constituting a basis of equivalence. Ti Jean is a hero whose exemplarity lies neither in any action he has accomplished nor in any saving narrative he may have heard, but in his stark and simple location in space, a bare proportionality: he is somewhere.

Critics are right, I think, to see in *Ti Jean L'horizon* a utopian text that conforms to Antillanité's prescription for disalienation and in its hero a projection of, in the words of Kathleen Gyssels, "what an Antillean conscious of his Antillanité could be." [56] But there is a rather gaping fissure in this collective projection, and that is the conspicuous absence of women. Ti Jean was, after all, prompted to enter the beast to search for his pregnant lover Égée Kaya, and while he spies her in visions throughout his journey she fails to return after the final destruction of the beast. This significant loose thread in an otherwise completed narrative unsettles one's reading of the novel's conclusion, which announces itself as a new beginning ("Mais il voyait maintenant nostr'homme, que cette fin ne serait qu'un commencement" [But he saw now, our man, that this ending would only be a beginning . . .] [*TJ*, 286]). In the absence of Égée Kaya and the unborn child she encloses, the future horizons of the collective hopes Ti Jean may embody seem strangely, prematurely truncated, for the novel ends or re-begins with two bodies still lost in space: the child in the enclosed monocosm of its mother, the woman in a realm of the dead strictly out of bounds, now that the cow has been vanquished.

Égée Kaya's final appearance in the narrative is ambiguous. Ti Jean last sees her in a vision at the very end of the novel; she is sitting in his own hut and she suddenly breaks into a melancholy song:

> On m'a appelée la femme sans chance
> On dit que je n'ai pas la couleur rose
> Mais si pas rose je suis verte
> Et ma chance viendra, car j'ai mon espérance . . .
>
> [They called me the woman with no luck
> They say I do not have the color pink
> But if not pink I am green
> And my luck will come, for I have my hope . . .]
> —(*TJ*, 285)

Finding her "as she is, a negress unadorned and without affectation" [telle quelle, négresse sans fard ni pose] (*TJ*, 285), a description that recalls Télumée ("Il me trouvait belle dans cette robe à ma forme sans fard ni mode" [He found me beautiful in this dress cut to form, unadorned and without fashion] [*TJ*, 215]), he shakes himself out of his three-month stupor, opens his eyes, and sets off toward the valley. If we emphasize the result of this encounter then we might propose that Ti Jean and *Ti Jean L'horizon* have assimilated Égée Kaya into their futures, but if we focus on her melancholy ditty that at once recapitulates racial self-denigration and affirms endurance with a hope projected into the future, she seems for all the world like a Télumée, enduring heroine of an autobiographical Antillean narrative whose conditions for emergence are yet to come.

Like *Pluie et vent sur Télumée Miracle*, this narrative ends with a stark reminder of a failed or incomplete couple, thus leaving the reader with a clear memory of how in each case the opposite sex, Élie in *Pluie et vent sur Télumée Miracle* and Égée in *Ti Jean L'horizon*, drops out of the narrative early and cannot be resolved back into it by the end. Égée Kaya clearly recalls Télumée, and indeed in her ability to conceive a child fulfills one of Télumée's thwarted desires, even as, in Ti Jean's story, she is denied a future. Ti Jean recalls Élie, the pursued one, except that his travels have the limit and telos of finitude given him by the heroic opportunity to say "yes" to death and thereby reverse the emasculating dialectic of enslavement.

Télumée's narrative has no place for this masculine contest, just as Ti Jean's has no place for the story of victorious survival within the island's own sufficiency. This complementary incompletion makes it difficult to set these texts squarely in opposition as mutually exclusive narratives or narratives offering equivalently divergent alternatives, even as they are also clearly not perfectly complementary or sequential. Though the symmetry of their oppositions invites the reader to set the two novels side by side, one would be hard put to find the basis of equivalence between them upon which to draw conclusions or value judgments from the comparison. Rooted as they are in the givenness of the folk tradition, they do not represent two strictly separable perspectives from which one might choose freely.

It's worth remembering that each novel draws from a different strain of the folk tradition and that the collectivity, the "us" that the folktales in each case give implicitly, to reinvoke Glissant, differs as does the manner and consequence of its appropriation into the modern present. In their introduction to an anthology of Antillean folktales, Ina Césaire and Joëlle Laurent remark that the major formal or public occasion for storytelling is the funeral wake where the storytellers are always men and the audience adult, whereas the major informal occasion for storytelling is evening, or bedtime when the tellers are usually women and the audience often children. A specific repertoire is also bound to each occasion so that stories of animals and sorcery belong to the bedtime tales women tell, whereas all others, including the Ti-Jean stories, belong to public occasions.[57] Judging by Raphaël Confiant's collection, *Les maîtres de la parole*, a celebration of living storytellers in Martinique, the gendered line of separation is still powerfully operative, for the many contemporary storytellers profiled in the book do not include a single woman. The oral tradition is understood implicitly and without question to refer to the public realm, or the realm of men, and to a distinct public vocation. Schwarz-Bart recounts that Stéphanie Priccin, the model for Télumée, was at one point so concerned over the rapid loss of the folk tradition among the younger generation that she organized storytelling evenings that, however, very few attended.[58] At the level of the folk tradition, then, there are two distinct realms, each associated with the particular speech of one gender, but in both of which both genders partake. Boys have bedtime, after all, and women attend funerals. In the space between them marked by their mutual incompletion, these two novels powerfully question the mutual exclusivity of fixed positions and singular perspectives, small and large, female and male, and call attention to the way such categories are implicitly presented as the choice of either/or, whereas they are lived in combination. The question raised in the cleavage between *Pluie et vent sur Télumée Miracle* and *Ti Jean L'horizon* is also one of worlds, for it suggests an internal incommensurability along the horizon of gender (and scale) in the literary imagination of a collective Antillean voice. Just as there is more than one oral tradition through which Fond-Zombi can be written and its people disalienated, so too the place contains more than one collective world and the two novels seem to me to testify to the impossibility of containing these worlds within a single work. The two Fond-Zombis are neither incompatible nor in contradiction but they are incommensurable in that they suggest a com-parative construction of community, one that partakes of the same space but is not mediated by a single common work or endeavor and that therefore cannot be contained in a single gendered subject.

What is so deeply instructive about the two novels is that each one breaks down the internal unity of its gendered perspective (the gendered determinations of the heroine and of the hero become less distinct as the narratives unfurl) even as it presents each gender as incomplete. Schwarz-Bart thus precludes a unifying resolution that would simply bring the separated genders together again in perfect complementarity. The masculine and the feminine, on the contrary, are caught up in a multitude of equivalences that do not unify, to recall Glissant's phrase, precisely because they share a ground of comparison but no basis of equivalence. Writing about these two novels together makes it quickly pointless to compare one gender (its experience, its perspective) to another because the objective of the exercise is perplexingly inadequate (is one better than the other, bigger, smaller, more enduring?) and yet to consider one novel in view of the other is to be immediately engaged in a ubiquity of com-parison that exceeds enumeration. In geography's rationalization of space, only one body can occupy any given space at a given time. Schwarz-Bart's novels suggest that if we want to take gender into account, we must do precisely the opposite and consider the full incommensurability of the co-presence of two bodies in the same space at the same time. The carving out of a separate, differently embodied perspective is not enough. This is ultimately the crucial dimension of her textual development of the figure of catastrophic miniaturization as the problem of collectivity. Michael Dash writes eloquently that the literature of the Caribbean in its many varied forms ultimately leaves its readers with the understanding that "insularity is not a kind of reductive polarity but the recognition of a field of relation."[59] Schwarz-Bart's novels remind us that this field of relation obtains between the island's own multiple worlds.

Notes

GROUNDS FOR COMPARISON

1. Lane Cooper, *Experiments in Education* (Ithaca, NY: Cornell University Press, 1942), 75. Cooper favored the name "Comparative Study of Literature."

2. René Wellek, "The Name and Nature of Comparative Literature," *Discriminations: Further Concepts of Criticism* (New Haven, CT: Yale University Press, 1970), 17. He proposes "general literature" or "literature" as a telos for the discipline in the popular handbook he co-authored with Austin Warren, *Theory of Literature* (1942). For a reflection on the affinities between Wellek and his successor at Yale, Paul De Man, see Samuel Weber, "The Foundering of Aesthetics: Thoughts on the Current State of Comparative Literature," in Clayton Koelb and Susan Noakes, eds., *The Comparative Perspective on Literature; Approaches to Theory and Practice* (Ithaca, NY: Cornell University Press, 1988), one of the only texts devoted to the discipline during the 1980s. I do not dwell much here on the ascendancy of "Theory" in comparative literature, in part because my focus is on the discipline's linguistic and cultural scope, which, if anything, underwent a narrowing as a result of Theory's attention to (Northern European) continental philosophy.

3. "Report on Standards," in Charles Bernheimer, ed., *Comparative Literature in the Age of Multiculturalism* (Baltimore: Johns Hopkins University Press, 1995), 41–42. Hereafter cited in the text as Bernheimer.

4. In *Comparative Literature in the Age of Multiculturalism*, see especially, Emily Apter, "Comparative Exile: Competing Margins in the History of Comparative Literature" (81–96), who elaborates on the exilic nature of the discipline, and Françoise Lionnet, "Spaces of Comparison" (165–174), who writes eloquently of the intrinsic comparatism of growing up in postcolonial, multilingual, multiracial Mauritius.

5. Charles Chauncey Shackford, "Comparative Literature," delivered at Cornell University in 1871 and published in *Proceedings of the University Convocation* (Albany: New York State University Press, 1876), 266–274. Reprinted in Hans-Joachim Schulz and Philip H. Rhein, eds., *Comparative Literature: The Early Years* (Chapel Hill: University of North Carolina Press, 1973), 42.

6. See Emily Apter, op. cit.

7. One would want to add Gayatri Chakravorty Spivak to this company, but her critical practice is so boldly transgressive of disciplinary and academic boundaries that containing her under the rubric of the discipline seems inadequate. May her presence in this footnote at least function as an interruption of the male humanist genealogy adumbrated here.

8. "The Concept of Evolution in Literary History," orig. publ. in *For Roman Jacobson*, (The Hague, Moulton, 1956), 653–661. Reprinted in *Concepts of Criticism* (New Haven, CT: Yale University Press, 1963), 37.

9. See, for instance, Ulrich Weisstein, *Comparative Literature and Literary Theory*, trans. William Riggan (Bloomington: Indiana University Press, 1968), which has a thorough and extensive appendix outlining the history of comparative literature in various countries.

10. Susan Bassnett's excellent *Comparative Literature: A Critical Introduction* (Oxford: Basil Blackwell, 1993) is an exception here. See especially her chapter "Beyond the Frontiers of Europe: Alternative Concepts of Comparative Literature," where she notes the explicitly nationalist framework for the establishment and practice of comparative literature outside Europe.

11. Anthony Kwame Appiah, "*Geist* Stories," *Comparative Literature in the Age of Multiculturalism* (Baltimore: Johns Hopkins University Press, 1995), 51–57.

12. Erich Auerbach "Philology and Weltliteratur," trans. Edward Said and Maire Said, *The Centennial Review* 13, no. 1 (1969): 1–17.

13. René Wellek, "Comparative Literature Today," *Discriminations* (1970): 52–53.

14. See René Etiemble. *Comparaison n'est pas raison: la crise de la littérature comparée* (Paris: Gallimard, 1963) and *Ouverture(s) sur un comparatisme planétaire* (Paris: Christian Bourgeois, 1988). It's worth remembering at least one major postcolonial intellectual, Maryse Condé, understood her doctoral work in comparative literature under Etiemble. His student Adrian Marino calls for an engaged postcolonial comparatism: "il me semble que notre devoir a nous comparatistes, c'est aujourd'hui d'étudier les problèmes de littérature comparée que posent la colonisation et la décolonisation: l'influence d'une langue dominante sur l'expression littéraire d'un peuple colonise; le bilinguisme des écrivains en période de décolonisation etc." Adrian Marino, *Etiemble ou le comparatisme militant* (Paris: Gallimard, 1982), 79.

15. Gerald Graff, *Professing Literature: An Institutional History* (Chicago: University of Chicago Press, 1987), 167. Hereafter cited in the text as Graff.

16. John Guillory, *Cultural Capital: The Problem of Literary Canon Formation* (Chicago: University of Chicago Press, 1993), 41. Hereafter cited in the text as Guillory.

17. Harry Levin assures us that unlike the Soviet Union, America is a safe place for comparatism: "There can still be a dash of adventure in the enterprise of comparative literature. It came to the surface in the Soviet Union not very long ago

when a concern for the literature of the West was attacked by official spokesmen for the prevailing nationalism, and so-called 'comparativism' became a charge of treason—or perhaps, through Western eyes, a gesture of liberation. *Fortunately, it has not been regarded as an un-American activity. On the contrary, it has been sponsored by our government through the support of teaching programs in foreign languages*" (my emphasis). Harry Levin, *Grounds for Comparison*, (Cambridge, MA: Harvard University Press, 1972), 72. Levin sees no conflict between the United States' national security apparatus and the aims of a cosmopolitan humanism.

18. The manifest disjunction between the polarities of cold war politics on the one hand and the increasing transnationalism of corporations on the other is thoroughly demonstrated in, for instance, Masao Myoshi's seminal essay. He argues that postcolonial studies participate in the kind of diversionary movement I ascribe here to comparative literature, particularly insofar as this discourse sets itself in opposition to an enemy (the imperial nation-state) long vanished. Masao Myoshi, "A Borderless World? From Colonialism to Transnationalism and the Decline of the Nation-State," *Critical Inquiry* 19 (Summer 1993): 726–751.

19. Gayley pointedly named the comparatist scholarly journal he founded *University of California Publications in Modern Philology*.

20. Charles Mills Gayley, "English at the University of California," William Morton Payne, ed., *English in American Universities* (Boston: D. C. Heath & Co., 1895), 106–109.

21. I find it perplexing that Graff takes up more than half of his discussion of this important curricular reform, hailed by a contemporary reviewer as the most advanced in its conception of any in the country, with the acerbic comments of a particularly disaffected early student (1890–1894), the future novelist Frank Norris. In part perhaps this is because Gayley doesn't fit well in the opposition between humanists and specialists Graff develops and, in part, it may also betray a certain bias toward elite institutions of the East Coast, which offer a much more distinct generational continuity than do the younger and public institutions. It is possible to place Gayley's counterpart, George Woodberry, in an unbroken line of humanists stretching from Matthew Arnold to Lionel Trilling. No such orderly descent attends Gayley's intellectual progress.

22. Charles Mills Gayley, *Idols of Education* (New York: Doubleday, 1910), 52.

23. See, for instance, Anne Douglas, *The Feminization of American Culture* (New York: Knopf, 1977).

24. Benjamin Putnam Kurtz, *Charles Mills Gayley* (Berkeley: University of California Press, 1943), 109. Hereafter cited in the text as Kurtz. This woman problem is without question also a particular obsession of this biographer, a student of Gayley's who received his Ph.D. around 1907–1910, and must thus have been one of the first crop of graduate students to emerge from Gayley's program.

25. Women's biographical accounts of their training in comparative literature overwhelmingly focus on intellectual questions rather than institutional social

relations. See, for instance, the contributions of Marjorie Perloff and Lilian R. Furst in Lionel Grossman and Mihai Spariosu, eds., *Building a Profession* (Albany: New York State University Press, 1994). Self-identified feminist writings on comparative literature focus on the question of how feminism as theory and discourse might affect the traditional subject areas of the discipline, but stay clear of the question of social relations within the academy. See Margaret Higonnet, ed., *Borderwork: Feminist Engagements with Comparative Literature* (Ithaca, NY: Cornell University Press, 1994). The attitudes reflected in Gayley and Kurtz suggest a social and cultural history of women's relation to humanist internationalism would be very interesting indeed.

26. I am thinking here of such "seminal" figures as Gayatri Spivak, Barbara Johnson, Peggy Kamuf, Avital Ronell, and Cynthia Chase, to name just a few. Certain native informants, however, point out that in the meantime "high theory" has become very much a male preserve, thus perhaps reasserting the line between the virility of ambitious abstraction and the femininity of smallness and particularity, especially associated with close reading.

27. Charles Mills Gayley, "What Is Comparative Literature?" First published in *The Atlantic Monthly* (1903). Reprinted in Hans-Joachim Schulz and Philip H. Rhein, eds., *Comparative Literature: The Early Years*, 84–103. Hereafter cited in the text as Gayley. Gayley first lays out his idea for the collaborative comparatism of a Society of Comparative Literature in an earlier essay, "The Society of Comparative Literature," *The Dial* (August 1, 1894): 57.

28. See, for instance, the idea of *Ansatzpunkt* in Erich Auerbach, "Philology and *Weltliteratur*," trans. Edward Said and Maire Said, *The Centennial Review* 13, no. 1 (1969): 13.

29. George E. Woodberry, Editorial, *Journal of Comparative Literature* 1 (1903): 3–9. Reprinted in full in Schulz, Rhein, *Comparative Literature: The Early Years*, 207–214.

30. Kenneth Bock, "The Comparative Method in Anthropology," *Comparative Studies in Society and History* 7 (1965–1966): 270. See also I. Schapera, "Some Comments on the Comparative Method in Social Anthropology," *American Anthropologist* 55, no. 3 (1953): 353–362; Johannes Fabian, *Time and the Other: How Anthropology Makes Its Object* (New York: Columbia University Press, 1983); and George Stocking, *Race, Culture, and Evolution; Essays in the History of Anthropology* (New York: Free Press, 1971).

31. See Kenneth Bock, "The Comparative Method in Anthropology," 278.

32. The comparative method, shorn of its exclusive evolutionary dimension but retaining its comprehensive scope, continued in some branches of anthropology and sociology well into the twentieth century, particularly concerning the compilation of the Human Relations Area Files at Yale and the work emerging from it. Ladislav Holy reflects on the shift from positivist comparative anthropology's objective of massive generalization to the current paradigm of thick description and concern with epistemological questions, a paradigm shift that in some ways

parallels that of literature. See Ladislav Holy, ed., *Comparative Anthropology* (Oxford: Basil Blackwell, 1987). In his *Big Structures, Large Processes, Huge Comparisons* (New York: Russell Sage Foundation, 1984), Charles Tilly advocates a reformed comparative method for sociology, one shorn of its "pernicious nineteenth-century postulates," especially the notion of evolution or development. Though generally discredited in academic circles, the idea of some kind of unified human development in culture and social organization seems broadly to inform not only ubiquitous media representations of various parts of the third world as "backward," but also the idea of "development" that subtends the U.S. government's massive aid programs. See especially Arturo Escobar, "The Making and Unmaking of the Third World through Development," and Ivan Illich, "Development as Planned Poverty," in Majid Rahnema, ed., *The Post-Development Reader* (London: Zed Books, 1997).

33. Charles Mills Gayley, "Lectures on the Aesthetics of Literature," delivered at the University of California, Berkeley, 1890–1891, typescript at Bancroft Library, University of California at Berkeley.

34. Charles Mills Gayley and Benjamin P. Kurtz, *Lyric, Epic and Allied Forms of Poetry*, vol. 2 of *An Introduction to the Methods and Materials of Literary Criticism* (Boston: Ginn and Co., 1920), x–xi. Hereafter cited in the text as Gayley and Kurtz.

35. A substitution that seems to have lost little of its sting judging by continuing reactions to Martin Bernal's *Black Athena: The Afroasiatic Roots of Classical Civilization* (New Brunswick, NJ: Rutgers University Press, 1987).

36. See Weisstein, *Comparative Literature and Literary Theory*, 212.

37. Edward Said, *Culture and Imperialism* (New York: Knopf, 1993), 46–48. Hereafter cited as *CI*.

38. René Wellek, "The Name and Nature of Comparative Literature," 31.

39. René Wellek, "The Concept of Evolution in Literary History," 34. See also Gayley on Brunetière in "What Is Comparative Literature?" in Schulz, Rhein, *Comparative Literature: The Early Years*, 31.

40. Hutcheson Macaulay Posnett, *Comparative Literature* (London: Kegan Paul, 1886), reprinted in René Wellek, ed., *Classics in Art and Literary Criticism* (New York: Johnson Reprint Corporation, 1970), 86. Hereafter cited in the text as Posnett.

41. Homi K. Bhabha, "Introduction," *The Location of Culture* (London: Routledge, 1994), 12.

42. Michel Foucault, *The Order of Things*, trans. unnamed (New York: Vintage, 1973), 245. Hereafter cited in the text as *Order*.

43. Michel Foucault, "Of Other Spaces," trans. Jan Miskowiec, *Diacritics* 16 (1986): 22. Hereafter cited in the text as *Spaces*.

44. Henri Lefebvre, *The Production of Space*, trans. Donald Nicholson-Smith (Oxford: Blackwell, 1991; first published in 1974), 12.

45. Lefebvre, *The Production of Space*, 356.

46. Fredric Jameson, "The Cultural Logic of Late Capitalism," in *Postmodern-*

ism or the Cultural Logic of Late Capitalism (Durham, NC: Duke University Press, 1991), 53.

47. Fredric Jameson, "Introduction," in *The Seeds of Time* (New York: Columbia University Press, 1994), xii.

48. "I am addressing a subject about which I know nothing whatsoever, except for the fact that it does not exist. . . . what kind of operation this will be, to produce the concept of something we cannot imagine." Fredric Jameson, "Cognitive Mapping," *Marxism and the Interpretation of Culture*, eds. Cary Nelson, and Lawrence Grossberg (Urbana and Chicago: University of Illinois Press, 1988), 347.

49. James Clifford, "Traveling Cultures," first published in Grossberg et al eds., *Cultural Studies* and reprinted in *Routes: Travel and Translation in the Late Twentieth Century* (Cambridge, MA: Harvard University Press, 1997), 18n. All references are to the latter and will hereafter be cited in the text as Clifford.

50. Interestingly enough, Lisa Lowe's recent essay, "The Intimacy of Four Continents" in Ann Laura Stoler, ed., *Haunted by Empire: Geographies of Intimacy in North American History* (Durham: Duke University Press, 2006) excavates precisely the history of the Asian laborer in the Caribbean that Clifford imagines as out of reach, but she does so not only in relation to European men, but also to Africans and East Asians.

51. See, for instance, Naoki Sakai, "The West and the Rest" in Iftikhar Dadi and Salah Hassan, eds., *Unpacking Europe: Towards a Critical Reading* (Rotterdam, The Netherlands: NAi Publishers, 2001), Pheng Cheah, "Universal Areas: Asian Studies in a World in Motion" in the inaugural issue of *Traces* 1 (2001): 37–70, and for a brief and particularly trenchant critique, Rey Chow, "In the Name of Comparative Literature," in Bernheimer, ed., *Comparative Literature in the Age of Multiculturalism*, 108.

52. The American Comparative Literature Association's latest report, just published as of this writing, would seem to confirm this. No longer calling itself a "Report on Standards," it comprises a set of essays meant to comment on the state of the discipline at the present time from various viewpoints. This format is admirably intended to avoid forced consensus; in practice, however, the essay of Haun Saussy, who chaired the committee, stands in for a full report because it is the only contribution to attempt a panoptic view of the discipline. The tone and objective of Saussy's learned and witty essay contrast sharply with those of the Bernheimer report. Whereas the Bernheimer report was ambitiously prescriptive, not to say tendentious, aiming much of its somewhat hectoring prose at what the discipline ought to be doing, Saussy's is descriptive, limiting itself to detailing the discipline's modest "triumph" over the last decade in the dissemination of its ideas and to commenting on its relation to current institutional and geopolitical trends. Saussy's essay seems to me largely a corrective document to the excesses of the Bernheimer report's sanguine exhortations. As a result, however, no clear purpose or direction for the discipline emerges from the essay, so that while the Bernheimer report, together with the collection of essays accompanying it, made a clear state-

ment about the place of comparative literature in "the age of multiculturalism," the link between the discipline and "an age of globalization" remains diffuse, if not coincidental. A fair number of the contributions remark upon and advocate the renewed attention to world literature, but without the intellectual gusto that animates Anderson and Moretti's projects. In his contribution, Jonathan Culler notes with his usual clarity that the heralded triumph of comparative literature seems distinctly to lack a triumphant tone. Such a tone may be precluded for a topical tome by the very air of these times of American unilateralism and resurgent imperialist war, a sentiment most fully and depressingly encapsulated in Djelal Kadir's contribution. See Haun Saussy, ed., *Comparative Literature in an Age of Globalization* (Baltimore: Johns Hopkins University Press, 2006).

53. Franco Moretti, "Conjectures on World Literature," *New Left Review* 1 (Jan/Feb 2000): 57. See also "Graphs, Maps, Trees: Abstract Models for Literary History—1," *New Left Review* 24 (Nov/Dec 2003): 67–94; "Graphs, Maps, Trees: Abstract Models for Literary History—2," *New Left Review* 26 (Mar/Apr 2004): 79–103; "Graphs, Maps, Trees: Abstract Models for Literary History—3," *New Left Review* 28 (July/Aug 2004): 43–63.

54. Several critics have remarked that this constellation, as well as the provocative idea of distant reading in which Moretti leaves the task of reading non-Western literature to non-Western scholars while reserving to himself the privilege of theorizing the unity of world literature, quite exactly duplicates the colonial division of labor underlying the division between the general humanities and area studies. See Jonathan Arac, "Anglo-Globalism?" *New Left Review* 16 (July/August 2002): 39–45; and Emily Apter, "Global *Translatio*: The 'Invention' of Comparative Literature, Istanbul, 1933," *Critical Inquiry* 2 (Winter 2003): 253.

55. Pascale Casanova, *La république mondiale des lettres* (Paris: Seuil, 1999). Wai Chee Dimock's "Literature for the Planet" *PMLA* 1 (Jan 2001): 173–188, another important contribution, presents an interesting contrast to Casanova's sociological approach and to Anderson's historical approach, to the extent that it takes as its starting point a certain transnational circulation of literature that is not reducible to the cause and effect of both institutional determinations of cultural capital and historical, empirically grounded influence.

56. Benedict Anderson, "In the World-shadow of Bismarck and Nobel," *New Left Review*, 28 (July/Aug 2004): 129.

57. See Benedict Anderson, *The Spectre of Comparisons: Nationalism, Southeast Asia and the World* (London: Verso, 1998), and the collection of essays devoted to it—Pheng Cheah and Jonathan Culler, eds., *Grounds of Comparison: Around the Work of Benedict Anderson* (New York: Routledge, 2003)—many of whose contributors, including Anderson himself, comment on the shortcomings of the two figures of comparison briefly outlined in the book: the inverted telescope and the specter. Might these subsequent essays be read as responding to the insufficiencies of these figures? Anderson suggests as much in this essay when he articulates one of its goals to be "to allow a new global landscape of the late nineteenth century to come into

view, from the estranging vantage point of a brilliant young man (who coined the wonderful expression *el demonio de las comparaciones*) from one of its least-known peripheries" (Anderson, "In the World-Shadow of Bismarck and Nobel," 85). Anderson's sequence of essays have recently been brought together in a book, *Under Three Flags: Anarchism and the Anti-Colonial Imagination* (London: Verso, 2006).

Perhaps the long-distance ocular metaphor of the telescope as well as the metaphor of haunting's doubleness, expressed in the notion of the "specter" (an odd translation of the Spanish *demonio* from Rizal's phrase *"el demonio de las comparaciones"*), have been replaced with an implicit method or figure of comparison grounded in the multiple branchings of narrative.

58. David Damrosch, *What Is World Literature?* (Princeton, NJ: Princeton University Press, 2003).

59. Naoki Sakai, *Translation and Subjectivity: On "Japan" and Cultural Nationalism* (Minneapolis: University of Minnesota Press, 1997); Walter Mignolo, *Local Histories/Global Designs: Coloniality, Subaltern Knowledges, and Border Thinking* (Princeton, NJ: Princeton University Press, 2000); Emily Apter, "Global *Translatio*: The 'Invention' of Comparative Literature, Istanbul, 1933," *Critical Inquiry* 29, 2 (2003): 253–282; Marcel Detienne, *Comparer l'incomparable* (Seuil: Paris, 2000); Gayatri Chakravorty Spivak, *Death of a Discipline* (New York: Columbia University Press, 2003).

60. Rodolphe Gasché, "Comparatively Theoretical," in *Germanistik und Komparatistik* (DFG-Symposion 1993) (Stuttgart: J. B. Metzler Verlag, 1993), 431.

61. Nick Nesbitt in the introduction to his *Voicing Memory: History and Subjectivity in French Caribbean Literature* (Charlottesville: University of Virginia Press, 2003) elaborates this logic most fully in terms of the idea of the aesthetic developed by the Frankfurt school.

62. Paul Gilroy, *The Black Atlantic: Modernity and Double Consciousness* (Cambridge, MA: Harvard University Press, 1993), 37.

63. Gayatri Chakravorty Spivak, *Death of a Discipline*, 31.

64. The most stringent of these critiques is to be found in Aijaz Ahmad, *In Theory: Nations, Classes, Literatures* (London: Verso, 1992), and Arif Dirlik, *The Postcolonial Aura: Third World Criticism in the Age of Global Capitalism* (Boulder, CO: Westview Press, 1997). These are strident polemical interventions from a Marxist position. For a more nuanced and multifaceted Marxist critique of postcolonial theory, see the fine essays in Crystal Bartolovich and Neil Lazarus, eds., *Marxism, Modernity and Postcolonial Studies* (Cambridge: Cambridge University Press, 2002).

65. See Dipesh Chakrabarty, *Provincializing Europe: Postcolonial Thought and Historical Difference* (Princeton, NJ: Princeton University Press, 2000).

66. Aamir Mufti writes compellingly of the great practical difficulties involved in the study of non-Western literatures within the framework of comparative literature, reminding us that whatever the success of postcolonial critique at the level

of institutional rhetoric, its implementation remains tenuous. See "Global Comparativism" in *Critical Inquiry* 2 (Winter 2005): 472–490.

67. David Scott, *Refashioning Futures: Criticism after Postcoloniality* (Princeton, NJ: Princeton University Press, 1999), 13.

68. David Scott, *Conscripts of Modernity: The Tragedy of Colonial Enlightenment* (Durham, NC: Duke University Press, 2004), 2.

69. The Chicago Cultural Studies Group, "Critical Multiculturalism," *Critical Inquiry* 3 (1992): 530–555.

70. Bill Readings, *The University in Ruins* (Cambridge, MA: Harvard University Press, 1996), 126.

71. See Dominick LaCapra, "The University in Ruins?" *Critical Inquiry* 1 (1998): 32–55.

72. Spivak, *Death of a Discipline*, 46.

73. David Lloyd and Lisa Lowe, in the introduction to their co-edited volume *The Politics of Culture in the Shadow of Capital* (Durham, NC: Duke University Press, 1997), 24–25, make strong claims for local culture as a potential locus of contradiction and therefore resistance, particularly in sites where capital encounters premodern or incompletely modern state formations and in which, therefore, the cultural is not marked off as a separate sphere. It is above all, however, Timothy Brennan's provocations in the first four chapters of *At Home in the World: Cosmopolitanism Now* (Cambridge, MA: Harvard University Press, 1997), 12–207, that make my own qualification here necessary. He punctures the inflated claims to oppositionality or subversiveness in so much of postcolonial criticism in the late 1980s and 1990s, showing that, given its number of proponents and its rapid institutionalization, it could easily be seen as, on the contrary, dominant. Moreover, and more damningly, he shows how postcolonial studies constructs or selects third world cultural objects that conform to its own postmodern (taken broadly) intellectual genealogy, with particular emphasis on complexity, discontinuity, multivocality, etc. In other words, "difference" is not so different at all. The field, thus, Brennan argues, severely distorts anticolonial and postcolonial histories, which are often invested in authenticity, master narratives—especially socialism—and totalizing forms—especially the nation-state. The argument seems unassailable to me, except in its polemical overstatement. Is it really possible, I wonder, to seek "real," absolute difference? Doesn't any object brought into the sanctioned discourse of the university by that very fact conform to some rule of recognizability? My own sense is that, while by no means revolutionary, the work of reading, teaching, and commenting on non-Western or postcolonial texts, whatever their level of recognizability, has its own limited value within literary scholarship and teaching in the university. For all the vaunted stardom of postcolonial critics and the success of their rhetoric, at the level of practice huge disparities remain. Many of the most recognized canonical anticolonial and postcolonial texts, for example, lack scholarly apparatuses and often fall quickly out of print.

74. For Lyotard the ultimate (flexible) standard of exchange value, its mode of equivalence, is time, a point that stands in an interesting relation to the commodification of space (Lefebvre) or the reduction of space through time (Harvey), which other thinkers privilege in their analysis of globalization. "La philosophie a pu publier ses réflexions sous le couvert de beaucoup de genre (artistique, politique, théologique, scientifique, anthropologique), au prix certes de méprises et de torts graves, mais enfin . . . —tandis que le calcul économique lui parait fatal. Le différend ne porte pas sur le contenu de la réflexion. Il touche a sa présupposition ultime. La réflexion exige qu'on prenne garde a l'occurrence, qu'on ne sache pas déjà ce qui arrive. Elle laisse ouverte la question: *Arrive-t-il?* Elle essaiye de maintenir (mot pénible) le maintenant. Dans le genre économique, la règle est que ce qui arrive ne peut arriver que s'il est déjà acquitté, donc arrivé. L'échange présuppose que la cession est annulée d'avance par une contre-cession. Le tirage du livre annulé par sa vente. Et plus vite c'est fait, mieux c'est." Jean-François Lyotard, *Le différend* (Paris: Minuit, 1983), 14.

UNGROUNDING COMPARISON

1. Eric Hobsbawm, *The Age of Empire. 1875–1914* (New York: Pantheon Books, 1987), 56–62.

2. Joseph Conrad, *Heart of Darkness*, ed. Robert Kimbrough (New York: W. W. Norton, 1971), 10. Hereafter cited in the text as *HD*.

3. See Ian Watt, *Conrad in the Nineteenth Century* (Berkeley: University of California Press, 1979), 167–161. Hereafter cited in the text as Watt.

4. See Patrick Brantlinger, *Rule of Darkness: British Literature and Imperialism* (Ithaca: Cornell University Press, 1988), 32–40.

5. Quoted in Watt, *Conrad in the Nineteenth Century*, 163.

6. F. R. Leavis, *The Great Tradition: George Eliot, Henry James, Joseph Conrad* (London: Chatto & Windus, 1948), 180.

7. See, for instance, Edward Said, *Culture and Imperialism* (New York: Knopf, 1993), 24–25.

8. Albert Memmi, *Portrait du colonisé* (Paris: Gallimard, 1985), 89. My translation. The work is better known (and perhaps better represented) by its English title, *The Colonizer and the Colonized*, trans. Howard Greenfeld (Boston: Beacon Press, 1991).

9. Frantz Fanon, *Les damnés de la terre* (Paris: Gallimard, 1991), 69. My translation.

10. Bette London, "Reading Race and Gender in Conrad's Dark Continent," *Criticism* 21 (Summer 1989).

11. Aaron Fogel, *Coercion to Speak: Conrad's Poetics of Dialogue* (Cambridge, MA: Harvard University Press, 1985), 19.

12. Gérard Genette, *Figures III* (Paris: Éditions du Seuil, 1972), 228. My translation.

13. Homi K. Bhabha, *The Location of Culture* (London: Routledge, 1994), 107. Hereafter cited in the text as Bhabha.

14. Watt, *Conrad in the Nineteenth Century*, 63.

15. Watt, *Conrad in the Nineteenth Century*, 63, 67.

16. See Norman Sherry, *Conrad: The Critical Heritage* (London: Routledge and Kegan Paul, 1973).

17. Joseph Conrad, *An Outcast of the Islands* (Middlesex, NY: Penguin Books, 1981; 1896), 129–130.

18. Joseph Conrad, *An Outcast of the Islands*, 289.

19. Joseph Conrad, "An Outpost of Progress," in *Selected Tales from Conrad*, ed., Nigel Stewart (London: Faber and Faber, 1977; 1897), 31.

20. Such early criticisms of Conrad's style are of a piece with the frequent charge of wordiness, overwriting, and excess leveled at him. In an anonymous review of *An Outcast of the Islands*, H. G. Wells wrote: "Mr. Conrad is wordy; his story is not so much told as seen intermittently through a haze of sentences. He has still to learn the great half of his art, the art of leaving things unwritten." (Quoted in V. S. Naipaul, "Conrad's Darkness," 211. Also quoted more briefly in Watt, *Conrad in the Nineteenth Century*, 126.)

21. Ford Madox Ford, *Joseph Conrad: A Personal Remembrance* (Boston: Little Brown, 1924), 36.

22. Watt, *Conrad in the Nineteenth Century*, 53.

23. J. Hillis Miller, *The Form of Victorian Fiction: Thackeray, Dickens, Trollope, George Eliot, Meredith and Hardy* (Notre Dame: University of Notre Dame Press, 1968), 67.

24. Quoted in Watt, *Conrad in the Nineteenth Century*, 214.

25. In George Levine, *The Realistic Imagination* (Chicago: University of Chicago Press, 1981), Levine puts Conrad in a chapter with George Eliot, reading him as the heir to realist narrative. Ian Watt (in *Conrad in the Nineteenth Century*) rigorously traces Conrad's relation to nineteenth-century aesthetic and intellectual currents. Facing the other direction, many studies of the modern novel give Conrad pride of place, e.g., Bette London, *The Appropriated Voice: Narrative Authority in Conrad, Forster, Woolf* (Ann Arbor: University of Michigan Press, 1990), and Perry Meisel, *The Myth of the Modern: A Study in British Literature and Criticism after 1850* (New Haven, CT: Yale University Press, 1987).

26. Fredric Jameson, *The Political Unconscious: Narrative as a Socially Symbolic Act* (Ithaca, NY: Cornell University Press, 1981), 74. Hereafter cited in the text as Jameson.

27. See, e.g., Zdzislaw Najder, *Joseph Conrad: A Chronicle* (New Brunswick, NJ: Rutgers University Press, 1983), 231; M. M. Mahood, *The Colonial Encounter* (London: Collings, 1977), 23. W. Y. Tindall puts it very nicely: [Marlow is] the Victorian gentleman, the embodiment maybe of Conrad's aspiration" ("Apology for Marlow" in *From Jane Austen to Joseph Conrad* (Minneapolis: University of Minnesota Press, 1958), 277). Francis Mulhern points out that the first stories written for *Blackwood's*

Magazine provided a welcome diversion from Conrad's tortured, stalled, and solitary writing of *The Rescue* (which he was to complete some twenty years later) and that Conrad himself understood writing for *Blackwood's* as an alternative to writing for the market. See Francis Mulhern, "Conrad's Inconceivable History," *New Left Review* 38 (March/April 2006): 63. Hereafter cited in the text as Mulhern.

28. Watt, *Conrad in the Nineteenth Century*, 212.

29. This fascinating word, "personate," which, while denoting the same meaning as "impersonate," to act the part of, to portray, has none of the connotation of exact imitation endowed by the prefix -im. It is, like "foil," another one of those slightly decentered Conradian word choices in which symmetrical equivalence is blurred or sidestepped. Conrad uses the word in his only comment regarding his infamous narrator, Marlow, in the author's note to *Youth*: "It is pleasant to remember that nobody had charged him with fraudulent purposes or looked down on him as a charlatan; but apart from that he was supposed to be all sorts of things: a clever screen, a mere device, a '*personator*,' a familiar spirit, a whispering 'daemon'" (*Heart of Darkness*, 159; my emphasis).

30. Joseph Conrad, "Youth," in *Youth and Two Other Stories* (New York: Doubleday, 1920). Hereafter cited in the text as *Y*.

31. Najder, *Joseph Conrad: A Chronicle*, 77–78. I might add that the fictional renaming of the *Palestine* as the *Judea* nicely recapitulates the story's retrospective cast and its attendant, though failed, transformation of history into "universal" legend that binds eternal communities.

32. "Karain: A Memory," in Nigel Stewart, ed., *Selected Tales from Conrad* (London: Faber and Faber, 1977; 1897), 81. Hereafter cited in the text as *K*.

33. Bhabha, *The Location of Culture*, 110.

34. Peter Brooks, *Reading for the Plot: Design and Intention in Narrative* (New York: A. A. Knopf, 1984), 29.

35. Watt, *Conrad in the Nineteenth Century*, 269.

36. Watt, *Conrad in the Nineteenth Century*, 269.

37. Joseph Conrad, *Lord Jim*, Thomas Moser, ed. (New York: Norton, 1968), 135–136. Hereafter cited in the text as *LJ*.

38. There is circumstantial evidence that Conrad may have conceived it as a response to a Polish intellectual's denunciation of him as a traitor to Poland, an artistic mercenary selling his talents to wealthy England. See Eloise Knapp Hay, "Lord Jim: From Sketch to Novel," reprinted in the 1968 Norton edition of *Lord Jim*, 429.

39. The captain's whole speech reads like a farce of *Heart of Darkness*, from colonial outposts "situated internally" to boats on their way upriver fired upon by "irresponsive parties." Is he a foil for Marlow as the latter appeared and discoursed in *Heart of Darkness*? Marlow as half-caste, Marlow robbed of any white pretensions to tragically unveiling the failures of noble civilizing missions? Marlow as mongrel, which is to say, Marlow as Conrad. . . .

40. Marlow associates "us" with an explicitly racial category: "Beloved, trusted, and admired as he [Dain Waris] was, he was still one of *them*, while Jim was one of *us*" (*LJ*, 267; Conrad's emphasis).

41. Geoffrey Galt Harpham, *One of Us: The Mastery of Joseph Conrad* (Chicago: University of Chicago Press, 1996), 12.

42. Raymond Williams, in *The English Novel from Dickens to Lawrence* (New York: Oxford University Press, 1970), 154, argues against the narrow critical emphasis on isolation in Conrad. Avrom Fleischman, as I have already mentioned, makes a strong case for organic community as a political ideal in the "manifest content" of Conrad's fiction. David Thorburn, in *Conrad's Romanticism* (New Haven, CT: Yale University Press, 1974), aligns Conrad's insistence on "solidarity" both in his artistic manifesto, the preface to *Nigger of the Narcissus*, and in his fictions with Wordsworthian constructions of communion. Finally, Benita Parry, though she doesn't explicitly link it to community, reads a distinctively romantic inclination in *Lord Jim*: "the fiction's vatic impulses are constrained to issue as illuminations of the human need to anticipate and possess the future, but without intimations of who the architects of the new age will be or what it is they are striving to construct" (*Conrad and Imperialism: Ideological Boundaries and Visionary Frontiers*, 98), making of the novel one of the instances of the "Visionary Frontiers" in her study's title.

43. Jean-Luc Nancy, *La communauté désœuvrée* (Paris: Christian Bourgeois, 1986), 72.

EMPIRE'S LOOSE ENDS

1. One letter begins: "I am a white educator from the inner city. . . ." Another, "As a black male. . . ." Another, "Having grown up white in a white middle-class neighborhood. . . ." *Los Angeles Times*, May 9, 1992. What is missing in this binary dissimilation between white and black or Asian and black is also what was missing from much of the coverage and commentary on the events—namely, the substantial Latino participation in the rebellion.

2. The essay first appeared as "An Image of Africa" in the *Massachusetts Review* 4 (1977), and was reprinted with the same title in *Research in African Literature*. A version of it appeared in the *Times Literary Supplement* 1 (1980): 193 and in the most recent Norton critical edition of Conrad's *Heart of Darkness*, ed. Robert Kimbrough (New York: Norton, 1988), 251–262. Citations within the text will be to *Research in African Literature* 9 (Spring 1978) and hereafter cited in the text as Achebe.

3. Joseph Conrad, *Heart of Darkness*, 37.

4. Ngugi is often deployed in critiques of Achebe's denunciation of Conrad. Ngugi wrote his Master's thesis and several articles on Conrad. See Peter Nazareth, "Out of Darkness: Conrad and Other Third World Writers," *Conradiana* 24 (1982): 171–187.

5. Harpham quips that such a text would drain the power of Conrad's vision and turn it into a "*Heart of Grayness.*" I think he misses the point, however, when he argues that what Achebe "admires in Conrad might finally be indistinguishable from what he condemns" and that this is yet another indication of Conrad's transcendent "greatness." Achebe isolates precisely those points in the text that manifest gratuitous racism and suggests quite unequivocally that a less racist depiction, one that would at least acknowledge the viability of African culture, would have been possible at the time. What he admires and what he condemns are clearly not identical. Moreover, my own argument is that what is at stake in the postcolonial readings of Conrad I analyze is precisely not a quality that transcends time, place, and perspective, but, on the contrary, that Conrad's "greatness," if that is still the right word, inheres precisely in his eloquent articulation of partiality.

6. See, for instance, Hunt Hawkins, "The Issue of Racism in *Heart of Darkness,*" *Conradiana* 3 (1982), 168. In addition to restating all the objections Achebe raises, Hawkins also makes a detailed case for the veracity of Conrad's representation of cannibalism. P. J. M. Robertson ("*Things Fall Apart* and *Heart of Darkness*: a Creative Dialogue" *International Fiction Review* 2 (1980),) adds that had Conrad had the benefit of *Things Fall Apart* perhaps his views would have been larger, but alas, "it would be another fifty years before the African's English would be such as to make possible the writing of *Things Fall Apart*" (Robertson, 110).

7. Cedric Watts, "'A Bloody Racist': About Achebe's View of Conrad," *The Yearbook of English Studies* 13 (1983): 196. Hereafter cited in the text as Watts.

8. Susan L. Blake, "Racism and the Classics: Teaching *Heart of Darkness.*" *CLA Journal* 4 (1982): 397–404, also invokes comparison to counter Achebe's proposition that *Heart of Darkness* should not be read, but with a very different aim from Watts. For her, a comparison between *Heart of Darkness* and African novels "throws the limitation of the work into relief without requiring the teacher to make a case against it," thus providing a way out of the quandary of teaching works whose position some might not endorse. It is a suggestion first made by Mahood in *The Colonial Encounter.* Though the intention may be laudable, there seems to me to be a problem in merely setting works into parity and reading them as different points of view about a single place. It displaces the focus from the asymmetry of power relations onto simply the multiplicity of points of view. It also relieves the reader from acknowledging racial interpellation. For a reading of white and black African writers together, which takes full account of this dissymmetry, see Abdul JanMohamed, *Manichean Aesthetics: The Politics of Literature in Colonial Africa* (Amherst, MA: Amherst University Press, 1983).

9. For a subtle account of racially bounded reading in the feminist American context, see Elizabeth Abel, "Black Writing, White Reading: Race and the Politics of Feminist Interpretation," *Critical Inquiry* 19 (Spring 1993): 470–498. The first part of the essay is a detailed account of two readings, one by a black woman and one by a white woman, of a short story by Toni Morrison in which the two main characters' race is left deliberately ambiguous. What is interesting is Abel's em-

phasis on how a critic's race necessarily determines her reading of the racial code. I have been thinking in terms of a text "marking" a reader, rather than a reader deploying a code. The process as I see it is more actively determined by the work itself, something that happens to a reader rather than something a reader does to a text—this has partly to do with the nature of the text in question (where Morrison deliberately scrambles racial codes, Conrad in *Heart of Darkness* does quite the opposite) and partly to do with the difference between racial identifications within a single nation and racial identification across imperial divides.

10. For the classic argument on the historical underpinnings of reader response, see Wolfgang Iser, *The Act of Reading: A Theory of Aesthetic Response* (Baltimore: Johns Hopkins University Press, 1978), 203ff. I will use the term "postcolonial" throughout the chapter, though to the extent that what is often at stake here is not one particular colonial history or another, but the condition of imperialism as such; "postimperial," the term Said uses in *Culture and Imperialism*, might be more exact. However, the sheer currency of the term "postcolonial" has by now made it a signifier for both of these meanings.

11. Wilson Harris, "The Frontier on Which *Heart of Darkness* Stands," *Research in African Literatures* 1 (Spring 1981): 86. Hereafter cited in the text as Harris.

12. V. S. Naipaul, "Conrad's Darkness," in *The Return of Eva Peron* (New York: Knopf, 1980). Hereafter cited in the text as Naipaul.

13. Sara Suleri, "Naipaul's Arrival," *The Yale Journal of Criticism* 1 (fall 1988): 25. Hereafter cited in the text as Suleri.

14. Louis Althusser, "Ideology and Ideological State Apparatuses," in *Lenin and Philosophy and Other Essays*, trans. by Ben Brewster. (London: New Left Books, 1971), 163. Hereafter cited in the text as ISA.

15. The Conradian conversation by no means stops with Harris and Naipaul. A notable contribution is Peter Nazareth's "Out of Darkness: Conrad and Other Third World Writers," *Conradiana* 24 (1982): 171–187. The author, a Goan Ugandan and a novelist, adds another layer to experiential readings of Conrad when he locates his own experience as a colonial between Naipaul's and Ngugi's readings of Conrad, with some affinities to Achebe and Harris.

16. See, for instance, Ebele Obumselu, "*A Grain of Wheat*: Ngugi's Debt to Conrad," *The Benin Review* 1 (1974): 80–91, and a response to it, Jabbi Bu-Buakei, "Conrad's Influence on Betrayal in *A Grain of Wheat*," *Research in African Literatures* 11 (1980): 50–83.

17. Edward Said, "Third World Intellectuals and Metropolitan Culture," *Raritan* 3 (winter 1990): 49. Hereafter cited in the text as Said. Many of the positions in this essay recur in slightly different form in his *Culture and Imperialism* (New York: Alfred A. Knopf, 1993).

18. Said, *Culture and Imperialism*, 54–56.

19. Homi Bhabha, *The Locations of Culture* (New York: Routledge, 1994), 175.

20. Ibid., 241. Emphasis in the original.

21. Jean-Luc Nancy, *La communauté désoeuvrée* (Paris: Christian Bourgeois,

1986). Hereafter cited in the text as Nancy. Nancy's main reference is to Bataille, with important points borrowed from Hegel and Martin Heidegger. The text as a whole, in addition, emerges in dialogue with Maurice Blanchot, whose *La communauté inavouable* (Paris: Editions de Minuit, 1983) is a response to one chapter and the starting point of a later chapter. The book itself is thus something of a communal endeavor, or should I say exposure. Though an English translation exists, I provide here my own translation. What is lost in awkwardness I hope will be partly regained in nuance.

22. There is no exact English equivalent to this use of the adjective "similar" as a substantive referring to a person. The word means comrade, colleague, co-conspirator, someone in the same position. All this is rendered in the very adjective for similarity, rather than through the Latin "con" ("with") and denoting shared activity. The sharing of the *semblable* is in similarity itself. I will therefore keep to the French word.

23. Mary Louise Pratt, in *Imperial Eyes: Travel Writing and Transculturation* (New York: Routledge, 1992), shows the ambiguities and mutual destabilization affecting even the most magisterial of the imperial travelers.

24. Celia M. Britton, *Edouard Glissant and Postcolonial Theory: Strategies of Language and Resistance* (Charlottesville: University of Virginia Press, 1999), 5.

25. Édouard Glissant, *L'Intention poétique* (Paris: Éditions du Seuil, 1969), hereafter cited in the text as *IP*; *Le discours antillais* (Paris: Éditions du Seuil, 1981), hereafter cited in the text as *DA*; *Poétique de la Relation* (Paris: Éditions Gallimard, 1990), hereafter cited in the text as *PR*; *Vers une poétique du divers* (Montréal: Presses de l'université de Montréal, 1995), hereafter cited in the text as *PD*; *Traité du Tout-Monde* (Paris: Éditions Gallimard, 1997); La cohée du Lamentin (Paris: Éditions Gallimard, 2005).

26. Lucien Taylor elaborates an important critique of Glissant's notion of the "Same" in "The Same Difference," *Transition* 63 (1993): 106–111. In the most concise and penetrating account of the Glissantian category of Relation to date, Jacques Coursil presents it as "a tool that a poetics proposes to the sciences of history, a tool which mediates the passage from the simplicity of the world understood as a unicity ("l'Un-monde") to the complexity of the world as totality ("Tout-monde") without falling into the hybrid amalgamations of relativism." See "La Catégorie de la relation dans less essais d'Edourard Glissant: Philosophie d'une poétique," in *Poétiques d'Edouard Glissant*, ed. Jacques Chevrier (Paris: Presses de l'Universite de Paris-Sorbonne, 1999), 100. My translation.

27. A subsequent work, *La comparution: Politique à venir*, in collaboration with Christophe Bailly (Paris: Christian Bourgois, 1991), poses the problem of community in the more explicit political context of the immediate time of writing (summer 1991), the Gulf War, and just beyond its limit, at the moment of publication, the fall of the Soviet Union, behind both of which, no doubt, stands the imminent European Community (1992). This text poses a meditation on community much more explicitly at the accomplished "end" of communism that is also figured here

as the end of revolution as such, but community still refers, as the title indicates, to a *coming* politics. It is notable that Nancy's main contribution to this volume is an extensive engagement with Marx.

28. While my argument here intersects with Peter Hallward's in *Absolutely Post-colonial: Writing Between the Singular and the Specific* (Manchester: Manchester University Press, 2001), in many ways, I emphasize the collective over the singular in Glissant and insist, reading him perhaps somewhat against the grain of his own abstraction, on the correlation of his texts with a distinct, material postcolonial itinerary.

29. See J. Michael Dash, *Édouard Glissant* (Cambridge: Cambridge University Press, 1995), and the very useful biographical passages in Bernadette Cailler, *Les conquérants de la nuit nue: Édouard Glissant et l'H(h)istoire antillaise* (Tübingen: Gunter Narr Verlag, 1988).

30. Chris Bongie, *Islands and Exiles: The Creole Identities of Post/Colonial Literatures* (Stanford, CA: Stanford University Press, 1998), 138. Hereafter cited in the text as Bongie.

RUINED METAPHOR

1. Derek Walcott, "What the Twilight Says: An Overture," in *Dream on Monkey Mountain and Other Plays* (New York: Farrar, Straus and Giroux, 1970), 4. Hereafter cited in the text as "Twilight."

2. Rei Terada, *Derek Walcott's Poetry: American Mimicry* (Boston: Northeastern University Press, 1992), 1–5.

3. For discussion on the term "postcolonial" see Anthony Kwame Appiah, "Is the Post- in Postmodernism the Post- in Postcolonial?" *Critical Inquiry* 17 (1991), and Ella Shohat "Notes on the "Post-Colonial" *Social Text* 31/32 (1992).

4. Chris Bongie, *Islands and Exiles: The Creole Identities of Post/Colonial Literatures* (Stanford: Stanford University Press, 1998), 66.

5. Tejumola Olaniyan makes a similar point in "Derek Walcott: Liminal Spaces/Substantive Histories," in *Caribbean Romances: The Politics of Regional Representation*, ed. Belinda Edmondson (Charlottesville: University Press of Virginia, 1999), 199–214.

6. Robert Hamner, *Epic of the Dispossessed: Derek Walcott's* Omeros (Columbia: University of Missouri Press, 1997), 8.

7. Mary Lefkowitz, "Bringing Him Back Alive," *The New York Times Book Review*, 7 October 1990: 1, 34–55. Reprinted in Robert Hamner, ed., *Critical Perspectives of Derek Walcott* (Washington, D.C.: Three Continents Press, 1993), 400. Hereafter cited in the text as Lefkowitz.

8. See the important essay by Eddie Baugh, "The West Indian Writer and His Quarrel With History," *Tapia* (February 20 and 27, 1977).

9. "The Caribbean: Culture or Mimicry," in *Journal of Interamerican Studies and World Affairs* 16.1 (February 1974): 5. Hereafter cited in the text as "Mimicry."

10. Derek Walcott, "The Muse of History," in *Is Massa Day Dead? Black Moods in the Caribbean*, ed. Orde Coombs (New York: Doubleday, 1974), 2. Hereafter cited in the text as "Muse."

11. Derek Walcott, "Another Life," in *Collected Poems 1948–1984* (New York: Farrar, Straus and Giroux, 1988), 212. Hereafter cited in the text as AL.

12. James Anthony Froude, *The English in the West Indies or The Bow of Ulysses* (New York: Scribner's Sons, 1888), 347. Hereafter cited in the text as Froude. West Indian responses to Froude's resounding condemnation began as early as the year after his book's publication with J. J. Thomas' *Froudacity* (1889).

13. See Ian Gregory Strachan, *Paradise and Plantations: Tourism and Culture in the Anglophone Caribbean* (Charlottesville: University of Virginia Press, 2002), 62–72, for an illuminating discussion of this period.

14. See, for instance, *The Antilles: Fragments of Epic Memory* (hereafter cited in the text as *Antilles*) and as an epigraph to the poem "Air" (1969) in *Collected Poems 1948–1984* (New York: Farrar, Straus and Giroux, 1986), 113.

15. V. S. Naipaul, *The Middle Passage* (New York: Anchor Books, 1962), 29. Hereafter cited in the text as "Passage."

16. Strachan, *Paradise and Plantations*, 183.

17. See Edward Kamau Brathwaite, "History, The Caribbean Writer and X/Self," in *Crisis and Creativity in the New Literatures in English*, eds. Geoffrey V. Davis and Hena Maes-Jelinek (Amsterdam: Rodopi, 1990), 29.

18. Patrick Chamoiseau, *Texaco* (Paris: Gallimard, 1992), 45.

19. Derek Walcott, "A Far Cry From Africa," in *Collected Poems 1948–1984*, 18.

20. See Paul Breslin, *Nobody's Nation: Reading Derek Walcott* (Chicago: University of Chicago Press, 2001), 39–40; and Bruce King. *Derek Walcott: A Caribbean Life* (Oxford: Oxford University Press, 2000), 255.

21. Tejumola Olaniyan has argued the former in "Derek Walcott: Liminal Spaces/Substantive Histories," *Caribbean Romances: The Politics of Regional Representation*, ed. Belinda Edmondson (Charlottesville: University Press of Virginia, 1999), 199–214. Édouard Glissant argues the latter, assimilating Walcott to his own position on History/histories, in *Le discours antillais* (Paris: Éditions du Seuil, 1981), 133. Simon Gikandi perhaps comes down in the middle when he writes that Walcott "seems to become enmeshed in history the more he tries to escape from it" (*Writing in Limbo: Modernism and Caribbean Literature* (Ithaca, NY: Cornell University Press, 1992), 9).

22. Breslin, *Nobody's Nation*, 4–6.

23. "History is a nightmare from which I am trying to awake" (James Joyce, *Ulysses* (New York: Vintage, 1961), 34). Less well-remembered is the humorous extension of this resounding statement: "From the playfield the boys raised a shout. A whirring whistle: goal. What if that nightmare gave you a back kick?" It's also worth remembering that this now iconic phrase so often used to express the relation of a certain modernist aesthetic to history is articulated in this novel in direct response to anti-Semitism.

24. Edward Baugh, *Derek Walcott: Memory as Vision: Another Life* (London: Longman, 1978).

25. "I met History once, but he ain't recognize me, / [. . .] I confront him and shout, 'Sir, is Shabine! / They say I'se your grandson. You remember Grandma, / your black cook, at all?' The Bitch hawk and spat. / A spit like that worth any number of words. / But that's all them bastards left us: words" ("The Schooner Flight," *Collected Poems 1948–1984*, 350).

26. George Seferis, "Thrush" (1946) in *Collected Poems*, translated, edited and introduced by Edmund Keeley and Philip Sherrard (Princeton, NJ: Princeton University Press, 1995), 164–165.

27. George Seferis, "Mythistorema 3" (1933–44), in *Collected Poems*. In a poem that finds an elaborate and baroque development in *Omeros*, "From This Far" (1981), Walcott seems to be addressing this particular poem: "but no stone head rolls in the ochre dust, / in the soil of our islands no gods are buried / They were shipped to us, Seferis, / dead on arrival" (*Collected Poems 1924–1955*, 414).

28. T. S. Eliot, "Tradition and the Individual Talent" (1919) in *Selected Essays* (New York: Harcourt, Brace and World, 1964), 5.

29. Gregson Davis, "'With No Homeric Shadow': The Disavowal of Epic in Derek Walcott's *Omeros*," *The South Atlantic Quarterly* 2 (1997): 321–333.

30. Paule Marshall's *Praisesong for the Widow* (New York: Plume, 1983), for instance, articulates the culture and class "roots" fantasy of that tourism, a deculturation or unassimilation from white culture and absorption back into a more authentic community.

31. Dean MacCannell, *Empty Meeting Grounds: The Tourist Papers* (New York: Routledge, 1992), 177.

32. *St. Lucia Star*, 26 August 1988, cited in Polly Patullo, *Last Resorts: The Cost of Tourism in the Caribbean* (London: Cassell, 1996), 2–3. The ironies in Patullo's brief and pragmatic account are so outlandish and multilayered they might be derived from some hitherto unknown manuscript of Jonathan Swift. The area in question, for instance, was sacred to St. Lucia's annihilated native Arawaks; the resort's tennis court now covers what was probably their burial ground. On the way to the Jalousie resort there is a home for the poor and the old named "Malgretout" (in spite of everything). "Local fishermen are no longer allowed to work the bay where guests now lie on imported sand" (p. 4).

33. ". . . as forgettable as a vacation" (Derek Walcott, *The Antilles*).

34. Jonathan Culler, *Framing the Sign: Criticism and Its Institutions* (Oxford: Blackwell, 1988), 156.

35. See, for instance, Roland Robertson, *Globalization: Social Theory and Global Culture* (London: Sage, 1992).

36. Henri Lefebvre, *The Production of Space*, trans. Donald Nicholson-Smith (Cambridge, MA: Blackwell, 1991), 353. Hereafter cited in the text as Lefebvre.

37. It's hard to resist quoting Naipaul casting a jaundiced eye on the scene in 1960: "Jamaica presents to the outside world two opposed images: the expensive

winter resort—turquoise sea, white sands, reverential bowtied black servants, sunglassed figures below striped umbrellas: *Tourism matters to you* is the theme of a despairing advertising campaign run by the Jamaica Tourist Board to diminish the increasing hostility to tourists—and the immigrant boat-trains arriving at London's gloomy railway stations: *Niggers go home* painted in large red letters in Brixton and *Keep Britain white* chalked everywhere" (*The Middle Passage*, 115).

38. A statistic to be found in a guidebook; Sarah Cameron and Ben Box, eds., *1994 Caribbean Islands Handbook* 5th ed., 533.

39. Jahan Ramazani, *The Hybrid Muse: Postcolonial Poetry in English* (Chicago: University of Chicago Press, 2001), 57. Hereafter cited in the text as Ramazani.

40. Jean-Paul Sartre, Preface in Frantz Fanon, *Les damnés de la terre* (Paris: Gallimard, 1991) 37–38. My translation.

41. See Peter Hulme, *Colonial Encounters: Europe and the Native Caribbean 1492–1797* (New York: Routledge, 1986) for a remarkable reading of this discourse through the early eighteenth century. See also Strachan, *Paradise and Plantation*, and Mimi Sheller, *Consuming the Caribbean: From Arawaks to Zombies* (London: Routledge, 2003).

42. Narda Graham, born, raised, and educated in Jamaica through high school, remarks on the profound (and colonial) irony of the fact that she discovered Kamau Brathwaite, one of the Anglophone Caribbean's two most accomplished and celebrated poets (the other is Walcott, of course), in the "Great Books" course she was required to take as a comparative literature major at Cornell University. See "Words, Pebbles and Other Fragments: The Poetry of Edward Kamau Brathwaite." Honors Thesis (Department of Comparative Literature, Cornell University, April 1999).

43. See, for instance, D. J. R. Bruckner, "A Poem in Homage to an Unwanted Man," *New York Times* (7 October 1991; natl. ed.): C13.

44. Breslin, *Nobody's Nation*, 266 and 272.

45. Derek Walcott, "Reflections on *Omeros*," *The South Atlantic Quarterly* 2 (1997): 238–239.

46. Gordon K. Lewis devotes a subsection entitled "The Caribbean and the Mediterranean" to this idea in his *Main Currents in Caribbean Thought: The Historical Evolution of Caribbean Society in Its Ideological Aspects, 1492–1900* (Baltimore: Johns Hopkins University Press, 1983), 16–20. Naipaul writes: "The Caribbean has been described as Europe's other sea, the Mediterranean of the New World. It was a Mediterranean which summoned up every dark human instinct without the complementary impulses towards nobility and beauty of older lands, a Mediterranean where civilization turned satanic, perverting those it attracted. And if one considers this sea, which the tourist now enlivens with his fantastic uniform as a wasteful consumer of men through more than three centuries . . . it would seem that simply to have survived in the West Indies is to have triumphed" (*The Middle Passage*, 224). Walcott himself used ancient Greek materials previously in his plays; see especially *Ione*, with its Homeric cast of characters, and a

play that remains unpublished but was produced under the title *The Isle Is Full of Noises*. See Breslin, *Nobody's Nation*, 37 and 246. C. L. R. James writes, "I believed that if when I left school I had gone into the society of Ancient Greece I would have been more at home than ever I had been since. It was a fantasy, but for me it had meaning. The world we lived in, and Ancient Greece" (*Beyond a Boundary* (New York: Pantheon, 1983), 152).

47. For what it's worth, the "boxer's broken nose" probably indicates that this is a reproduction of a portrait of Homer in the Boston Museum of Art and not the more familiar portrait from (I believe) the Vatican, which is the model for the tourist souvenirs sold in Greece.

48. See Frederick Treves, *The Cradle of the Deep: An Account of a Voyage to the West Indies* (New York: EP Dutton and Company, 1928), first published in 1908: "There can hardly be a spot, that, for its size, has played a more stirring part in the history of arms or in the chronicles of the British navy and army. There is no dot of land that has been so desperately fought over, so savagely wrangled for, as this too fair island. St. Lucia is the Helen of the West Indies, and has been the cause of more blood-shedding than was ever provoked by Helen of Troy" (p. 109).

49. Aristotle, *Poetics*, 1459a7.

50. Jacques Derrida, "White Mythology: Metaphor in the Text of Philosophy," in *The Margins of Philosophy*, trans. Alan Bass (Chicago: University of Chicago Press, 1982), 239. Hereafter cited in the text as "White."

51. Homer, *Iliad*, trans. Richmond Lattimore. All citations from the *Iliad* will be from Lattimore's translation unless otherwise indicated. Hereafter cited in the text as *Iliad*.

52. This simile, along with one other in the *Iliad* that also clearly contradicts its subject (*Iliad* XII, 40–49), has drawn its share of attention; see Carroll Moulton, *Similes in the Homeric Poems* (Göttingen: Vandenhoeck and Ruprecht, 1977), 46.

53. Ancient critics tended to analyze the similes by focusing on the *Vergleichspunkt*, the point of resemblance or correspondence. See A. Clausing, *Kritik und Exegese der Homerischen Gleichnisse im Altertum* (Parchim: Druck von H, Friese, 1913), 50–51. In the glory days of the analysts this emphasis on points of correspondence fueled many arguments for interpolation. It wasn't until the publication of Hermann Fränkel's *Die Homerischen Gleichnisse* (Göttingen: Vandenhoeck and Ruprecht, 1921; 1977) that a more capacious sense of the similes' breadth of reference and their multiple functions came into modern criticism, though his rather impressionistic readings have been minutely and systematically contested, in, for instance, D. J. N. Lee, *The Similes of the Iliad and the Odyssey Compared* (Melbourne, Australia: Melbourne University Press, 1964).

54. For an analysis of the simile in terms of oral composition, see W. C. Scott, *The Oral Nature of the Homeric Simile* (Leiden: Brill, 1974). For more literary-minded interpretations that take account of orality see, for instance, Charles Segal, "The Theme of the Mutilation of the Corpse," *Mnemosyne* (1973), and Steven H.

Lonsdale, *Creatures of Speech: Lion, Herding, and Hunting Similes in the Iliad* (Stuttgart: B. G. Teubner, 1990).

55. Susanne Lindgren Wofford, *The Choice of Achilles: The Ideology of Trope in the Epic* (Stanford, CA: Stanford University Press, 1992). Hereafter cited in the text as *Choice*.

56. See Jean-Pierre Vernant, *Mythe et pensée chez les grecs* (Paris: Éditions la découverte, 1990), 109–137. See also Andrew Ford, *Homer: The Poetry of the Past* (Ithaca, NY: Cornell University Press, 1992).

57. The only notable exception I can muster is Achilles' final pursuit of Hektor through the landscape just outside the walls of Troy in book XXII.

58. Wolfgang Schadewalt, "Die Homerische Gleichniswelt und die Kretisch-Mykenische Kunst," in *Von Homers Welt und Werk* (Stuttgart: KF Koehler Verlag, 1959), 130–136.

59. I am grateful to Michael Nagler for pointing this out to me.

60. Gregory Nagy, *The Best of the Achaeans: Concepts of the Hero in Archaic Greek Poetry* (Baltimore: Johns Hopkins University Press, 1979), 115–116.

61. Rei Terada introduces the adjective "Omeric" in her inspiring study, *Derek Walcott's Poetry*, 187.

62. Jamaica Kincaid, *A Small Place* (New York: Penguin, 1988), 81. Hereafter cited in the text as Kincaid.

63. The terms post-colonizer and post-colonized are developed by Simon During in "Postmodernism or Post-Colonialism Today," *Textual Practice* 1 (1987), 45.

64. My reading of Kincaid here owes much to Ian Bogost's outburst in a seminar (November 1998, Cornell University) discussion of the text against what he perceived as her utter negation of any possible relation of hospitality between self and other.

65. Roger Caillois, "Mimicry and Legendary Psychasthenia," trans. John Shepley, in *October* 31, (Winter 1984): 30.

66. John B. Van Sickle, "A Poet's St Lucia," *Los Angeles Times*, February 22, 1998, L13.

67. Van Sickle doesn't seem to be aware that this could be the real-life Hector who has a cousin named Achille, as Walcott recently revealed: "But the shopkeeper named Hector—this is true—had a cousin named Achille. Somebody in St. Lucia must have decided to call one child Hector and the other Achille. Obviously, that's what happened. If you asked Hector what Hector did, he wouldn't know; if you asked Achille what Achilles did, he wouldn't know either" (Derek Walcott, "Reflections on *Omeros*," *The South Atlantic Quarterly* 2 (1997): 238–239).

THE GIFT OF BELITTLING ALL THINGS

1. Voltaire, *Essai sur les moeurs et l'esprit des nations* (Paris: Garnier, 1963), 380; also quoted in Kathleen Gyssels, *Filles de solitude: Essai sur les (auto-)biographies fictives de Simone et André Schwarz-Bart* (Paris: L'Harmattan, 1996), 181.

2. De Gaulle's comment is cited with this wording as an epigraph to Édouard Glissant's *Le discours antillais* (Paris: Éditions du Seuil, 1981). It occurs with a slightly different wording ("Entre l'Amérique et l'Europe, il n'y a que l'Océan et quelques poussières!" [Between Europe and America there is only the ocean and a few specks of dust!]) in René Ménil's essay, first delivered as a lecture in June of 1964, three months after de Gaulle's visit. I cite Ménil's text at some length in order to give a sense of the statement's immediate neocolonial resonance within the political context of Martinique's struggle to gain some form of autonomy:

> "'Surtout,' répètent les Assimilés à l'adresse du pouvoir colonial, 'gardez-vous de confier aux Martiniquais la direction politique de leur pays! Les Martiniquais ne peuvent pas, ne doivent pas gouverner la Martinique!' La valeur n'est pas chez nous, elle est ailleurs. Elle est en France: La culture, l'homme, tout.'
>
> Et le Général de Gaulle, dont on connaît les ruses et les astuces, comprenant vite le profit que le colonialisme peut encore tirer d'une telle idéologie, dira, comme un écho qui répond à son écho: *'Entre l'Amérique et l'Europe, il n'y a que l'Océan et quelques poussières!'*
>
> En apprenant que la Martinique n'était rien de la bouche même de l'Oracle, les fonctionnaires assimilés, les descendants des anciens maîtres d'esclaves—les Békés—poussèrent un cri de triomphe!"
>
> ["Above all," repeat the Assimilated ones to the address of colonial power, "don't grant Martinicans the power to chart the political direction of their country! Martinicans cannot and must not govern Martinique!"
>
> And General de Gaulle, whose ruses and wiles are well known, quickly understanding the advantage colonialism could still draw from such an ideology will say, like an echo responding to its echo: *'Between Europe and America there is only the Ocean and a few specks of dust!'*
>
> Learning that Martinique is nothing from the very mouth of the Oracle, the assimilated functionaries, the descendants of former slave masters—the Békés—shouted out in triumph! René Ménil, *Tracées: Identité, négritude, esthétique aux Antilles* (Paris: Éditions Robert Laffont, 1981), 27 (italics in the original).

3. Edward Said, *Culture and Imperialism* (New York: Knopf, 1993), 225.

4. For a full elaboration, see Abdul JanMohamed, *Manichean Aesthetics: The Politics of Literature in Colonial Africa* (Amherst, MA: Amherst University Press, 1983), 152–157.

5. Frantz Fanon, *Peau noire, masques blancs*, préface et postface Francis Jeanson (Paris: Éditions du Seuil, 1952), 190–191. My translation. Hereafter cited in the text as Fanon. For a fuller elaboration of this paradox, see my "Versions of Incommensurability," *World Literature Today* (1995): 275–280.

6. The term "corporal schema" is drawn from Maurice Merleau-Ponty's classic work, *Phénoménologie de la perception* (Paris: Gallimard, 1945), 114–117.

7. Susan Stewart, *On Longing: Narratives of the Miniature, the Gigantic, the Souvenir, the Collection* (Durham, NC: Duke University Press, 1993), 43.

8. Gaston Bachelard, *The Poetics of Space*, trans. Maria Jolas (Boston: Beacon Press, 1994), 165. Hereafter cited in the text as Bachelard.

9. Ashis Nandy, *The Intimate Enemy: Loss and Recovery of Self under Colonialism* (Oxford: Oxford University Press, 1983).

10. Gaston Bachelard, *La Poétique de l'espace* (Paris: Presses Universitaires de France, 1998), 150. My translation.

11. Aimé Césaire, *The Collected Poetry*, trans. and ed. Clayton Eshleman and Annette Smith (Berkeley: University of California Press, 1983), 34. Translations modified. Hereafter cited in the text as Césaire.

12. I should clarify that in referencing Bachelard, I am not proposing a Bachelardian reading of the *Notebook*'s imagery, but rather exploring the phenomenological dimensions of subjective embodiment in their absence. For a Bachelardian study of Césaire's poetry, see Keith Walker, *La Cohésion poétique de l'oeuvre césairienne* (Paris: J-M Place, 1979).

13. Interview with J. Sieger in *Afrique* 5 (1961), cited in Georges Ngal, *Aimé Césaire: Un homme à la recherche d'une patrie* (Dakar-Abidjan: Nouvelles Editions Africaines, 1975), 28.

14. Interview with Anne Guérin, cited in Ngal, *Aimé Césaire*, 82.

15. Personal communication, May 2004. Savage and slave of Prospero in Shakespeare's *The Tempest*, whose obdurate resistance invites constant corporal punishment, Caliban has by now garnered a dense postcolonial genealogy, which includes Césaire's own 1969 version or topical revision of Shakespeare's play. The lines that have become an emblem and a motto of sorts for this figure concern his relation to the master's language: "You taught me your language; and my profit on't is, I know how to curse" (act 1, scene 2, lines 365–366).

16. Abiola Irele, ed., *Aimé Césaire: Cahier d'un retour au pays natal*, 2nd ed. (Columbus: Ohio State University Press, 2000), xlix. Irele points to the elements of oral poetics in the *Cahier* and also to oratory. The latter seems particularly illuminating when we consider that the poem begins with the speaker recounting to himself the expulsion of his interlocutor ["Beat it," I said to him, "you dirty pig, you cow, I hate the flunkies of order . . ." (*Notebook*, 34)]. The poem can be read as a declamatory fantasy, the plenitudinous invective, recrimination, and also hope hurled into the wake of the departed interlocutor; all that, in its fullness, could only be spoken when he isn't there.

17. I am grateful to Trevor Pinch for drawing this to my attention.

18. A. James Arnold, in *Modernism and Négritude: The Poetry and Poetics of Aimé Césaire* (Cambridge, MA: Harvard University Press, 1981), 136, calls this a "corrosive poetics." Nick Nesbitt, *Voicing Memory: History and Subjectivity in French Caribbean Literature* (Charlottesville: University of Virginia Press, 2003), 79, discusses the voice in terms of DuBois' double-consciousness.

19. See Nesbitt, *Voicing Memory*, 92, for a similar argument.

20. This line was not removed until the "final" 1956 edition of the poem pub-

lished by Présence Africaine. For an invaluable record of the variations between the first three editions of the poem (1939, and the two editions of 1947), see Lilian Pestre de Almeida, "Les Versions successive du *Cahier d'un retour au pays natal*," in M. a M. Ngal and Martin Steins, eds., *Césaire 70* (Paris, Éditions Silex, 1984), 73.

21. Hedy Kalikoff, "Gender, Genre and Geography in Aime Cesaire's 'Cahier D'un Retour au Pays Natal,'" *Callaloo* 2 (Spring 1995), 496–498.

22. See Ronnie Scharfman, *Engagement and the Language of the Subject* (Gainesville: University of Florida Press, 1980), 58–61.

23. Nesbitt, *Voicing Memory*, 86.

24. See Abiola Irele, ed., *Aimé Césaire*, xlvii. Arnold points out that the sections added in 1947 are among the most recognizably surrealist and notes: "In view of the composite nature of the text, which has grown by accretion, it makes little sense to continue to consider the *Notebook* that is actually read as though it were a prewar poem" (Arnold, *Modernism and Négritude*, 147). For an important account of the international black culture of the 1930s, out of which the poem and the ideology of negritude most directly emerged, see Brent Hayes Edwards, *The Practice of Diaspora: Literature, Translation and the Rise of Black Internationalism* (Cambridge, MA: Harvard University Press, 2003).

25. Toumson and Henry-Valmore cite the following comments from the pages of the newspaper *Le Franc-Tireur* on 12 April 1946: "The discussion of the articles relative to the French Union allowed the delegated reporter Senghor and the Martinican deputy Aimé Césaire to intervene in a very brilliant manner. Our overseas friends proved that, when it comes to the art of oratory, one Black is worth two Whites." Roger Toumson and Simonne Henry-Valmore, *Aimé Césaire: Le nègre inconsolé* (Paris: Syros, 1993), 84. My translation.

26. "Longtemps j'ai porté en moi votre *Cahier d'un retour au pays natal*, tel un 'garde-corps,' un talisman . . ." "Par la grâce de votre parole, vous habitiez en moi, vous habitiez en chacun d'entre nous et votre place était celle de l'ancêtre fondateur. Celle du Nègre fondamental." Raphaël Confiant, *Aimé Césaire: Une traversée paradoxale du siècle* (Paris: Stock, 1993), 39, 41.

27. For a useful overview, see Richard Burton, "Ki Moun Nou Ye? The Idea of Difference in French West Indian Thought," *New West Indian Guide* 67, no. 1&2 (1993): 5–32.

28. Mireille Rosello, *Littérature et identité créole aux Antilles* (Paris: Karthala, 1992), 75.

29. Maryse Condé, "Négritude Césairienne, Négritude Senghorienne," in *Revue de Littérature Comparée* 3, no. 4 (1974): 409–419.

30. Glissant, *Le discours antillais*, 15. Hereafter cited in the text as DA.

31. Simone et André Schwarz-Bart, "'Sur les pas de Fanotte': Interview avec Simone et André Schwarz-Bart," by Héliane and Roger Toumson, in *Textes et documents* special issue on *Pluie et vent sur Télumée Miracle* 2 (1979): 18.

32. Simone Schwarz-Bart's *Pluie et vent sur Télumée Miracle* (Paris: Éditions

du Seuil, 1972), 11. Ellipses in the original. My translation. Hereafter cited in the text as *Télumée*.

33. Jean Bernabé, "Contribution a l'étude de la diglossie littéraire: Le cas de *Pluie et vent sur Télumée Miracle* de Simone Schwarz-Bart," in *Textes et documents* special issue on *Pluie et vent sur Télumée Miracle*, 104. My translation; emphasis in the original. Hereafter cited in the text as Bernabé.

34. Kathleen Gyssels, *Filles de solitude*, 19. Hereafter cited in the text as Gyssels.

35. It is not possible to consider the structure of the remainder within systems of domination without thinking of the pioneering work of Zita Nunes in *Resisting Remainders: Race and Democracy* (University of Minnesota Press, forthcoming).

36. Richard Matheson wrote the screenplay for *The Incredible Shrinking Man* based on his own novel of the same name. I am grateful to Bertram and Jean Salzman for introducing me to this film and to other earthly and unearthly delights.

37. See, for instance, Ronnie Scharfman, "Mirroring and Mothering in Simone Schwarz-Bart's *Pluie et vent sur Télumée Miracle* and Jean Rhys' 'Wide Sargasso Sea,'" *Yale French Studies* 62 (1991); and Patrice J. Proulx "Situer le 'moi' féminin dans *Pluie et vent sur Télumée Miracle*," in Susanne Rinne and Joëlle Vitello, eds., *Elles écrivent des Antilles . . . (Haiti, Guadelopue, Martinique)* (Paris: l'Harmattan, 1997), 135–143.

38. Hortense Spillers, "Mama's Baby, Papa's Maybe: An American Grammar Book," *Diacritics* (Summer 1987), 67.

39. Beverley Ormerod, *An Introduction to the French Caribbean Novel* (London: Heinemann, 1985), 129.

40. Aimé Césaire, *The Collected Poetry*, 256–257.

41. Maryse Condé, *La parole des femmes: Essai sur des romancieres des Antilles de langue française* (Paris: L'Harmattan, 1979), 25. On the particular quality of Télumée's heroism in the context of the problematic construction of the hero in Antillean literature, see Rosello's illuminating discussion in *Littérature et identité créole aux Antilles* (Paris: Karthala, 1992).

42. Abena P. A. Busia, "This Gift of Metaphor: Symbolic Strategies and the Triumph of Survival in Simone Schwarz-Bart's *The Bridge of Beyond*" in *Out of the Kumbla: Caribbean Women and Literature*, Carole Boyce Davies and Elaine Savory Fido, eds. (Trenton, NJ: Africa World Press, 1990), 301n.

43. For a brief account, see Rosello, *Littérature et identité créole aux Antilles*, 72–73.

44. Maryse Condé, "Order, Disorder, Freedom and the West Indian Writer," *Yale French Studies* 83 (1998): 121–135.

45. Clarisse Zimra, "In the Name of the Father: Chronotopia, Utopia and Dystopia in *Ti Jean L'horizon*," *L'Esprit Créateur* 2 (1993): 64.

46. Simone Schwarz-Bart, *Ti Jean L'horizon* (Paris: Éditions du Seuil, 1979), 9; ellipsis in the original. Hereafter cited in the text as *TJ*. All translations mine. An

English translation exists, now unfortunately out of print: *Between Two Worlds*, Barbara Bray, trans. (New York: Harper Row, 1981).

47. Simone Schwarz-Bart, *Ti Jean L'horizon*, 9.

48. Clarisse Zimra, "Righting the Clabash: Writing History in the Female Francophone Narrative," in *Out of the Kumbla*, 143–159.

49. G. W. F. Hegel, *Phenomenology of Spirit*, trans. A. V. Miller with foreword and analysis by J. N. Findlay (Oxford: Oxford University Press, 1977), ch. 4, part A, §186–196, 113–119. See also Alexandre Kojève, *Introduction à la lecture de Hegel* (Paris: Gallimard, 1947).

50. Orlando Patterson, *Slavery and Social Death* (Cambridge, MA: Harvard University Press, 1982).

51. Kathleen Gyssels elucidates a great variety of mythological sources for the novel in "Oralité antillaise: Conte, mythe et mythologie" in *Présence Franco-phone* 44 (1994): 127–147. Elizabeth Mudimbe-Boyi shows the complex structuration of the text's mythological dimension in a comparative study, in "The Poetics of Errancy and Exile: Ken Bugul's *Le Baobab fou* and Simone Schwarz-Bart's *Ti Jean L'horizon*" in *Yale French Studies* 2 (1993): 196–212.

52. See *DA*, 192. This argument has many affinities with Georg Lukacs' *Theory of the Novel*, with which it shares a pronounced Hegelian bent.

53. Bernadette Cailler, "*Ti Jean L'horizon* de Simone Schwarz-Bart, ou la leçon du royaume des morts," *Stanford French Review* (Fall / Winter 1982): 290. I should note that the author later recants the strong claims she makes here for *Ti Jean L'horizon* as an exemplary Antillean novel. See Bernadette Cailler, *Conquérants de la nuit nue: Édouard Glissant et l'H(h)istoire antillaise* (Tübingen: Gunter Narr Verlag, 1988), 173–174. Hereafter cited in the text as Cailler.

54. See "Ti Jean la fortune" in Ina Césaire and Joëlle Laurent, trans. and intro., *Contes de mort et de vie aux antilles* (Paris: Nubia, 1976), 235–245. See also Derek Walcott's play, *Ti Jean and His Brothers*.

55. See Joëlle Laurent and Ina Césaire, *Contes de mort et de vie aux antilles*, 224–231, for the version I summarize here. In Patrick Chamoiseau's retelling, the story has the same basic plot but very different episodes: see his *Creole Folktales* (New York: The New Press, 1994).

56. Kathleen Gyssels, "Oralité antillaise: Conte, mythe et mythologie," 142.

57. Laurent and Césaire, *Contes de mort et de vie aux antilles*, 8.

58. Simone et André Schwarz-Bart "'Sur les pas de Fanotte': Interview avec Simone et André Schwarz-Bart," 15.

59. Michael Dash, *The Other America: Caribbean Literature in a New World Context* (Charlottesville: University Press of Virginia, 1998), 164.

Bibliography

Abel, Elizabeth. "Black Writing, White Reading: Race and the Politics of Feminist Interpretation." *Critical Inquiry* 19 (1993): 470–498.

Achebe, Chinua. "An Image of Africa." *Research in African Literatures* 9, no. 1 (1978): 1–15.

———. *Things Fall Apart*. New York: Anchor, 1959.

Adorno, Theodor and Max Horkheimer. *Dialectic of Enlightenment*. New York: Herder and Herder, 1972.

Ahmad, Aijaz. *In Theory: Nations, Classes, Literatures*. London: Verso, 1992.

Althusser, Louis. *Lenin and Philosophy and Other Essays*. Translated by Ben Brewster. London: New Left Books, 1971.

Anderson, Benedict. "In the World-Shadow of Bismarck and Nobel." *New Left Review* 28 (2004): 85–129.

———. "Jupiter Hill: José Rizal: Paris, Havana, Barcelona, Berlin—3." *New Left Review* 29 (2004): 91–120.

———. "Nitroglycerine in the Pomegranate." *NLR* 27 (2004): 99–118.

———. *The Spectre of Comparisons: Nationalism, Southeast Asia and the World*. London: Verso, 1998.

Appiah, Anthony Kwame. "Is the Post- in Postmodernism the Post- in Postcolonial?" *Critical Inquiry* 17 (1991): 336–357.

Apter, Emily. "Global Translatio: The Invention of Comparative Literature, Istanbul, 1933." *Critical Inquiry* 29, no. 2 (2003): 253–282.

Aristotle. *Poetics*. Translated by S. H. Butcher. New York: Hill and Wang, 1961.

Arnold, A. James. *Modernism and Négritude: The Poetry and Poetics of Aimé Césaire*. Cambridge, MA: Harvard University Press, 1981.

Auerbach, Erich. "Philology and *Weltliteratur*." Translated by Edward Said and Maire Said. *The Centennial Review* 13, no. 1 (1969): 1–17.

Bachelard, Gaston. *The Poetics of Space (La poétique de l'espace)*. Translated by Maria Jolas. Boston: Beacon Press, 1994.

Bassnett, Susan. *Comparative Literature: A Critical Introduction*. Oxford, UK: Blackwell, 1993.

Bartolovich, Crystal and Neil Lazarus, eds. *Marxism, Modernity and Postcolonial Studies*. Cambridge: Cambridge University Press, 2002.

Baugh, Edward. *Derek Walcott: Memory as Vision: Another Life.* London: Longman, 1978.

———. "The West Indian Writer and His Quarrel with History." *Tapia* (Feb. 20, 1977): 6–8.

Beckett, Samuel. *The Unnamable.* New York: Grove Press, 1958.

Bernabé, Jean. "Le Travail de l'écriture chez Simone Schwartz-Bart: Contribution à l'étude de la diglossie littéraire créole-français." *Textes et documents* special issue on *Pluie et vent sur Télumée Miracle* 2 (1979).

Bernal, Martin. *Black Athena: The Afroasiatic Roots of Classical Civilization.* New Brunswick, NJ: Rutgers University Press, 1987.

Bernheimer, Charles, ed. *Comparative Literature in the Age of Multiculturalism.* Baltimore: Johns Hopkins University Press, 1995.

Bhabha, Homi K. *The Location of Culture.* London: Routledge, 1994.

Blake, Susan L. "Racism and the Classics: Teaching *Heart of Darkness." CLA Journal* 4 (1982): 397–404.

Bock, Kenneth E. "The Comparative Method in Anthropology." *Comparative Studies in Society and History* 7 (1965–1966): 269–280.

Bongie, Chris. *Islands and Exiles: The Creole Identities of Post/Colonial Literatures.* Stanford: Stanford University Press, 1998.

Brantlinger, Patrick. *Rule of Darkness: British Literature and Imperialism.* Ithaca, NY: Cornell University Press, 1988.

Brathwaite, Edward Kamau. *The Development of Creole Society in Jamaica, 1770–1820.* Oxford: Clarendon Press, 1971.

———. "History, The Caribbean Writer and X/Self," In *Crisis and Creativity in the New Literatures in English,"* edited by Geoffrey V. Davis, and Hena Maes-Jelinek. Amsterdam: Rodopi, 1990.

Brennan, Timothy. *At Home in the World: Cosmopolitanism Now.* Cambridge, MA: Harvard University Press, 1997.

Breslin, Paul. *Nobody's Nation: Reading Derek Walcott.* Chicago: University of Chicago Press, 2001.

Britton, Celia M. *Edouard Glissant and Postcolonial Theory: Strategies of Language and Resistance.* Charlottesville: University of Virginia Press, 1999.

Brooks, Peter. *Reading for the Plot.* Cambridge, MA: Harvard University Press, 1984.

Bu-Buakei, Jabbi. "Conrad's Influence on Betrayal" In *A Grain of Wheat." Research in African Literatures* 11 (1980): 50–83.

Burton, Richard. "Ki Moun Nou Ye? The Idea of Difference in French West Indian Thought." *New West Indian Guide* 67, no. 1&2 (1993): 5–32.

Busia, Abena P. A. "This Gift of Metaphor: Symbolic Strategies and the Triumph of Survival in Simone Schwartz-Bart's *The Bridge of Beyond." Out of the Kumbla: Caribbean Women and Literature.* Edited by Carole Boyce Davies and Elaine Savory Fido. Trenton, NJ: Africa World Press, 1990.

Cailler, Bernadette. *Conquérants de la nuit nue: Edouard Glissant et l'H(h)istoire antillaise.* Tübingen: Gunter Narr Verlag, 1988.

———. "Ti Jean l'Horizon de Simone Schwarz-Bart, ou la leçon du royaume des morts." *Stanford French Review* (1982): 283–297.

Caillois, Roger. "Mimicry and Legendary Psychasthenia." Translated by John Shepley. *October* 31 (1984): 17–32.

Cameron, Sarah, and Ben Box, eds. *1994 Caribbean Islands Handbook*, 5th ed. Chicago: Passport Books, 1994.

Casanova, Pascale. *La république mondiale des lettres.* Paris: Seuil, 1999.

Césaire, Aimé. *The Collected Poetry.* Translated and edited by Clayton Eshleman and Annette Smith. Berkeley: University of California Press, 1983.

Chakrabarty, Dipesh. *Provincializing Europe: Postcolonial Thought and Historical Difference.* Princeton, NJ: Princeton University Press, 2000.

Chamoiseau, Patrick. *Creole Folktales.* Translated by Linda Coverdale. New York: The New Press, 1994.

———. *Texaco.* Paris: Gallimard, 1992.

Cheah, Pheng and Jonathan Culler, eds. *Grounds of Comparison: Around the Work of Benedict Anderson.* New York: Routledge, 2003.

The Chicago Cultural Studies Group. "Critical Multiculturalism." *Critical Inquiry* 18, no. 3 (1992): 530–555.

Clausing, A. *Kritik und Exegese der Homerischen Gleichnisse im Altertum.* Parchim: Druck von H, Friese, 1913.

Clifford, James. *The Predicament of Culture.* Cambridge, MA: Harvard University Press, 1988.

———. *Routes: Travel and Translation in the Late Twentieth Century.* Cambridge, MA: Harvard University Press, 1997.

Condé, Maryse. *Heremakhonon.* Translated by Richard Philcox. Washington, D.C: Three Continents Press, 1982.

———. "Négritude Césairienne, Négritude Senghorienne." *Revue de Littérature Comparée* 3, no. 4 (1974): 409–419.

———. "Order, Disorder, Freedom and the West Indian Writer." *Yale French Studies* 83 (1993): 121–135.

———. *La parole des femmes: Essai sur des romancières des Antilles de langue française.* Paris: L'Harmattan, 1979.

Confiant, Raphaël. *Aimé Césaire: Une traversée paradoxale du siècle.* Paris: Stock, 1993.

Confiant, Raphaël, David Damoison, and Marcel Labielle. *Les maîtres de la parole.* Paris: Gallimard, 1995.

Conrad, Joseph. *Heart of Darkness.* Edited by Robert Kimbrough. New York: W. W. Norton, 1971.

———. "Karain: A Memory." In *Selected Tales from Conrad,* edited by Nigel Stewart. London: Faber and Faber, 1977; 1897.

————. *Lord Jim*. Edited by Thomas Moser. New York: Norton, 1968.

————. *An Outcast of the Islands*. Middlesex, NY: Penguin Books, 1981; 1896.

————. "An Outpost of Progress." In *Selected Tales from Conrad*, edited by Nigel Stewart. London: Faber and Faber, 1977; 1897.

————. *Youth and Two Other Stories*. New York: Doubleday, 1920.

Cooper, Lane. *Experiments in Education*. Ithaca, NY: Cornell University Press, 1942.

Coursil, Jacques. "La Catégorie de la relation dans les essais d'Edouard Glissant: Philosophie d'une poétique," in *Poétiques d'Edouard Glissant*. Edited by Jacques Chevrier. Paris: Presse de l'université de Paris: Sorbonne, 1999.

Culler, Jonathan. *Framing the Sign: Criticism and Its Institutions*. Oxford: Blackwell, 1988.

Dadi, Iftikhar and Salah Hassan, eds. *Unpacking Europe: Towards a Critical Reading*. Rotterdam, The Netherlands: NAi Publishers, 2001.

Damrosch, David. *What Is World Literature?* Princeton, NJ: Princeton University Press, 2003.

Dash, J. Michael. *Édouard Glissant*. Cambridge: Cambridge University Press, 1995.

————. *The Other America: Caribbean Literature in a New World Context*. Charlottesville: University Press of Virginia, 1998.

Davis, Gregson. "With No Homeric Shadow." *The South Atlantic Quarterly* 2 (1997): 321–333.

Derrida, Jacques. "The Double Session." *Dissemination*. Chicago: University Press, 1981.

————. *The Margins of Philosophy*. Translated by Alan Bass. Chicago: University of Chicago Press, 1982.

Detienne, Marcel. *Comparer l'incomparable*. Seuil: Paris, 2000.

Dirlik, Arif. *The Postcolonial Aura: Third World Criticism in the Age of Global Capitalism*. Boulder, CO: Westview Press, 1997.

During, Simon. "Postmodernism or Post-Colonialism Today." *Textual Practice* 1, no. 1 (1987): 32–47.

Edwards, Brent Hayes. *The Practice of Diaspora: Literature, Translation and the Rise of Black Internationalism*. Cambridge, MA: Harvard University Press, 2003.

Eliot, T. S. *Selected Essays*. New York: Harcourt, Brace and World, 1964.

Etiemble, René. *Comparaison n'est pas raison: la crise de la littérature comparée*. Paris: Gallimard, 1963.

————. *Ouverture(s) sur un comparatisme planétaire*. Paris: Christian Bourgeois, 1988.

Fabian, Johannes. *Time and the Other: How Anthropology Makes Its Object*. New York: Columbia University Press, 1983.

Fanon, Frantz. *Les damnés de la terre*. Paris: Gallimard, 1991.

———. *Peau noire, masques blancs*, préface et postface Francis Jeanson. Paris: Éditions du Seuil, 1952.

Fleishman, Avrom. *Conrad's Politics: Community and Anarchy in the Fiction of Joseph Conrad*. Baltimore: Johns Hopkins Press, 1967.

Fogel, Aaron. *Coercion to Speak: Conrad's Poetics of Dialogue*. Cambridge, MA: Harvard University Press, 1985.

Ford, Andrew. *Homer: The Poetry of the Past*. Ithaca, NY: Cornell University Press, 1992.

Ford, Ford Madox. *Joseph Conrad: A Personal Remembrance*. Boston: Little Brown, 1924.

Foucault, Michel. *The Order of Things: An Archaeology of the Human Sciences*. New York: Vintage, 1973.

———. "Of Other Spaces." Translated by Jan Miskowiec. *Diacritics*. 16 (1986): 22–27.

Fränkel, Hermann. *Die Homerischen Gleichnisse*. Göttingen: Vandenhoeck & Ruprecht, 1921; 1977.

Froude, James Anthony. *The English in the West Indies; or The Bow of Ulysses*. New York: Scribner's Sons, 1888.

Gasché, Rodolphe. "Comparatively Theoretical." *Germanistik und Komparatistik* (DFG-Symposon 1993). Stuttgart: J.B. Metzler Verlag, 1993.

Gayley, Charles Mills. *Idols of Education*. New York: Doubleday, 1910.

Gayley, Charles Mills, and Benjamin Putnam Kurtz. *Methods and Materials of Literary Criticism Lyric, Epic and Allied Forms of Poetry*. Boston: Ginn and Company, 1920.

Genette, Gérard. *Figures III*. Paris: Éditions du Seuil, 1972.

———. "Rhetoric Restrained." *Figures of Literary Discourse*. Translated by Alan Sheridan. New York: Columbia University Press, 1982.

Gikandi, Simon. *Writing in Limbo: Modernism and Caribbean Literature*. Ithaca, NY: Cornell University Press, 1992.

Gilroy, Paul. *The Black Atlantic: Modernity and Double Consciousness*. Cambridge, MA: Harvard University Press, 1993.

Glissant, Édouard. *Le discours antillais*. Paris: Éditions du Seuil, 1981.

———. *L'intention poétique*. Paris: Éditions du Seuil, 1969.

———. *Poétique de la relation*. Paris: Éditions Gallimard, 1990.

———. *Vers une poétique du divers*. Montréal: Presses de l'université de Montréal, 1995.

Grossberg, Lawrence, Cary Nelson, and Paula A. Treichler, eds. *Cultural Studies*. New York, London: Routledge, 1992.

Grossman, Lionel, and Mihai Spariosu, eds. *Building a Profession: Autobiographical Perspectives on the Beginnings of Comparative Literature in the United States*. Albany, NY: State University of New York Press, 1994.

Guillory, John. *Cultural Capital: The Problem of Literary Canon Formation*. Chicago: University of Chicago Press, 1993.

Gyssels, Kathleen. *Filles de solitude: Essai sur les (auto-)biographies fictives de Simone et André Schwarz-Bart*. Paris: L'Harmattan, 1996.

———. "Oralité antillaise: Conte, mythe et mythologie." *Présence Francophone* 44 (1994): 127–147.

Hallward, Peter. *Absolutely Postcolonial: Writing Between the Singular and the Specific*. Manchester: Manchester University Press, 2001.

Hamner, Robert D., ed. *Critical Perspectives on Derek Walcott*. Washington, D.C.: Three Continents Press, 1993.

———. *Epic of the Dispossessed: Derek Walcott's* Omeros. Columbia: University of Missouri Press, 1997.

Harpham, Geoffrey Galt. *One of Us: The Mastery of Joseph Conrad*. Chicago: University of Chicago Press, 1996.

Harris, Wilson. "The Frontier on Which *Heart of Darkness* Stands." *Research in African Literatures* 12, no. 1 (1981): 86–93.

Hawkins, Hunt. "The Issue of Racism in *Heart of Darkness*." *Conradiana* 15, no. 3 (1982): 163–171.

Hegel, G. W. F. *Phenomenology of Spirit*. Translated by A. V. Miller. Oxford: Oxford University Press, 1977.

Henry-Valmore, Simonne, and Roger Toumson. *Aimé Césaire: Le nègre inconsolé*. Paris: Syros, 1993.

Higonnet, Margaret R. *Borderwork: Feminist Engagements with Comparative Literature*. Ithaca, NY: Cornell University Press, 1994.

Hobsbawm, E. J. *The Age of Empire 1875–1914*. New York: Pantheon Books, 1987.

Hobson, J. A. *Imperialism, A Study*. Ann Arbor: University of Michigan Press, 1902; 1965.

Holy, Ladislav, ed. *Comparative Anthropology*. Oxford: Basil Blackwell, 1987.

Homer. *Iliad*. Translated by Richmond Lattimore. Chicago: University of Chicago Press, 1974.

Hulme, Peter. *Colonial Encounters: Europe and the Native Caribbean 1492–1797*. New York: Routledge, 1986.

Irele, Abiola. ed. *Aimé Césaire: Cahier d'un retour au pays natal*, 2nd ed. Columbus: Ohio State University Press, 2000.

Irigaray, Luce. *An Ethics of Sexual Difference*. Translated by Carolyn Burke and Gillian C. Gill. Ithaca, NY: Cornell University Press, 1993.

Iser, Wolfgang. *The Act of Reading: A Theory of Aesthetic Response*. Baltimore: Johns Hopkins University Press, 1978.

Jabbi, Bu-Buakei. "Conrad's Influence on Betrayal in *A Grain of Wheat*." *Research in African Literatures* 11 (1980): 50–83.

James, C. L. R. *Beyond a Boundary*. New York: Pantheon Books, 1983.

Jameson, Fredric. "Cognitive Mapping." *Marxism and the Interpretation of Cul-*

ture. Edited by Cary Nelson and Lawrence Grossberg. Urbana and Chicago: University of Illinois Press, 1988.

——. *The Political Unconscious: Narrative as a Socially Symbolic Act.* Ithaca, NY: Cornell University Press, 1981.

——. *Postmodernism and the Cultural Logic of Late Capitalism.* Durham, NC: Duke University Press, 1991.

——. *The Seeds of Time.* New York: Columbia University Press, 1994.

——. "Third World Literature in the Era of Multinational Capital." *Social Text* 15 (1986): 65–88.

JanMohamed, Abdul R. *Manichean Aesthetics: The Politics of Literature in Colonial Africa.* Amherst, MA: Amherst University Press, 1983.

Joyce, James. *Ulysses.* New York: Vintage, 1961.

Kalikoff, Hedy. "Gender, Genre and Geography in Aime Cesaire's 'Cahier D'un Retour au Pays Natal.'" *Callaloo* 2 (Spring 1995).

Kincaid, Jamaica. *A Small Place.* New York: Penguin, 1988.

King, Bruce. *Derek Walcott: A Caribbean Life.* Oxford: Oxford University Press, 2000.

Kojève, Alexandre. *Introduction à la lecture de Hegel.* Paris: Gallimard, 1947.

Kurtz, Benjamin P. *Charles Mills Gayley.* Berkeley and Los Angeles: University of California Press, 1943.

LaCapra, Dominick. "The University in Ruins?" *Critical Inquiry* 25, no. 1 (1998): 32–55.

Laurent, Joëlle, and Ina Césaire, trans. and intro. *Contes de mort et de vie aux Antilles.* Paris: Nubia, 1976.

Leavis, F. R. *The Great Tradition: George Eliot, Henry James, Joseph Conrad.* London: Chatto & Windus, 1948.

Lee, D. J. N. *The Similes of the Iliad and the Odyssey Compared.* Melbourne, Australia: Melbourne University Press, 1964.

Lefebvre, Henri. *The Production of Space.* Translated by Donald Nicholson-Smith. Oxford: Blackwell, 1974.

Levin, Harry. *Grounds for Comparison.* Cambridge, MA: Harvard University Press, 1972.

Levine, George, *The Realistic Imagination.* Chicago: University of Chicago Press, 1981.

Lewis, Gordon K. *Main Currents in Caribbean Thought: The Historical Evolution of Caribbean Society in Its Ideological Aspects, 1492–1900.* Baltimore: Johns Hopkins University Press, 1983.

Lloyd, David, and Lisa Lowe, eds. *The Politics of Culture in the Shadow of Capital.* Durham, NC: Duke University Press, 1997.

London, Bette. *The Appropriated Voice: Narrative Authority in Conrad, Forster, Woolf.* Ann Arbor: University of Michigan Press, 1990.

————. "Reading Race and Gender in Conrad's Dark Continent." *Criticism* 21 (Summer 1989).

Lonsdale, Steven H. *Creatures of Speech: Lion, Herding and Hunting Similes in the Iliad*. Stuttgart: B.G. Teubner, 1990.

Lukacs, Georg. *The Theory of the Novel: a historico-philosophical essay on the forms of great epic literature*. Cambridge, MA: MIT Press, 1971.

Lyotard, Jean-François. *The Differend*. Translated by Georges Van Den Abbeele. Minneapolis: University of Minnesota Press, 1988.

————. *The Postmodern Condition*. Minneapolis: University of Minnesota Press, 1984.

MacCannell, Dean. *Empty Meeting Grounds: The Tourist Papers*. New York: Routledge, 1992.

Mahood, M. M. *The Colonial Encounter*. London: Collings, 1977.

Marino, Adrian. *Etiemble ou le comparatisme militant*. Paris: Gallimard, 1982.

Meisel, Perry. *The Myth of the Modern: A Study in British Literature and Criticism after 1850*. New Haven, CT: Yale University Press, 1987.

Melas, Natalie. "Versions of Incommensurability." *World Literature Today* (1995): 275–280.

Memmi, Albert. *Portrait du colonisé*. Paris: Gallimard, 1985.

Ménil, Réné. *Tracées: Identité, négritude, esthétique aux Antilles*. Paris: R. Laffont, 1981.

Merleau-Ponty, Maurice. *Phénoménologie de la perception*. Paris: Gallimard, 1945.

Mignolo, Walter D. *Local Histories/Global Designs: Coloniality, Subaltern Knowledges, and Border Thinking*. Princeton, NJ: Princeton University Press, 2000.

Miller, J. Hillis. *The Form of Victorian Fiction: Thackeray, Dickens, Trollope, George Eliot, Meredith and Hardy*. Notre Dame: University of Notre Dame Press, 1968.

Moretti, Franco. "Conjectures on World Literature." *New Left Review* 1 (2000): 54–68.

————. "Graphs, Maps, Trees: Abstract Models for Literary History—1." *New Left Review* 24 (2003): 67–94.

————. "Graphs, Maps, Trees: Abstract Models for Literary History—2." *New Left Review* 26 (2004): 79–103.

————. "Graphs, Maps, Trees: Abstract Models for Literary History—3." *New Left Review* 28 (2004): 43–63.

————. "More Conjectures." *New Left Review* 20 (2003): 73–81.

Moulton, Carroll. *Similes in the Homeric Poems*. Hypomnemata, 49. Göttingen: Vandenhoeck and Ruprecht, 1977.

Mudimbe-Boyi, Elizabeth. "The Poetics of Errancy and Exile: Ken Bugul's *Le Baobab Fou* and Simone Schwarz-Bart's *Ti Jean l'Horizon*." *Yale French Studies* 2 (1993): 196–212.

Mulhern, Francis. "Conrad's Inconceivable History." *New Left Review* 38 (March/ April 2006): 59–93.

Mufti, Aamir. "Global Comparativism." *Critical Inquiry* 2 (Winter 2005): 472–490.

Myoshi, Masao. "A Borderless World? From Colonialism to Transnationalism and the Decline of the Nation-State." *Critical Inquiry* 19 (Summer 1993): 726–751.

Nagy, Gregory. *The Best of the Achaeans: Concepts of the Hero in Ancient Greek Poetry*. Baltimore: Johns Hopkins University Press, 1979.

Naipaul, V. S. "Conrad's Darkness." *The Return of Eva Peron*. New York: Knopf, 1980.

———. *The Middle Passage*. New York: Anchor Books, 1962.

Najder, Zdzislaw. *Joseph Conrad: A Chronicle*. New Brunswick, NJ: Rutgers University Press, 1983.

Nancy, Jean-Luc. *La communauté désoeuvrée*. Paris: Christian Bourgeois, 1986.

Nancy, Jean-Luc, and Christophe Bailly. *La comparution: Politique à venir*. Paris: Christian Bourgeois, 1991.

Nandy, Ashis. *The Intimate Enemy: Loss and Recovery of Self Under Colonialism*. Oxford: Oxford University Press, 1983.

Nazareth, Peter. "Out of Darkness: Conrad and Other Third World Writers." *Conradiana* 24 (1982): 173–187.

Nesbitt, Nick. *Voicing Memory: History and Subjectivity in French Caribbean Literature*. Charlottesville: University of Virginia Press, 2003.

Ngal, Georges. *Aimé Césaire: Un homme à la recherche d'une patrie*. Dakar-Abidjan: Nouvelles Editions Africaines, 1975.

Nunes, Zita. *Resisting Remainders: Race and Democracy in the Literature of the Americas*. Minneapolis: University of Minnesota Press, forthcoming.

Obumselu, Ebele. "*A Grain of Wheat*: Ngugi's Debt to Conrad." *The Benin Review* 1 (1974): 80–91.

Olaniyan, Tejumola. "Derek Walcott: Liminal Spaces/Substantive Histories." *Caribbean Romances: The Politics of Regional Representation*. Edited by Belinda Edmondson. Charlottesville: University Press of Virginia, 1999.

Ormerod, Beverley. *An Introduction to the French Caribbean Novel*. London: Heinemann, 1985.

Parry, Benita. *Conrad and Imperialism: Ideological Boundaries and Visionary Frontiers*. London: Macmillan, 1983.

Patterson, Orlando. *An Absence of Ruins*. London: Hutchinson, 1967.

———. *Slavery and Social Death*. Cambridge, MA: Harvard University Press, 1982.

Patullo, Polly. *Last Resorts: The Cost of Tourism in the Caribbean*. London: Cassell, 1996.

Payne, William Morton. *English in American Universities*. Boston: D. C. Heath & Co., 1895.

Pestre de Almeida, Lilian. "Les Versions successive du *Cahier d'un retour au pays natal.*" *Césaire 70.* Edited by M. a M Ngal and Martin Steins. Paris, Éditions Silex, 1984.

Posnett, Hutcheson Macaulay. *Comparative Literature.* London: Kegan, Paul and Trench, 1886.

Pratt, Mary Louise. *Imperial Eyes: Travel Writing and Transculturation.* London: Routledge, 1992.

Proulx, Patrice J. "Situer le 'moi' féminin dans *Pluie et vent sur Télumée Miracle.*" *Elles écrivent des Antilles . . . (Haiti, Guadelopue, Martinique).* Edited by Susanne Rinne and Joëlle Vitiello. Paris: l'Harmattan, 1997, 135–143.

Rahnema, Majid, and Victoria Bawtree, eds. *The Post-Development Reader.* London: Zed Books, 1996.

Ramazani, Jahan. *The Hybrid Muse: Postcolonial Poetry in English.* Chicago: Chicago University Press, 2001.

Readings, Bill. *The University in Ruins.* Cambridge, MA: Harvard University Press, 1996.

Renan, Ernest, *L'Avenir de la science: Pensées de 1848.* Paris: Calmann-Lévy, 1890.

Robertson, P. J. M. "*Things Fall Apart* and *Heart of Darkness*: A Creative Dialogue." *International Fiction Review* 7, no. 2 (1980): 106–111.

Robertson, Roland. *Globalization: Social Theory and Global Culture.* London: Sage, 1992.

Rosello, Mireille. *Littérature et identité créole aux Antilles.* Paris: Karthala, 1992.

Said, Edward. *Culture and Imperialism.* New York: Knopf, 1993.

——. *Orientalism.* New York: Pantheon Books, 1978.

——. "Third World Intellectuals and Metropolitan Culture." *Raritan* 3 (1990).

Sakai, Naoki. *Translation and Subjectivity: On "Japan" and Cultural Nationalism.* Minneapolis: University of Minnesota Press, 1997.

Saussy, Haun, ed. *Comparative Literature in an Age of Globalization.* Baltimore: Johns Hopkins University Press, 2006.

Schadewalt, Wolfgang. *Von Homers Welt und Werk.* Stuttgart: KF Koehler Verlag, 1959.

Schapera, I. "Some Comments on the Comparative Method in Social Anthropology." *American Anthropologist* 55, no. 3 (1953): 353–362.

Scharfman, Ronnie. *Engagement and the Language of the Subject in the Poetry of Aimé Césaire.* Gainesville: University of Florida Press, 1980.

——. "Mirroring and Mothering in Simone Schwarz-Bart's *Pluie et vent sur Télumée Miracle* and Jean Rhys' *Wide Sargasso Sea.*" *Yale French Studies* 62 (1991): 88–106.

Schulz, H. J., and P. H. Rhein, eds. *Comparative Literature: The Early Years.* Chapel Hill: University of North Carolina Press, 1973.

Schwarz-Bart, Simone. *Pluie et vent sur Télumée Miracle.* Paris: Éditions du Seuil, 1972.

——. *Ti Jean L'horizon.* Paris: Éditions du Seuil, 1979.

Scott, David. *Refashioning Futures: Criticism after Postcoloniality*. Princeton: Princeton University Press, 1999.

———. *Conscripts of Modernity: The Tragedy of Colonial Enlightenment*. Durham, NC: Duke University Press, 2004.

Scott, W. C. *The Oral Nature of the Homeric Simile*. Mnemosyne, 28. Leiden, Netherlands: Brill, Biblioteca Classica Batavia, 1974.

Seferis, George. *Collected Poems*. Translated, edited and introduced by Edmund Keeley and Philip Sherrard. Princeton, NY: Princeton University Press, 1995.

Segal, Charles. "The Theme of the Mutilation of the Corpse." *Mnemosyne* (1973).

Sheller, Mimi. *Consuming the Caribbean: From Arawaks to Zombies*. London: Routledge, 2003.

Sherry, Norman. *Joseph Conrad: The Critical Heritage*. London: Routledge and Kegan Paul, 1973.

Shohat, Ella. "Notes on the "Post-Colonial." *Social Text* 31/32 (1992): 99–114.

Spillers, Hortense. "Mama's Baby, Papa's Maybe: An American Grammar Book." *Diacritics* (Summer 1987): 65–81.

Spivak, Gayatri Chakravorty. *Death of a Discipline*. New York: Columbia University Press, 2003.

Stewart, Susan. *On Longing: Narratives of the Miniature, the Gigantic, the Souvenir, the Collection*. Durham, NC: Duke University Press, 1993.

Strachan, Ian Gregory. *Paradise and Plantation: Tourism and Culture in the Anglophone Caribbean*. Charlottesville: University of Virginia Press, 2002.

Suleri, Sara. "Naipaul's Arrival." *The Yale Journal of Criticism* 2, no. 1 (1988): 25–50.

Taussig, Michael. *Mimesis and Alterity*. New York: Routledge, 1993.

Taylor, Lucien. "The Same Difference." *Transition* 63 (1993): 98–111.

Terada, Rei. *Derek Walcott's Poetry: American Mimicry*. Boston: Northeastern University Press, 1992.

Thoburn, David. *Conrad's Romanticism*. New Haven, CT: Yale University Press, 1974.

Thomas, J. J. *Froudacity*. London: New Beacon, 1969.

Tilly, Charles. *Big Structures, Large Processes, Huge Comparisons*. New York: Russell Sage Foundation, 1984.

Tindall, W. Y. "Apology for Marlow." *From Jane Austen to Joseph Conrad*. Minneapolis: University of Minnesota Press, 1958.

Treves, Frederick. *The Cradle of the Deep: An Account of a Voyage to the West Indies*. New York: EP Dutton and Company, 1928.

Toumson, Héliane and Roger Toumson. "'Sur les pas de Fanotte:' Interview avec Simone et André Schwarz-Bart." *Textes et documents* special issue on *Pluie et vent sur Télumée Miracle* 2 (1979): 18.

Urry, J. *The Tourist Gaze: Leisure and Travel in Contemporary Societies*. London: Sage, 1990.

Vernant, Jean-Pierre. *Mythe et pensée chez les grecs*. Paris: Éditions la découverte, 1990.

Walcott, Derek. *The Antilles, Fragments of Epic Memory* (*Nobel Lecture*). New York: Farrar, Straus and Giroux, 1992.

———. "The Caribbean: Culture or Mimicry." *Journal of Interamerican Studies and World Affairs* 16, no. 1 (1974): 3–13.

———. *Collected Poems 1948–1984*. New York: Farrar, Straus and Giroux, 1986.

———. "The Muse of History." *Is Massa Day Dead? Black Moods in the Caribbean*. Edited by Orde Coombs. New York: Doubleday, 1974.

———. *Omeros*. New York: Farrar, Straus and Giroux, 1990.

———. "Reflections on *Omeros*." *The South Atlantic Quarterly* 2 (1997).

———. *Ti Jean and His Brothers. Dream on Monkey Mountain and Other Plays*. New York: Farrar, Straus and Giroux, 1970.

———. "What the Twilight Says: An Overture." *Dream on Monkey Mountain and Other Plays*. New York: Farrar, Straus and Giroux, 1970.

Walker, Keith. *La cohésion poétique de l'oeuvre césairienne*. Paris: J-M Place, 1979.

Warren, Austin, and René Wellek. *Theory of Literature*. New York: Harcourt Brace and World, 1942;1956.

Watt, Ian. *Conrad in the Nineteenth Century*. Berkeley: University of California Press, 1979.

Watts, Cedric. "'A Bloody Racist': About Achebe's View of Conrad." *The Yearbook of English Studies* 13 (1983): 197–209.

Weber, Samuel. "The Foundering of Aesthetics." In *The Comparative Perspective on Literature*, edited by Clayton Koelb and Susan Noakes. Ithaca, NY: Cornell University Press, 1988.

Weisstein, Ulrich. *Comparative Literature and Literary Theory*. Translated by William Riggan. Bloomington: Indiana University Press, 1968; 1973.

Wellek, René. *Concepts of Criticism*. Edited by Stephen G. Nichols, Jr. New Haven, CT: Yale University Press, 1963.

———. *Discriminations: Further Concepts of Criticism*. Yale University Press, 1970.

Williams, Raymond. *The English Novel from Dickens to Lawrence*. Oxford: Oxford University Press, 1970.

Wofford, Susanne Lindgren. *The Choice of Achilles: The Ideology of Figure in the Epic*. Stanford, CA: Stanford University Press, 1992.

Zimra, Clarisse. "In the Name of the Father: Chronotopia, Utopia and Dystopia" in *Ti Jean l'Horizon*." *L'Esprit Créateur* 32, no. 2 (1993): 59–72.

———. "Righting the Clabash: Writing History in the Female Francophone Narrative" in *Out of the Kumbla: Caribbean Women and Literature*, edited by Carole Boyce Davies and Elaine Savory Fido. Trenton, NJ: Africa World Press, 1990, 143–159.

Index

Cultural Memory | *in the Present*

James Phillips, *Heidegger's Volk: Between National Socialism and Poetry*

Frank Ankersmit, *Sublime Historical Experience*

István Rév, *Retroactive Justice: Prehistory of Post-Communism*

Paola Marrati, *Genesis and Trace: Derrida Reading Husserl and Heidegger*

Krzysztof Ziarek, *The Force of Art*

Marie-José Mondzain, *Image, Icon, Economy: The Byzantine Origins of the Contemporary Imaginary*

Cecilia Sjöholm, *The Antigone Complex: Ethics and the Invention of Feminine Desire*

Jacques Derrida and Elisabeth Roudinesco, *For What Tomorrow . . . : A Dialogue*

Elisabeth Weber, *Questioning Judaism: Interviews by Elisabeth Weber*

Jacques Derrida and Catherine Malabou, *Counterpath: Traveling with Jacques Derrida*

Martin Seel, *Aesthetics of Appearing*

Nanette Salomon, *Shifting Priorities: Gender and Genre in Seventeenth-Century Dutch Painting*

Jacob Taubes, *The Political Theology of Paul*

Jean-Luc Marion, *The Crossing of the Visible*

Eric Michaud, *The Cult of Art in Nazi Germany*

Anne Freadman, *The Machinery of Talk: Charles Peirce and the Sign Hypothesis*

Stanley Cavell, *Emerson's Transcendental Etudes*

Stuart McLean, *The Event and Its Terrors: Ireland, Famine, Modernity*

Beate Rössler, ed., *Privacies: Philosophical Evaluations*

Bernard Faure, *Double Exposure: Cutting Across Buddhist and Western Discourses*

Alessia Ricciardi, *The Ends of Mourning: Psychoanalysis, Literature, Film*

Alain Badiou, *Saint Paul: The Foundation of Universalism*

Gil Anidjar, *The Jew, the Arab: A History of the Enemy*

Jonathan Culler and Kevin Lamb, eds., *Just Being Difficult? Academic Writing in the Public Arena*

Jean-Luc Nancy, *A Finite Thinking*, edited by Simon Sparks

Theodor W. Adorno, *Can One Live after Auschwitz? A Philosophical Reader*, edited by Rolf Tiedemann

Patricia Pisters, *The Matrix of Visual Culture: Working with Deleuze in Film Theory*

Andreas Huyssen, *Present Pasts: Urban Palimpsests and the Politics of Memory*

Talal Asad, *Formations of the Secular: Christianity, Islam, Modernity*

Dorothea von Mücke, *The Rise of the Fantastic Tale*

Marc Redfield, *The Politics of Aesthetics: Nationalism, Gender, Romanticism*

Emmanuel Levinas, *On Escape*

Dan Zahavi, *Husserl's Phenomenology*

Rodolphe Gasché, *The Idea of Form: Rethinking Kant's Aesthetics*

Michael Naas, *Taking on the Tradition: Jacques Derrida and the Legacies of Deconstruction*

Herlinde Pauer-Studer, ed., *Constructions of Practical Reason: Interviews on Moral and Political Philosophy*

Jean-Luc Marion, *Being Given That: Toward a Phenomenology of Givenness*

Theodor W. Adorno and Max Horkheimer, *Dialectic of Enlightenment*

Ian Balfour, *The Rhetoric of Romantic Prophecy*

Martin Stokhof, *World and Life as One: Ethics and Ontology in Wittgenstein's Early Thought*

Gianni Vattimo, *Nietzsche: An Introduction*

Jacques Derrida, *Negotiations: Interventions and Interviews, 1971–1998*, edited by Elizabeth Rottenberg

Brett Levinson, *The Ends of Literature: The Latin American "Boom" in the Neoliberal Marketplace*

Timothy J. Reiss, *Against Autonomy: Cultural Instruments, Mutualities, and the Fictive Imagination*

Hent de Vries and Samuel Weber, eds., *Religion and Media*

Niklas Luhmann, *Theories of Distinction: Re-Describing the Descriptions of Modernity,* edited and introduced by William Rasch

Johannes Fabian, *Anthropology with an Attitude: Critical Essays*

Michel Henry, *I am the Truth: Toward a Philosophy of Christianity*

Gil Anidjar, *"Our Place in Al-Andalus": Kabbalah, Philosophy, Literature in Arab-Jewish Letters*

Hélène Cixous and Jacques Derrida, *Veils*

F. R. Ankersmit, *Historical Representation*

F. R. Ankersmit, *Political Representation*

Elissa Marder, *Dead Time: Temporal Disorders in the Wake of Modernity (Baudelaire and Flaubert)*

Reinhart Koselleck, *The Practice of Conceptual History: Timing History, Spacing Concepts*

Niklas Luhmann, *The Reality of the Mass Media*

Hubert Damisch, *A Childhood Memory by Piero della Francesca*

Hubert Damisch, *A Theory of /Cloud/: Toward a History of Painting*

Jean-Luc Nancy, *The Speculative Remark: One of Hegel's bon mots*

Jean-François Lyotard, *Soundproof Room: Malraux's Anti-Aesthetics*

Jan Patochacka, *Plato and Europe*

Hubert Damisch, *Skyline: The Narcissistic City*

Isabel Hoving, *In Praise of New Travelers: Reading Caribbean Migrant Women Writers*

Richard Rand, ed., *Futures: Of Jacques Derrida*

William Rasch, *Niklas Luhmann's Modernity: The Paradoxes of Differentiation*

Jacques Derrida and Anne Dufourmantelle, *Of Hospitality*

Jean-François Lyotard, *The Confession of Augustine*

Kaja Silverman, *World Spectators*

Samuel Weber, *Institution and Interpretation: Expanded Edition*

Jeffrey S. Librett, *The Rhetoric of Cultural Dialogue: Jews and Germans in the Epoch of Emancipation*

Ulrich Baer, *Remnants of Song: Trauma and the Experience of Modernity in Charles Baudelaire and Paul Celan*

Samuel C. Wheeler III, *Deconstruction as Analytic Philosophy*

David S. Ferris, *Silent Urns: Romanticism, Hellenism, Modernity*

Rodolphe Gasché, *Of Minimal Things: Studies on the Notion of Relation*

Sarah Winter, *Freud and the Institution of Psychoanalytic Knowledge*

Samuel Weber, *The Legend of Freud: Expanded Edition*

Aris Fioretos, ed., *The Solid Letter: Readings of Friedrich Hölderlin*

J. Hillis Miller / Manuel Asensi, *Black Holes / J. Hillis Miller; or, Boustrophedonic Reading*

Miryam Sas, *Fault Lines: Cultural Memory and Japanese Surrealism*

Peter Schwenger, *Fantasm and Fiction: On Textual Envisioning*

Didier Maleuvre, *Museum Memories: History, Technology, Art*

Jacques Derrida, *Monolingualism of the Other; or, The Prosthesis of Origin*

Andrew Baruch Wachtel, *Making a Nation, Breaking a Nation: Literature and Cultural Politics in Yugoslavia*

Niklas Luhmann, *Love as Passion: The Codification of Intimacy*

Mieke Bal, ed., *The Practice of Cultural Analysis: Exposing Interdisciplinary Interpretation*

Jacques Derrida and Gianni Vattimo, eds., *Religion*